Ask Sir James

Ask Sir James

Michaela Reid

ELAND

This edition published by Eland Publishing,
61 Exmouth Market, London EC1R 4QL in July 2009

First published in Great Britain by Hodder & Stoughton 1987

First published in the USA by Viking Penguin 1989

First published by Eland Publishing in 1996

© Michaela Reid 1987

ISBN 978 1 906011 15 4

Printed in Great Britain by Clays Ltd, St Ives Plc

TO

Sandy and Vicky

An honest man is the noblest work of God.
ALEXANDER POPE

Self-confidence is the first requisite to great undertakings.
SAMUEL JOHNSON

Acknowledgements

I am most grateful to Her Majesty the Queen for her gracious permission to quote from the Royal Archives, and for allowing me to visit Balmoral Castle. I should like to thank the Royal Librarians past and present, Sir Robin Mackworth-Young and Mr Oliver Everett, Miss Jane Langton, formerly Registrar of the Royal Archives, and Mr Robert Fellowes, Assistant Private Secretary to Her Majesty, for their help.

My particular thanks must go to Lady Longford who has not only supplied me readily with invaluable source material, but also has given, unstintingly, her time, advice and encouragement. I am most grateful to Mrs Daphne Bennett who, in the early stages of preparation, gave me much useful advice and nobly read and commented on my first draft. I have benefited too from the counsel of Dr David Cannadine, of Christ's College, Cambridge. Warm thanks are due to Mr Hugo Brunner who initially persuaded me to write the book and helped me in numerous ways throughout its often painful gestation.

I should like to thank the following: Mrs Roma Barber for permission to quote from her grandmother, Mary Reid's letters; Mr David Reid for the generous loan of Susan Reid's scrapbooks; Lady Margaret Douglas Home, Mrs Helen Foster, Mrs Jean Francis, and the late Lady Delia Peel for giving me their personal recollections of Sir James Reid; Mrs Greta Bowering for German translation; Mr Michael Cory-Smith for his advice on the Whitaker Wright case; Surgeon Captain and Mrs R. D. McDonald for generously giving me their time and hospitality on two occasions at Osborne; Dr Arthur Rook, for advice on medical literature; Dr Grahame Swan for answering my medical queries, and his wife Rosemary for suggesting the title; and Professor Charles Shute for his visits to the Medical Faculty Library at Cambridge on my behalf.

The following have helped me in various ways for which I thank them: Mr Jeffrey and Dr Mary Archer, Mr Philip Barber, Mr Adrian Bridgewater, Miss Felicita Busby, Mrs Elizabeth Chaize, Mr Michael Dobell, Mr Peter Fawcett, Mr Simon Houfe, Mr Richard Ingrams, Mrs Helen Lewsey, Surgeon Rear-Admiral Godfrey Milton-Thompson, Mr and Mrs James Tomlinson, Mrs Sarah Worboys, and my daughters Tina, Jennifer and Alexandra.

With Mr Ion Trewin and Miss Margaret Body I have had the greatest fun preparing for publication. I could not have had a more sympathetic, tactful and generous editor than Margaret. I should like, too, to thank my indexer, Mrs Stephanie Darnill.

Very special thanks are owed to Mrs Victoria Ingrams, Sir James Reid's daughter, whose interest and enthusiasm have never flagged throughout many years and vicissitudes. My greatest debt of gratitude is to my ever patient husband who has helped me in too many ways to enumerate, and without whom this book would never have been written.   MR

Author's Note

All quoted material without source notes at the back of the book can be deemed to have been taken from the Reid papers. Much of this is dated in the text, but where further information is required, the author may be referred to. The letters and diary entries have not been edited, so that the spelling of names in quoted matter will not necessarily correspond with a possibly more accepted version in the index. Queen Victoria's frequent underlining for emphasis has been printed in italics. A medical glossary has been provided on p. 280.

MR

Contents

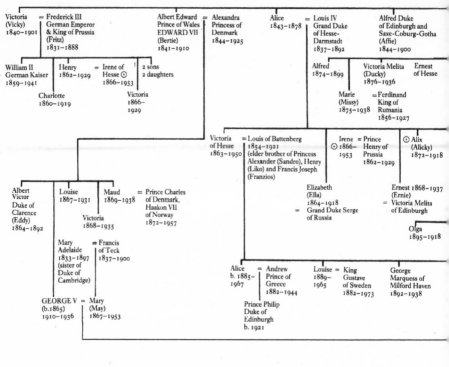
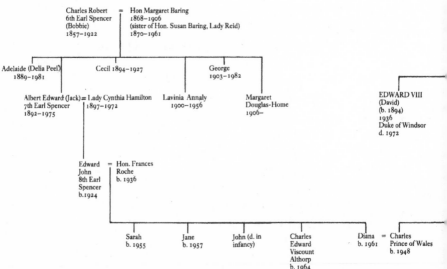

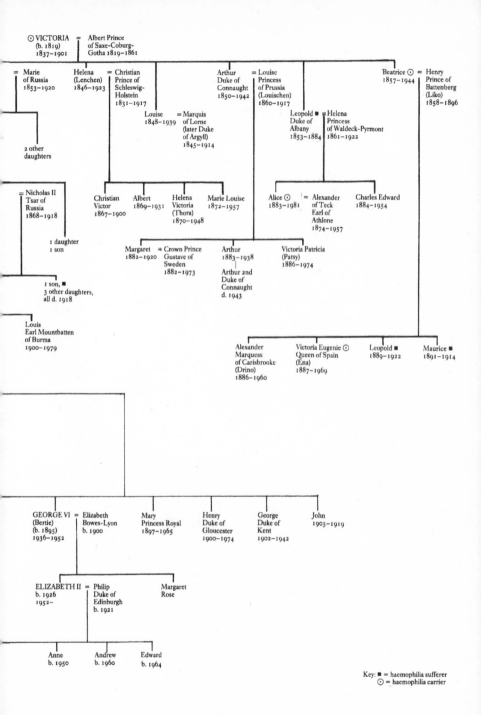

Key: ■ = haemophilia sufferer
⊙ = haemophilia carrier

Princess Louise's drawing of Queen Victoria, 1881

Foreword

BY

Elizabeth Longford

Summon up the image of a woman of strong character and personality who is none the less dependent for her happiness on male support. Conceive of it all beginning in a fatherless childhood. At eighteen this girl becomes a queen. Three years later she marries and for the next twenty years is utterly dependent on her consort. When she is widowed at forty-two she cannot get on alone, goes to pieces. Another twenty years on and she has virtually recovered, having found a new male support in a Scottish servant. Twenty years later and he too is dead. The poor lady is now sixty-two and sick. But in her new doctor she has found her final male support. He also is Scottish and though not strictly a *servant*, is not exactly a gentleman either. At first he is not permitted to take his meals with the royal Household, who are all strictly gentlemen. He remains her indispensable male support for another twenty years; in fact until the end of her reign.

This is of course a highly schematic approach to the supporting roles of three males in Queen Victoria's life: Prince Albert, John Brown, Dr James Reid. Much is rightly known about her admirable consort; a good deal about her gillie, who was tolerated by the Household and criticised by her family about equally; but hitherto very little indeed about her doctor. Lady Reid, married to the doctor's grandson and possessed of his papers, has most convincingly filled the gap, building up a fascinating new picture of Queen Victoria's last years.

The young Jamie Reid, buoyed up with first-class medical degrees but totally ignorant of Courts, arrived at Windsor Castle exactly twenty years, less five months, after Prince Albert's death. Another illness and death was to cement his friendship with the Queen: that of John Brown. She presented Reid with a locket containing Brown's portrait and an inscription commemorating the 'terrible' event. Lady Reid emphasises two attractive qualities in the Queen that this episode brought out. Despite her own overwhelming grief she sent special enquiries after Reid's bereaved mother. And she showed her appreciation of Reid's honest answers to whatever questions she put to him. Like the gillie, as Lady Reid also points out, the doctor 'would say

13

what he thought and not what he thought the Queen would like to hear'. Unlike Brown, however, the doctor was tactful and discreet where the gillie had been rough and drunken.

Dr Reid was soon immersed in the round of royal brides and babies, the Queen being particularly grateful for his care of Princess Beatrice after the difficult birth of her second child. He was rapidly proving himself a most skilful physician as well as a friendly and humorous person.

Where Reid failed (as anyone else would almost certainly have failed too) was in persuading his august patient of the connection between indigestion and appetite. Of course her hearty appetite has long been legendary, testified to, among others, by the Aga Khan. We have also already heard the entertaining story of Reid's attempt to substitute a bowl of light, milky Benger's Food for some of Her Majesty's more indigestible dishes; the net result being, yes, she did like the Benger's – and ate both. But Dr Reid's diaries show in all seriousness the problems of keeping an imperious old lady healthy as well as hearty. Never hungry.

With the best known episodes – some of them tragic – Lady Reid is lucid in her narrative and sensitive as well as sensible in her judgments. The death of the Queen's son-in-law the German Emperor (Vicky's husband) from throat cancer wrings our hearts all over again. The chapter on Abdul Karim the Queen's Munshi or 'Indian secretary' is a positive contribution to social history, answering as it does many hitherto puzzling queries. Why, for instance, were the courtiers apparently so prejudiced about colour, while their royal mistress was unbiased? This very detailed account, filled with new material, manages to achieve the seemingly impossible. It leaves us with more understanding both of the Queen *and* of her harassed Household, some of whom were beginning to say, Come back, John Brown, all is forgiven. The Munshi himself, alas, is revealed as unpleasantly domineering towards his fellow Indian servants and therefore unpopular with them as well as with the courtiers. But with Queen Victoria never. Loyalty was her second name.

Among the Queen's children, Reid found Princess Louise far the most sympathetic. Beautiful and gifted, aspiring and faintly Bohemian, she was also the saddest. Her unhappy childless marriage prompted her to accept consolation elsewhere, whether from Princess Beatrice's husband or from the Queen's favourite sculptor Edgar Boehm. It would be wrong to think of Princess Louise as a frustrated, predatory female, ready to snap up anything in her path. Nevertheless, the fact that she and Reid maintained a close but platonic relationship a long as they lived is a credit to them both.

The account of Reid's well-earned knighthood in 1895 brings to light many intriguing aspects of honours and pay, though the story is picturesque enough to stand alone. Being in Balmoral at the time, Reid was knighted by Her Majesty with a claymore! And after she had wielded this unexpected weapon, she made another telling thrust at the new *Sir* James. 'She has never seen the top of my head before, and was surprised, she said, to see my hair so nearly gone!'

If the Queen had never before seen her doctor's bald patch, her doctor never saw her undressed until she was dead. This suggests that her 'Victorian' ultra-modesty was no prudish affectation, but a part of her nature; strong enough to make her bear gynaecological ills that a quick strip would have revealed and cured. This is all the more surprising because sixty years earlier her gynaecologist Dr Locock had commented on her total lack of reticence about pregnancy and childbirth. Of course it is always possible that she preferred to keep her later ills secret rather than risk surgery.

The tale of Sir James's late but supremely happy marriage is presented as a charming idyll with a setting of wit and humour. Clearly the Queen hoped that Sir James, having avoided the contagion so long, would never have another woman but her in his life. Yet he not only married at fifty but married her own maid-of-honour, and married above his station – committed hypergamy – to boot. (His wife was Susan Baring, sister of the first Lord Revelstoke; but as Jamie was by now a baronet, the hypergamy was not so 'hyper' as it might have been.) The description of the Queen's reluctant acceptance of the situation is one of the most effective in the book.[1]

As a doctor's biography, built up mainly from his diaries, this book naturally has its full share of medical *rapportage*. Yet it in no way lacks variety. If one chapter ends with old Donald Stewart's 'hemiplegic stroke', another finishes triumphantly with Jamie and Susan honeymooning in the Royal Suite of the Ocean Hotel, Sandown, Isle of Wight.

There are two death-bed scenes of special note: Queen Victoria's and King Edward VII's; for Sir James continued as a royal doctor after the Queen's death. Apart from the interest of comparing Reid's account of the Queen's last hours with others now available (Frederick

---

[1] On the other hand, the famous anecdote about Reid's winning over H.M. to his marriage by promising her 'never to do it again' turns out to be semi-apocryphal. Lady Reid tells me that he made the joke, according to a note in Susan's handwriting, to Harriet Phipps the Queen's secretary, not to the Queen herself.

Ponsonby's, for instance, and Dr Barlow's) there is Reid's riveting description of his royal mistress's coffin, the arranging of whose contents was Reid's secret – and sacred – duty. 'To be placed in the coffin were rings, chains, bracelets, lockets, photographs, shawls, handkerchiefs, casts of hands etc.; all souvenirs from her life – early, middle, and late. No friend or servant was forgotten, and each member of her family was remembered. It was truly a burial worthy of a Queen and Empress.' A Queen and Empress indeed. But with so much dear luggage assembled to travel with her into the next world, it must have seemed like the preparations for a royal journey to the Valley of the Kings in ancient Egypt, rather than Frogmore.

The Prince Consort's plaster hand, cloak and dressing-gown (surely the celebrated one in which he did his last good deed, re-drafting the Trent Dispatch?) were secreted with all the other treasures beneath a cushion under her body, while John Brown's lock of hair and photograph were hidden under Queen Alexandra's nosegay in the Queen's left hand – the hand that she had once placed on 'honest Brown's' arm when she had been stricken with rheumatism and walked with a stick. She trusted Reid and his three women assistants not to tell her family, for they would never have understood.

Before the Brown saga was over, it was Reid's further duty to get back for the new King a packet of letters Queen Victoria had written about Brown to another royal doctor, Dr Profeit, whose son was trying to blackmail Edward VII. No doubt they were about John Brown's alcoholism. As Lady Reid perceptively writes:

> When Hugh Brown, John Brown's brother, died in 1896 Reid was 'commanded by the Queen on no account to tell the Ladies and Gentlemen that Hugh Brown had died of alcoholic poisoning!!' ... As she was so particular on all other matters regarding behaviour this quirk of the Queen's is somewhat curious. It can perhaps be attributed to her persistent championship of the underdog. She thought that the lot of a servant was hard, and that they needed an outlet; in consequence she felt concern for, rather than contempt of, the inebriate. This feeling, of course, did not extend to those better placed in society.

Lady Reid makes no attempt to conceal the faults of her two major characters. The Queen's concentration on her own health was some-times morbid and always a burden to her doctor; he could never count on not being called back in the middle of an all too brief and rare holiday. When on duty he must not be long out of her sight. Though one feels that Reid was a noble character, he was also human. He tried to cure himself of heavy smoking but failed; he was naïve enough to get mixed up in the notorious Whitaker Wright financial scandal; he had a nickname for the Queen (like Lord Clarendon earlier on but not the same one) – Bipps – perhaps chosen to rhyme with her secretary Phipps? Nevertheless, the relationship of the old Queen and young doctor was a genuine and touching one: he was never tempted to leave and she could not bear to be without him.

Immediately after Queen Victoria's death, Edward VII expressed his gratitude to Reid: 'You are an honest straightforward Scotchman.' Reid was that and much more. His grandson's wife has described all the rest in an equally 'honest straightforward' manner that is also graceful and penetrating. She satisfies a long-felt want and her balanced but often surprising story will be absorbing to the general reader and historian alike.

Author's Preface

When Ellon Castle, in Aberdeenshire, was handed over to my husband about twenty years ago, we inherited a housekeeper by the name of Rosie Cooper. She was invaluable; as a mere Sassenach or, worse still, a complete foreigner, I could never have coped without her. She knew everyone and everything about the place and told me, with the bluntness customary in Aberdeenshire, what was expected of me. She was obsessed by cleanliness and tidiness, virtues I applaud, but which, when carried to excess, can lead to disaster. 'Possessions, possessions, who'd want possessions?' she would say, throwing her arms in the air.

I peered into a dark cupboard and found about sixty large dusty mouldy volumes, a mass of photographs in Victorian frames, bundles of papers tied up with pink tape, and a large cash box. 'Och,' said Rosie, 'a' dam' neer threw them oot the ither week fan I haed a bonfire, but thocht better o't.' On further inspection, I found that here was a remarkable collection of family scrapbooks which I had heard about but never seen. The large cash box, when opened, revealed forty small pocket diaries written in the minutest, neatest handwriting. I was busy with a young family and unwilling at that stage to probe further, so, with the assistance of a muttering Rosie, who could not imagine why I should want to keep such rubbish, I moved the tómes from the dirty cupboard downstairs to a clean one upstairs, intending to study them some other time.

Many years passed, Ellon Castle was sold, and now the scrapbooks occupy pride of place in our library in Cambridgeshire. Five or six years ago I started working through them and, as I did so, it became clear to me that Sir James, as he is called by everyone, even by his daughter Victoria Ingrams, had not compiled this meticulous archive purely for the benefit of his family, but had intended it to be published. His discretion was such that we know little about him from other sources, despite the fact that he was Queen Victoria's personal physician for twenty years. Nothing went unremarked – all his letters, papers and accounts have been preserved as well as a large amount of photographic material, newspaper cuttings, menu cards, railway timetables, programmes for concerts, lectures, plays and operas, and even, in some cases, his train tickets! The first few volumes Sir James compiled himself, but after he married he left this work to his wife who applied herself to the daunting task with great enthusiasm, ably assisted by her niece, Lady Delia Peel. My husband remembers the two of them, his grandmother and cousin, sitting at The Chesnuts, in Ellon, poring over scraps of paper and dabbing from pots of Gripfix, using Sir James's professional brass door plate from 72 Grosvenor Street as a weight to hold the pieces in position whilst they dried.

The most important material in the scrapbooks comprises the collection of approximately 200 letters and notes written by Queen Victoria to Reid. Some of the letters are long, some of the notes are short; some of them are formal, and others are more intimate; but whichever they are, they throw light on her character. Also contained in the scrapbooks are Reid's weekly letters about their royal patient written to Sir William Jenner, and returned to him after Jenner's death, and all his correspondence with his mother, regaling her with details of Court life. Here Reid exposes himself more than he does in his diaries, revealing a distinct personality. There are also numerous letters from Morell Mackenzie written at the time of Emperor Frederick III's fatal illness. In addition, whenever Reid himself sent an important letter, he made a copy for his own records.

Reid's medical diaries were burnt by my father-in-law, Sir Edward Reid, according to the instructions contained in his father's will, as was the Green Memo Book referred to in the extant diaries, which contained material Sir James never intended for publication. Although we tried often to prise from my father-in-law the secrets written in this book, his discretion equalled his father's, and we learnt nothing.

In order to read the pocket diaries, I had to use a magnifying glass. These forty small volumes provide a factual account of Reid's daily life at Court. Some of the related facts, if not hitherto unknown, have at least not previously been published. Because the tone of the diaries is unemotional, surprising information does not shock; nothing is exaggerated and unimportant details like 'had my hair cut', mingle with a significant deathbed scene. Reid rarely expressed his views in his diaries, with the result that there is little room for psychological analysis but, to counterbalance this loss, there is the certitude of reliability.

The content of the book is focused mainly on the material from these diaries and scrapbooks, and from his wife Susan's scrapbooks, now in David Reid's possession, but inevitably I have looked to other sources for both social and, to a less extent, political background. Where I have quoted directly, a reference is given in the notes at the back of the book, but for general material I am indebted particularly to the following authors: Tom Cullen, David Duff, Christopher Hibbert, Lady Longford, Sir Philip Magnus-Allcroft, John Matson, Kenneth Rose, R. Scott Stevenson and E. E. P. Tisdall. The titles of their books can be found in the Bibliography.

There are still a few relations alive today who knew Sir James. To his daughter, Victoria Ingrams, his only surviving child, he seemed more like a grandfather than a father. He was approaching the age of sixty when she was born, and he had died before she had reached maturity. Her nursery life, remote from her parents' activities, precluded her from getting to know her father intimately. Nevertheless, she remembers hearing him say 'that's all humbug' on several occasions. She recollects also his bluntness in society, and certain fads. He insisted that milk should not be boiled (unusual in those days), and that potatoes should be unpeeled. In this he was avant garde. He was pernickety about details and could not bear it if a loaf of bread were not cut straight, a fad shared by his grandson, my husband!

Mrs Roma Barber and Mrs Jean Francis, his great-nieces (grandchildren of James's brother John), were eleven and nine years old respectively when he died. Jean Francis writes her impressions to Victoria Ingrams:

> I can visualise him standing in front of my grandmother's huge fire, with his back to it warming his coat tails! I see him as stocky, short, rosy cheeked, and feel that on this occasion [Christmas Day] he was very jovial. His voice I think was jerky – Roma says he 'barked'. My mother told me once he was an extremely impatient man, but that your mother managed him wonderfully. She never lost her equanimity but would quietly say something like, 'that's enough, Jamie' and he would subside.

To the Baring nieces and nephews on his wife's side of the family 'he used to appear *very* SCOTCH'. Mrs Nellie Foster recalls: 'He looked rather frightening and the archetypal Dr – frock coat and glasses.' Lady Margaret Douglas-Home, both a niece and a patient, who saw more of him than the others mentioned, says that 'he was quite different from all my other relations, a provincial Scot and "too clever" for words!' She remembers going to the Reids' house in Grosvenor Street for French lessons, and even at her tender age she was aware of the academic pressure put upon the children. Marks mattered. To be top of the form was paramount. While this attitude would be normal in many households today, it was alien to a child living during the early part of this century whose milieu was Spencer House and Althorp. On occasions he remarked that she looked pale,

21

and prescribed quantities of milk and roast beef, neither of which his niece cared for.

But these are the views of children about an old man who clearly lacked the art of pleasing the very young. To the late Lady Delia Peel, Lady Margaret Douglas-Home's much older sister, he appeared quite different. He was in no way formidable to her and she spoke of him with the greatest affection and respect. She was old enough to appreciate his sense of humour and intellect, and recalled that when nervous before an operation he remained by her bedside comforting her and giving her confidence. 'He was so pointful,' she would say.

Letting him speak for himself in quotation from his own archive will, I hope, provide a convincing picture of a man who filled a unique niche at Queen Victoria's Court.

Michaela Reid
January 1987

1

The Making of a Doctor

Chill winds blow in from the North Sea up the estuary of the River Ythan, which flows through the small, grey, granite town of Ellon, in the Buchan district of Aberdeenshire. As the centre of a rich agricultural area it entirely escaped the demoralising effects of the Industrial Revolution so strongly felt in other parts of Scotland. In 1849 Ellon could boast four grocers, three hotels and seven inns for a population of between 700 and 800. Dreary as this bare north-east coast would be to many, to James Reid the Buchan countryside was to act as a magnet all his life and he hurried back to it whenever opportunity arose.

Geographical background has a profound influence upon the development of a community, and nowhere is this more true than in Aberdeenshire. The rigours of the climate in Buchan and the strict puritanical propensities of its inhabitants have bred a tough and resilient people. Thoroughly practical by nature and habit, they do not readily express their feelings. James was a product of this way of thinking and in accepting life's caprices with equanimity he was following in the tradition of his heritage.

His father, also James Reid, the second of ten children, was the local Ellon doctor, a highly respected and conscientious practitioner who covered vast areas on horseback to visit his patients. The life of a country doctor in the middle of the nineteenth century was rugged to say the least. He was called out day and night, in all weathers, sometimes having to plod through the snow to an outlying farm only to find a sick cow awaiting him; and he would be expected to try his hand at dentistry as well as veterinary surgery. As he had been brought up on his father's farm, he was well acquainted with the vagaries of animals and could cope with veterinary cases with the same skill that he showed in his treatment of humans.

Devoted as he was to his doctor father, it was to his mother and her family that young James felt a deep and lifelong affection. Beatrice, James's mother, was the eighth of ten children born to John Peter of Canterland in Kincardineshire, factor for the Earl of Kintore, and in addition an able classical scholar. A kind, sensible homely woman, Beatrice Reid, though a doting mother and especially proud of her clever elder son, was never possessive. The serenity which emanated from her large comfortable frame gave him a sense of security and self-confidence which were to serve him admirably in future life.

James Reid was born on 23 October 1849 at The Chesnuts, the Ellon house which was to be his home for the whole of his life. A modest typical country doctor's establishment, James enlarged and embellished it as his circumstances became grander, but he never thought of parting with it.

From the first James showed signs of precocity and an ambitious nature, but those characteristics never overshadowed a naturally kind and sanguine disposition. Education was much prized in Aberdeen-shire and at the local school in Ellon he flourished under the tutelage of Dr John Davidson, a teacher of outstanding ability. Before the age of seven James had written to his grandmother, Barbara Peter, in his bold neat handwriting: 'I am at the top of my class.' And so he was to remain throughout his school career, leaving Aberdeen Grammar School in 1865 covered in glory, having been awarded the Gold Medal for the best scholar.

At the age of sixteen James was still too young to embark upon medicine, his chosen career. So for three years he followed an arts curriculum at Aberdeen University where he acquitted himself with great distinction, once again receiving the Gold Medal. All his life he held firmly to the view that a training in the arts was essential to a scientist.

James had not spent all his childhood and youth bent over his books, however. His father leased a small farm at Hillhead of Fechil, just outside Ellon, where James, and his younger brother John, spent much of their spare time. They fished on the Ythan, one of the finest sea trout and salmon rivers in Scotland. Not only was there pearl-mussel fishing too, but the whole area along the river banks was an ornithologist's paradise. Occasionally there were day trips to the coast, not far away, to Newburgh, the sands of Forvie, and even to Cruden Bay. During their school holidays James and John stayed with their uncles, George and James Peter, who were Presbyterian ministers living in their respective manses in Kemnay and Old Deer, a day's journey from Ellon in a horse and buggy. Both were bachelors responsible not only for their human flock but also for their glebe land and stock. Here the boys could indulge in the country pursuits so dear to them and being spoiled by Aunt Barbara Peter who kept house for Uncle George. The Reverend James Peter, known as 'the Abbot', had a twinkle in his eye and was a gifted artist who illustrated, with great charm, journals of his travels abroad. From Kemnay and Old Deer James wrote regularly to his parents using such words as

Dr Reid Ellon			
1861	To Reid brothers	£	s	D

		£	s	D
May 7th	To 4 mice @ £ & 1 rat at 2	0	0	4
„ 8th	To 4 mice & 1 rat	0	0	4
„ 9th	To 2 mice	0	0	1
„ 10th	To 1 mouse & 1 rat	0	0	2
„ 18th	To 1 rat	0	0	2
„ 24th	To 4 mice & 1 rat	0	0	4
„ 26th	To rat	0	0	2
June 5th	To 2 rats & 1 mouse	0	0	4
„ 7th	To 1 rat	0	0	2
„ 11th	To 3 rats	0	0	6
„ 26th	To 3 rats	0	0	6
„ 27th	To 3 rats	0	0	6
July 23rd	To 1 mouse	0	0	½
„ 24th	To 4 mice	0	0	2
Oct 14th	To 2 mice	0	0	1
„ 15	To 1 mouse	0	0	½
„ 18	To 1 mouse	0	0	½
		£0	4	3

Youthful enterprise, a rat-catching bill addressed to Dr Reid senior by his sons.

bass (doormat), brose (porridge) and lead (harvested), and telling them that he 'got fine fun at the Backgammon'. Some of his vocabulary would be incomprehensible to a Sassenach or, even in some cases, to a Scot outside Buchan. To the locals the dialect is known as 'the doric'. The sounds are guttural, as in Scandinavian languages, in contrast to the soft melodious brogue of the West Highlands.

At nineteen, now at the Aberdeen Infirmary, Reid was on the brink of an unusual medical career. He had bright blue twinkling eyes, wavy brown hair, and a beard. He was short (five feet eight and a half inches) and sturdy, and, as has been observed, spoke with a strong Aberdonian accent which never left him, though with time some local expressions were modified and his style of writing became Anglicised. He enjoyed exceptionally good health and, judging from his reports, he never missed a single lecture during his time at University.

Once while he was a medical student Reid went to London, and wrote to his mother in great excitement: 'I think London is by far the best place I have ever been to – I have been driving about with Mrs Cruickshank a great deal and making calls with her. Today we drove in the Park and saw all the aristocracy of England in their carriages. It is a sight really worth seeing and which you have no Idea of.' In those days London would have seemed as remote to the inhabitants of Ellon as the moon is to most of us today.

At the Aberdeen Infirmary he continued to achieve great heights academically. Alex Harvey, the Professor of Materia Medica and Consulting Physician to the Aberdeen Royal Infirmary, wrote a glowing letter to Reid's father after his son's final pre-clinical examinations. 'Last Wednesday, on announcing the prize-list, I did, what I believe I never did before, on an occasion of the kind, namely this – compliment your son in the face of the clap – I could not help doing so. I was so pleased with the style and substance of his exercises.' His parents had good reason to be proud of him.

In his final year as a medical student he was top of his class and obtained the first prize in Botany, Chemistry, Materia Medica, Anatomy, Zoology with Comparative Anatomy, Physiology, Surgery, Midwifery and Medical Jurisprudence. After Reid had graduated in April 1872, James Brazier, Professor of Chemistry and Secretary to the Medical Faculty in the University, wrote in his testimonial: 'On presenting himself for the medical professional examinations, Dr Reid obtained the highest mark in each of the branches comprised in the three separate divisions of the examinations, and necessarily thereafter graduated with the highest academic honours that the University could confer.' So ended an exceptional academic career.

With glowing testimonials to support him, Reid decided to seek his fortune in his favourite city, and joined Dr William Vacy Lyle's practice at 6 Westbourne Terrace, Paddington. Here he had considerable experience in practical medicine, managing large dispensaries and dealing with a great number of midwifery cases. Vacy Lyle was absent through illness much of the time so Reid was left in charge of a busy practice in what was then not a salubrious district. Yet he found time to contribute two articles to the *British Medical Journal*.[1] He also enjoyed London and told his mother he went 'to the Park for a little to see the swells. I was rather in luck as on my way down I met the Queen and Duchess on their way to the station for Windsor.' But after nine months in London Reid became restless and dissatisfied with his prospects. Vacy Lyle offered him a partnership on favourable terms, being afraid to lose him, but even this did not induce him to remain.

He determined instead to consolidate his studies in Vienna which then boasted one of the highest medical reputations in Europe. But first he must learn German. In November 1874 he left London for the Continent and wended his way slowly via Antwerp, Cologne, and Munich to Klagenfurt, in southern Austria, where he took up a position as tutor to the eight-year-old Karl, Count de Lodron.

It was Reid's first visit abroad and he made the most of the opportunity to see the fine churches in Antwerp, and the cathedral in Cologne. He was immensely impressed by the scenery along the Rhine, and then even more by the Alps, writing to his parents: 'The Tyrolese Alps by the Brenner Pass beats hollow everything I have ever seen, Rhine and all being nothing to it in my opinion. It must cost ever so much to keep the line clear of snow in winter. There seemed a man every few yards enveloped in fur and up to the ears in snow.'

By now he had 'got into a country where nobody knew English or French and I was a little at sea. The second-class carriages are quite as good and comfortable as our first class. All the higher middle classes here travel second class, only fools and Dukes and adventurers go first class, a German gentleman told me.'

At last he arrived at Klagenfurt and was gratified to find himself thrown into a social life more exciting and elegant than any he had hitherto encountered, for Karl's father was Civil Governor of Carinthia, and represented the Emperor Franz Joseph in that province. Karl was precocious, being an only child, and a little spoiled, but he was amiable and they soon became firm friends. It was not long before

---

[1] 'Case of Aortic Embolism (1873), and Erysipelas during Puerperal Condition (1874).

Reid was writing home: 'I can lingo away quite well now and have no trouble with the Chamber maid!'

Although reasonably assiduous in attending church on Sundays, he was not deeply religious and he was openly tolerant towards denominations other than Presbyterian. He light-heartedly regaled his Uncle James, 'the Abbot', with a description of Lenten fare:

> But inner man has been on short commons here the last two days, that is to say that we have been fasting and nothing but fish and slops on the go. In my desperation I have been driven to make onslaughts on fried 'puddocks' [frogs] and the soup made from the same lively little animals, and (would you believe it) I actually rather like the fare! Glory be to Allah! However the fast is over, and today we shall revel in the wing of the ox.

In summer Reid accompanied Karl on a round of visits to de Lodron relations, moving from one fine castle to another, and, now that he could 'lingo away' with greater ease, he enjoyed himself among these charming jolly country-loving aristocrats. From the Tyrol he wrote home to his parents: 'It is a pity you could not have seen us climbing like Chamois among the rocks, and then sitting on the top, all three puffing at our cigars and taking in the magnificent view.'

By December 1875 Reid felt confident in his ability to tackle a few medical courses and wrote to his father asking his advice and outlining what he hoped to study in Vienna:

> Some of the subjects that seem to me to be of more likely future advantage to me are:- practical pathology, electro-therapeutics, practical laryngoskopy and rhinoskopy, diseases of larynx and windpipe, theoretical and practical aurology, diseases of children, syphilis, pathology and therapeutics of the nervous system, and treatment of electricity in various forms, etc. etc. Such are a few selected at random, and which I have at present little or no knowledge of. There are many other departments I should also like to give a little attention to, as chest and abdominal diseases, operations etc:, to make a comparison between our and Vienna ideas and treatment. I shall just select a few for this winter when I arrive, but will leave the main work till next winter, when my previous knowledge of the place and more complete mastery of the language will of course enable me to 'make a better job' of it.

It is not known what advice his father gave him but he did send him vaccination plates with which Reid vaccinated himself, thinking it important to do so, 'especially in a place like this [Vienna] where people take no care'.

So Reid took temporary leave from the de Lodrons and settled in a small hotel in Vienna, from where he wrote to 'the Abbot': 'I feel as much at home in the place as I do in the city of Old Deer!' He enjoyed the independence of living on his own, free from the restrictions imposed upon him in Klagenfurt, and declared, 'this existence suits me to a T'. The General Hospital was a good place at which to acquire further skills. A sprawling mass stretching over many acres of the city, it was a refuge for more than 3,000 patients who came not only from the capital itself, but from the furthest parts of the Empire, and even from Asia and Africa. Here cases which normally would be seen only once in a lifetime, or never at all, would crop up frequently, and for an ambitious doctor there were few, if any, better places in Europe in which to gain experience. But in spite of the great reputation of Viennese medicine the conditions in the hospital were appalling. There was only limited gaslighting, so that during the winter months patients spent a good deal of the time in the dark, and operations were sometimes carried out by candlelight. Defying these conditions, doctors flocked from all over the world to glean from a handful of eminent professors new theories of medicine, both physiological and psychological. (In 1876 Sigmund Freud, seven years younger than Reid, was at the Vienna School of Medicine.) For the first winter session in 1876 Reid followed courses in gynaecology with Dr Marcus Funk, and aural diseases under the auspices of Dr Politzer with, according to his testimonials, outstanding results.

He found time to enjoy the opera season to the full and, before returning to Klagenfurt for the summer, took a steamer down the Danube to Budapest, reporting to his Uncle James that the vast plain of Hungary was 'a fine place for "fairmers"'. Before leaving the de Lodrons in November 'the Count had up a bottle of champagne to drink my health'. Young Karl wrote to him a week later, 'If I had a thousand tutors I should always like you best. Mama also misses you very much.'

Back in Vienna Reid applied himself to studying ear, nose and throat diseases, and worked at Pathology as well. Like Freud, he disapproved of *'female* medical students', and found their appearance 'anything but attractive'! Perhaps he merely reflected accepted opinions in nineteenth-century Europe and Vienna in particular (the students referred to were American), but he was always conservative in his attitude to women, and as public opinion became more liberal Reid still voted against accepting women into the Royal College of Physicians, and became a positive anti-suffragist. During the summer session he attended lectures on dermatology and syphilis with the famous Professors Hebra and Moriz Kaposi. Under Professors

Gruber, Schrötter and Stoerk he was to gain practical experience in operating on ears, noses and larynxes. He learnt both the theory and practical use of the ophthalmoscope, and performed eye surgery several times, as well as acquiring considerable skill in surgery at the clinic of Professor Billroth who first introduced the use of sterile dressings.

By the beginning of July 1877 Reid had finished his medical training in Vienna, having collected more glowing references, and was ready for his journey home after more than two and a half years' absence. He decided to return to Scotland via Prague, Dresden, Berlin and Hamburg, first sending an anxious plea to his mother: 'Don't eat all the strawberries till I come!'

For many the change from the gay, stimulating life in Vienna to the hard daily slog of a country doctor would have been difficult, but Reid threw himself into his work with enthusiasm and good humour. Following in his father's footsteps he had a reputation to maintain. His medical qualifications were more than adequate, but it is doubtful whether, at first, he was equipped to deal with the languishing cow or sheep with the same skill as his father had done for the past forty years, though, no doubt, he learnt quickly enough.

In October 1878 Reid joined the Aberdeen Rifle Volunteers as Acting Surgeon, which involved attending drills occasionally but could not, otherwise, have been onerous in peacetime. But as he plodded through the countryside on his Highland pony to see his patients in outlying farms and cottages he must have wondered, as the years passed by, whether he was making the most of his education and abilities. Surely greater things were meant for him. He could not be expected to remain in remote Buchan for ever. Fortunately, his patience was rewarded, and in April 1881, nearly four years after he had left Vienna, he arrived at the great turning point in his life.

Queen Victoria was looking for a successor to Dr William Marshall as Resident Medical Attendant to the Queen and the royal Household. Her Majesty stipulated that the person selected should be a Scotsman, and preferably a native of her beloved Aberdeenshire. He should be highly qualified and conversant with German so as to be capable of communicating with the vast numbers of visiting relations who, from time to time, descended upon the Queen at Windsor, at Balmoral, and at Osborne. Dr Profeit, Her Majesty's Commissioner, or Factor, at Balmoral was given the task of finding a suitable candidate, and the Reverend George Peter was approached on the matter by his friend John Charles of Inverurie. Uncle George immediately thought of Reid as being the ideal man for the post, and came to Ellon to discuss the proposal with his nephew. It was arranged that Reid should meet John Charles and Dr Profeit in Aberdeen for further consultation on 20 April. But it was not until 2 June that he received a communication from Dr Profeit which said: 'I have today received Her Majesty's commands to ask you to come here on any day convenient to yourself. You do not need to bring any change of dress with you. I should advise you to wear an ordinary morning coat (dark). As to the other garments they may be anything you choose.' On 8 June Reid went to Balmoral for the day, and saw the Queen for the first time. He has not recorded his feelings before, or what went on during the interview, but despite his self-confidence Reid must have felt a little nervous with so much at stake. He had his audience with the Queen in the morning soon after his arrival at Balmoral. Her Majesty recorded the occasion in her Journal:

> 8 June: Saw Dr Reid from Ellon, who has *the very* highest testimonials, having taken very high honours at Aberdeen and studied for two years at Vienna; he also practised for a short time in London and is now helping his father at Ellon, who has been doctor there for many years. He is willing to come for a time or permanently in Dr Marshall's place.

All was well. Queen Victoria was a good judge of character and Reid had not only impeccable medical qualifications but also many qualities which appealed to the Queen, such as shrewdness, tact, honesty and a great sense of humour.

There was, however, one more bridge to cross before he was home and dry. The Queen would not engage him until he had seen her trusted Physician-in-Ordinary, Sir William Jenner. His word was law. On 11 June Reid went to London where he had an interview with the great man himself. He passed muster and Sir William telegraphed to the Queen his approval. Reid was requested to appear '*in propria persona*' at Windsor Castle on 8 July to embark upon his duties. Thus, at the age of thirty-one, this Scot of modest origin found himself catapulted to a position far beyond his wildest dreams.

2

Arrival at Court

On the appointed day in July 1881 the young doctor left the obscurity of his remote practice in Aberdeenshire to take up his position as Resident Medical Attendant to Queen Victoria at Windsor Castle. Self-assured as he was, it would have been unnatural for him not to have felt some anxiety at the prospect before him. The Queen was held in awe by all those who had met her and even by the public at large who had only heard about her but never seen her. Small, plain and dumpy, dressed invariably in her widow's weeds and white cap, she nevertheless commanded great respect, and often succeeded in reducing sophisticated statesmen to incoherence in her presence. Even the garrulous Gladstone was silenced by a cold stare from the Monarch.

When Reid took up his duties at Windsor Castle the Queen was sixty-two years old, had been on the throne for forty-four years, and had been a widow for twenty. For years after the death of her husband, Prince Albert of Saxe-Coburg-Gotha, she had retired completely from public life and nursed her wounds in an orgy of self-pity which nearly, some said even then, cost her her throne. Slowly and by degrees she emerged from her gloom and began once more to take an active interest in life. Perhaps it was the visits of her numerous grandchildren which restored her to something like her former self. In 1881 the Queen had twenty-six grandchildren and was to have nine more while Reid was with her, many of whom he regularly attended and cared for. Although rarely completely at ease with her own children, with the possible exception of Princess Beatrice, her youngest, the Queen was never happier than with her grandchildren whom she indulged freely and who, in return, adored her. Young people found the Queen fascinating and the unpredictability of the ideas she expressed endeared her to them. The Queen not only commanded respect, but she engendered love. Dowdy as she was to look at, she nevertheless had a great aura about her, possessing a beautiful melodious voice and brilliant smile, which would, on occasions, appear across her otherwise glum face to enchant its beholder.

Perhaps the most illuminating portrait of the Queen by a contemporary is that of Randall Davidson, who became Dean of Windsor a couple of years after Reid took up his post at Court.[1]

[1] He became Bishop of Rochester in 1891, Bishop of Winchester in 1895, and Archbishop of Canterbury in 1903.

What exactly it was which constituted the irresistible charm attaching to her, I have never been able quite clearly to define, but I think it was the combination of absolute truthfulness and simplicity with the instinctive recognition and quiet assertion of her position as Queen and of what belonged to it. I have known many prominent people, but with hardly one of them was it found by all and sundry so easy to speak freely and frankly after even a very long acquaintance. I have sometimes wondered whether the same combination of qualities would have been effective in a person of stately or splendid appearance. May it have been that the very lack of those physical advantages, when combined with her undeniable dignity of word and movement, produced what was in itself a sort of charm? People were taken by surprise by the sheer force of her personality. It may seem strange, but it is true that as a woman she was both shy and humble. Abundant examples will occur to those who know her. But as Queen she was neither shy nor humble, and asserted her position unhesitatingly.

Such was the favourable side of the character of Reid's new patient. There were also flaws. Although she was by nature thoughtful and considerate, there were times when she exhibited a selfish streak which she was freely able to indulge on account of her unassailable position. She could be extremely stubborn on occasions and would refuse to admit an error in spite of irrefutable proof. On the other hand she could also be magnanimous and admit her shortcomings, even revealing remorse and humility rare in a royal person of her standing. She was intuitive rather than rational, guided by common sense and emotion rather than intellect. Normally a sound judge of character she did, however, throughout most of her widowhood, form what Randall Davidson described as 'unwise' relations with two of her servants. Like most women she needed a man in her life, someone to cherish and in whom she could confide. Fundamentally innocent as her friendships may have been, they did not always appear to be so, and led to much detrimental speculation.

When Reid travelled to Windsor to embark upon his new life in the royal Household the Queen was still mourning the loss of her favourite Prime Minister, Benjamin Disraeli, Lord Beaconsfield, who had died three months earlier. The exotic Disraeli had appealed to the romantic side of Queen Victoria's character. He had introduced her to the wonders of the Orient, and had been largely responsible for creating her Empress of India in 1876. She was his 'Faery' Queen who sent him spring flowers, especially his favourite primroses, picked from the castle slopes at Windsor.

The Queen was a creature of habit who followed a strict routine, daily and yearly. She travelled a good deal, but so regular were her movements from place to place that it was nearly always possible to tell where she would be at any given moment merely by glancing at a calendar. Christmas and New Year were invariably spent at Osborne on the Isle of Wight, where she stayed enjoying the milder climate until the middle of February, when the Court moved to Windsor Castle. Although at the hub of events there, the Queen liked Windsor the least of her three residences. It had not been created by Albert as a family home, as had Osborne and Balmoral, and being close to London she had far less privacy than she had in either of the other places. During the second or third week in March the Queen went abroad for about six weeks, usually to the South of France, though she frequently combined her holiday in France with a visit to one or other of her numerous relations in Germany. On three occasions she went to Florence. A short time at Windsor in May would prelude a late spring visit to Balmoral, her Highland home, which lasted two or three weeks. Then the Court moved back to Windsor again for a few weeks in July before proceeding once more to Osborne, where the Queen spent the rest of July and the whole of August. On about 30 August she travelled to Balmoral, where she remained until the middle of November. From then on her Court would reside at Windsor until it was time once more to move to Osborne for Christmas. Buckingham Palace was visited but rarely. Occasionally the Queen attended a Drawing Room there, but whenever possible she delegated this duty to the Prince of Wales. The only variations to this rigid regime were State visits to industrial cities in the North of England, and brief journeys to Edinburgh, to Wales, and to Ireland. Such was the Queen's programme during the last twenty years of her life. Wherever she went she took her Resident Medical Attendant with her.

Throughout her long life the Queen enjoyed remarkably good health, though in her later years she suffered from rheumatism, exacerbated by various falls. Indigestion gave her cause for complaint from time to time, but this was hardly surprising considering the quantity of food she consumed (she had a penchant for heavy puddings), and the speed with which she devoured it. She had an obsession with fresh air which had been instilled in her by Sir James Clark, a previous physician.

As a young medico he had offered a thesis entitled *De Frigoribus Effectis*. On Queen Victoria the effects of Clark's enthusiasms were at first beneficial but later excessive. She gradually came to endow 'Frigor' with almost divine properties, dogmatically asserting that cold was always good for people, warmth bad. She ruthlessly sacrificed on its altar the convenience of her less hardy husband and courtiers, establishing as its priesthood a vast array of wall thermometers.

Whatever the weather the Queen would drive out in her carriage accompanied by a shivering and long suffering lady-in-waiting or maid-of-honour. Poor Princess Beatrice became a victim of rheumatism at a very early age, which was hardly to be wondered at when one considers the swirling icy mist that must have filled the rooms at Balmoral in November. Disraeli and Lord Salisbury, for whom an enforced sojourn in the north was anathema, had doctors' orders to have their rooms specially heated for them. Elsewhere the Queen forbade open fires and insisted that windows should be kept wide open.

The Queen's 'nerves' did not play up as much in the 1880s and '90s as they had done formerly. But there were still times when she used them for her own ends as a hedge between herself and her politicians. Whereas Sir James Clark and Sir William Jenner had been compliant to her whims, James Reid did not succumb so readily and, when he thought the occasion demanded, did not hesitate to oppose her, albeit tactfully.

The Queen, who tended to see everything in terms of black and white, liked doctors, who were white, as opposed to bishops, who were definitely black.[2] The smooth bedside manner did not impress her, but she was interested in illness and would talk without reserve on the subject with her doctors. She was courteous to them, dependent on them, but often exhibited a snobbishness towards them. According to Lady Longford, 'She treated them with meticulous respect as regards fees and titles, but though she liked them far better than, say, cavalry officers, she never regarded them as the officers' social equals.'

---

[2] During the Diamond Jubilee celebrations the Queen had to receive both Houses of Convocation as well as the various bishops and ecclesiastical dignitaries from overseas. When it was all over she went for her usual afternoon drive. Edith, Lady Lytton, was in waiting and accompanied her. There was rather a prolonged silence at first, and then the Queen said, 'A very ugly party.' Black shovel hats, black gaiters, black silk aprons, and the whole rather gloomy tailoring of these worthy divines was a striking contrast to the gorgeous and colourful Indian and Eastern guests she had been entertaining. Then, after a pause, the Queen said, 'I do not like Bishops!' Lady Lytton nearly fell out of the carriage in surprise and horror at the very outspoken verdict of the Queen concerning the so-called pillars of the Church. 'Oh, but your dear Majesty likes *some* bishops, for instance, the Bishop of Winchester, [Randall Davidson] and the Bishop of Ripon [Boyd Carpenter].' 'Yes,' said Her Majesty, 'I like the man but *not* the Bishop!'
See H.H. Princess Marie Louise, *My Memories of Six Reigns*, Evans Brothers, 1956 (p.146)

Lady Longford goes on to suggest that 'apart from tradition, it was probably the subject matter of the medical profession which caused Queen Victoria to rank her doctors a little lower than the Household. She once warned her eldest daughter against "too great intimacy with 'Kuntsler' [art] as it is very seductive and dangerous!" The study of anatomy seemed to her a good deal more dangerous, and less seductive. As she informed her second daughter, it was "disgusting".'

At this stage something should be mentioned about the composition of Queen Victoria's Medical Household. In England and Scotland, the Physicians- and Surgeons-in-Ordinary were consultants to the Queen, but at times acted as her general practitioners.[3] The senior of the physicians was styled Head of the Medical Department and the senior surgeon Sergeant Surgeon. The numbers varied, but usually three physicians and three surgeons held office at a time, so that in an emergency there would be at least one available.

Under them were the Physicians and Surgeons Extraordinary. They formed a second line and were in a sense on probation. Many, but not all, were in due time promoted to being in-Ordinary, and a few of those in-Ordinary, usually because they had become incapacitated by age or ill health, reverted to being Extraordinary. This was a compliment paid for long service. Besides these there were various specialists, *accoucheurs*, oculists, and aurists, who might be called upon from time to time.

Finally, there were the apothecaries. This branch of the profession had originally prepared and dispensed drugs, but since the Apothecaries Act of 1865 they had become general practitioners. For the Queen's Apothecaries the nomenclature was variable and their duties not always clearly defined. Sometimes styled Apothecary to the Household or, from 1864, Surgeon Apothecary, they were general practitioners and were of two classes. There were the Apothecaries to the Household up to but not including the royal family, and Apothecaries to the Person, who acted as general practitioners to the Queen and any members of the royal family who might require medical attention while staying with her. In Scotland there were no appointments as Apothecaries, but there were Resident Physicians at Balmoral, who fulfilled much the same functions.

The Physicians- and Surgeons-in-Ordinary were senior men recognised as leaders of their profession, and they served for an average

[3] Reid became Physician Extraordinary in 1887 and Physician-in-Ordinary in 1889, but still continued to act as the Queen's general practitioner at Balmoral, Windsor and Osborne, remaining as Resident Medical Attendant at all the Queen's residences until her death in 1901.

period of only twelve years. During Queen Victoria's reign at least fifty-seven were at some time Presidents of the appropriate Royal Colleges; forty-two were Fellows of the Royal Society, including two Presidents, Lord Lister and Sir Benjamin Collins Brodie. The Apothecaries, on the other hand, were younger men when appointed and served for an average of twenty-two years, some, like John Merriman and Sir William Carter Hoffmeister, serving for over forty years. They were appointed in pairs, and were local general practitioners, often with family connections. While Reid was with Queen Victoria the Ellisons, a father and son, were Surgeon Apothecaries at Windsor, while the Hoffmeisters, a father and four sons, served at various intervals at Osborne.

Reid's post did not fit precisely into any of the categories just described. His position was unique in that he was the first physician to remain constantly at the Queen's beck and call, and to travel with her wherever she went at home or abroad. For twenty years, until her death, he was a permanent member of the Household, starting his time as Resident Medical Attendant and eventually becoming the Queen's senior Physician-in-Ordinary. Of all the Queen's Apothecaries and Medical Attendants he was the only one to achieve the position of either Physician Extraordinary or Physician-in-Ordinary.

A memorandum from the Privy Purse Office stating the new doctor's conditions of employment reached Reid just before he set off on his journey to Windsor Castle. These instructions are in line with the Queen's views, mentioned above, concerning the social position of her doctors. The memorandum is as follows:

Dr Reid will be appointed Resident Medical Attendant on the Queen at a salary of Four Hundred Pounds (£400) per annum.

He will not be an official member of the Royal Household, but will have breakfast and luncheon with the Ladies and Gentlemen in Waiting.

He will not dine with them, unless especially invited by the Queen's orders, excepting at Balmoral, when he will always dine at the Household dinner.

He will be in constant attendance upon the Queen, and will at Her Majesty's convenience receive six weeks' leave in the Year.

He will attend the Members of the Royal Family who are residing with the Queen, if required, and will at any time visit any person whatever if directed by Her Majesty.

He is to take medical and surgical charge of all the personal attendants on the Queen (her dressers and maids) and Royal Family, of all Scotch servants, and of all other servants who may desire him to attend them.

He is to attend any lady or gentleman in the Palace who may ask for his professional assistance.

He will maintain a constant communication with Dr Ellison, or Dr Hoffmeister,[4] when at Windsor or Osborne, and will report· all special medical matters to Sir William Jenner.

Dr Reid will come into attendance on the Queen at the beginning of July for three months on the condition mentioned in the enclosed paper.

At the beginning of October the agreement will either cease or be made permanent.

Reid was put in no doubt as to the terms of his employment. Although the memorandum was issued from the Privy Purse Office the hand of the Queen can be clearly detected as the author of these instructions, from both their tone and their content. For the first eight years of his employment with the Queen Reid was responsible to Sir William Jenner, the Queen's chief physician, and had to report to him when anything untoward arose concerning his patients. Sir William Jenner had succeeded Sir James Clark as Physician-in-Ordinary to the Queen in 1862, shortly after the death of Prince Albert. Born in 1815, he was a man of great medical distinction, a Fellow of the Royal Society, and President of the Royal College of Physicians from 1881 to 1888. His claim to fame lay in his recognition of the distinction between typhoid and typhus fever which had hitherto been treated as one and the same disease. As an expert in typhoid fever he had been called in at the time of Prince Albert's ʹfatal illness. He had failed to treat the Prince successfully, but this may well have been because it is questionable whether the Prince Consort did in fact die of typhoid fever. In any event, being a new boy at Court, and in awe of Sir James Clark, Jenner would have maintained a respectful silence, probably realising that his patient, having no will to live, was beyond cure.

With his robust common sense and jovial good humour, Jenner was the most virulent Tory. His kindliness, honesty and lack of pretence were characteristics which appealed to the Queen. Though his reactionary attitude to women entering the medical profession influenced the Queen unfavourably, on the question of vivisection, to which she was strongly averse, he acted as a moderating influence. He was Reid's mentor until he assumed ultimate responsibility for the Queen's health in 1889, and clearly they were birds of a feather, combining many of the same qualities – including the ability to tell racy stories which amused the Queen. Their regular correspondence shows a mutual

---

[4] Dr Ellison and Dr Hoffmeister were Surgeon Apothecaries to the Queen at Windsor and Osborne respectively.

trust and admiration. Jenner rarely found it necessary to proffer advice on medical matters since Reid invariably anticipated him and treated the patient in the same way that he would have done. At first the Queen was reticent with her young doctor, preferring to reserve her medical problems for Jenner's weekly visits, but very soon she felt able to rely more and more upon the advice of the man who was closer at hand.

On 8 July 1881, on his arrival at Windsor, Reid wrote to his mother: 'I have got very comfortable quarters here with a splendid view right down what they call "the Long Walk". I don't think, so far as I can judge, that I am likely to suffer from want of either comfort or good living. There is a sentry just under my window, so there's no fear of any night bird coming in upon me.' He had barely time to accustom himself to his new surroundings, for within ten days of his arrival at Windsor it was time to move to Osborne. He was impressed by the speed of the journey and wrote again:

> We came very quickly, about three hours altogether. We travelled very luxuriously in saloon carriages with blocks of ice in them: but the heat was terrific. It was very pleasant crossing [the Solent] in the Queen's Yacht. I had no trouble packing and unpacking, as the man who waits on me did it all for me, being evidently a fellow who will save me no end of trouble. My quarters here are very comfortable, but not so commodious as at Windsor. I think I am getting on pretty well, though altogether I have not done *one day's* work since I left you!

Reid had found no difficulty in settling down to his new life. In spite of being an outsider in an enclosed environment (for it must be remembered from the memorandum that he was neither a servant nor an official member of the Household) he had made friends easily, aided by his charm and sense of humour. He found himself in the midst of a closely-knit circle of aristocrats, most of them connected to each other through kinship, and it was to his credit that he was immediately accepted by them on equal terms. Although inferior socially he was superior intellectually, and realising this gave him the confidence he needed to tackle his new life.

Who comprised the Queen's Household? There were the fluctuating members who were in attendance upon the Queen in rotation. Of these there were eight ladies of the bedchamber, eight women of the bedchamber, eight maids-of-honour, eight lords-in-waiting, eight grooms-in-waiting, and eight equerries. All these, except seven of the eight lords-in-waiting, were appointed by Her Majesty independent of political party. The Mistress of the Robes, and the ladies in her department, changed with the government, and received their salaries from the Lord Chamberlain, as did the lords and grooms-in-waiting. The equerries were in the department of the Master of the Horse. All these ladies and gentlemen Reid saw from time to time when they were on duty.

Then there was the hard core of the Household, the permanent members, with whom he was in constant communication. Most of the gentlemen of the Household were retired army officers, many of whom had been in the cavalry in their youth. Major-General Sir John Cowell was Master of the Household, and had served in the Baltic and the Crimea. He was a friend of General Gordon, and a capable soldier of the scientific sort, having been in the Royal Engineers. He had been governor to Prince Alfred and also to Prince Leopold. Randall Davidson described him as a 'man of deep religious earnest-ness . . . essentially something of a martinet, and [he] strangely lacked adaptability or ingenuity in effecting his excellent purposes for and in the Royal Household. His splendidly high tone and serious views of life were appreciated by the Queen, although she came personally to be tired of him and certainly did not follow his advice.' On many occasions he came to blows with John Brown, the Queen's Highland Servant, on the question of the amount of alcohol consumed by the servants. The Queen, who was indulgent on this point, always sided with Brown.

More congenial to Reid, or Jimmy as he came to be called by the Household, was Lord Bridport, the permanent lord-in-waiting, a charming, elderly, retired General, with whom Reid spent many an hour sightseeing and 'loafing about' during the Queen's spring hol-idays abroad. Sir John McNeill, an Equerry since 1874, and yet another Major-General, was a favourite with Reid, too. He had served both in the Indian Mutiny and in the Ashanti Expedition of 1873-4, and had become ADC to the Duke of Cambridge when Commander-in-Chief. He was a delightful man with a great sense of humour, but was apt to be abrupt with servants. He also crossed swords with the redoubtable John Brown.

The most important and the most loved and admired member of the Household was Sir Henry Ponsonby, the Queen's Private Sec-retary. Sir Henry had served the royal family for many years, having been Equerry to the Prince Consort, and had succeeded to the secretaryship from his wife's uncle, General Grey, in 1870. In spite of their difference in age and background a warm friendship grew up between Ponsonby and Reid, whose foundation lay in a shared sense of the ridiculous. With his over-acute sense of humour Ponsonby knew he could get a response from Reid and that he would be able to share with him his very occasional relaxations. Their approach to life enabled them both to put up with Her Majesty's manifold foibles, and to submit to all the petty restrictions imposed upon them by Court life under a strict headmistress.

With great skill Sir Henry acted as a liaison between the Queen and her Ministers, using tact and discretion when conveying despatches and, where necessary, tempering the tone, if not the content, of her messages so as not to offend her Ministers, and vice versa. Although a convinced Liberal himself (his wife Mary had radical views), he never allowed politics to interfere in his work as Private Secretary, as Disraeli's tribute to him testifies: 'I believe that General Ponsonby used to be a Whig, but, whatever his politics may once have been, I can only say that I could not wish my case better stated to the Queen than the Private Secretary does it. Perhaps I am a gainer by his Whiggishness as it makes him more scrupulously on his guard to be absolutely fair and lucid.'

Ponsonby's task was not made easier by the Queen's insistence that all communications between him and members of the Household should be in writing. This involved a great deal of extra work for her already overburdened Secretary. Ponsonby was also miserable at Balmoral so far away from his wife whom he dearly loved. He was not a countryman, nor a sportsman, and for the routine pursuits of a country gentleman he simply had not time. Besides, at Balmoral the atmosphere was more enclosed than ever, and domestic disputes more numerous; and there was the added difficulty of carrying on the affairs of State from such a remote establishment. Ponsonby was the man who bore the brunt of all this inconvenience.

Perhaps the most apposite summary of his character is that of Arthur Bigge, who was his colleague for fifteen years.

The longer I live and the more I look back, the more remarkable man he seems to me. One of, if not the greatest gentleman I have known: the entire effacement of *self*: the absolute nonexistence of conceit, side or pose: the charming courtesy to strangers old, young, high, low, rich, poor. His extraordinary wit and sense of the ridiculous, his enormous powers of work – too much – it killed him, but I never heard him say he was hard-worked or had too much to do, nor did I ever hear him say 'Oh, don't bother! Come back in five minutes; I am writing an important letter to the Queen or Prime Minister or Archbishop of Canterbury, Cardinal Manning, Mrs Langtrey, etc:' The letter was put down and he listened patiently and considered whether the Crown Equerry or the Equerry-in-

Waiting should ride on the right of the Queen or whether next Sunday's preacher should refer to this or that.

Sir Henry Ponsonby had two Assistant Private Secretaries and Keepers of the Privy Purse, Captain Fleetwood Edwards and Captain Arthur Bigge. The former was seven years older than Reid but Bigge was an exact contemporary, which must have been refreshing for Reid who, during his early years at Court, was forced to spend most of his time with men much older than himself. Like Sir John Cowell, Fleetwood Edwards had been an officer in the Royal Engineers. He had accompanied General Sir John Simmons to the Congress of Berlin, and was an efficient and businesslike person. The Queen showed her trust in, and respect for, him by making him an executor of her will, the only non-royal person to be honoured in this way. Edwards, like Reid, enjoyed walking and they were often seen together in this daily pursuit.

With Arthur Bigge Reid was to form a deep and lifelong friendship. Bigge had been an officer in the Royal Artillery and had served in the Zulu War as A.D.C. to Sir Evelyn Wood. He had also been the Prince Imperial's intimate friend at Woolwich and in the Artillery, and, but for a serious illness, Bigge would have been with his friend at the time of his death in a skirmish on the banks of the Ityatosi River. Bigge had brought the Prince's body to England where it was interred at Chislehurst by the side of his father, Napoleon III. He was later selected by the Queen to accompany the grief-stricken Empress Eugénie on a pilgrimage to Zululand to see the spot where her beloved son had died. The journey, lasting many weeks, through inhospitable country and in the most difficult circumstances, was an unusual and responsible task which Bigge nevertheless undertook to the satisfaction of both Majesties. The Empress remained his friend for forty years, until her death, and it was through him that Reid came to know this charming and beautiful lady. So impressed was the Queen by the way in which Bigge had handled this tricky operation that on his return from Zululand she appointed him as Assistant Private Secretary to the overworked Ponsonby. Bigge soon learnt the ropes. A man of diligence and good judgment, he had a talent for distinguishing between the molehills and mountains as well as an appreciation of the lighter side of Court life. He, Reid, and Ponsonby were able to derive a good deal of amusement from a life which could have become intolerable without a sense of humour.

More indispensable to the Queen even than Ponsonby was her servant John Brown. A great deal has been said and written about

John Brown and his relationship with Queen Victoria, which to many remains an enigma to this day. What is undisputed is that his influence upon the Queen, and his effect upon those around him, was considerable. Born in 1826, in Crathie on the Balmoral estate, his father, Jamie, was a small crofter, his mother the daughter of the local blacksmith. From the first John Brown distinguished himself by being one of the strongest and most agile lads in that wild district. He was tall, handsome, and had a strong personality. When the Queen and Prince Albert first came to live at Balmoral, Brown, who had been a stable-lad to Sir Robert Gordon, became Albert's gillie. In this capacity he always accompanied the Queen and her Consort on their various expeditions into the Highlands, where his rough common sense, agility and calm efficiency in the face of danger appealed to his royal employers. After Prince Albert's death in 1861 the Queen, inconsolable and delirious in her grief, shut herself away from public view. In 1864, still wretched and depressed, and showing no sign of overcoming her sorrow, her condition caused grave concern. Sir William Jenner had a sudden inspiration. Why not bring John Brown down to Osborne to act as her groom? This was immediately arranged, and from that moment until his death Brown, having been promoted rapidly from groom to personal attendant, remained constantly at her side. He was often peremptory and rude to her, he was far too fond of whisky, he was intolerable to visitors at Balmoral and Osborne, patting Ministers on the back and being familiar with the family; but no matter how appalling his behaviour, the Queen always forgave him, and came to depend upon his close personal attendance in a manner that was both touching and ludicrous. Furthermore, he was her link with her husband and those happy days in the Highlands.

The two ladies most closely attached to the Queen were Lady Ely and Lady Churchill, both Janes, who had been ladies of the bed-chamber since the 1850s. Lady Ely, widow of the third Marquis of Ely, had neither specialised knowledge nor particular discretion for so important a role, but she was pretty and charming and adored the Queen, who bullied her mercilessly. She delivered the Queen's instructions in a 'mysterious whisper' which so vibrated with awe that sometimes it was incoherent. Being too polite to cross-examine her, people sometimes did the wrong thing, which led at times to petty rows in the Household. She whispered everything to the Queen, who seemed to weave a hypnotic spell over her.

Lady Churchill, wife of the second Baron Churchill, was quite different. She was vigilant and helpful, and had great common sense. She, too, was frightened of the Queen, but hid her feelings and if possible avenged herself by disturbing somebody else. The Queen liked to entrust to her the writing of royal reprimands, which went down to the offices of the Private Secretary or Master of the Household. There was no mistaking the meaning in her concise messages, which were often ill-appreciated. Some at Court liked her, and all respected her.

Another lady of the bedchamber was Lady Erroll, whose family seat, Slains Castle, was close to Ellon. During his holidays Reid used to stay with the Errolls and became a friend of the eccentric owner of the castle, the Lord High Constable of Scotland, Lord Erroll. Lady Erroll was a kindly, rather stupid woman, who frequently annoyed the Queen by her tactlessness. She suffered from an overdose of evangelical fervour and supported all kinds of odd philanthropic causes.

The circle would not be complete without mentioning Hermann Sahl, the Queen's German secretary. Sahl was rather a character, clever in his way, but absurdly touchy, always looking out for slights, and sometimes absenting himself from meals in a huff. He was supposed to carry on the work begun by Prince Albert's mentor, Baron Stockmar – cataloguing correspondence – but as the correspondence increased with such rapidity he soon found the burden intolerable and gave up, placing the papers he was given in cupboards without attempting to sort them. Another of his duties was to draft official letters of condolence and congratulation to foreign sovereigns.

When Reid first joined the Household he and Hermann Sahl were a species apart, and had to dine in a special room allotted to them as they were considered to be 'below the salt'. Very soon Reid began to entertain his friends and members of the Household in his room, where they would be sure of a lively evening – a change from the Queen's rather dull, formal dinners. It was not long before the Queen heard about this: 'I hear Dr Reid has dinner parties!' She did not approve of this rival attraction, and decided that the only way to put a stop to these entertainments was to permit the culprit to join the Household dinners, which he did, to the benefit of its members. On 23 December 1882 Reid was ordered by the Queen to dine with the Household at Osborne. Eventually he was included in the Queen's own dinner parties. After years at the Queen's table Reid complained he found himself 'excited about small things which when he got away he didn't care a damn for'.

After her beloved Balmoral, Osborne was the place the Queen most enjoyed. It was the first home of their own which she and Prince Albert had created together. The house, designed by Thomas Cubitt in 1846 in the Italian style with campaniles, alcoves and terraces, was inspired by Albert. His rooms, untouched since his death, were a constant reminder of happier days when the royal children played at being mothers and fathers in the Swiss Cottage, and where they were allowed freedom to romp, unusual in mid-Victorian times. Here Reid was enjoying himself, not doing '*one day's* work', and reported to his mother that he saw 'a constant succession of swells here, and had a good look at them'. While at Osborne he was introduced to Disraeli's brother, who 'is rather like the pictures of his late brother'. On 28 August 1881 Reid's temporary appointment was, after six weeks' trial, made permanent. This was well before the contracted time laid out in his conditions of employment.

On 24 August Reid went on his first journey with the Queen, as a member of her Suite, to Edinburgh to stay at Holyrood Palace. He was present at a Review of the Scottish Volunteers by Her Majesty. It rained torrents the whole day.

From Edinburgh the Court moved to Balmoral where, as a result of getting thoroughly wet at the Review, the Queen caught a chill and, most unusual for her, failed to attend the Braemar Gathering. In Aberdeenshire Reid was on his home ground and, unlike many of the courtiers, he enjoyed being there. He was used to the cold, harsh climate and did not at first mind the cramped conditions as much as some of his more spoilt colleagues. He did, however, after a spell at Balmoral look forward to his more 'commodious quarters' at Windsor.

Balmoral, the Queen's favourite residence, was in reality no more than a typical Scottish baronial country house. The estate was bought by Victoria and Albert from the Fife Trustees in 1852, after much searching around Scotland for somewhere to settle. The existing house was pulled down and the foundation stone of the new one laid in September 1853. William Smith of Aberdeen was the architect who, with the help of the chief mason, James Beaton, created a perfect monument in the vernacular style. The house lies in the valley of the Dee, surrounded by hills and forest, whose romantic scenery reminded Albert of his childhood home in Thuringia.

The Court was inevitably, both on account of the smallness of the place and its remoteness, more closely knit than at Windsor. Royalty were thrown into close contact with the Household, who felt the Queen's petty restrictions more keenly here than elsewhere. One evening at dinner the Household were served a special wine which Reid for some reason refused. The waiter leant forward and whispered, 'The Prince Consort's birthday', to which Reid responded with alacrity, 'Well, I have no objection', to the amusement of all present. The Queen, never one to forget the past, clung to it more tenaciously than ever at Balmoral. Sir Henry Campbell-Bannerman, a Minister-in-Attendance in the 1890s, thought the castle was like a convent. 'We meet at meals and when we are finished each is off to his cell.'

The Queen was an inveterate scribbler who filled volume upon volume of journal, and page upon page of black-edged paper, with her bold illegible handwriting. She remained invisible most of the time, communicating with the inmates of her establishment by note only, and kept the footmen busy delivering her messages to various members of the Household, including her secretary who, likely as not, would be sitting in the next room. Invisible she might be, but nothing escaped her notice. Discipline was strict. No one was allowed to leave the castle until the Queen had gone out. Gladstone ignored this rule and was severely reprimanded in consequence.

Reid received his first handwritten instruction from the Queen while he was at Balmoral. It is a typical example of the type of message the Queen would send scattering in all directions. The note of authority is always there. 'Let Dr Reid go out from quarter to 11 to one, unless the Queen sends before to see him, and from 5 till *near* 8. If he wishes on any particular occasion to go out sooner he shd. ask. These are the regular hours. But I may send *before* to say he is not to go out before I have seen him shd. I not feel well or want anything. This every Doctor in attendance has done and must be prepared to do.'

During Reid's first Christmas and New Year sojourn at Osborne Sir Henry Ponsonby received a note from the Queen requesting that 'Dr Reid shd. go to see the Netley Hospital sometime'. The Royal Victoria Hospital at Netley, near Southampton, had been built on Queen Victoria's instructions in 1856, and one of Reid's duties was to keep her regularly informed as to the state of this large military hospital and show important visitors around the premises. On this occasion he went to Netley with Princess Beatrice and the Empress Eugénie. 'On board the Yacht I was presented to the Empress at her desire, by Baron Corvisart, and I had the honour of a short conversation with her both going and coming. She is very like her photographs and seems in fair spirits,' he reported to his mother.

Back at Windsor, the Queen attended a Drawing Room at Buckingham Palace and as her carriage left Windsor Station on her return a man called Roderick MacLean fired a revolver and the shot passed uncomfortably close to John Brown, who was in the rumble seat. 'I had just got out of the train with the other members of the Suite, and was standing near the Queen's carriage when the shot was fired,' Reid informed his mother. Fortunately he was not required to carry out any first aid as no one was hurt. The Queen remained calm throughout the whole proceeding, and on her return to Windsor wrote:

> Took tea with Beatrice, and telephoned to all my children and relations. Brown came in to say that the revolver had been found loaded, and one chamber discharged. Superintendent Hayes, of the Police here, seized the man, who was wretchedly dressed, and had a very bad countenance. Sir H. Ponsonby came in to tell me more. The man will be examined tomorrow. He is well-spoken and evidently an educated man. Then came Lord Bridport, who repeated the same thing, saying that the man's intentions seemed very clear. An Eton boy had rushed up, and beaten him with an umbrella. Great excitement prevails. Nothing can exceed dearest Beatrice's courage and calmness, for she saw the whole thing, the man take aim, and fired straight into the carriage, but she never said a word, observing that I was not frightened.

That night the Queen 'slept well as usual, and never once thought of what had occurred'.

Some weeks before the incident Reid had written to his mother about his proposed journey to Mentone, in France, with the Queen in March.

> It will be a nice trip for me, though of course it will be rather a heavier responsibility to have medical charge of the Queen so far from Jenner. There will be a very small Suite, only two ladies and three gentlemen, the latter being Lord Bridport, Sir H. Ponsonby, and myself. We three, as the village is not large enough, are to live in a Hotel about four minutes' walk from the Queen's villa: only the ladies live in the villa.

On the eve of his departure for Mentone Reid wrote:

> [I] slipped away from the Drawing Room to write a line before going to bed. I have been very busy the last day or two, as besides my ordinary work and overlooking the packing of my baggage by Vaughan [his valet], I have to make sure that I have all the drugs and professional appliances of every kind that I might want. We start tomorrow morning at 10 o'clock. We dine and sleep on board, and start next morning for our 30 hours' run by rail to Mentone. Of course the journey will be as comfortable and luxurious as possible!

The following evening from Cherbourg Harbour Reid wrote to his mother:

> We had a most lovely passage across, the day being fine and the sea like

47

a pond. We have just dined, and I am going to smoke with the officers. I have a most comfortable cabin and everything I can think of. This is a splendid yacht, not the small one we go to Osborne in, but the large one. They say there is not another like it in existence. The run across took up to 5½ hours, and we were accompanied by three other steamers, so it was rather a pretty sight.

The saloon carriages in which the Queen and her entourage travelled from Cherbourg to Mentone were her own property and the passengers on the royal train numbered between sixty and a hundred. Her slow progress along the Continental lines was a spectacle. The speed of the train was limited to thirty-five miles per hour by day and twenty-five by night. It was halted between eight and nine in the morning so that the Queen could dress in comfort, and stops were made for meals. Gentlemen requiring hot water for shaving sent word ahead and a jug awaited them at a convenient station. The Queen even brought food packed in special containers from Windsor but on the whole the French menus were preferred by the more discerning of the Suite. Although she travelled so-called incognito under the title of Madame la Comtesse de Balmoral, the Queen's progress had a distinctly royal flavour. She preferred to be mistress of her own Household rather than a guest when on the Continent. She took her own furniture with her; her bed and desk, her chair and couch, and a gallery of family pictures. She drove out only in her own carriage, drawn by her own horses and, latterly, the donkey which she acquired on one of her travels always went with her.

The Queen stayed at the Châlet des Rosiers, to the east of the town, which had a fine view facing the sea. Not far from Her Majesty's villa was the Hôtel des Anglais where Ponsonby, Bridport and Reid resided. 'Our Hotel is a capital one,' Reid wrote home, 'and from my bedroom window I could throw a stone into the Mediterranean. Our three bedrooms are all in a line, and we have a very nice sitting and dining room. We have all gone in for white umbrellas to keep off the sun, that being most indispensable in the heat of the day.' John Brown even went as far as to wear a topee to keep the sun off his face, which aroused the curiosity of the local inhabitants. 'I go to the Châlet twice a day, and am free all the rest of the day; so it is very nice for me. Bridport is also pretty idle, so we loaf about a good deal together. We have a special carriage told off for us (the three gentlemen) so I suppose we shall go somewhere every day.'

The *Inflexible* warship had just arrived in the bay and was to remain there for some time. Reid went on board with Lord Bridport and the

King of Saxony and his Suite, who were staying at Mentone. A further diversion was provided by a trip to Monte Carlo.

> Yesterday, Prince Leopold, Bridport, Ponsonby, Royle[5] and I drove to Monte Carlo. We went through the gambling establishment and saw the gaming going on. The place was quite crowded at the different tables, and a very motley crew the people are, all nations, ages and classes being represented, and half the players being women! In the evening Mentone was illuminated in honour of the Queen, and, as it is built on the slope of a hill, it looked first rate. The sea was covered with boats carrying Chinese lanterns, and the *Inflexible* was lit up with electricity. There was also a display of fireworks.

Reid was thoroughly enjoying himself. He always relished being abroad, unlike John Brown who hated it and made difficulties for the Queen. Apart from the change of climate, food and customs, the fact that Brown was unable to communicate with anyone made him feel insecure and ineffective in keeping people off the carriage when he was out driving. He also disliked the exposed grounds and lack of privacy at the Châlet des Rosiers, but this problem was solved by a Dr Bennet, author of *Spring on the Shores of the Mediterranean*, who put his fine secluded garden at the disposal of the Queen. Here she and Princess Beatrice were able to walk and sketch undisturbed. Reid, a gardening enthusiast, made friends with Dr Bennet, who showed him round his magnificent eight-acre garden and he went on several excursions with him.

In spite of enjoying a leisurely time at Mentone there were, nevertheless, one or two minor medical problems which had to be dealt with. On one occasion Reid received an urgent message from the Queen: 'The stopping having quite suddenly come out of the Queen's tooth, she wishes him to bring up something to stop it with *if possible* this evening before dinner.' Reid hastened to the Châlet des Rosiers and succeeded in stopping the tooth 'with complete and permanent success!' His training as doctor cum vet and dentist in Ellon no doubt served him in good stead on this occasion, as it did on others.

Another time the Queen suffered from a sore throat, but the prescription caused some discomfort. In a note to Reid she complained: 'In spraying her throat with tannin before dinner, the Queen found it made the part near the right ear burn, and it is sore. She

---

[5] Arnold Royle was physician to Prince Leopold, Duke of Albany, who needed a doctor in permanent attendance as he suffered from haemophilia, inherited through his mother, Queen Victoria.

wishes to know if she had better not spray with cold water instead?' The throat does not hurt at all in swallowing but the ear still aches a little. Should the poultice be *only linseed*?'

Once back at Windsor everyone was in a state of great excitement over the wedding of the Queen's youngest son, Prince Leopold, Duke of Albany, to Princess Helen Frederica Augusta of Waldeck-Pyrmont, which was to take place in St George's Chapel on 27 April 1882. The Queen was, quite naturally, concerned not only for her son who suffered from haemophilia, but more particularly for the bride who would be committing herself to an incurable invalid. Princess Helen disregarded all warnings for she was determined to marry her Leopold. She had great personality and was the one member of the royal family who was not in the least afraid of Queen Victoria. On the day of the wedding the Queen wrote in her Journal: 'It was very trying to see the dear boy, on this important day of his life, still lame and shaky, but I am thankful it is well over. I feel so much for dear Helen, but she showed unmistakably how devoted she is to him.'

For Reid there was a different worry. What should he wear? The Lord Chamberlain had decided that either uniform or Court Dress had to be worn, instead of morning dress as stated on the invitation cards. He was relieved to find that he was permitted to appear in his Volunteer Uniform and wrote an urgent note to his mother to send it. 'I am very glad indeed, as it settles all about my dress and will leave me no bother on that score. It also saves me getting a Court Uniform which is very expensive and would be little use to me afterwards; so that being a Volunteer has been some use to me after all. It is a good thing that I had not resigned! I suppose the wedding will be a pretty sight: but I am not very enthusiastic about these grand ceremonies.'

Reid had spent his first eighteen months at Queen Victoria's Court enjoying what we might be tempted to consider one long holiday. Fortunately, every aspect of his life was a novelty. However, had this state of affairs continued indefinitely a man of his calibre and intellect might have become restless. The fascination of meeting royalty, politicians and the elite, and of living in the lap of luxury, could not compensate for ever for the lack of interesting medicine, but early in 1883 events occurred which were to test the young medical attendant's capability to its utmost.

James as a fourteen-year-old grammarschoolboy.

The country doctor, James Reid senior, in 1862.

Reid with his mother, Beatrice Reid,
September 1884.

The Rev. James Peter (Uncle James), the Rev.
George Peter (Uncle George), Reid's mother,
Miss Peter (Aunt Barbara), photographed in May
1885 during a visit to Windsor.

'There is a sentry just under the window (marked with an x) so there is no fear of any night bird coming in upon me.'

The Queen at the time Reid came to court.

Household group at Balmoral, November 1884, l to r: Reid, Sir Henry Ponsonby, Dowager Duchess of Roxburghe, Sir John McNeill, Hon. Evelyn Moore, Dr. Profeit, Major Arthur Bigge (seated).

Captain Arthur Bigge, Assistant Private
Secretary and Equerry to the Queen, 1881.

Major General Sir John Cowell, Master
of the Household until 1894, in 1881.

The signed photograph of the Queen in court dress which she
presented to Reid after the birth of Princess Ena in 1887.

Major Fleetwood Edwards, Groom-in-
Waiting and Assistant Private
Secretary to the Queen, 1884.

General Sir Henry Ponsonby, the
Queen's Private Secretary and
Keeper of the Privy Purse, 1884.

Miss Dittweiler, the Queen's Chief Dresser, in 1882.

Mrs Tuck, Head Dresser, 1881.

Annie MacDonald, Wardrobe Maid, who served the Queen for forty-one years

The Queen setting out for a drive at Balmoral, September 1889.

'Friend more than Servant, Loyal, Truthful, Brave, Self less than Duty, even to the Grave.' The redoubtable John Brown in 1882.

The Brown clan in 1883.
Back row, l to r: Archibald, bust of John, Hugh; front row: William, James, Donald.

Sir Joseph Edgar Boehm, sculptor, 1884.

Randall Davidson, Dean of Windsor and later Archbishop of Canterbury.

Dr William Hoffmeister, Surgeon Apothecary to the Queen at Osbourne, 1882.

Sir James Paget, Bt., Sergeant Surgeon
to the Queen, 1883.

Sir William Jenner, Physician-in-Ordinary to
the Queen in 1881, wearing his robes as
President of the Royal College of Physicians.

Dr James Ellison, Surgeon Apothecary to the Queen at Windsor, 1884.

Sir John Williams, accoucheur to Princess
Beatrice, 1887.

Princess Victoria of Hesse who married Prince Louis of Battenberg.

Prince Louis of Battenberg at the time of his wedding in 1884.

Princess Louise, Marchioness of Lorne, 1890.

The Grand Duke of Hesse, 1884.

Madame Kolemine, for a few days the morganatic wife of the Grand Duke of Hesse.

Prince and Princess Henry of Battenberg at Balmoral soon after their marriage in 1885.

Princess Henry (Beatrice) with her 'Battenbunnies' in 1899, l to r: Princess Victoria Eugenie (Ena), Prince Leopold, Prince Maurice, Prince Alexander, Marquess of Carisbrooke (Drino).

The four royal dukes, l to r: Duke of Rothsay (Prince of Wales), Duke of Edinburgh (Prince Alfred), Duke of Connaught (Prince Arthur), Duke of Albany (Prince Leopold).

Five Victorias, behind: Princess Victoria of Wales, Princess Victoria of Prussia; in front, Queen Victoria, Princess Victoria of Edinburgh, the Crown Princess Victoria of Germany.

Three Deaths

The year 1883 opened with great activity for Reid. In February he wrote to his mother: 'The Connaughts have gone to Mentone and left their children under my medical care. I have quite enough to do at present, as there is scarlet fever in the town and Dr Ellison is prohibited from coming here in the meantime, so I have all the 300 people in the Castle to take care of in addition to my usual work.' There was the added inconvenience of floods. 'In the lower parts of Windsor the water came half up the ground floor rooms: and it is funny to see boats plying in the streets taking people to and from houses!'

On 25 February Princess Alice of Albany was born at Windsor Castle. There was a constant stream of notes to Reid before and after the birth (at which he was present) in which the Queen fussed over the sleeping arrangements of the royal parents, and the condition of the mother as though she herself were giving birth. As the mother of nine children there was little that the Queen did not know about confinements, and she made quite sure that her doctors should have the benefit of her experience.

Then there were two royal injuries to attend to. While Princess Helen was recovering from the birth of her first child, her husband sprained his leg and was confined to his room. Rather more serious was the Queen's fall. On 17 March she slipped on the stairs and injured a knee. His letter home reported: 'She is confined to her couch and has me in to see her very often. I have just written a paragraph for the Court Circular about her.' Several times a day Reid had to walk round Her Majesty's sitting room while she held his arm for support. He evidently enjoyed his new role. 'I am always getting on very well, and like my post *immensely*. It suits me to a T.'

There were scenes between Brown and his royal mistress about her being carried downstairs, but these did not last long for on 25 March Brown awoke with erysipelas of the face and was 'quite helpless all day'. He had caught a severe chill on his drive to The Fisheries, near Windsor, to see Lady Florence Dixie with a message from the Queen to enquire after her as reports had reached the Castle that Lady Florence had been attacked by two men, dressed as women, and stabbed with a knife. Apparently one of the men thrust a handful of mud in her mouth and eyes, and was about to renew the onslaught with the knife, when her St Bernard dog came to her rescue and threw himself upon the assailants, whereupon the two men fled. The whole affair was most mysterious as there was no apparent motive for the attack. Reid was sceptical about the event: 'As to Lady Florence Dixie, most of the Gentlemen here seem to think the story is an invention of her own; she is rather a queer customer,' he confided to Mama.

Nevertheless, according to some, Brown lost his life on her account. The afternoon was damp and an icy wind swept across the flat countryside as Brown drove over to The Fisheries in an open dogcart, having scorned the offer of a closed carriage. After he had heard an account of the incident from Lady Florence, he insisted upon going to the scene of the crime and searching every inch of the ground, with great thoroughness, for clues which the police had failed to find. So engrossed was he in his task that he never noticed the biting wind, and when he climbed into the dogcart to return to Windsor he was chilled to the bone, his resistance to infection thereby being greatly diminished.

This was not the first time that Brown had suffered from erysipelas. As early as 1865 he had cut his legs during an outing at Balmoral and one of his limbs became 'so inflamed and swelled so much that he could hardly move', the Queen noted. In 1877, while accompanying the Queen on a tour of the Dreadnought HMS *Thunderer*, he fell through an open space inside a gun turret and severely damaged his shins. But these were no ordinary shin barks and took an inordinately long time to heal. There had been occasions, too, at Balmoral, when Brown had come out in blotches, and once his face had swelled to such an extent that his eyes were shut. Dr Hal Yarrow, a specialist in skin diseases and Fellow of the Royal Society of Medicine, wrote: 'It is very likely that the sudden change from the healthy outdoor life formerly led by Brown to that of the comparatively soft living as the Queen's personal attendant would make him more prone to recurrent attacks, once the condition had manifested itself.' Chronic alcoholism which Brown suffered from towards the end of his life was an additional factor in reducing his resistance to bouts of erysipelas, and affords an explanation for his surliness and irritability, which caused him to make enemies at every hand.

This time Reid noted that, 'by the evening of 26 March he was worse, and suffered from delirium tremens'. Sir William Jenner slept overnight at the Castle, but Reid – as native of Aberdeenshire – was the favoured doctor and more constantly in attendance upon the dying man. The Queen, who was deeply concerned about Brown's condition, was, nevertheless, totally unaware of its gravity. She sent a note to Reid suggesting that 'Dr Profeit might be acquired to help nursing our good Brown. If you thought so too I could telegraph to him and have him say he had come up on business. I think it might be a relief to you as he knows his family so well.' In her anxiety the Queen had lapsed into the first person, which was most unusual in her notes to members of her Household, normally written in the more formal third person.

On the morning of 27 March Reid received a telegram from Dr Fowler, his father's fellow practitioner, to say that his father was seriously ill, and a little later another telegram from his uncle, George Peter, announcing that his father had died the previous evening. With Brown at death's door the Queen felt unable to release her doctor, but she wrote a mitigating letter which went some way towards comforting Reid in his distress:

It is with the deepest concern that the Queen has just heard of the terrible loss which Dr Reid has sustained in so awfully sudden a manner and additionally so as he was not able to be with him and his poor mother at the last. Dr Reid has been kind and attentive, and so *indefatigable* in his care of the faithful Brown and herself, that she feels doubly grieved and distressed at this great sorrow and trouble which have come upon him. Now she grieves so that he could not start off instantly on knowing the sad news. The Queen is so thankful that Dr Profeit D.V. will be here tomorrow and able to relieve him and enable him to go to his mother.

On the same day Reid wrote his mother a letter which, in the circumstances, seems matter of fact and even lacking in sympathy. In his defence it must be said that he was preoccupied with what for him was a great crisis, and he was, in any event, not a man to indulge strong emotion. His observations are honest if not over filial.

When I got Fowler's letter this morning, I had a presentiment of what it meant. I fancy you must sometimes have thought something sudden might happen and have been in a measure prepared: and you must now bear up as well as you can, especially as you have got John and me left who will always be devoted to you as long as we live, and do all we can to make you happy. I am awfully sorry I can't come off at once, and only something of the utmost importance would have prevented me; that something is the very dangerous illness of John Brown, the Queen's servant. He has got erysipelas of the head and I fear will die. The Queen is in a great state of grief about him. I have hardly a moment to myself day or night, or I would have been writing you sooner; and now it is rather hard not to be able to get away: it could not have occurred at a more inopportune time, as the

Queen herself is not nearly well yet. Now you must take it calmly and keep up. I fancy after all it is better than if he had had a long and painful illness. I must go now and help the Queen into a carriage.

On the evening of 27 March John Brown died. The next day Reid was still unable to leave the Queen and go to his mother, but he wrote to her again: '*Brown is dead*. The Queen is in a great way about it. Jenner was here last night when he died and comes again tonight; but still the Queen was anxious I should stay till Profeit comes tomorrow, and as I could not see Papa alive, and also knew that you had uncle and aunt with you [George and Barbara Peter], I thought it best to comply with Her Majesty's wish, though had I pressed it she would have let me go tonight.' It was not until 30 March, three days after his father's death, that Reid was able to be with his mother who, throughout her own tragedy had remained sympathetic and understanding, never resenting his absence at a time when she most needed him.

With the death of his father Reid was suddenly burdened with extra responsibility, not only for the welfare of his mother, but also for The Chesnuts and the family farm at Hillhead. It was not easy to manage a farm from such a distance and the vagaries of the Aberdeenshire climate merely added to the problems which were to plague Reid for the next few years. His constant references to the weather in his letters to his mother were not so much polite small talk as based on an interest in the mundane business of profit and loss. Good weather meant profit, bad weather loss, which he could ill afford as he struggled to pay off his father's debts.

On 2 April a telegram arrived at The Chesnuts from the Queen: 'Anxious to know how you and your mother are, thought much of you yesterday, am very miserable and stunned.' There is something touching and thoughtful about this message, sent while the Queen was wrapped up in her own grief, although there is an underlying current of remorse. Being a highly emotional person she was able to identify with the tragedies of others and was warmly sympathetic towards them. For the widow she had a special understanding, and in her later letters to Reid she frequently enquired after his mother.

A couple of months later he received a letter from the Queen with a small, silver-framed portrait of his father, painted on enamel, with an inscription on the back of the frame. The letter reads: 'The Queen hopes Dr Reid will accept the accompanying recollection of a day so terribly sad to him and her, the remembrance of which will ever be one of the most painful ones in her life.'

From the time of John Brown's illness there developed a closer bond between the Queen and her doctor. The Queen came to trust Reid implicitly and she always knew that, when asked for an opinion, he would say what he thought rather than what he thought the Queen would like to hear. In this respect, if in no other, he was like John Brown, though he expressed himself with greater tact and in a more gentlemanly manner.

The Queen mourned deeply the loss of her Highland servant. 'Weep with me for we all have lost the best, the truest heart that ever beat. My grief is unbounded, dreadful, and I know not how to bear it, or how to believe it possible,' she wrote to Hugh Brown's wife (John Brown's sister-in-law). To Sir Henry Ponsonby she described herself as 'utterly crushed. The loss of the strong arm and wise advice, warm heart and cheery original way of saying things and the sympathy in any large and small circumstances is most cruelly missed.' She wrote to her grandson, Prince George, the future George V, 'Never forget your poor sorrowing Grandmama's best and truest friend.'

While Reid was at Ellon with his mother John Brown lay in state for six days in the Clarence Tower, Windsor, before being given what amounted to a hero's funeral. The Court Circular obituary bore the unmistakable signs of the Queen's composition. On 29 March the *Daily Telegraph* informed the public of the 'grievous shock' sustained by the Queen in the loss of this 'honest, faithful and devoted follower' who had secured for himself her 'real friendship', and on 3 April the Queen hobbled across to the Clarence Tower, leaning heavily on Princess Beatrice, to attend his funeral service. Her wreath of myrtle and choice white flowers lay alongside one from the Empress Eugénie. Nothing less than a tribute from two Empresses was good enough for Brown.

There were those close to the Queen who thought that Her Majesty, Brown, and the spirit of Albert formed some mystic triangle. The cult of Spiritualism and the occult was rife in the latter half of Queen Victoria's reign, and the Queen was not beyond conducting 'willing' seances in her drawing room with Princesses Beatrice and Irene, and the Duchess of Roxburghe, or whoever was available; sometimes even Reid was persuaded to join in, but being a sceptic his heart was not in it, and whenever possible he refused to partake in these sessions. Boyd Carpenter, the Bishop of Ripon and a favourite cleric of the Queen's who often came to see her, wrote to Reid in a light-hearted vein in 1885: 'I hope that later on we may be able to fix the "spiritualist". I shall still look forward to an evening when we can join hands across the table and find out what is beneath us.'

Although they were only lightly dabbling in the occult, what went on behind the scenes? More than twenty years after the death of John Brown Reid once more became involved, albeit indirectly, with the Queen and her servant, this time over the contents of a black trunk which contained more than 300 letters written by Queen Victoria to Dr Profeit about John Brown, 'many of them most compromising', as Reid recorded in his diary. The contents of these letters will never be known. Their secret was contained in Reid's green memorandum book which was burnt by his son after his death, but they involved a case of blackmail from which Reid extricated Queen Victoria's successor. Could the Queen have been communicating with Albert, using Brown as a medium, or do these numerous letters contain matters of a more intimate nature? The former possibility seems unlikely in the light of what we know about the respective characters of Queen Victoria and John Brown. The Queen could be morbid and often dwelt on the subject of death, but she was essentially practical and down-to-earth, the very antithesis of a mystic. John Brown was a true native of Aberdeenshire, a rough and tough Highlander, a loyal servant full of common sense, but devoid of imagination or a single speck of mystery, 'stuff and nonsense' being his attitude to anything that smacked of the supernatural. As to the latter possibility, no one will ever know.

Once recovered from the initial shock of Brown's death the Queen turned her attention to Brown memorials. They ranged from plaster of Paris busts to gold tiepins. Reid was presented with a blue and gold enamel locket containing a likeness of Brown and inscribed on the back, 'In recollection of the 27th March 1883 from V.R.I.' But the most imposing monument to the Highlander was the life-size bronze statue of Brown by the Viennese sculptor, Sir Edgar Boehm. It was placed alongside the garden cottage at Balmoral and stood guard over the Queen when, in fine weather, she sat out working on her despatch boxes.[1] Lady Erroll, a strict Calvinist, disapproved of this graven image which she likened to that which Nebuchadnezzar raised to the pagan idol Baal. Boehm had depicted the Brown of former days, before he had gone to seed, a fine rugged man dressed in his native costume, with his chest festooned with medals awarded to him by his grateful royal mistress for services beyond the call of duty. On the plinth upon which he stands are carved the enigmatic words suggested to the Queen by her friend, the poet Alfred, Lord Tennyson:

[1] Edward VII had the statue removed and it is now hidden from view amongst trees on the hillside behind Baile-na-Coile, the house which the Queen had built for John Brown shortly before he died.

Friend more than servant, Loyal, Truthful, Brave,
Self less than Duty, even to the Grave.

Sir Edgar Boehm saw in Reid a useful liaison between himself and the Queen. He had enjoyed Reid's company at Balmoral on hill walking expeditions, where they could reminisce together about life in Vienna, and he had consulted Reid about how best to approach the Queen on the subject of Brown's statue. Even at this early stage in his career Reid was finding himself involved in matters which were entirely unrelated to medicine, as courtiers and outsiders began to realise that he had easy access to the Queen. Since her fall in March he had seen her several times a day.

Apart from the stiff and swollen knee which Sir James Paget, Her Majesty's Sergeant Surgeon, came to see in the middle of April the Queen temporarily lost the use of her legs. This had occurred on other occasions in moments of great emotional stress – in 1861 for instance – when, according to Lady Clarendon, the Queen seemed 'hardly able to move one leg before the other'. A few days after Brown's death Victoria wrote to Sir Henry Ponsonby: 'The Queen can't walk the least and the shock she has sustained has made her very weak – so that she can't stand.' In the present instance, the Queen's wrenched knee made it impossible for her to walk unaided, but when her helplessness persisted after the swelling in her knee had gone down it was thought by her doctors that the symptoms were of psychogenic origin. All male members of the Household were banned from the Queen's dinners in the weeks immediately following Brown's death, as she complained to Ponsonby: 'How can I see people at dinner in the evening? I can't go walking about all night holding on to the back of a chair?'

Remedies from the public poured in to Ponsonby, and it was even suggested that the Queen should try her hand at riding a tricycle. 'Fancy the Queen on a tricycle,' Ponsonby wrote to his wife! Six months after her fall Lady Ely wrote from Balmoral to Reid, who was at Ellon, that 'Charlotte [the Queen's masseuse] has finished her treatment this morning. The Queen has borne it wonderfully, but it is enough. I think H.M. certainly walks and moves about better.' Nevertheless, she had still not completely recovered by 26 January 1884, ten months after the death of Brown. According to the Court Circular, 'Her Majesty is able to take short walks out of doors, but she can stand only for a few minutes.' A year was to pass before the Queen returned to normal, although for the rest of her life she was to suffer from rheumatism in her knee.

If she was back on her feet, the Queen was certainly not going to let the memory of John Brown fade. In February 1884 she published *More Leaves from a Journal of our Life in the Highlands*, which she had dedicated to her faithful gillie. On the first anniversary of Brown's death she presented Reid with a copy, inscribed with the following words: 'To Doctor James Reid M.D. whose kindness during those dreadful days last year, and at a time of deep grief to himself she can never forget, from Victoria R.I. Windsor Castle, March 24th 1884.' Her family clearly did not approve of the exposure of her private life and thoughts to her people, especially since Brown's name appeared in the pages all too frequently. The public, however, received the book warmly; indeed it was such a success that the Queen was spurred on to write a *Life of John Brown*, which she planned to publish for private circulation (although it would certainly have reached the public before long), together with excerpts from the gillie's diaries. News of this latest undertaking left the Household thunderstruck. Something had to be done to prevent it. Reid had discussions with Ponsonby and Lady Ely on the subject but it was Randall Davidson, the new Dean of Windsor, who finally brought things to a head.

From the very first time that the Queen set eyes on Randall Davidson in December 1882 she was impressed by him, and wrote to Gladstone the following day: 'He is singularly pleasing both in appearance and manner, very sympathetic and evidently very intelligent – wise and able.' This was praise indeed for a young man of thirty-four years. Davidson combined charm with intellectual ability, though sometimes he made difficulties for himself by assessing problems from too many viewpoints, thereby leaving his questioner baffled by his solutions. The new Dean was naturally favoured with a copy of *More Leaves from a Journal of our Life in the Highlands*. But while thanking the Queen for her gift, he seized the opportunity of suggesting that a further volume would be inadvisable. The Queen took offence at Davidson's presumption, banished him from her sight and filled his place in the pulpit with another cleric, at the same time letting it be known that in spite of all objections she intended to publish the *Life of John Brown*. She asked the young Dean to withdraw his remarks, and apologise for the pain which he had caused her. Davidson was willing to apologise for the pain but refused to withdraw his remarks about the book and, having stood his ground, offered to resign. After a few weeks the Queen saw sense and, having summoned Davidson to her presence on an entirely different matter, she was, in his own words, 'more friendly than ever' to him. 'My belief is that she liked and trusted best those who incurred her wrath provided that she had reason to think their motives good,' he said. The unfortunate memoir and Brown's diaries, which had remained with Ponsonby throughout the furore, were referred to no more, and Ponsonby quietly disposed of them.

Just as the Queen was beginning to recover from one great sorrow another afflicted her a year almost to the day, after the death of John Brown. On 17 March 1884 the Prince of Wales held a levée on behalf of the Queen at Buckingham Palace and Reid, as an Acting Surgeon of the 2nd Volunteer Battalion of the Gordon Highlanders, was presented by Prince Leopold, Duke of Albany. A day or two later Prince Leopold went to Cannes for a holiday while his wife was waiting for her second baby. On the anniversary of Brown's death the Queen heard that her youngest son had hurt his knee. The following day Reid had to decypher a telegram for the Queen from Arnold Royle, the Duke of Albany's doctor. 'Fits quite sudden, probably unconnected with fall. Results sinking pulse. We are brokenhearted.' The same day Prince Leopold died from a haemorrhage of the brain. The Queen, although grief stricken, was philosophical on this occasion: 'Too too dreadful!' she wrote in her Journal. 'But we must bow to God's will and believe that it is surely for the best. The poor dear boy's life had been a very tried one, from early childhood! He was such a charming companion, so entirely the "Child of the House".' Prince Leopold was the son most like Albert, intelligent and intellectual, serious-minded and public spirited, but thwarted at every turn by the hereditary disease which caused his death at the early age of thirty.

Leopold's death kept Reid busy. 'I get lots of letters of condolence from various people which I have to show the Queen and answer, and several wreaths are being sent to me to see to, so I am very busy in addition to my ordinary work,' he informed his mother. On 5 April Reid attended the funeral. According to Prince Leopold's wishes, expressed in a letter to Princess Helen, he was buried in St George's Chapel and was given a military funeral. 'Of course I could say nothing against this, as I consider a wish of that kind as sacred. But personally, I should have liked the Mausoleum,' wrote the Queen.

On 10 April Reid was sent by the Queen's order 'into the Royal Vault to examine the Duke of Albany's coffin which was emitting offensive gas'. Evidently the coffin-makers at Cannes had not done a satisfactory job. Two days later he was entrusted with the task of rearranging the Prince's coffin in the vaults of St George's Chapel. There is a signed document written in his hand containing a detailed account of what occurred beneath the Chapel on 12 April. It is inscribed on black-edged paper addressed Windsor Castle, and on the outside is a note in the Queen's hand, written in purple pencil, saying 'Relative to dear Leopold's remains 1884'.

> This day, at 12 o'clock noon, the undersigned went down with Mr Howe, Clerk of the Works, into the Royal Vault under St George's Chapel, for the purpose of seeing the coffin containing the remains of the late Prince Leopold, Duke of Albany, placed in a new leaden coffin which had been prepared so as to afford extra protection to the remains.
>
> The new leaden coffin having been made to fit accurately the one containing His Royal Highness's body, the latter with the wooden casing over it (which was so closely connected with the leaden one that it was considered better not to remove it) was lifted in, and found to fit exactly. The leaden lid was then put on and securely soldered down, and the whole made ready to be deposited in the outer oak coffin.
>
> 1. Leaden coffin made at Cannes
> 2. Wooden coffin
> 3. Leaden coffin made at Windsor to which, in a few days, will be added
> 4. Oak coffin made at Windsor
>
> James Reid, M.D.

The placing of the lead coffin within the oak container took place on 21 April in the presence of Sir William Jenner, while the Queen and Reid were in Darmstadt for the wedding of Prince Louis of Battenberg to the Queen's granddaughter, Princess Victoria of Hesse.

This, however, was not to be Prince Leopold's final resting place for on 23 June 1885 his remains were removed from the vaults at St George's Chapel to the Memorial Chapel.

On 28 June Reid asked the Queen whether 'he should be present at the closing of the sarcophagus, which he had heard from the Dean takes place tomorrow morning at 6 o'clock'. The Queen's reply was brief and to the point: 'Yes, and Hugh and Archie Brown *also*.' While the rest of the inhabitants of the Castle were sleeping, four of the Queen's Scots, her Dean, her doctor, and her two Highland servants (John Brown's brothers) were present in the Memorial Chapel at Windsor to see the closing of her son's sarcophagus.

Another of Reid's duties was more reminiscent of his Ellon apprenticeship. When the Queen's favourite collie, Noble, became ill he was called in to prescribe for him. On one occasion she was anxious that Noble should be fed at night, for 'I have such a dread that he may sleep away!' Rotherham, the vet, came to see the collie in consultation with Reid and declared: 'I think you will have him for a long time yet, if he does not get any bones and is regularly, but not overfed.' Three years after this advice was given the Queen's faithful friend, who always guarded her gloves, died at Balmoral aged sixteen. Reid was present at his death and recorded the occasion in detail.

> The Queen's old dog Noble died about 11.30 p.m. of convulsions which came on suddenly after his supper, and went on for two hours at intervals of two or three minutes till he died. Her Majesty was much upset, and cried a great deal, said she was so fond of those that were gone, and that everything in the world comes to an end: that she believes dogs have souls and a future life: and she could not bear to go to see his body, though she would have liked to kiss his head. Kingsley and many people, she says, believe dogs have souls. I had to increase the strength of her sleeping draught, and only left her at 12.45 a.m. when she gave me the accompanying note of instructions for his burial:

>> I just write down what was done in the case of the Prince's beloved old dog, *EOS* who died 43 years ago and is buried in the slopes in a small bricked grave under *her statue* at the top of the slopes at Windsor. The grave was bricked, and coins were placed in the bag in which the dear dog (who was only 10 years old) was placed. I wish the grave to be bricked. The dear dog to be wrapped up in the box lined with lead and *charcoal*, placed in it, as well as some coins. I feel as if I could not bring myself to go and choose the spot. Dr Profeit would perhaps suggest it. I will then tell Mr Profeit to write to Mr Boehm to get a repetition of his statue of the dear Dog in bronze to be placed over the grave.

Whether it be for a son, for a servant, or for a dog the Queen always attended minutely to the details of the burial. In her eyes each and every one of God's creatures deserved a memorial. Her sculptor was kept perpetually busy creating effigies to Queen Victoria's dear departed. It was as if she loved them all the more when they were beyond reach, and though she never ceased to grieve for them, in her heart she knew that one day she would be reunited with them. Meanwhile she entrusted the problem of dealing with the earthly remains to her medical attendant, for who was more suited than a doctor to tend a body whether alive or dead?

4

Two Marriages

Less than a month after Prince Leopold's death the Queen and her entourage set off for Darmstadt to attend the wedding of her granddaughter, Princess Victoria of Hesse, to Prince Louis of Battenberg.[1]

Reid was pleased to be in Germany and wrote to his mother: 'I have to go and see the Queen at 10 o'clock in the morning and 7 o'clock at night; all the rest of the day I am free. We drive about a good deal, and as I know the Grand Duke's people very well and know the language, I feel quite at home.'

However, as the days passed Reid found Darmstadt 'a dull place, and none of us will be sorry to return'. Fortunately he managed to venture further afield and visited Frankfurt with Lord Bridport, and Heidelberg with Lord Carlingford, the Lord Privy Seal and Minister in Attendance upon the Queen, Lieutenant von Plöskow, who at 6 feet 8 inches had the distinction of being the tallest man in the German army, and Herr Muther, who had replaced Hermann Sahl as the Queen's German secretary. These excursions provided light relief from the confined atmosphere of Darmstadt.

A few days before the wedding the royal guests started to arrive: the Crown Prince and Princess of Germany and Prince William, their son; the Prince and Princess of Wales with their daughters; and other royal relations, who were packed tightly into the *Schloss*. Apart from the excitement and preparations for the wedding, which was to take place on 30 April, there was more than a hint that all was not quite as it should be. Reid reported home with relish:

> There is a scandal being whispered about here which I may tell you, as it is true, but you had better not publish it till it is in the newspapers, viz: that the Grand Duke of Hesse is going to marry a Polish lady of rather doubtful reputation, who is divorced from her husband, a Russian baron. The Queen does not yet know all the trouble, but she will be furious, and I don't expect we will ever come back here again, so I am seeing all there is to see here about, while we have the chance.

Reid, practical as ever, was evidently amused, but the Queen, when eventually she discovered the truth, was not.

[1] They later became Marquis and Marchioness of Milford Haven, parents of Earl Mountbatten of Burma, and grandparents of Prince Philip, Duke of Edinburgh.

Madame Alexandrine de Kolémine had been the Grand Duke's mistress for some time. She was beautiful and accomplished, and, furthermore, liked by the Grand Duke's children, who thought it would be a good idea for their father to be looked after when they had married and left Darmstadt. It would have been wise if, from the first, the Grand Duke had informed the Queen of his intentions, but his fear of upsetting his mourning mother-in-law or possibly, lack of moral courage, prevented him from doing so. How could she countenance the fact that the Grand Duke had been unfaithful to the memory of her daughter?

Romance was definitely in the air. The engagement was announced between Princess Elizabeth (Ella) of Hesse, the bride's younger sister (who had previously rejected the proposal of the future Kaiser Wilhelm II of Prussia), and the Grand Duke Serge of Russia. The wedding was to take place in St Petersburg in June. A mutual attraction had also sprung up between Prince Henry (Liko), Prince Louis' younger brother, and Princess Beatrice, which gave the Queen cause for anxiety. Finally, the young Prince of Bulgaria, Alexander (Sandro) of Battenberg, another of Louis' brothers, was deeply and hopelessly in love with the Crown Prince and Princess Frederick's daughter, Princess Victoria of Prussia. The Emperor and Empress of Germany, Bismarck, and Prince William were dead set against the marriage, not wishing to offend the Czar with whom Sandro had quarrelled, while the Crown Princess and the Queen were equally determined that this love match should take place. The Queen even sent Reid to see Prince Alexander, who was in bed with a sore throat and had lost his voice.

Anxieties, undercurrents and family feuds were all set aside on the day of the wedding. Despite his secret, the Grand Duke was in high spirits, for never before had Darmstadt been the centre of such a royal gathering. The streets were gaily decorated, the Hessians in a holiday mood, and there was a splendid and festive marriage programme. The groom, referred to by the Emperor of Germany as the most handsome man in Europe, was thirty years old, an officer in the British Navy, intelligent and amusing, with a gift for impersonation that could be wickedly funny at the expense of his victim. His bride was an attractive girl of twenty-one, with intellectual propensities, who through sheer determination, and with the aid of Reid's potions, managed to reach the altar at the appointed time.

There had been a minor crisis just before the wedding, which was due to take place at four thirty p.m. At three o'clock Reid had been sent for urgently to see the bride. It appeared that Princess Victoria had been so engrossed with preparations for the wedding during the past few days that she had not allowed herself enough time for eating. On the eve of the wedding she had indulged in a late night feast of lobster which, devoured on an empty stomach and in conjunction with a natural nervousness, had caused violent indigestion and sickness. The Queen had sent Reid to restore the bride at the eleventh hour, which he did with success, though there is no evidence of what he prescribed. As if this were not enough, the poor bride had sprained her ankle in a moment of high spirits whilst endeavouring to leap over a coal scuttle.

The Times described the wedding ceremony as a 'simple and yet touching and imposing spectacle, in which the Queen of England may be said to have herself formed the chief figure in the picture through standing out of a dark and sombre background'. Reid was present and he also partook in the wedding festivities which followed. The Queen, in mourning, did not attend the wedding banquet, but stayed in her room where Reid went to see her at ten thirty p.m., as he usually did.

On the evening of the wedding the Grand Duke of Hesse was married in secret to Madame de Kolémine. It was three days before the news leaked out, and the Prince of Wales had the unenviable task of informing his mother. The Queen was furious and insisted that her son should interview the unfortunate Madame de Kolémine instantly. She also peremptorily ordered the Grand Duke to put an end to his marriage, and demanded that Madame de Kolémine sign a paper agreeing that the marriage was null and void. This was a formidable task, even for the most tactful of Princes. There were hysterics and floods of tears from Madame de Kolémine, but the Queen had her way, the marriage was duly annulled, and the son of the union was adopted as a brother by the Empress of Russia. The Queen did not advance her date of departure and behaved as though nothing had occurred, but gloom descended upon the hitherto festive Darmstadt. On 7 May she returned to Windsor taking the Grand Duke with her! Such was the force of her personality.

In 1885 the summer visit to Osborne was distinguished by an event of very special importance to the Queen, namely the wedding of Prince Henry of Battenberg to her favourite daughter, Princess Beatrice, at Whippingham Church. The poor Princess had been through a great ordeal before the marriage. She had met and fallen in love with Prince Henry at the Darmstadt marriage the previous year. Once back at Windsor she had confessed to her mother that she wished to marry him. The Queen, afraid of losing her beloved and indispensable prop, showed a ruthless and selfish streak in her character by refusing to talk to her daughter. For six months all communication between them was channelled through notes pushed across the breakfast table. Princess Beatrice, although behaving like the dutiful daughter that she was, nevertheless remained firm in her intentions. It was not the marriage that worried the Queen, but the fear that Prince Henry would insist upon continuing his military career, and take the Princess away to Potsdam. Prince and Princess Louis decided that action must be taken to break the impasse, and invited Prince Henry to stay with them at their home, Sennicotts, near Chichester. Prince Henry was persuaded to give up his military career and live in the Queen's Household. The Queen, on hearing this, relented, and the couple became officially engaged.

The press was outspoken in its criticism of the impending marriage, describing Prince Henry as a 'German pauper', expecting to be kept at government expense. However, as the years went by, the Prince won over the hearts of the English people, through his charm, good looks and assiduous attention to royal duties.

The wedding took place on 23 July, the service being taken by the Archbishop of Canterbury, the Bishop of Winchester, the Dean of Windsor and Canon Prothero, Rector of Whippingham. The limited space in the small parish church gave the Queen an excellent excuse for not sending invitations to those whom she did not wish to attend. Gladstone was omitted from the list, and was deeply hurt. There was a crush, too, at Osborne, and many guests stayed on boats in Osborne Bay. Princess Beatrice wore the Honiton lace which the Queen had worn at her wedding forty-five years earlier, the only daughter to be granted such a special favour. The handsome Prince Henry was strikingly dressed in the white uniform of the Prussian Garde du Corps, which was rather overwhelming in a parish church, and caused the Princess of Wales to describe him as 'Beatrice's Lohengrin'.

Reid, also in dress uniform,[2] had been put in charge of the omnibus taking members of the Household to and from the church. 'At 5,' the Duke of Cambridge wrote in his dairy, 'we saw the young couple drive

---

[2] Reid had two dress uniforms. The Household uniform consisted of a tail coat with gold buttons and braid and square tails. The Windsor uniform differed in having scarlet collar and cuffs and wearing it was a privilege awarded to very few. Reid's diary for 19 July 1885 states, 'Told by Duke of Connaught that Queen had granted me the Windsor uniform.' It would be pleasing to think that a dexterous Court tailor allowed him to wear this exclusive finery four days later at the royal wedding. But perhaps it would not have been appropriate at Osborne. Today Windsor uniform is only worn at Windsor in the presence of the monarch or consort.

after lunch

Reid off duty, a post-prandial sketch by Major S. Waller.

off for their honeymoon to Lady Cochrane's Villa near Ryde.[3] We all dined in uniform in the two large tents. The Queen was again present and seemed wonderfully cheerful and well. The gardens were beautifully illuminated and the *Hector* and Royal Yacht, besides being illuminated, gave a very pretty display of fireworks.'

The Queen had every reason to be content. The day had been a triumph for her and for her youngest daughter. In the solitude of her sitting room, while guests were still celebrating and her tenants were enjoying their own ball, she wrote in her Journal:

> A happier looking couple could seldom be seen kneeling at the altar together. It was very touching. I stood very close to my dear child, who looked very sweet, pure and calm. Though I stood for the ninth time near a child and for the fifth time near a daughter, at the altar, I think I never felt more deeply than I did on this occasion, though full of confidence. When the blessing had been given, I tenderly embraced my darling 'Baby'.

There was the usual autumn migration to Balmoral that year, but this time Prince Henry was there to add zest to the royal party, and the Queen delighted at seeing her daughter, who normally found Deeside cold and miserable, looking radiant. For Reid the visit was not without its diversions, as he wrote to Sir Henry, who was taking the waters at Aix-les-Bains:

> You are well away from Balmoral at present as the atmosphere is highly charged with electricity, and there are frequent discharges all around and in all directions! *Even I* have had my row, as the Queen sent me one day to tell Muther (who had sent in word that he was going to stalk with his charge)[4] that she did not wish him to go out; and although I adopted my suavest manner and most honied words, the honourable gentleman got into such a passion that he wished at once to resign his post, and – what astonished me even more – not go down to luncheon. It was only by inviting him to the Royal dinner (an honour he had never before enjoyed) that his injured dignity was satisfied. He told me the Darmstadt papers have all published that he is here alone in charge of the heir, and that 'the eyes of all Darmstadt are on him at present', so that he will stand no nonsense. However, we are good friends again, and, as I leave on Tuesday, he will have one less thorn in his flesh.

A week before the Court was due to leave Balmoral, Princess

---

[3] Quarr Abbey, where a modern house has been built on the site of the historic ruin.

[4] Queen Victoria's grandson, Prince Ernest, heir to the Grand Duke of Hesse.

Beatrice had a miscarriage which for a day or two gave Reid 'much anxiety'. On 11 November he noted in his diary: 'At home all day with the Princess: at 6 p.m. removed contents of uterus.' He had been hoping to spend a few days with his mother before leaving for Windsor, but felt that he should postpone his holiday in order to look after the Princess. 'It would have made the Queen and the Princess uneasy had I gone away: and as I am in such favour with both of them, it was better not to insist on going away. It will be made up to me another time.' It was just as well that Reid remained at Balmoral: 'The Princess was not quite right in the afternoon and wanted me a good deal. Had I been away she and the Queen would have been a good deal anxious.' Nevertheless, Princess Beatrice managed to travel south on the night of 17 November, and bore the long journey well.

Jenner wrote Reid a letter of sympathy and encouragement: 'I have felt for you very much, knowing something of what you must have gone through.' He congratulated Reid on the 'successful progress of the case' and hoped that 'Her Majesty will not press too much about the Princess going out.' The Queen invariably tried to cut short convalescence against her doctors' wishes.

The following autumn Princess Beatrice was expecting another baby, which necessitated an early departure from Balmoral. 'The Queen says it is *dreadful* to have to leave so early,' Reid wrote to Jenner on 2 November. During the last week of her pregnancy the Princess had taken to having her dinner in her room. The Queen did not hold with this and sent Reid a memorandum in which she expressed her views forcibly:

> It is for the Princess's sake, *not* mine (Princess Irene[5] is here) that I urge her coming to dinner, and not sitting moping in her own room which is very bad for her. In my case I came regularly to dinner, excepting when I was really unwell (even when suffering a good deal) up to the very last day, and the Prince never would have let me keep in my room unless I was very suffering. The dinners were earlier, 8.15 p.m. to 8.30 p.m. but then we always went to bed before 12, often at 20 minutes past 11, so that it was not different. The dinner can easily be at 8.45 *now*. But I (the Mother of 9 children) must *know* what is wise and right and not young inexperienced people who know *nothing*.

On 22 November the 'young and inexperienced' Princess Beatrice was 'taken ill about eight thirty p.m., the rupture of the membranes occurring unexpectedly'. Reid sent for Dr Williams, the Queen's

[5] Her granddaughter, third daughter of the Grand Duke of Hesse.

obstetrician, who arrived at twelve thirty a.m. and a son was born at five a.m. on the 23rd. Although the Queen had become a grandmother on thirty previous occasions, no addition to the family had given her more pleasure than the birth of a child to her own beloved Baby. She knew that he would become part of her daily life, and not just a visitor to her home as all the other grandchildren were. But there were drawbacks already. The Queen never liked having to alter her set way of life, and as she had hated leaving Balmoral before her time was up, so she was annoyed at having to forgo her usual Christmas at Osborne, having decided that it would be unwise for the Princess and her baby son to undertake the journey.

On 18 December the baby was christened by the Dean in the White Drawing Room at Windsor. He was given the names Albert Alexander (Drino), and later became the Marquis of Carisbrooke, a suitable title for a son whose father was made Governor of the Isle of Wight. Prince Alexander of Battenberg, the deposed ruler of Bulgaria after whom the baby had been named, acted as sponsor, as did the Queen, the Prince of Wales, Prince Alexander of Hesse, and Princess Irene of Hesse. Reid, who had been present at the birth, was also asked to attend the christening. Now that Dr Williams had left, he was in charge of the welfare of mother and baby.

Less than a year later, Reid was in attendance at Balmoral on 24 October at the birth of another Battenberg baby, a daughter Victoria Eugénie (Ena) who later became Queen of Spain. The birth was not an easy one. The day before the confinement the Princess complained of a great deal of pain. The following day at seven a.m. she began having regular labour pains. Reid gave her chloroform and the baby was delivered by Dr Williams 'at 3.45 p.m. (after 40 minutes of forceps)'. Four days later the Princess was still suffering from severe uterine pains and Reid was in constant attendance upon her. The pains gradually subsided, after which she rapidly recovered. On 6 November the Queen gave Reid a photograph of herself in full Court dress, wearing the Order of the Garter and a coronet, as a token in recognition of the part he had played towards the Princess's recovery: 'I hope you will accept this photograph and these books (*Leaves* and *More Leaves from a Journal of our Life in the Highlands*) in recollection of the birth of my dear little Granddaughter, as well as my best thanks for all your care and attention to my beloved child.'

This year the alteration to her programme was in the Queen's favour, for in order to allow Princess Beatrice the necessary period of recuperation, she decided to extend the autumn holiday at Balmoral. Victoria Eugénie's baptism took place in the Castle on 23 November 'by a parson of the "Auld Kirk"'. This departure from the usual procedure delighted all Deeside and pleased the Queen, who was at heart a Presbyterian. It was the first royal christening to be held in Scotland since Charles I's in 1600. The service was taken by the Very Reverend Dr Cameron Lees, Dean of the Thistle and Chapel Royal of Scotland, Chaplain to the Queen, and the water used for the baptism came from the River Jordan.

On 21 May 1889 Princess Beatrice gave birth to her third child, another son, Prince Leopold. This time the confinement was easier and the labour pains lasted for only four hours. Prior to the birth there had been a vitriolic attack by the press condemning the Princess's fecundity:

> What is this we hear! Another Battenberg on the way! well!! well!! One cannot help drawing a comparison between the plague of rabbits in Australia and the plague of Battenbergs in Europe. And after all there is a close resemblance between the two visitations. The former, as well as the latter, 'gather where they have not strawed', are abnormally prolific, and cause an amount of mischief which is in inverse proportion to their size and importance. Europe would gladly give £25,000 to a political Pasteur who would undertake to rid it of the Battenbunnies.

Once again Reid administered chloroform and 'the baby boy was born at 2.5 a.m. The Queen was present all the time as well as Prince Henry[6] and Countess Erbach.' 'The little boy is a particularly pretty child, large, fat and with darkish hair. He weighed 8lb. which is more than Ena did. The children are not at all pleased with their little brother saying "won't kiss that",' wrote the Queen.

Three days later the Queen had her seventieth birthday, but she had not forgotten about her own pregnancies and had firm ideas on postnatal care which she insisted that her doctor adhere to. The smallest detail occupied her attention and she remembered exactly what had happened after the birth of Drino: 'I find she went on her sofa for the 1st time on the 9th day but it was a very uncomfortable narrow one and she disliked it and could not remain till night. Then she got a wide soft one and she remained all day till she went to bed. That one is *here now*. I hope she may go on it, on the 8th day but she will refuse *pushing on*.' Princess Beatrice, much more placid than her mother, wanted to recover in her own time.

On 6 June the Queen set off for Balmoral leaving the Princess and

---

[6] Though the Queen would have been giving bedside advice, Prince Henry would have been behind a screen.

little Prince Leopold at Windsor in Reid's care. He was instructed to inform the Queen regularly of the Princess's progress and she in turn wrote back giving him advice.

I am very glad the Princess had been out, tho' I did not quite understand why she did not go out on Friday, as I thought you expected – perhaps the weather – After the 1st day I always went out twice and that was earlier in the year (in April or beginning of May) – and if it rained, in the close carriage – only always got out. And after Tuesday she should walk up and downstairs. Perhaps she could walk *up* on Tuesday afternoon and then walk down on Wednesday and discard the carrying chair. It will be 3 weeks on Tuesday. She should now begin to use the sofa for *rest* merely. Perhaps *still* 4 hours in the course of the day till *Thursday* and then gradually less, and not for very long at a time.

I mention what my 9 experiences have taught me from a most excellent nurse who always attended me, and in whom the physicians had the greatest confidence. The baby will I suppose also be going out tomorrow or next day if it is fine.

Balmoral did not have the usual lustre for the Queen. 'The Princess and the children are terribly missed and it is very dull.'

On Saturday, 8 June Reid and Prince Henry carried the Princess downstairs into the garden chair. On the Sunday Reid carried the Princess into the garden both in the morning and in the afternoon. On Monday, as it was cold and wet, he did not let the Princess out, in spite of the Queen's suggestion that she should go in the 'close carriage'. On Tuesday the Princess graduated to the pony chair, and on Thursday, 13 June, 'Princess Beatrice was at both lunch and dinner'. On Friday, three and a half weeks after her confinement, she was fit enough to go with Prince Henry and her other children to a military parade at Aldershot.

On 29 June the infant Prince was christened Leopold Arthur Louis in St George's Chapel by the Dean of Windsor. Princess Louise, one of his many sponsors, held the baby, who was named Leopold after his uncle the Duke of Albany, the brother whom she sorely missed. Unhappily, the young baby had inherited the same unfortunate disease from which his namesake had died. For Reid this was to be an additional worry and responsibility. Nevertheless he was able to enjoy the christening free from the knowledge that his latest charge was a haemophiliac.

The fourth and last Battenberg child was born at Balmoral on 3 October 1891. Reid was up most of the night with the Princess and, as before, gave her chloroform. The baby boy 'was born at 6.45 a.m.

in the presence of the Queen, Prince Henry and Princess Christian'. The birth of a Prince in Deeside was cause for great celebration. *The Times* reported: 'In the evening a bonfire was lighted at Craig Gowan; a torchlight procession was formed on the hill, and proceeded to the front of the castle.'

As usual Reid's holiday was delayed. 'The Queen made a special request for me to stay a few days longer, as she does not feel easy at leaving Princess Beatrice in the hands of Hoffmeister until she has been out and resumed her usual habits to some extent. Of course I could not refuse, or even appear to be annoyed, as it is in my interest to keep in with her and to be as necessary to her as I can!' he wrote to his long suffering mother. On 30 October, the day before the christening, he was released. 'I am asked to stay for the Baptism if I like; but I told H.M. that as I had been at the last one here, and as it is to be the same thing, I would not stay for it unless otherwise required. I am anxious to get home now as every day I lose will be a day off my time with you!'

The christening followed the same pattern as Princess Ena's four years earlier. Dr Cameron Lees took the service and the baby, who was held at the font by the Queen, was named Maurice Victor Donald, the last name a compliment to Scotland.

The Battenberg tribe was complete. Their father's position had not been easy at first. He was half German and half Russian by birth, and neither country was popular with the British public. He had to play second fiddle to his wife and submit to the authority of a self-willed, powerful old lady. Pleasant, genial, and full of fun, Prince Henry was a first-rate sportsman, excelling at sailing, riding, shooting and tennis, as well as being expert at skating. He was blessed with a good deal of tact and was able to wheedle his way with the Queen to such an extent that he managed to persuade his mother-in-law, who thought smoking was an obnoxious habit, to set aside more comfortable rooms at Osborne and Balmoral for indulging his vice with his fellow Princes, visitors and members of the Household. Many an evening Reid, who was a heavy smoker, enjoyed puffing away into the early hours of the morning with Prince Henry and others. Previously the miscreants had had to cross an open yard to enter a cubby hole with bare boards and hard wooden chairs. They must have been desperate to escape either for a smoke, or from female domination, to undertake such an expedition.

The four Battenberg children gave the Queen an endless source of joy as well as moments of uneasiness. The latter were usually the result of accident or illness – for which Reid had the responsibility, and shared her anxiety. The ten years which followed the Battenberg marriage were in some ways the Queen's happiest. She had become popular and revered throughout the country and she was no longer averse to appearing in public; she was emotionally more stable, and her health had not yet begun to decline. In her various Households she always had with her a closely-knit, happy family, the four young children helping her to remain youthful in outlook.

5

The Queen's Health

The Queen enjoyed remarkably good health for her age and had energy and stamina, but having a doctor constantly at hand meant that she could indulge in hypochondria. She liked nothing more than a daily discussion of her discomforts with her doctor.

She suffered from indigestion, which led to heated discussions between her and her physician, Reid being more outspoken on her eating habits than any of her previous doctors. He prescribed Benger's Food as a palliative, which proved to be ineffective as the Queen insisted on taking this in addition to her other food, rather than instead of it. Her subjects showed great concern for her welfare, and inundated Reid with cranky letters containing helpful suggestions. John Goodman from Youngstown, Ohio, described at length how he had lost weight, and in a letter to Reid he implored the Queen to do the same. Tristam Hill wrote: 'To the Queen's Most Excellent Majesty; may it please your Majesty to accept of the accompanying box of Tristam's Liver Pills. Whilst your Majesty's dutiful and subscribing servant is of the opinion that he can send no more valuable present (if *needed*) in commemoration of this year of Jubilee, yet he trusts Your Majesty may be many years before requiring them.'

The 'colicky' pains from which the Queen suffered were not invariably the result of over-indulgence. They occurred, too, when she succumbed to 'fits of nervousness' due to anxiety. There were her 'political nerves', her 'family trouble' nerves, and, worst of all, nerves emanating from 'Indian affairs', involving the Munshi.

In July 1884, when Reid was called upon to attend the birth of the fatherless Duke of Albany at Claremont, the Queen arrived just in time to witness the event, but was far from well and was suffering from headache and sickness. Reid recorded in his diary that he saw her eight times. Six months later the Queen's health was bothering her again. Reid wrote to Jenner from Osborne in January 1885 that: 'The Queen had a headache and flatulence the last two days, but is somewhat better again. She had salt both yesterday and today, and the bowels were acting well; she thinks the podophyllin pill has upset her.'

In February the Queen postponed her journey to Windsor because she had a severe neuralgic headache. Reid confided to Jenner:

Her cough and expectoration have been troublesome all this week, and she has been rather impatient about it. I proposed today to take her temperature, but she said she preferred to leave it alone! I believe that one great cause of the headache today was that last night she was much upset at saying goodbye to Colonel Ewart (who has been in waiting). Yesterday he got orders to leave at once for Egypt, and the Queen, who likes him very much, felt the parting severely. Then this morning, on getting up, she heard of General Earle's death, as well as of the two Colonels who were killed; and she also had a telegram saying Sir Herbert Stewart is *not* doing well. When she told me all this she broke down and cried a good deal. Between the war[1] and the Government, and the Princess's marriage, she really has had a great deal to worry her lately.

As he was neither a member of the family, nor in any way connected with politics, the Queen could open her heart to Reid as an outsider, knowing that she could trust him to be discreet.

Jenner, who always feared for the Queen's 'nerves' more than Reid did, arrived at Osborne and Reid, while sending 'primrose buds and Windsor violets' to his mother, wrote: 'Jenner's presence makes it much easier for me, as he has the responsibility.' In spite of her seediness the Queen managed to attend the birth of her great-granddaughter, Princess Alice, at Windsor on 25 February.

In March the Queen asked Reid to request Jenner to write to Sir Henry Ponsonby, saying: 'For the sake of her health she ought to go abroad now. She thinks there may be some question of her not going; but she wishes to go. She thinks you might say (in order that they [the Cabinet Ministers] may not think she is going simply for her amusement) that unless she goes where she can have some rest she might break down, that she suffers from over-work.' The next time Jenner heard from Reid he was at Maison Mottet in Aix-les-Bains.

Aix-les-Bains had pleased the Queen and she returned to England via Darmstadt, where she and Reid attended the confirmation of the Hereditary Grand Duke of Hesse, Prince Ernest Ludwig and the baptism of Princess Alice of Battenberg, feeling greatly restored.

On 9 June, the Queen heard that Gladstone had resigned as a result of a split in the Liberal party on Irish policy which led to a Budget defeat occasioned by a combination of Tories and Irish Nationalists voting against a proposal for the increase of taxes on beer and spirits. To take his place the Queen sent for Lord Salisbury who

---

[1] The war in the Sudan. General Gordon had been murdered by the Mahdi's followers on 26 January and the Queen blamed Gladstone for his delay in sending reinforcements to Khartoum and sent him a telegram *en clair* rebuking him, Granville and Hartington. Gladstone contemplated resignation.

arrived at Balmoral a few days later. The Queen had never made any attempt to hide her dislike of Gladstone, who lacked the art of pleasing women which his rival Disraeli cultivated to such perfection, and her complaint that he addressed her as though she were a public meeting is well known.

Queen Victoria was a night owl and Reid regularly attended her between ten thirty p.m. and midnight to see if she required anything before retiring to bed. It was during these nocturnal encounters that she unburdened herself. When the conversations were of particular interest, Reid recorded them verbatim. Two days after Gladstone's resignation she complained to Reid: 'I asked Mr G. to come here, and he refused. He said he had to prepare to remove from his house, and he coolly wishes me to come South at once. He is most impertinent, and forgets I am a Lady. He seems to think I am just a machine to run up and down as he likes.' On an earlier occasion she had said petulantly to Reid, 'I am told his voice is nearly gone. I only hope it will go altogether. The letter I wrote him offering him a peerage was not at all the one I would have written had I for a moment dreamt he would decline it.[2] I was anxious to do something to keep him quiet.'

On 2 September Reid began his autumn holiday in Ellon, when he substituted for the grandeur of Court life the simple pleasures of home, where his mother spoiled him. His time was spent attending to farming affairs with the grieve, gardening, and walking with his mother. But he had only been home five days before he received a letter from the Queen about her husky throat and insomnia, written in such indecipherable writing that he complained to Jenner, 'it took me quite *one hour* to make it out!'

> The essence of it is that as her voice still becomes a little husky for a *few minutes* from the presence of a little mucus about the vocal cords, Dr Profeit had suggested her inhaling iodine, and the external application of 'something strong'. She seems unwilling to do this without asking me, and said I was to write my opinion. I have done so, deprecating the use of any strong external application on the ground of the extreme sensitiveness of Her Majesty's skin. As to the iodine, I have said I thought it might be

---

[2] In 1882, after fifty years in the House Commons, Gladstone had considered retiring in favour of Lord Hartington, but his colleagues, while wishing him to remain in office, insisted that he could only leave if he were to take a seat in the House of Lords, which he was reluctant to do. In January 1883, on the advice of Lord Granville, the Queen offered Gladstone a peerage, which he declined, being overcome by a renewed desire to do his duty towards pacifying Ireland.

tried, but that the quantity ought to be *small* lest the fumes should cause irritation. I have written both Profeit and Hoffmeister about it, and have been very careful to avoid the possibility of their feeling hurt; but as the Queen wrote me about it herself I was obliged to communicate with them on the subject.

The Queen says she is quite well: but that sometimes she does not sleep well, and that I was to write to Hoffmeister about increasing the night draught. In my note tonight I have given him the exact limits of the Bromide and of the Henbane which I never exceed without consulting you. I have told him also that I never even go up to these limits if it can be avoided.

The Queen, always nervous about her health when Reid was away, wrote again on 17 September, this time almost pleading for him to come to Balmoral to see her:

You said you would kindly be ready to come for a day or a few hours to see me if anything was required. There is nothing perhaps necessary or pressing, but there are one or two things which are just hanging about me, which I should be glad just to ask you about, for if I do the others [Drs Profeit and Hoffmeister] they sometimes make more of it than is really necessary, and I should therefore be thankful if you could come over either merely for a few hours or for one night. I have this tiresome huskiness which every now and then causes me to cough, and then almost immediately after you left I got this pain between my shoulders which *generally* leaves me after a day or two, but which returns again and again, and which I feel right through me and extending to the muscles of the chest. Dr Profeit thought it was indigestion, and so I thought too. But still there is little oppression with it, and when I think it is gone it reappears. I have no *cold*, but I have a little more rheumatism and the walking has been less. Please telegraph an answer.

Reid could hardly refuse her request. 'I thought it was the right thing to leave all engagements here and run up to Balmoral tonight. I fancy Her Majesty had flatulence, and that she is a little nervous. I shall not frighten her in any case, and I fear that to propose using the stethoscope could seriously alarm her.' At Balmoral Reid was able to reassure Jenner that he found the Queen looking very well, 'but she has been feeling very nervous, and fearing she had something wrong with her heart. I do not see any special indication of this: her pulse is as usual, she can walk upstairs as well as before; there is no symptom of any local or general congestion, nor is her voice altered in any way.' As he dared not use the stethoscope, Reid could not say 'anything about physical signs. I have recommended the *soda, sal volatile* and *ginger* draught twice or thrice daily after meals, and an occasional dose of salt in the morning.'

Reid was told by the Queen to tell Jenner 'not to be at all alarmed about her, as it was only a little indigestion, and that she had got a little nervous, but was better now'. From Reid's letters it struck Jenner that 'it is really flatulence from indigestion. I remember once an attack of indigestion from Cranberry tart and cream when Sir James Clark's only remark to Her Majesty was "Don't eat it again", whereat Her Majesty was very much annoyed.'

Back at Ellon, where Reid continued his interrupted holiday, the Queen inundated him with a series of barely decipherable letters describing her ailments. There were headaches, eye-strain, and even a touch of lumbago, or 'rather pain in my hip, just the sciatic nerve, but I hope a poultice of Colchicum will remove it, as I felt it on getting up today'. Was she suffering from hypochondria? Or did she miss her consultations with her young doctor? The 'others' did not seem to understand her as he did. But that was not all. The poor Queen was upset, Reid told Jenner:

> Not so much by public affairs as by family squabbles and misunderstandings, and today she told me she was much worried and had hardly courage to go on. I could not but feel sorry to see her evidently unhappy, but one can do nothing in these matters. Sometimes she is quite bright and cheery, but then something occurs to upset her; but *physically* she is very well indeed.

Early in 1886 Reid wrote in great excitement to his mother: 'The Queen opens Parliament on Thursday, and I shall see it all as I am to have a place in the House of Lords, which is a great privilege, as very few people can be accommodated.' On 21 January the Queen, supported by Princess Beatrice and Prince Albert Victor, opened Parliament – for what turned out to be the last time.

Her visit to London was brief, as usual, and the following day she returned to Osborne where she was faced once more with a political crisis. The Conservatives were forced to resign over their policy in Ireland, but the Queen would not let them go without a fight. Reid received an urgent undated note from the Queen: 'Please see Lord Salisbury and press on him not to resign in a hurry – could not accept it.' Whether she was simply using Reid as a messenger or whether she wished him to offer her health as an excuse is not quite clear, but she was desperate and would clutch at any straw to avoid having to accept Gladstone once more.

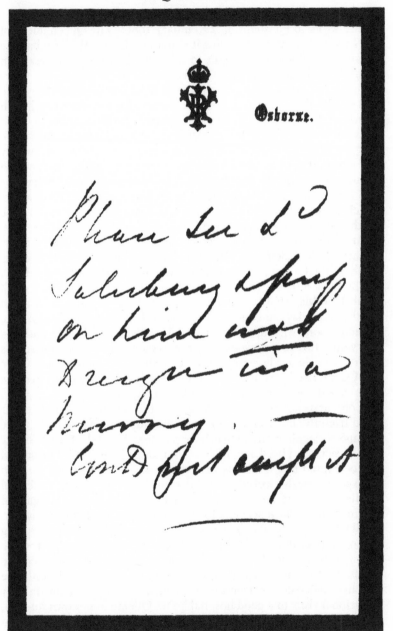

The Queen uses Reid as a political emissary to Lord Salisbury, 1886.

She wrote to Ponsonby on 29 January 1886: 'The Queen does not the least care but rather wishes it should be known that she has the greatest possible disinclination to take this half crazy and really in many ways ridiculous old man – for the sake of the country.'

In the end, after much criticism from the Liberals at her delay, she had to submit to the inevitable. But she still kept in close touch with Lord Salisbury, sometimes through Jenner, who brought her news on his weekly visits. Since he was a confirmed and dogmatic Tory there was no difficulty in using him as her messenger, though frequently she wrote directly to Lord Salisbury, seeking his advice on how she should deal with the government. This unconstitutional behaviour was inexcusable and she admitted to feeling a twinge of conscience, which tempered her rejoicing when Gladstone's ministry fell in June on the defeat of the Home Rule Bill.

At Balmoral the political crisis affected Reid and delayed his departure for Ellon. 'At 9 o'clock this morning,' he informed his mother, 'the Queen sent to say she would like me to stay till tomorrow, as she felt a little out of sorts: so of course I could not say No. I don't think Her Majesty likes being without me!' A second letter written on the same day announced, 'I am put off this time till *Friday*. The Queen is somewhat upset and agitated by the political crisis, and says she would feel very nervous if I were to go tomorrow. Of course it is my duty to do as she wishes, as she is always so kind to me.' Once the Queen had heard that the Home Rule Bill had been defeated she immediately felt better and let Reid off a day earlier.

Content as he was with his life at Court, there were difficulties for Reid from the medical point of view. In January 1887 he had to face advanced examinations to qualify for membership of the Royal College of Physicians. His daily routine with the Queen and Household scarcely fitted him for the severe test ahead. While he could study in his spare time he lacked practical experience on a wide variety of medical cases. It was not easy, either, for him to keep abreast of advances in medical science. In desperation he applied to Lady Ely: 'Will you kindly ask the Queen if Her Majesty will sanction my going to London one day weekly (Fridays) when she is at Windsor, to resume hospital work. It is of considerable importance for me, and of course indirectly for Her Majesty, that I should keep in touch with the practical advances in medical science; and this I can do only by occasional visits to a good hospital.' The Queen, in her own interest, could hardly deny this reasonable request and, thereafter, Reid spent as many Friday afternoons as he was able at Charing Cross Hospital, watching operations and demonstrations. After 1889 when Jenner, on account of failing health, ceased to be a regular visitor to Windsor Reid was more than ever involved with Court affairs, and his visits to the Charing Cross became less frequent, until finally they ceased altogether.

He was most anxious about the results of his examinations, for in his position he could hardly afford to fail. 'I hope I get through,' he wrote to his mother, 'but I can't be sure as it is a very stiff business.' However, on 27 January he triumphantly informed her: 'I have passed the examinations and am now a member of the R.C.P. of London, at least I shall be after being formally admitted tonight. It is a tremendous relief, and I shall never have any more examinations, as there is nothing higher than this. Jenner who is President of the College has been most kind and I should not wonder if he helped to get me through, as he was most anxious for me to pass.' The Queen too was 'delighted' and told Jenner 'to tell him so'.

A few months later Reid was appointed one of Her Majesty's Physicians Extraordinary. The Queen wrote: 'Besides Sir William Jenner there is no Physician in whom she has more confidence than in Doctor Reid.' What greater compliment could he have received? But Arthur Bigge viewed the honour from a more practical angle: 'My dear Extraordinary Physician, my sincere congratulations on your promotion; I hope it carries with it a large salary!' Sadly it did not, and it was several years before Reid received remuneration commensurate with his position and responsibility.

In October 1889 Reid informed Jenner that the Queen had a 'very severe attack of acute indigestion with gastric pain and nausea. I was up with her till 5.30 a.m. It was caused, I believe, by her eating among other things a very heavy indigestible sweet at dinner; and I trust she will be more careful in future.' A few days later, when he went on holiday, the royal indigestion once more pursued him to Ellon.

Since you left my indigestion seems not very good. I had no pain but rather an oppression after meals, and a rising after all I eat and acidity, as well as a slight headache most mornings, which goes off later. The bowels are right, upon the whole, but there is an inclination to griping and the day before yesterday there was a good deal of bile. I think that perhaps tomorrow evening that powder with a little salt the next morning will be a good thing.

Despite the fact that the Queen had a locum during Reid's holidays, she frequently bypassed him, preferring to inundate her regular doctor with details of her ailments by post. He was never left in the slightest doubt as to the exact state of her health.

There were also times when the Queen suffered from bouts of sleeplessness or, more accurately, what she conceived to be so. In July 1889 she went through a bad patch. 'The Queen complained very much last night and was in a very bad humour,' Reid wrote to Jenner.

> I was obliged to give her 5 grains of Dover with one of Calomel, as she insisted on having something of the sort. She had an excellent night, but Mrs MacDonald says she is dreadfully cross today, and that they can hardly get on with her at all. I believe it is entirely owing to the Royal Grants Committee not getting on as she wishes, for she has been in a vile humour since Wednesday evening when she got a box on the subject from Lord Salisbury. Ponsonby told me yesterday that the Royal Grants Committee do not quite see their way to recommending grants to any of Her Majesty's children, except the Wales family, and that this had made the Queen angry. I am afraid to give her more Dover's Powders for fear of establishing a habit. The Queen said again that she could not sleep. Nonetheless she declined to go to bed till the usual time, 1.30; and as her undressing, etc., takes an hour, it was about 2.30 when she got to bed. She could have quite enough if she would sleep when she can, but she *won't* and *refuses* to sleep either earlier at night or later in the morning than her usual hours.

By the end of July the Queen was still not sleeping.

> I gave the Queen last night no Dover's Powder, but a draught with 25 grains of Ammonium Bromide and 30 drops of Tincture of Henbane. After grumbling about her very bad night she said that perhaps after all she had more sleep than she thought, as, except once, she did not think she remained awake longer than five or six minutes at a time! Every time she wakes, even for a few minutes, she rings for her maids, who of course don't like it, and naturally call the night a 'bad' one. She has got into the habit of waking up at night, and I fear it may not be easy to break this habit. Meantime I shall go on with Bromide and Henbane, and give no opium.

It was hardly surprising that Mrs Tuck, the Queen's chief dresser, had a nervous breakdown. The Queen was an exacting mistress.

The Queen was a nervous traveller, especially at sea. Fortunately for her, Reid was an intrepid sailor and suffered 'only from *hunger* at sea, a malady that is easily remedied'. In 1896 there was a rough crossing and Reid's diary records he was 'sent for thrice by the Queen, who was very emotional and nervous'. Two years later, on her penultimate journey to France, Reid wrote to his mother: 'We had a fair passage across yesterday, but the Queen, whose nerves are rather depressed at present, was very nervous, and I had to stay nearly the whole of the six hours' passage with her in her cabin! She did not like to be alone, and would not have anybody but me with her. She described the passage in the Court Circular as "rough" but it was not at all a bad one, and only made me very hungry!'

Apart from the usual heavy and feverish colds and the occasional bout of influenza, from which the Queen recovered with amazing rapidity and which carried with them no side-effects, she was plagued with rheumatism. This was not helped by her insistence on a surfeit of fresh, usually damp, air in her rooms. When telling him about the Queen's lumbago, Reid complained to Jenner that she wore thinner clothing at Balmoral than she wore at Windsor, 'and put on nothing thicker, even for breakfast outside'.

She was given regular massage and always employed a French masseuse from Aix-les-Bains – Charlotte Nautet being succeeded by Marie Angelier. Reid was in charge of their engagement, their welfare and their remuneration, which the Queen discussed with him. They were employed for periods of two or three weeks at a time during the months when the baths at Aix-les-Bains were closed, which was from the middle of October until the beginning of April, unless the Queen suffered from a severe attack of rheumatism leading to crippling lameness, when they were called back from France. Not surprisingly, she needed their services most at Balmoral. From Ellon Reid wrote to Jenner in November 1889 that the Queen was complaining of rheumatism, 'notwithstanding the massage that has been going on all the time I was away. The masseuse has assured H.M. that "it always brings out the rheumatism at first and it is a sign that it is doing good", so she is quite satisfied!'

In June 1893, while at Balmoral, the Queen was suffering so severely from rheumatism that she had to be carried up and down the stairs. As she was unable to walk, she insisted upon riding instead. 'I have no discomfort to mention in riding, and no difficulty in getting on or in getting off (I have ridden three times). I think there is more pain afterwards that is stiffness, and more than on a day when I have not ridden. But I shall continue it all the same.' By November there was a marked improvement, and the Queen wrote, '[I] was able to walk down the whole staircase yesterday and today without pain. I have also walked better in the evening, and this tho' we have had two days of snow showers and thaw, and several inches of snow on the ground!'

The following year in August the Queen's rheumatism was so bad again that she was forced to postpone her journey from Osborne to Balmoral for a few days. Reid noted that, 'her nerves were much upset, and she cried much when she saw me in the forenoon and at other times'. As with all rheumatics she had bad periods and better moments, but for many years she relied on a stick or her Indian servants for support, finally resorting to a wheelchair for all but the very shortest distances.

The Queen also had trouble with her teeth and relations with her dentists were not always easy. She refused to have Dr Fairbank 'as he is so slow', Reid wrote to Jenner. 'I fear H.M. expects impossibilities from the dentists.' In May 1897 Mr Charles Tomes came to see the Queen about making some false teeth: 'He gave a favourable opinion about her mouth, but H.M. would not let him take a cast of her mouth yet!' A year passed before she allowed another dentist, Harry Baldwin, to examine her, and he took a cast of her lower jaw. In January 1899 Reid noted that the Queen was 'very troublesome about her artificial teeth, which she constantly wishes me to alter!'

What concerned and vexed her far more than her teeth were her eyes. By the end of 1892 her sight was beginning to deteriorate noticeably. In one of her long, illegible letters, written to Reid at Ellon, she complained: 'My eyes are troublesome. I can get none of the spectacles to suit; they are wrongly focused, and at night reading is very trying and difficult, though I still at times find dark print not too unreadable. I can see much better without glasses. I am sure some can be got to suit.'

The following June the problem was still unsolved, when she wrote to Reid rather pathetically, 'The eyes are dim, and the loss of the power of reading books or papers is a terrible privation.' Her eye specialist, George Lawson, thought that the lens was at fault, and not the nerve, and suggested to Reid: 'You might have a 1 per cent solution of cocaine in a drop bottle and drop into the eye once a day, and note the effect.'

In August, while the Queen was at Osborne, Reid recorded, 'Lawson arrived from London and after luncheon examined the Queen's eyes in the Prince's room with an ophthalmoscope. He found the lens clear, but the disc rather red, and the eyes indistinct, (slight neuritis), vessels healthy, and no haemorrhages.' After this consultation George Lawson wrote to Reid that 'in accordance with your suggestion, I have had a letter written to Mr F. Fritsch of Vienna, the leading Optician, requesting them to send two pair of spectacles with +2.5d and +2.d, and I hope to have them to send to you in about a week. I do not know of a French optician in London, but I can easily get a pair from Paris.'

In spite of the infinite trouble taken, in November the Queen complained that the new spectacles seemed just like the others. 'I could read, however, very clearly yesterday, tho' the afternoon was very dark, an article in a magazine without glasses! I can't read fresh writing or see well what I write!'

Eighteen months later, in June 1895 Reid wrote to Jenner that 'the Queen's defective eyesight is now a serious hindrance to her writing letters'. By this time her writing had become almost totally illegible, and Reid spent hours trying to decipher her notes to him.

In May 1896 Lawson, together with a colleague, Edward Nettleship, came to Windsor to examine the Queen's eyes and found a nuclear cataract in both eyes. They made suggestions for improving her glasses and prescribed eyedrops, but said that 'the affection must be progressive'. The Queen was not satisfied that all that could be done had been done, and having heard from many sources of the miraculous cures effected by the German professor, Hermann Pagenstecher, declared that she wished to see him. This demand put Reid in an awkward position as it would appear to be a slight upon the two leading ophthalmic surgeons she had already consulted. A third opinion seemed excessive. However, the Queen was adamant although it was agreed that Nettleship should be present at the consultation. Nettleship was needled, as his letter to Reid illustrates:

> I thought the principle of a consultation had been conceded by Her Majesty, and I am extremely sorry if this should not be so. The case seems to me eminently one in which, if further advice is desired, a quiet consultation would be more likely to help the patient than another separate opinion, and this is not less true because the patient is the Queen. I fully appreciate and sympathise with the difficult position in which you are placed.

Professor Pagenstecher's visit was arranged for 24 August at Osborne. Reid wrote detailed notes on the consultation and Pagenstecher's conversations with him while everything was still fresh in his mind. (See Appendix I) They make interesting reading, throwing light not only on the psychology and principles of treatment in medicine, but also on the Queen's attitude to the individuals who treated her. While she spurned the smooth bedside manner, she disliked equally the more withdrawn, remote and businesslike attitude of Nettleship. A friendly confident bearing such as Pagenstecher's reassured her. Reid was amused that 'she evidently thinks him much before English oculists!'

In his official report, Pagenstecher stated that if the Queen's condition were to deteriorate 'there is an excellent prospect that an operation would restore a good vision'. George Lawson was more cautious in his opinion. In a letter to Reid on the subject he expressed his views:

> The advice which I always give with reference to operations for cataract is, that so long as the sight of one eye is sufficient for the requirements of the patient, which does not include reading and writing, no operation should be performed, but when the sight of the latter eye is so dim that the patient runs against chairs or mistakes the food on his plate, as the potato for the meat, then the most defective eye should have the cataract extracted. In following out these directions it should be remembered that while success is probable, failure is possible. As far as the Queen is concerned, I would not advise an operation until absolutely necessary. The restraint and the period of darkness, if only two or three days, would be difficult for her.

Her predicament did not pass unnoticed by her loyal subjects. On 26 September a letter, written in very large copy-book style, arrived from Ireland from a man who rejoiced in the name of Julius Leckie MacCulloch Craig, recommending a cure for 'fading vision': 'Stew one handful of Velvet Horehound, one of She-Dandelion, with one quart of pure Spring water, one hour's time. Add $^{1}/_{16}$ Teaspoonful of Cayenne Pepper. Drink two cupfuls per day. Preserve in bottle without alcohol. Improved vision by October 10th.' Enclosed in the letter were Dandelion and Horehound leaves. The effect this recipe might have had upon the Queen's eyes is a matter for conjecture since her doctor was not prepared to risk impairing her digestive system with such a curious concoction.

In spite of all the expert advice the Queen still complained that, 'the goggles do not answer, because they do not fit and fall over the eyelids. Something must be done to make them fit closer to the eyes.' She was satisfied with the drops, but found that Mrs Tuck was not adept at applying them. Once again she needed her doctor, who was once again on holiday in Ellon.

Reid also received a letter from Nettleship from which he learnt that Pagenstecher had told Dr Frank of Cannes about his visit to the Queen, and given details of the case. Nettleship was annoyed at this breach of etiquette: 'It is too bad of Pagenstecher to have told even Frank after the careful manner in which you enjoined secrecy on him. I do not suppose the incident in itself has any importance, but it throws a not too pleasant light on Pagenstecher's conduct. I must say I thought better of him.' Pagenstecher's behaviour surprised and disappointed Reid, too, who all along had tried to give the German surgeon the benefit of the doubt.

After 1899 Reid received no further communications in writing from the Queen. Harriet Phipps, the Queen's personal secretary, and Princess Beatrice became her scribes. To them she dictated her instructions to her Ministers and they read the newspapers and the contents of her daily boxes to her. For those who had had the problem of trying to decipher her letters over the previous decade, it was a relief, but to the inveterate scribbler herself it remained a great deprivation.

6

Royal Health

Apart from the Queen herself, Reid was often called upon to attend members of her family to whom, in some cases, he acted not only as doctor, but also as friend and counsellor. His relations with other members of the royal family were not so dramatic; nevertheless he became involved, albeit indirectly, in one of the most complicated and sadly mismanaged royal medical cases in history, namely that of Crown Prince Frederick of Germany's cancer of the throat. Historically, as well as medically, the outcome of the case was vital. Had the Crown Prince, who became Emperor for a mere ninety-eight days, survived his illness and lived to a ripe old age, the whole course of history could have been altered. Unlike his autocratic, unstable and pro-vocative son, Prince William, Prince Frederick was a peace-loving, gentle being, whose relatively liberal views were encouraged by Vicky, his wife (Queen Victoria's eldest daughter). He might have helped to ensure stable relations between Germany and the rest of Europe and so have avoided the Great War in 1914. As it was, the unfortunate Prince's illness also led to a war between the doctors. (See Appendix II.)

The Crown Prince's malady first became evident in January 1887 when he exhibited a slight but persistent hoarseness. In March Dr Wegner, the Crown Prince's Physician-in-Ordinary, called in Dr Gerhardt, Professor of Clinical Medicine at the University of Berlin, a well-known authority on diseases of the throat. He examined the Crown Prince's throat with a laryngoscope and diagnosed a polypoid thickening of the left vocal cord. Several attempts to remove the nodule failed and it continued to grow. Gerhardt began to have vague suspicions that the growth might be cancerous, and called in Professor von Bergmann, Professor of Surgery in Berlin and President of the Association of German Surgeons. Bergmann came to the conclusion that a thyrotomy was necessary for the purpose of exploration and thorough removal of the growth. He minimised the risk of the oper-ation, which he said was 'no more dangerous than an ordinary tracheotomy'. After discussion with Gerhardt and von Bergmann, Wegner broached the subject of consulting a laryngologist and it was agreed to invite Morell Mackenzie, the English laryngologist. The Crown Princess also sent Queen Victoria a telegram begging her to send Morell Mackenzie at once. So Reid was duly despatched to

Mackenzie's house at 19 Harley Street to convey the urgency of his starting for Berlin as soon as possible.

When Mackenzie arrived he announced, after examining the patient, that he disagreed with the German doctors' decision to operate and thought that he should remove a piece of growth for microscopic inspection by Professor Rudolf Virchow of the Institute of Pathology in Berlin, the leading authority and founder of the modern science of pathology. The German doctors submitted to Mackenzie's suggestion. Virchow declared that there was no evidence of cancer or malignancy, but as the specimen was so small he would like to have a further piece for examination.

Reid was given detailed information on the progress of the case both by Wegner and Mackenzie, and requested to give explanations to the Queen, whose main concern was that the Crown Prince should be fit to represent the German Emperor at her Jubilee celebrations to commemorate her fifty years' reign. He was ordered by the Queen to cypher to Jenner that it was 'most important for family and political reasons that the Crown Prince should come to England even if he cannot appear. Mackenzie should be made to insist on treatment in England: frequent visits and stay at Berlin almost impossible and very costly. Sir William could write strongly to the Crown Princess on medical grounds.' Once again the Queen was using doctor's orders to serve her purpose.

During the examination for the further removal of the growth Mackenzie was accused by Gerhardt of damaging the right vocal cord with his forceps. This incident marked the beginning of the feud between the German doctors and Mackenzie. On 7 June Mackenzie, with specially constructed forceps, succeeded in removing more than half the growth on the vocal cord for inspection by Virchow who, having examined it, still maintained that there was nothing to arouse suspicion of a graver disease. After this second report from Virchow, it was agreed in a unanimous decision, and with the patient's consent, that the Crown Prince should be handed over to Mackenzie for treatment. Mackenzie from the first had been optimistic about the outcome of the case. As early as 29 May, he had written to Reid, 'If I could stay in Germany so as to have complete charge of him for some time I should be able to make a perfect cure *per vias naturales.*' Reid thought differently, and confided to Jenner: 'I can't say I feel free from some apprehension, notwithstanding the last telegrams – but this I keep to myself. The Queen is quite satisfied.'

The Queen's satisfaction turned into joy when she received a telegram from the Crown Princess announcing that they would come over to England for the Jubilee. Her Majesty was anxious about how her son-in-law would stand the strain of the festivities and Reid was constantly pestered to telegraph to Berlin to find out from Mackenzie 'how he finds the patient'. On 14 June the royal party arrived from Germany.

A week later, when the Queen led the Jubilee procession from Buckingham Palace to Westminster Abbey, 'there rode in the cavalcade of thirty-two princes the towering Lohengrin-like figure in white uniform, silver breast plate and eagle crested helmet, of the Crown Prince of Germany – a tragic figure, outwardly the embodiment of princely grace and splendour, but inwardly conscious that if it was indeed cancer that had laid its stranglehold upon him, his span of life was drawing to a close'. Reid was, meanwhile, waiting in the Abbey for the procession to arrive for the Thanksgiving Service. Dressed in his new Household uniform he thought he looked 'quite a personage!'

While enjoying all the Jubilee festivities – the banquets, concerts and reviews – to the full, Reid was aware all the time that the Queen was under a great strain and that it was his responsibility to see that she was not overtaxed. It was hardly surprising, therefore, that after ten days of ceremonial and celebration she complained of dyspepsia and exhaustion. As a result, he was obliged to forgo his conversazione at the Royal College of Physicians. 'I felt I could not ask to stay behind in London, as she would have thought I had no consideration for her: accordingly I thought my duty was to return with her to Windsor, so that I should be here if wanted: and in point of fact she did want me,' he wrote to Jenner. In all the excitement at seeing the Queen the people never stopped to think what a heavy programme she had to accomplish and how gruelling an experience it was for the little old lady. Her doctor understood only too well.

Reid had advised his mother to remain in Ellon during the Jubilee celebrations and was glad that he had done so. 'You could not have walked: and to go along in cabs is impossible. I have hardly ventured out!' he wrote to her in the midst of the festivities. She was not forgotten though, for he sent her a parcel containing a large slice of the Queen's Jubilee Cake. 'It was presented to her by Gunther, the great man in London for these things, and said to be the grandest cake ever made. It is, I think, fifteen feet high: and the actual *eating part* of it (without all the appendages) weighed over half a ton!!'

Meanwhile, at Osborne there were further Jubilee celebrations which took the form of a naval review. Reid was among the Suite which accompanied the Queen on board the *Victoria and Albert*, and sailed through the lines of war at Spithead. Osborne House was full to overflowing, a predicament which evoked a cutting series of comments from the reporter for the journal *Society*.

The silly etiquette which forbids a royal or even a demi-semi-royal personage to move a yard, without a military officer being in attendance upon him, has converted Osborne House into a fifth-rate Margate lodging house. On the nights before and after the naval review, many of the bedrooms had to be doubly and trebly tenanted, owing to the limited accommodation of the Queen's marine residence, which is really little more than a villa. The Grand Duke of Hesse, albeit just now in such favour at Court, had to allow his equerry, General von Westerweller, to sleep on a sofa at the foot of his bed: the Princess Irene and Alix of Hesse shared the same couch; and where Colonel Ewart, Major Bigge, and Dr Reid slumbered on those two eventful nights is a mystery they alone can solve. There are also rumours that the equerries consorted with their steeds in the stables.

Morell Mackenzie was not among those squeezed into Osborne House. He stayed at Carlton Villa in West Cowes, where Reid called on him. The Crown Prince and Princess spent two months in England after the close of the Jubilee festivities, dividing their time between Norwood, Norris Castle on the Isle of Wight, and Braemar. On 8 August the Queen received a personal letter from Mackenzie concerning the Crown Prince's progress, which irritated Reid as not being strictly within the code of medical practice, where convention demanded that all communication concerning patients should pass through doctors. 'I suppose as the Queen did not see him, he thought he would get at her by writing direct!' Reid commented to Jenner. For his part Mackenzie sought to set the royal mind at rest:

I found everything so satisfactory that I cannot forbear writing to inform Your Imperial Highness how pleased I am. Since I first examined the throat I have never seen it look so nearly quite well. In fact from a condition in which there was great and immediate danger to life the case has changed to one of slight chronic inflammation or rather congestion, the cure of which is humanly speaking only a *question of time*.

Clearly the German doctors Wegner and Landgraf (Professor Gerhardt's laryngological assistant), who were travelling in the Crown Prince's suite, did not share Mackenzie's optimistic view of the case. Two days after the Queen had received Mackenzie's report Dr Wegner informed Reid that the growth on the Crown Prince's larynx was again increasing. This news did not surprise Reid who, all along, had failed to be convinced by Mackenzie's sanguine diagnosis. He was not only peeved that Mackenzie was bypassing him and Jenner and conferring directly with the Queen, but he was angered by Mackenzie's habit of issuing statements to medical and other journals. 'I don't think he has any right to make known Her Majesty's wishes to the editors of the *Lancet* and the *British Medical Journal*,' Reid wrote angrily to Jenner.

While Reid castigated Mackenzie, the Crown Prince and Princess continued to put their trust in him, so much so that he was knighted by the Queen on 2 September, at the request of the Crown Prince, who wrote to thank his mother-in-law from Braemar:

> Dear beloved Mama, I thank you most heartily for acceding so readily to my request to confer the honour of Knighthood upon Dr Morell Mackenzie, to whom I am much indebted. Your favour will not be bestowed unworthily and, moreover, this mark of appreciation and distinction before all the world will not be grudged to my benefactor except perhaps by those whose talent and experience were not equal to his own [i.e. the German doctors]. As you know my love for England and Scotland you must also know how happy it makes me to have recovered my health in your country.

There was increasing pressure from Berlin for the Crown Prince to return in view of the failing health of the nonagenarian Emperor. It was felt inadvisable for events to be left in the hands of his son, the volatile Prince William. The royal couple left Scotland for Toblach in the Tyrol on 3 September, accompanied by Mark Hovell, senior surgeon to the Throat Hospital in London, although he was joined a few days later by Major Schrader, the Surgeon-in-Ordinary to the Crown Prince.

A short time later, in search of a warmer climate, they moved on to the Villa Zirio, in San Remo, in spite of grumblings from Berlin (based partly on the royal couple's continued insistence upon having English doctors). During the two months since they left England there had been little indication of significant change in the patient, but they had barely been twenty-four hours at the Villa Zirio when Hovell observed a 'small growth below the left cord about half an inch below and in front of the situation of the growth removed in May and June', which was confirmed by Mackenzie on his arrival hot foot at San Remo. Mackenzie at once 'told the Crown Prince that the disease *looked* like cancer, though it is impossible to be certain as to its nature without taking a microscopic examination after removal of a portion of the growth.' He added, 'I advised that the German specialists should be called in, not because I wanted their advice, but for the purpose of satisfying public opinion in Germany.' Cancer was confirmed and excision of the whole larynx recommended by the German specialists.

The Crown Prince was acquainted with the doctors' views about the various possibilities in the way of treatment. After considering the gloomy prospect he replied that he declined to have his larynx excised, but would submit to tracheotomy, should it become necessary. It was agreed that this would be performed by Bergmann unless difficulty in breathing came on suddenly, when it should be carried out by someone on the spot.

The Crown Princess still clung tenaciously to Morell Mackenzie, and throughout the unfortunate affair exhibited hostility towards the German doctors, which did her little credit and did nothing to ease the patient's position.

Meanwhile, at Balmoral Reid, who did not share the Crown Princess's view of Mackenzie, was using every means within his power to persuade the Queen to see the case objectively. 'The Queen talks as if Mackenzie were infallible, and the German Surgeons all wrong, the wish being Father to the thought as is often the case with Her Majesty.' In a long letter to Jenner Reid stated his own opinion of the case, and showed how he succeeded in convincing the Queen that the German doctors might be correct in suggesting an operation for the excision of the larynx as the only possibility for a complete cure.

I added what I really feel, that if I were told I had commencing cancer of the throat, which if let alone would surely kill me in time even if I did live in pain and discomfort for a year or so, but which I was assured by eminent surgeons of my own country might *possibly* be removed entirely by an operation which involved some risk, and which would seriously and permanently impair my voice, I should prefer being operated on. This seemed to let in light on Her Majesty and to make her realise the situation at last. She said the Crown Prince alive with an impaired or even no voice, would be infinitely better than no Crown Prince at all.

The Queen then asked Reid if he would write to Mackenzie to 'hint' at the possibility of an operation, which he readily agreed to do. But Reid had other suspicions about Mackenzie. He mistrusted his integrity and openly admitted it to Jenner.

He does not like now to draw back after having once said the Germans were wrong in wishing to operate, as it would be tantamount to acknowledging that they were right, and he wrong, and he would be discredited to some extent. But if the Germans think there is a chance of saving the Prince's life, I think it would be monstrous that Mackenzie's feelings should stand in the way, especially as his proposed plan gives no hope of averting a fatal issue. Of course I fancy the operation has less chance now than at the time they wished to do it, when Mackenzie prevented it. If the disease is really cancer, I fear removing parts of it from the inside, as Mackenzie proposed, with instruments, will tend to stimulate the growth.

Reid of course was making a judgment a thousand miles away from the scene of action, and had failed to realise that the situation had been carefully put before the Crown Prince, who had made his own decision. He also underestimated the risk involved in an operation on the larynx (see Appendix II). Nevertheless, he was justified in persuading the Queen 'to consider and weigh the arguments on *both* sides'.

The extent to which Reid had influenced the Queen is evident in her Journal entry for 14 November 1887: 'Dr Reid showed me his answer to Sir M. Mackenzie which is excellent. He is so afraid that both sides of the question may not have been duly weighed, for it must be borne in mind that palliatives cannot eradicate the disease, whereas the operation of opening the throat and removing all the growths might do so.' In answer to Reid's letter requesting to know whether the alternatives (palliative treatment versus operation) had been 'carefully and fully put before His Imperial Highness, and if he has deliberately resolved to elect the former', Mackenzie replied at length, stating his own case against operation with clarity and confidence, and illustrating his arguments with examples:

> The merits and demerits, the dangers and advantages of the various operations have been placed before the Crown Prince in writing, under the signature of all the physicians and surgeons recently in consultation, and explanations and details have been orally given to His Imperial Highness by Professor Schrötter. I have absolutely abstained from discussing the question with the Crown Prince either before or since his determination.

The next day he sent Reid an extract from the *Gazette de France*, 'which places the relative merits of simple tracheotomy and ablation of the larynx before the reader, with that logical precision which is so characteristic of the best French writers'.

This should have put Reid's mind at rest. But the truth was that he neither trusted nor approved of Mackenzie. Their characters and dispositions were diametrically opposed. Reid was intelligent but prosaic, discreet and unobtrusive: a man whose integrity was inviolable. Mackenzie, on the other hand, although possessing a kindly and generous nature, was ambitious and self-willed. He had an artistic and extravagant temperament. His self-esteem was titillated by being the friend and confidential adviser to the Crown Prince and Princess, and he cultivated newspaper correspondents and editors, supplying them freely with information given from his point of view. He had a smooth, plausible and ingratiating manner. In fact, everything about him was calculated to arouse animosity in Reid, as is amply illustrated in the following letter to Sir William Jenner which is one of a series written in the same vein.

> It is *solely* Mackenzie, who now, as in the spring, has been the means of thwarting the German surgeons in carrying out their views: also, though he has done this he wishes it kept secret! To me it will always be incomprehensible why, in the face of the highest German professional opinions, he has assumed such gigantic responsibility: but that, having done so, he should wish the fact concealed and the onus thrown on the Prince, is to my mind rather discreditable to put it mildly. I fear you will think I am writing with an 'animus' against Mackenzie. I trust I am not: but I can't conceal from you or myself that, judging from his former letters and from what has come to my knowledge in various ways, I don't think his conduct has been that of an honourable and upright gentleman.

Meanwhile, Mackenzie still continued to air his views in the newspapers. Even the Queen was disturbed by this and requested Reid to write to him and say, 'that I would suggest as little being published about the Crown Prince's state as possible, that is as to details, as it led to such wrangling and discussions on the part of German Physicians and Surgeons and was so very painful to her and to everyone'.

Mackenzie's answer to Reid was:

> The Crown Princess is very anxious that I should defend my position to the utmost of my ability, as she considers that the attacks on me are really, very often, blows directed at herself. At some future time if I am attacked by Gerhardt and Bergmann, it may be necessary for me to make a detailed statement in the medical journals assigning the various shades of responsibility to different persons. I imagine, however, that Her Majesty would not object to this.

Clearly Mackenzie foresaw hard times ahead, and was marshalling his lines of defence.

No wonder Reid was sceptical about Mackenzie's diagnosis, for he continued to receive contradictory letters and telegrams. On 7 December Mackenzie wrote: 'There is no doubt chronic inflammation and perichondritis, but I fear there is cancer also.' Ten days later, on 17 December: 'The present growth does *not look* malignant, but has the appearance of most inflammatory swellings or granulations (proud flesh) which I have described in my book on *Growth in the Larynx* (pub. 1871) as false excrescences.' While there was no doubt in the minds of the German doctors, Mackenzie continued to vacillate and fill all concerned with false hope (thereby, it must be said in his favour, allowing the royal couple a degree of peace at Christmas time).

For Reid the new year brought a change at home which was cause for rejoicing. The lease of the farm at Hillhead had been sold and, as he wrote to his mother, 'I feel much relieved now that we are clear of the farm and out of debt.'

For the Crown Prince and Princess of Germany, however, the new year began with gloomy forebodings. On 5 January Mark Hovell wrote to Reid from San Remo saying that a new swelling had appeared below the right vocal cord and was causing loss of voice. Early in February the doctors diagnosed perichondritis and decided to insert a cannula into the patient's throat, so as to enable him to breathe more freely. The operation of tracheotomy was to have been performed by von Bergmann but, as Mackenzie wrote to Reid, 'the dyspnoea increased so much that I was obliged to ask Dr Bramann [Bergmann's first assistant] to do the operation. He performed it in a most satisfactory way. The Crown Princess was terribly agitated during the operation. I persuaded her not to be in the room as I feared it might make Bramann nervous.' The Crown Prince had chloroform for the operation, 'though Mackenzie wished him to have none, but Bramann insisted on it', Reid informed Jenner.

The news of the operation at once excited Berlin, and the rumour quickly spread that the Crown Prince was on the point of death, if not actually dead. The Crown Princess, however, still would not believe that the malady was cancer and asked Mackenzie to draw up a report for the Emperor, which was published in the *British Medical Journal* and the *Lancet* as well as in German newspapers. Mackenzie continued to insist that there was no proof of the existence of cancer. 'In my opinion, the clinical symptoms have always been entirely compatible with a non-malignant disease, and the microscopic signs have been in harmony with this view. At this moment medical science does not permit me to affirm that any other disease is present than chronic interstitial inflammation of the larynx combined with perichondritis.'

At Osborne, Reid reported to Jenner:

The Queen speaks a great deal of the operation having been 'successful'. I try to impress on her that, so far as it goes, it could not well be otherwise; and that the mere fact of it being necessary only proves that the original ailment has been going on extending and is now more advanced than it has yet been: and that this real ailment is left untouched by the operation. I think she now *does* understand: but these people are in such matters very obtuse.

On 16 February Reid received a telegram from Mackenzie giving news of complications in the Crown Prince's treatment: 'Crown Prince not had a good night. Cannula irritated trachea, causing slight haemorrhage. Not dangerous at present but may cause trouble in future. After treatment entirely in hands German Surgeons, who are unwilling to receive suggestions from me. I only remain here at urgent desire of Crown Princess. I am entirely dissatisfied with treatment.' A few days later the telegram was followed by a letter in which Mackenzie told a tale of the German doctors' incompetence.

At the beginning of March there were signs that the Emperor's long life was drawing to a close. The Queen flooded Reid with solicitous notes to cypher to the Crown Princess. She was anxious about the Crown Prince having to move to the cold climate of Berlin. 'We all implore you to run no risk. I think of the awful consequences of a cold or bronchitis, and the mountains of papers are full of such. What would happen if Fritz got dangerously ill? In his state refusal seems a duty. He must be very decided, and allow nothing to be done behind his back. Trust he won't move until it is safe, and then to Wiesbaden.'

On 9 March Emperor William died and Fritz became Emperor Frederick III. In spite of Queen Victoria's advice to the contrary, Fritz proceeded at once to Berlin, arriving at Charlottenburg on 11 March. The day before the Emperor's funeral was to take place the Queen issued a further decree to Reid: 'Pray cypher to Sir M. Mackenzie and ask what part of the funeral the Emperor will take part in. The Queen trusts not in the procession on foot on account of the great cold.' She need not have worried for the new Emperor, unable to attend, watched the funeral cortège from his palace window.

On 21 March Reid set off for Florence in the Queen's Suite. From Portsmouth, where he spent the night on the Royal Yacht, he wrote to his mother in his matter of fact way: 'I don't think the German Emperor can live much longer: he is undoubtedly dying of cancer of the throat. I think it is very likely that if he is still alive we shall come back to England by way of Berlin as the Queen will want to see him

POST OFFICE TELEGRAPHS.

Government Dispatch №   Inch 9   18.

Given in at **San Remo**   This message has passed through the handing

at **4.40 pm**   O Bathurst   Telegraphist

Received in   at   Writer

Sent out for delivery at

TO { Dr Reid
     Windsor=Castle
            England

Emperor		*says*	*state*	*reasons*
n Ŀ C m v D V		X w U	X n w	v m w x D T
make	*it*	*absolutely*		*necessary*
‖ C W F M	g n	w g x d z y n m z u		a m x x w v u
for him	*to*	*return*	*to*	*Berlin*	*He think*
K d v h g e	n d v m n	y v t	n d q m v z g t	‖ m n ‖ W T
the	*Queen*	*for*	*her*	*kind*	*thought*
= ⨍ x n h m	b y m m t	K d v h m v	f g t o	n h d y i h ?
of	*him*	*I have*	*taken*	*every*
d ' K h g c	g h w r r m	n w ⨍ m t	m r m v u
precaution		*to ensure*	*that*	*railway*
c v m p w y n g d t		n d m ⨍ x y v m	n h i v n;	v w g z a w u
carriage		*shall*	*be kept*
p w v v q w i m	x h w z z	~~q~~	q m f m c n
properly	*heated*	*during*	*entire*
⁚ v d c m v z u	h o w n m o	o y g u ⨍ i	m t n g v n
journey		
g d y v t m v		m c K e n z i e

Morell Mackenzie kept Reid in touch with the treatment of the Emperor
Frederick by cyphered telegraph.

once again.' Then with his usual concern for his mother's welfare he added: 'Be sure not to want anything that can add to your comfort, as I am now saving money and getting rich by degrees!' Although his salary was not great, his expenses were few and he could well afford to indulge his mother, who tended to stint herself unless persuaded to do otherwise.

The Queen and her Suite settled in at the Villa Palmieri, which had been lent by the Countess of Crawford and Balcarres. For weeks prior to her visit it had been the scene of great activity. Not only had the house been painted outside and redecorated within, but a special water supply had been connected, and there was even a telephone. The Via Boccaccio which led up to it had been narrow and unlit, but now was widened to allow carriages to pass to and fro, and street lamps had been put up so that the royal party and members of the Household could return late at night without fear of being molested. The Queen enjoyed all the Easter festivities and Reid, who had more leisure than usual, spent his time in art galleries and looking at churches. He also accompanied the Queen when she was shown over the principal hospital in Florence by a doctor whom he knew.

From Florence the Queen was busy preparing for her journey to Berlin, to see her son-in-law for what she suspected would be the last time. Reid was required to send off regular cyphers to the Empress at Charlottenburg about family and domestic matters: 'I shall bring my own matrass [sic] – leave it to you to say who I must see or *not* besides my Grandchildren and Great Grandchildren, but beg not many, as have had to see so many here, and am much tired.' The Queen had indeed had numerous royal visitors in Florence, including the King and Queen of Italy and the Empress of Brazil.

En route to Berlin from Florence the Queen and her entourage stopped at Innsbruck, where she was greeted by the Austrian Emperor, Franz Joseph. A luncheon was served at the station, where Reid joined the Austrian Household. Karl Lodron, now a young officer in the Austrian army, and his mother came to the station to meet him. It was the first time he had seen them since he left Vienna in 1877, so there was much news to exchange in a short time.

In Berlin Reid was quartered at the Schloss Charlottenburg, where he met his German counterpart, Dr Wegner, who drove him round the city to leave cards on von Bergmann and Gerhardt. He encountered Bismarck and was given a photograph by the dying Emperor.

On 12 May at Windsor Reid received a letter from Mackenzie saying that there was a slight improvement in the Emperor's condition: 'Today he walked from his bedroom into his sitting room, only resting slightly on my arm, whilst on the other days he has always been wheeled in his chair. He takes his nourishment well, though he has not much appetite.' For a year Mackenzie had been sending telegrams to Reid in code; now they decided to adopt a new one in case the current one had become too familiar with the postal messengers. 'I think it would be better to keep the new cypher for *important occasions*. When I am going to use it I will always commence with the word *special*. Then you will know it refers to the new cypher,' wrote Mackenzie. For several months Reid had been receiving daily telegrams about the Emperor's condition which read like a barometer in the English climate, but on 10 June Dr Wegner, the Emperor's personal physician, wrote Reid a letter in which he allowed no room for hope of recovery. The disease had taken its course.

> Around the wound of the trachea, in which the cannula is inserted, is formed a prominent granulation, whose character shows that it originates from a seriously ill ground. The purulent discharge is abundant and wants frequent dressing. But, and I wish you will prevent this notion from being known by anybody besides Her Majesty, since two days fluid food, for instance milk, shows itself partially flowing out of the tracheal wound after having been swallowed. You will judge by this symptom that from the larynx the illness has spread further on. The Emperor has an admirable patience and greatness of mind to bear this sad state. He never complains, though I am convinced he knows the sadness of his condition. The Empress keeps him up, even with the great sorrow she feels, and makes him hope to recover. I must really admire her.

The full horror of the Emperor's condition is described by the anguished Empress in a letter to her mother:

> But what it is to see my poor darling so changed! He is a perfect skeleton now and his fine thick hair is quite thin. His poor throat is such a painful and shocking sight, and I can often hardly bear to look at it, when it is done up, etc: I have to rush away to hide my tears often! It is very difficult to keep the air pure in the room, so it is a great comfort that the weather permits his being on the terrace!

On 14 June broncho-pneumonia developed, and the following day he died peacefully, and free from pain, after a long and courageous struggle, at Friedrichskron, in the house where he had been born and spent the greater part of his married life.

During the final drama Reid was at Ellon with his mother. He was summoned back to Balmoral immediately upon the Emperor's death. 'The Queen seemed very glad to see me again and did not bully me for not coming sooner!' he wrote to his mother. Meanwhile, at Friedrichskron, rechristened by Frederick and restored to its old name of Neue Palais by Emperor William II, the dead Emperor was not allowed to rest in peace, for within an hour of his death the lying-in-state was to begin. A hurried *post mortem* was carried out and revealed that the whole of the larynx (except the epiglottis) had been destroyed and it now consisted of one large, flat gangrenous ulcer; patches of septic broncho-pneumonia were present in the lungs.

The death of Emperor Frederick III, far from ending the wrangling between the doctors, started a fresh battle. Mackenzie injudiciously spoke freely to a reporter of a Dutch newspaper, giving his account of the case. This in turn was published in Bismarck's semi-official newspaper, the *Norddeutsche Allgemeine Zeitung*, and not only infuriated the Germans but also brought down the wrath of Colonel Leopold Swaine, Military Attaché at the British Embassy in Berlin. Reid entirely agreed with Colonel Swaine's reaction and took steps to inform the presidents of the Royal Colleges of Medicine of the German attitude towards the British medical profession. For whatever Mackenzie's conduct during the affair, and there were arguments both for and against him, in publicly reporting a medical case he broke the Hippocratic oath, and eventually was forced to resign from the Royal College of Physicians.

Though the part played by Reid in the German Emperor's illness was interesting in that it influenced the Queen and the medical profession in England, he was not directly involved in the case. With other members of the royal family it was different. While he saw more of Princess Beatrice, who dwelt permanently with the Queen, and Princess Christian, who lived close by at Cumberland Lodge and was a frequent visitor, Princess Louise was the one with whom he had the closest relationship.

Of all the Queen's five daughters she was the most beautiful and alluring to men; a talented sculptress, she had an artistic temperament with Bohemian tendencies. Not as intellectual as her oldest sister, the Empress Frederick, she had, nevertheless, an interesting personality and was, like her mother, emotional and full of warmth. She had an unhappy childless marriage (to the Marquis of Lorne) and suffered from a restlessness common in the unfulfilled. Marie Mallet, first a maid-of-honour and then lady-in-waiting to Queen Victoria, thought that Princess Louise was at her best when people were in trouble, 'and this is a redeeming feature in her most complex character'. She also considered her a 'dangerous woman' who to gain her end would stick at nothing. 'She is fascinating but oh, so ill-natured I positively dread talking to her, and not a soul escapes.' Certainly Princess Louise did stir up trouble amongst her sisters, and she was often at odds with the Queen, who found her the most difficult of her daughters. She was, however, devoted to her brother and sister-in-law, the Prince and Princess of Wales.

On 2 September 1891 at Balmoral, Reid noted in his diary that whilst out walking he found white heather, some of which he gave to Princess Louise 'who wore it at dinner'. Three days later he went 'with Princess Louise to fish in the Gelder and stood by her putting on worms, disentangling the hook and line, etc., all the time. She caught two little trout. Walked home with her.' Thus began a friendship which was to last for the rest of his life. When in trouble each sought the other for advice and comfort. Princess Louise knew that she had a sympathetic and unprejudiced listener she could trust to be wise, fair, and discreet.

When a royal person was required for the opening of the new Royal Infirmary buildings in Aberdeen, therefore, Reid did not miss the golden opportunity of asking Princess Louise to perform the ceremony. The Princess was only too pleased to assist, although she wrote to Reid: 'If they want an "Eclat", as Mr Littlejohn says, I fear I am not the right person. At the same time I would much like to do anything to help you in assisting a work you yourself are interested in.' The opening ceremony duly took place on 4 October 1892. 'The whole thing was beautifully done and everyone was most kind,' remarked Princess Louise. 'I was able often to watch your face and was glad to notice an expression of perfect contentment on it! I need hardly say it had been a pleasure to me to be able to do anything for you in some way to show the gratitude we must all feel for your constant devotion to, and exertions for, our Queen.'

When staying with the Queen, Princess Louise spent hours talking with Reid not only about her own grievances but also about Household matters. She doubted whether Arthur Bigge and Fleetwood Edwards would be suitable successors to Sir Henry Ponsonby; she discussed the Munshi problem endlessly; and she even thought that the Queen should abdicate in favour of the Prince of Wales as she was no longer fit to reign. 'The people are learning to do without her and the government tell her very little, and she is reducing the future role of the Prince of Wales to a nonentity.'

In November 1895 Reid had to deal with a situation which involved the most delicate handling. Princess Beatrice sent for him:

to speak about Princess Louise's relations with Bigge and said that it was a scandal and something must be done. The Princess of Wales had written to her about it. Also Princess Christian she said was much exercised about it. Lady Bigge was in despair; she had ruined the happiness of others and would his. Prince Henry had seen Bigge drinking Princess Louise's health at the Queen's dinner. She had him in her toils. If the Queen knew all she would not keep Bigge. His manner was changed for the worse etc: etc:

While Randall Davidson, by now Bishop of Winchester, had been charged by the Queen and Princess Beatrice to speak to Bigge about his relations with Princess Louise, Reid not only had to face the Princess on the subject, but was also required to treat the distraught and outraged Lady Bigge. He had tea with her daily and soothed her – with potions and, more effectively, by being a sympathetic recipient of her woes. The scandal blew over as quickly as it had arisen, the parties in question having learnt the error of their ways.[1]

As far as Reid was concerned, however, it was not the end of the matter. Privately, Princess Louise continued to pour out her grievances to him regularly. 'She complained much of the Queen's unkindness to her, and especially of Princesses Christian and Beatrice. They had laid their heads together to ruin her position here [at Court], and had succeeded.' What could Reid do but listen? He was not in a position to dismiss the Princess from his room, nor could he deny her entry. His only hope was to try to alleviate her persecution mania by instilling common sense into her. The problem was insoluble, since the temperaments of the Princesses were incompatible and Princess Beatrice, at least, was jealous of Princess Louise.

The reason for Princess Beatrice's continued unkindness was eventually revealed to Reid in June 1898 when Princess Louise confessed to him, during one of her 'long talks', about 'Prince Henry's attempted relations with her, which she had declined', and his subsequent efforts to expose her and Bigge out of revenge. Finally she could stand the situation no longer and composed a letter to the Queen 'complaining of her treatment', which she sent to Reid to read first before sending on to the Queen. The letter appears to have had the desired effect, for after 12 August 1898, the 'long talks' between Princess and doctor ceased, and relations between Princess Louise

[1] There is no mention of this incident in the Royal Archives or in the papers belonging to the descendants of Arthur Bigge. The word 'relations' is ambiguous, and what was possibly a mild flirtation may have been blown up into a scandal by a notoriously jealous sister.

and her family improved. (Prince Henry had died in January 1896.)

Away from her family Princess Louise was quite a different person, as Maggie Ponsonby, Sir Henry's daughter, Magdalen, relates in a letter to Reid, written from Bordighera in the spring of 1896. 'Princess Louise is here, quite the retired saint, but full of prescriptions. She told Mama that to enjoy thoroughly good health you must boil your knees in whisky every night. I am so glad I wasn't there as I should have burst out laughing. She bikes with Lady Adela Larking all day, and does it very badly.' By Christmas Princess Louise had become proficient enough to cycle with Reid at Osborne.

With the other members of the royal family Reid was less intimate, although they often sought his advice on countless matters – sometimes related to medicine, but often not. As the Prince of Wales had his own personal physician, Sir Francis Laking, Reid was not required to attend him professionally, but they frequently communicated and when Jenner died in December 1898, Reid took his place as Physician-in-Ordinary to the Prince of Wales. He saw Princess Beatrice and Prince Henry daily, and was always trying to effect cures for the Princess's rheumatism, which had attacked her at an early age. There was never a great rapport between them; Reid found her remote and unsympathetic, and when Prince Henry invited him on a journey to Norway he told his mother that he did not want to go as he thought he should get bored with him.

He was, however, responsible for their children, who suffered from the usual childish ailments, whilst Prince Leopold, being a haemophiliac, was a constant cause of worry to his parents, the Queen, and his doctor. In January and February 1894 Reid was preoccupied with both Prince Leopold and Princess Ena, whose cases were serious. Prince Leopold, not quite five years old, was suffering from 'symptoms of haemophilia diathesis, in the form of swellings and subcutaneous haemorrhages. For the first time he had a severe attack of epistaxis, without any apparent cause.' The nostril was plugged successfully, but the nose-bleeds persisted at intervals, and Reid could never risk being far away from his patient.

Even more serious was the six-year-old Princess Ena's riding accident.

When out riding on Saturday and going at a canter the Princess's pony fell and pitched her on her head. She was stunned at first, but quickly recovered and walked home (a few hundred yards). When I saw her she was complaining of severe pain in her head, and had been sick. There was no mark of any injury to her head (nor has any bruise developed; I suppose her hat partially prevented this). I at once put her to bed. There were no local or general symptoms but what I have mentioned, pupils equal and reacting to light, no paralysis, consciousness clear, pulse quick but regular.

After being some time in bed she was sick again repeatedly, began to get drowsy, and after an hour or two could not be roused. Her pulse began to get irregular, her teeth were clenched, and she ground them at intervals. Her right pupils got dilated and sluggish. I at once told the Queen that there were dangerous symptoms developing, and that I thought Powell ought to be sent for. I got leave to telegraph to Powell who arrived at 3.0 a.m. on Sunday morning. The above signs had meanwhile increased and she was quite unconscious, with, in fact, evident signs of brain pressure, probably a haemorrhage. [Douglas] Powell [Physician Extraordinary] shared my anxiety on arrival and said there was, in all probability, a haemorrhage. This we have since localised as being probably on the right crus about the exit of the third nerve, as in addition to the dilated pupil there is ptosis and divergent squint. Today she has to some extent recovered consciousness, and can swallow. (We have been sustaining her hitherto by nutrient enemata). The general signs are also improving, and I trust all will go well. It has been a very anxious case, and I am feeling tired, but I hope to go to bed tonight (the first time since the accident), as we have a trained nurse and the condition is no longer so critical a one. I *think* she is going to do well, but of course I am still very anxious.

It was hardly surprising that Reid was exhausted, as he had been on duty for two and a half days continuously. His rest was well earned.

In spite of the fact that Jenner had retired Reid still liked to keep him informed of his cases, with details of his treatment of them. He knew that Jenner appreciated his communication and, as he felt that he owed his present position to Jenner, he thought it was the least he could do, besides which it had become a habit with him to confide his thoughts and actions to paper. Two days later he wrote to Sir William again.

The little Princess is much better than she was but I am still anxious about her. She is quite conscious when awake, but rambles a little when asleep. She now swallows food quite easily so that the nutrient enemata are no longer required. She also passes water herself, and the catheter is no longer necessary. The dilatation of the right pupil and the ptosis persist unaltered. Her temperature is normal or slightly subnormal. Respiration rather slow for a child of her age – 18 to 20. The pulse last night was as slow as 65 and very irregular. Today it is 70-75, and more steady, though the irregularity is still marked. I trust the improvement may go on steadily, but I tell them [the Queen and Prince and Princess Henry] that she is not yet out of danger, and I watch her very closely both when she is asleep and awake.

In his next letter Reid wrote, with a feeling of relief, 'I think she is now safe.' The pulse was more regular, and she was able to move 'the right upper eyelid *slightly* and the dilatation of the pupil is less than it was. She is quite herself mentally, and today is getting a little obstinate and troublesome!' On the same day Reid informed his mother that 'the accounts in the papers of the Princess's progress have been more favourable than was the case, but H.M. always makes the best of everything!' Just as she had refused to believe that Prince Albert and John Brown were dying, so the Queen would not admit that Princess Ena had been in grave danger.

Reid had little other than social contact with the Queen's third son, Arthur, Duke of Connaught and his family, although he was put in charge of their children while they were in India, and he attended Princess Patricia when she was seriously ill in 1892. Princess Christian, whom he saw regularly on the other hand, was kindly, if indiscreet, and on occasions suffered from 'imaginary ailments'. She was given to taking drugs such as opium and laudanum. Both Prince Christian and the Queen spoke frequently to Reid about her habits. Reid noted in his diary that on one occasion at Balmoral when 'the royal family and the Household were in the Queen's room after dinner, dancing to the music of Curtis's band, Princess Christian was rather queer.' On another occasion, 'After dinner smoked cigarettes with Princess Christian in her room.' He was a heavy smoker, though once or twice he made a real but unsuccessful attempt to give it up. However, it would not have been *comme il faut* for a lady to smoke in public, and certainly not in front of the Queen, hence the secret smoking sessions in which the smokers at Court indulged.

By 1894 Princess Christian was causing grave concern, and Prince Christian begged Reid to talk to her to see if he could induce her to refrain from taking drugs. Once again he had to play the role of confidant, but this time he notes in his diary after one of Princess Christian's sessions with him in his room that she was 'a great bore'. In 1896, whilst at Cimiez, Princess Christian was 'very ill with facial neuralgia or pretending?!' Three days later she was 'still pretending neuralgia' so that Reid decided that the best way to put an end to her malingering was 'to stop all her narcotics and stimulants', which he did.

Quite different from Princess Christian was the Empress Frederick. While he mistrusted her judgment as far as people and politics were concerned, he found her an interesting personality, intellectually lively, and, as a patient, she did not suffer from hypochondria. In February 1895, while the Empress Frederick was staying with the Queen at

Osborne, she sent for Reid who had a 'long interview with her. Afterwards was asked by the Queen what she had said, and if she had spoken about Her Majesty!' It is easy to see how misunderstandings arose at Court. The secret meetings and endless discussions and intrigue amongst courtiers and royalty, all interfering in each other's business while living in close proximity to one another, must have been stifling. Reid, who by the nature of his position was deeply entangled in all Court affairs, appears to have given the impression of being quite open, while concealing a great deal. 'Sir James is so open, I like him much, now many at Court are so "boutonné" as if they knew many secrets they will not tell,' Lady Lytton recalls.

The Queen always showed Reid her family letters when any question of health was mentioned in them. In June 1895 he received a note from the Queen which said: 'I forgot all along to show you this letter from the Empress Frederick about her health, giving an account of her sensations. I had these flushings thirty years ago with distressing restlessness but no palpitation. I hope it is chiefly nerves.' Nerves for the Queen covered a multitude of ailments, but this would seem to be a clear case of *le temps de la vie*, the Victorian euphemism for menopause.

Much more serious was Sir John Williams, the Queen's gynaecologist, and Reid's diagnosis of breast cancer in the Empress on 4 December and when Reid told the Queen 'she was much upset and cried a good deal'. At first it was hoped that the cancer would be operable, but on 13 December the Empress showed Reid a statement written by Sir Thomas Smith (Surgeon Extraordinary from 1895) and Frederick Treves (Surgeon Extraordinary from 1900) that her 'breast cancer was far too advanced for operation'.

The Queen and Princess Beatrice were not satisfied with this report and wished the Empress to employ a quack cancer curer, Roberts of Plymouth. Reid expressed strong disapproval and, as usual, his judgment proved to be sound. He was vindicated a month later by a report from Lady Ponsonby who wrote to him on 11 January 1899, having the same day had a visit from the Empress, and just after Roberts had been exposed in the newspapers.

Now he is proved to be a quack, and worse than that, I hope they will leave the matter alone, but ignorance and obstinacy are strong factors to oppose, and one fact like that in the Devonshire Newspaper is worth in such a case far more than the best of arguments. I have had tea this evening with the Empress Frederick, and I am glad to be able to tell you that we never approached the subject of Roberts. I am sure she will avoid all quack remedies. I am afraid the idea that the Queen is made to listen to these tales must annoy you very much. I thought the Empress looking wonderful, but she was not hopeful. Wonderfully brave, I think her, and so gentle and kind.

Brave she was until the end, which came two and a half years later. All the time she tried to hide her acute suffering from her mother, minimising the seriousness of her malady, but when she became bedridden, the cancer having attacked her spine, and could no longer use her hands, the truth could not be concealed. She survived the Queen by little more than six months.

The Queen's second son, Prince Alfred, Duke of Coburg, also had problems with his health. On 17 October 1894 Reid received a note from Ponsonby enclosing a letter from Sir Condie Stephen, Private Secretary to the Duke of Coburg, concerning the Duke's drinking habits and the effect that they had had upon his health. The letter was to be shown to the Queen, but Ponsonby 'objected to these details being talked about to her'. Condie Stephen wrote that, 'unless he can moderate the quantity of stimulants he takes, his health will soon entirely break down, and unless he is frightened he will not change his mode of living – the kidneys are already slightly affected. He is very touchy just now about his health, but I think he would consult a specialist in London if the Queen asked him to do so.'

Over the years there was no improvement and, while staying at Windsor in November 1897, the Duke of Coburg sent for Reid to discuss his health, and said that Reid 'gave good advice'. Reid noted that he also 'saw his servant Farquharson, who gave me a dreadful account of the Duke's drinking habits. Had a talk with the Queen on the subject.' He wrote to the Prince of Wales about his brother, and they agreed between them that, for the Duke's own good, he must be persuaded to leave the social life of London and go to Egypt to recuperate.

In March 1898 when the Duke was at Villefranche, staying on board his yacht the *Surprise*, Reid, who was at nearby Cimiez, was sent for. He found Prince Alfred suffering agonies with a 'developed rectal inflammation' which required urgent surgery. The following day he was operated on by Anthony Bowlby and warned by the Queen in a telegram: 'He must be most careful, and after such an attack must not travel without a doctor. Bertie joins me in thinking this absolutely necessary.' For once the Queen and her eldest son were in accord.

Reid wrote to his mother that the Duke 'was in a broken down state from too much drink, and that the place is swarming with Royalties and other big people, with whose affairs I am always having to do!' A few days later the Duke of Coburg reported satisfactory progress to Reid from the Château de Fabron at Rizza, where he was staying, and the Queen demanded to see his medical notes – which would seem to be a breach of medical etiquette, but there is no evidence that Reid forbore to show them to her. He was congratulated by the Prince of Wales 'on having made such excellent arrangements, and it was indeed fortunate that you were able to obtain the services of as able a Surgeon as Mr Bowlby'. [Anthony Alfred Bowlby, F.R.C.S.]

However, the Duke's general health deteriorated, his decline largely brought about by his own bad habits. On 25 July 1900 Reid had received 'definite news that the Duke of Coburg is suffering from inoperable cancer of the tongue and throat'. He died in Coburg on 31 July at the age of fifty-six, six months before his mother. For some time, unbeknown even to his wife, he had been fed through a tube, and the Queen had been kept in the dark as to the serious nature of his illness. 'I think they should never have held the truth from me as long as they did. It has come as such an awful shock. It is so merciful that dearest Affie died in his sleep without any struggle, but it is heartrending,' she wrote in her Journal on the day of his death.

7

Perquisites and Promotion

Attending to royal whims and ailments did not normally absorb the whole day, and one of Reid's great pleasures in his spare time was to wander through the gardens at Windsor with Owen Thomas, the head gardener. Inside two miles of wall at Frogmore lay magnificent vegetable and fruit gardens, divided into eight partitions, each under a foreman. There were also conservatories and glasshouses for every imaginable exotic fruit and flower. Thomas frequently gave Reid bouquets of flowers and bunches of grapes to send to his mother, and during the gooseberry and strawberry season he was allowed to indulge himself freely. Although he no longer farmed himself, Reid took great interest in the Queen's farms. He was a frequent visitor to the Dairy and to Shaw Farm, where he made friends with Tait the farmer who proudly showed him a 21 cwt Shorthorn, on its way to Smithfield. He liked animals generally, and when his brother John gave the Queen a Chinese Chow, he visited it regularly at the Royal Kennels where he had long chats with the kennelman. In turn, the Queen gave Reid a three-month-old white Pomeranian puppy named Vicky, which stayed at Ellon with his mother. When she saw photographs of Vicky the Queen always complained that she was 'too fat'.

At Balmoral, too, Reid was on excellent terms with the gardeners and gillies, being regularly plied with gifts of salmon and venison. He would warn his mother, 'Don't stock up the larder when I come as I shall be bringing a Dee salmon with me.' The gardeners kept him supplied with trees and plants for his garden at The Chesnuts, which he was continually altering and enlarging with his gardener, old James Marr. In 1899 the deer keeper at Richmond Park received a warrant, signed by Lord Edward Pelham Clinton, who had succeeded Sir John Cowell as Master of the Household in 1894, requiring him 'to kill one fat buck per season', for Reid. At Christmas he received munificent presents: a solid silver salver or a silver coffee pot from the Queen, a silver cigarette case from Princess Beatrice, or 'a lovely warm dressing gown, which I mean to use' from Princess Louise. Each year Reid wrote to his mother describing what he had been given; 'a pretty good haul this Christmas', he wrote in 1889, the first year he was actually bidden to eat Christmas dinner at the Queen's own table. By the time he had been with the Queen for twenty years, he had accumulated enough paraphernalia to furnish a house. Visiting royalty, too, showered him with gifts in lieu of fees, which led to a false impression that he must be a rich man. The opposite was the case, for since the gifts were of royal origin and in most cases inscribed, he was unable to sell them, had he wanted to, and he was never given remuneration in cash for attending patients. He lived solely on his salary which, until 1894 – when it was doubled – was meagre in relation to other medical men of his professional standing. As a Fellow of the Royal College of Physicians, where he was elected in 1892, it was well below what a consultant physician in London, or one of the larger provincial cities, would have earned – even after the Queen had given him a substantial rise.

Since his illness in 1889, Sir William Jenner had, to all intents and purposes, handed over his responsibilities to Reid, who in May of that year had been promoted to Physician-in-Ordinary. In addition, on her birthday – 24 May – the Queen had conferred upon him the Order of the Companionship of the Bath. Reid wrote to his mother:

> Unfortunately neither of these honours carries any extra pay: but it is a great rise in *status*. Jenner told me I might have a knighthood instead of a C.B. but I preferred the latter, and he quite approved of my choice. It is not much of an honour to be a common Knight Bachelor, as it is given to anybody, such as tradesmen who are Mayors of towns and so on: but only *gentlemen* get the C.B., and should I ever have the fortune to be promoted to K.C.B., I shall have a Knighthood that is worth having.

In January 1894 Sir William Jenner tendered his resignation to the Queen. 'Ponsonby told me yesterday that the Queen had accepted your resignation and has given you a pension of £500,' Reid wrote to Jenner. 'It is useless for me to comment on this, as it is in keeping with the Queen's pecuniary ideas where doctors are concerned. But it removes my feelings of delicacy in asking for a rise of pay, as I think Her Majesty will never think of it unless I do. Do you see any objection to my writing to Ponsonby? I mean to do so unless you advise me not to.' Jenner declined to give his advice and Reid sent a long letter to Ponsonby asking for an addition to his pay, which Ponsonby showed to the Queen. Next time he wrote to Jenner it was to announce that 'Her Majesty is willing to give me a material increase of pay. It only remains for the sum to be fixed. Ponsonby has asked me to think it over, which I am doing. I do not intend to suggest anything very small, as I find from experience that I am not likely to get much if I leave it to them, but on the other hand they may not accept my view as to figures.'

The Queen could not fail to be impressed by the points put forward in Reid's letter to Ponsonby, which is a model of clear thinking, and is worth quoting, since it illustrates not only the wide range of duties, but also the considerable responsibility, which devolved upon the Queen's personal physician. None of her other doctors had ever been required to fill a similar position. Previously both duties and responsibility had been shared between several men.

The conditions under which I serve the Queen have changed so greatly since I first came here that I feel myself constrained, after long reflection, to write to you on the subject of my remuneration. My duties during the last few years have steadily become more and more onerous and responsible: all that used to be referred to, and done by, Sir William Jenner has gradually drifted to me: I have to take cognisance of, and to control, the working of Her Majesty's medical men at Windsor and at Osborne, a difficult and delicate task involving frequent correspondence and bothers that are never known to anyone else: different members of the Royal Family consult me and write me, and refer matters to me for my decision: I have a large amount of responsible correspondence on many diverse subjects, often of a confidential nature, to conduct: Crown medical appointments and questions of Royal Patronage of Hospitals and benevolent Institutions, for which I get frequent applications, are investigated by me, with much expenditure of time and labour: I am daily besieged by people in trouble or in difficulty for my advice and assistance: I do much that is really the duty of the Medical men at Windsor, at Osborne, and at Balmoral, as it is difficult, and in fact impossible, for me to refuse to give medical or other assistance to the servants and dependents who come to me with their various troubles: the Indians, and matters connected with them, require no small share of my time and attention, so do the Royal nurseries: and, in addition, all sorts of miscellaneous duties and questions fall to my lot. Besides all this, and as my chief duty, I have for years had the sole care of the Queen's health, which involves a responsibility not only to herself and her family, but also to the country which, of itself, would be by some considered quite an ample duty and responsibility for one man. That my duties should, as the years go on, thus grow in extent and importance is but natural in the circumstances, and I do not regard it otherwise than as a privilege that my sphere of usefulness has widened so considerably. Of late years, I have been advised, oftener than once, by friends who take an interest in my welfare, to resign my post here and to settle in London where they tell me I should, as a Fellow of the College, and for other reasons which I need not mention, reap, with less wear and responsibility, more material advantages than I do here. But this I have refused to do. I know well that it would take years for anyone else to acquire and grow into the necessary knowledge of Her Majesty's health, temperament and constitution, and to become acquainted with the various family particulars, and the inner working of this place, so as to be able to cope satisfactorily with all that has to be done, and at the same time to steer clear of matters that had better not be meddled with, and on which, though they may be forced on his observation, the doctor should be reticent. I know too that many men, even of the highest professional attainments (and the Queen could, I think, have no one but a man whose medical status was such as to command the confidence of the Profession and the Country) might come and go before Her Majesty was satisfied, or before they could reconcile themselves to the peculiar and intricate knowledge of people and of things there which a stranger could not possibly acquire without long experience; I believe too that Her Majesty trusts me, and believes in my honesty of purpose. Were it otherwise, I should have followed the advice that has been urged on me; but I would not do anything that would cause the Queen personal inconvenience, or leave her in the hands of strangers, or that might savour of ingratitude or disloyalty. I think, however, that as I have devoted, and am still devoting to her and to her interests the best years of my life, when I should otherwise have been building up a practice for the future (like *all* her other medical men) that would enable me to provide for the time when I can no longer work, I should have that fact taken into consideration, and that it is not unreasonable to ask that the part of the salary resigned by Sir William Jenner should be added to mine. The time has come when I *must* look to the future as a matter of common prudence with my advancing years, seeing that I have no other source of income than my own exertions.

Her Majesty's medical men at Windsor, London and Osborne are paid for (at most) a few hours' work daily much higher proportionately than I am, and they conduct lucrative practices besides; while I, with higher diplomas and professional rank than any of them am by the necessities of my position, absolutely precluded from supplementing my income by extraneous work. I may add that of late years I have had several letters from Sir William Jenner, expressing his opinion on this point, but I have, from motives of delicacy, refrained from moving in the matter until now.

For all his work and responsibility Reid received the paltry sum of £800 per annum. He could, therefore, afford to be bold, and even demanding, and he had never lacked self-confidence, nor felt diffident about his capabilities. The Queen replied sympathetically to Reid's long letter on 26 January.

What Dr Reid says is true and he certainly should have his salary increased and by and by some further honour, but not yet. But what he should be relieved from is the constant applications of the servants and others all day long who ought to be attended by the doctors at Windsor, Osborne and Balmoral. The Queen's *own* personal people, male and female, he was always to attend, but not the others except in emergencies. And he should have stated hours to see people and except in any dangerous illness or emergency not receive them at other times. The Queen must insist on this, or else he will be worn out. The Indians really cannot give him much to do, as they fortunately are generally well, but of course from having different constitutions they require him. The fact is the servants and everyone have great confidence in him.

On 2 February he wrote jubilantly to his mother:

Ponsonby has just informed me that for the future my salary is to be what Jenner had, viz. £1500 a year. This is capital, and I consider I am now well paid. I hope to be able in future to save at least £1000 a year; so now you must on no account deny yourself any luxury or any travelling about that you feel you would like, as I can well afford you *anything*!

The £1500 from the Privy Purse was augmented by a further £200 from the Lord Chamberlain's Department, this being the amount paid annually to Physicians-in-Ordinary, which meant that Reid had more than doubled his original salary. He had every reason to be content. Although his salary was, by many standards, still on the low side, his expenses were minimal. He had no overhead charges, and his luxurious life-style cost him nothing. There was his mother to support, but her way of life was frugal, and The Chesnuts to keep up, but he could now count himself if not rich, at least comfortably off.

But what mattered to Reid more than anything else was the Queen's recognition of his services to her and her family. On 4 February she wrote a complimentary note to him: 'The Queen has had much pleasure in increasing remuneration as a mark of her great confidence in his zeal and unremitting attention and able treatment of herself and family, and many Members of her Household. She hopes he will not allow his time to be taken up by needless calls on his attention.'

Three months later Lord Rosebery, then Liberal Prime Minister, in the course of conversation with Reid at Windsor, proposed to offer him a knighthood on the Queen's Birthday. Reid promptly but courteously declined the offer, restating his reasons for doing so to Jenner:

Of course if it had been a K.C.B., I should have been proud to accept it; but being already a C.B. I could not well, as you say, accept something which is lower. A simple knighthood is, as you know, rather looked down on here, and *no one* holds one: the fact of its being offered me shows that I am not put on the same platform as the rest of the people here, though my services to the Queen are more arduous and responsible than those of most of the men here who have got K.C.B. (Edwards for instance).

To his mother he wrote simply: 'If ever I am to be a knight, it shall be K.C.B. and not a common knighthood, which is given to all sorts of common fellows.' His snobbishness was blatant, and there were those who disapproved of his declining such an offer. 'Since I declined the knighthood, I think I am under a cloud, and Ponsonby expressed to me his disapproval of what I had done,' he wrote to Jenner.

It did not take long for the cloud to blow over. On 23 May 1895 Lord Rosebery told Reid that he should have been made a K.C.B. on the Queen's Birthday, 'were it not that Bigge has to be made one, and his [Rosebery's] Radical people would make a row if *two* were given at once to members of the Court. But he says I am to have it on the anniversary of the Queen's accession a month hence,' Reid informed his mother, adding with his usual caution, 'do not speak of it to anyone in case of accidents.' There were no mishaps, and on 20 June at three o'clock, at Balmoral, Reid was knighted. He described the ceremony in detail to his mother:

> I was 'introduced' to the Queen's presence by Edwards, and went down on one knee, when Her Majesty touched me on each shoulder with a sword and said 'Sir James'. (She insisted on doing it with a Claymore, instead of an ordinary sword, as this place is in the Highlands!). I then kissed her hand and remained kneeling, when she put round my neck the red ribbon and badge of the Bath, and handed me the star which is worn on the coat. I then kissed hands again and got up, and it was all over. She had never seen the top of my head before, and was surprised, she said, to see my hair was so nearly gone! I dined last night with the Queen, and should not wonder if I do so again tonight in my new warpaint!

The press was full of praise for the new knight. One cutting which found its way into his scrapbook, albeit unattributed, described the Queen's physician as 'a Scotsman, middle-aged, rather stern of feature, and decidedly "plain" in manner and speech. To the Queen he is always a most valuable and faithful servant, while his faintly brusque ways have never made him unpopular at Court. He talks with a considerable accent, but his somewhat curt manner of addressing people is but a slight veil to a kindly heart and sympathetic nature. His promotion has been well earned at a most fitting moment.'

But it was Thomas Barlow, Reid's medical friend who became Physician Extraordinary in 1899 and who sometimes filled his place while he was on holiday, who understood the full significance of the honour: 'You have sacrificed, not only of personal ease, but of what I may call scientific happiness in your unremitting service to the Queen. This recognition takes some cognisance of your sacrifices.'

Reid's professional skill, too, was acknowledged. *The Practitioner* noted that: 'Everyone who has come into contact with Sir James Reid professionally has recognised that behind the tact of the courtier there lie the knowledge and clinical insight of the highly skilled physician. It is the surest proof of the solid work of the man that he has the confidence of the Queen and the high esteem of Sir William Jenner, two of the best judges of men in existence.'

In October Reid received recognition from his own University. He went to Aberdeen where, 'robed in gown and trencher', in the presence of his proud mother, an honorary LL.D. was conferred on him by the Dean of the Law Faculty, Professor Dove Wilson. At the precise moment when he was being 'capped and hooded' 'God Save the Queen' was sung lustily by the students who, throughout the Rectorial Address, behaved in a very unruly fashion!

Reid was honoured on the Continent as well as in England and Scotland. In April 1894, while staying in Coburg during the wedding celebrations of Victoria Melita of Saxe-Coburg-Gotha and the Grand Duke Ernest Ludwig of Hesse, he was offered two orders. Prince Alfred, Duke of Coburg, presented him with the Ritterkreuz (1st Class) of the Saxe Ernestine order, and the Kaiser bestowed the Order of the Red Eagle (3rd Class) upon him. 'So far, I am the only one of our suite who has got a decoration from the Emperor, so I am rather proud of it!' he wrote to his mother.

One duty Reid had not listed in his letter to Ponsonby in pursuit of a pay rise was a chore he would gladly have forgone, as indeed would Ponsonby. This was taking part in *tableaux vivants*. But as the Queen herself took a lively interest in the organisation of these domestic entertainments there was no escaping participation for either of them. The introduction of Prince Henry into the intimate family circle had done much to reawaken a royal interest which had ceased with the death of Albert. Prince Henry was a suitable candidate for hero opposite Princess Beatrice's heroine, for the Queen insisted that royalty should take the main parts in a production as it would not be fitting for a member of the Household to outshine them. Soon there were plays being acted by the Household.

The producer was usually the Hon. Alex Yorke, a jaunty and much-favoured groom-in-waiting. The Queen, far from leaving the Household to organise their own entertainments, insisted upon choosing the play, attending the rehearsals, cutting and altering the script to suit herself, and even went so far as to supervise the costumes and the making of scenery. She threw herself wholeheartedly into the enterprise and when the day arrived for the first performance she knew the play by heart – and sometimes was the only person who did, owing to the numerous interpolations she had added during rehearsals.

On 30 September 1889 Reid wrote to his mother from Balmoral: 'I am every day obliged to rehearse for theatricals that are being got up for Prince Henry's birthday on the 5th. They have given me a part to play, and I could not get out of it, though I tried to, as it takes up so much time.' Reid played the part of Fennel, a lawyer, in a comedy called *Used Up*, which was an adaptation of *L'Homme Blasé* by Charles Matthews. The anticipation was always worse than the reality, and he wrote to his mother afterwards: 'I was very shy of it as I never did anything of the kind before; however I got through it better than I could have expected.'

From one point of view Reid thought that the theatricals were salutary, as he explained to his mother: 'The *tableaux* begin tomorrow and will, I hope, keep the people from thinking of at least their *imaginary* ailments, which are very common among the sort of people I have to deal with.' He exercised a great deal of patience and tact in his treatment of minor discomforts which those with plenty of time on their hands tended to enlarge into major ailments. His impatience is occasionally discernible, but in most cases rigidly controlled.

However, not all the ailments were imaginary, and Christmas 1891 and January 1892 were particularly fraught as a result of mishaps of a more serious nature. After Christmas, whilst out shooting at Osborne, Prince Christian was accidentally shot in the eye by the Duke of Connaught. George Lawson, the Queen's eye specialist, was sent for immediately and declared that it was necessary to remove the globe of the damaged eye in order to save the other eye. Reid had to seek the Queen's permission to operate. 'I had much trouble with the Queen,' he informed Jenner.

> Her Majesty said that it [the operation] was quite unnecessary as formerly she knew several people with shot eyes who did not have it done and who did not become blind: that nowadays doctors were always for taking out eyes; and in short she spoke as if Lawson and I wished to do it for our own brutal pleasure! At last, however, she gave a reluctant consent, when I told her that Mr Lawson would be quite willing to leave the eye, provided he were not to be afterwards blamed or held responsible, in the event of the Prince becoming blind. This seemed to influence the Queen in withdrawing her refusal.

Prince Christian was operated on with complete success, and the globe duly removed. Reid was told by Mrs Macdonald that 'the Queen is now quite reconciled to what we have done, and she is glad all is over: but that Mr Lawson is not to feel hurt if she does not see him, and I am not to speak of the operation when I see her!!' She did not want to admit, even to herself, the appalling reality of an eyeless Prince Christian, preferring not to be reminded of it, either by Reid, or by the presence of the man who had, of necessity, removed the eye. Her behaviour may have been illogical, but there was something rather endearing and human about it.

A further accident occurred when early in the new year the Queen caught her foot in a piece of loose carpet and fell, with some violence, flat on the ground. Reid reported again to Jenner. 'She was unable to rise for a little, but was then assisted to her feet by the Indians and was able to walk upstairs to her room. I saw her at once, and found her a good deal shaken and agitated, but with no injury except a little bruising and pain in both knees. Her pulse was raised to over 100, but it is most fortunate that she escaped without any injury to a bone or joint.'

No sooner had the Queen recovered from her fall than she received the news of the illness (at Sandringham) of her grandson, Prince Albert Victor, Duke of Clarence. The Prince had influenza which rapidly developed into pneumonia, and Reid received in all thirteen telegrams from Doctors Laking and Broadbent, Physicians-in-Ordinary to the Prince of Wales, informing him of the patient's state. On top of all this the Household at Osborne was in the grip of a bout of influenza which attacked princes, princesses, non-royals and even the Munshi. 'As they all want to see me every few minutes, my time is pretty full. Two days ago I walked by my pedometer *9 miles* without leaving the house,' Reid informed his mother. As if this were not enough he had, as he wrote to Jenner, 'to appear in a *Tableau* in half an hour, and must now rig out in stage costume! Under the circumstances I am forcibly reminded of Solomon's saying "Vanities of Vanities", etc.!'

Reid could not wait for the Queen's royal guests to leave Osborne. Prince Christian in particular was not an easy patient. 'He is very nervous and fidgety about himself and sends for me very often during the day, and sometimes at night, to reassure him,' he wrote to Jenner. 'The people are now clearing out from here, but the Royalties all remain till Tuesday, when the Connaughts and Christians go – I wish they were gone now, for they are troublesome.'

On 14 January the young Duke of Clarence, recently engaged to Princess May of Teck, died, leaving his parents, the Prince and Princess of Wales, prostrate with grief. The Queen bore the tragedy well. She had been deeply attached to the charming but apathetic young man, but no doubt drew some comfort from the fact that the Duke of Clarence's younger brother, Prince George, was a more suitable candidate for the throne. She was, however, determined to attend the funeral at Windsor. As there was a severe epidemic of influenza there, Reid was equally adamant that she should not go.

> I mentioned the depressing effect of the service. She replied that was all nothing, and that she was never depressed at a funeral (!!). In fact, she rather lost her temper and was angry, so I said that of course I could not prevent her going, but that it was my duty to tell her what was my opinion, and that I could not be responsible for any untoward result. I found out that there had been a split on the subject among the Princesses, Louise and Helena being against her going, whilst Princess Beatrice urged it. I told Princess Beatrice about the puffiness in the Queen's ankles as a result of the fall and frightened her so that she turned round from urging the Queen to travel.

The Queen may have been annoyed with Reid but, once again, by combining firmness with tact he persuaded her to see reason, and she remained quietly at Osborne where, after the funeral was over, the Wales family came to see her.

In January 1893 Reid was spared the ordeal of appearing on the stage, having been struck down with what was diagnosed as subacute rheumatism, which laid him low for nearly a month. 'For five nights I could not sleep for pain,' he wrote to his mother, and confessed to her after he had recovered: 'I took so much opium for so many nights to deaden the pain that now I have left it off I feel the want of it!'

The Queen told the Duchess of Connaught he had only himself to blame: 'It is his own imprudence for he went on the sea wall without an overcoat when there was a strong N.East wind and caught a thorough chill, and then he went about with a high temperature and very unwell when he ought to have been in bed.' The roles had been reversed for it was usually Reid who chided the Queen for sitting out of doors at Balmoral without wearing sufficiently warm clothes. This was the first time that he had been ill since joining the royal Household twelve years earlier, and the case was considered so serious that no one, with the exception of his brother John and his wife Mary, was allowed to see him.

Reid managed to evade all appearance in *tableaux vivants* or plays after October 1893, and after the tragic death of Prince Henry in 1896 there is no further mention of any form of amateur theatricals being performed at Court. The Queen, by this time an old lady, was rapidly losing her sight and with it her former enthusiasm, and Princess

Beatrice, a main prop in the theatrical game, was grief-stricken at the loss of her husband.

Other forms of entertainment at Court included performances by professional players such as Henry Irving, Ellen Terry, and John Hare; but what the Queen enjoyed most was the Covent Garden Opera Company which came on several occasions to perform at Windsor. Reid was present at all these events, but he preferred an excursion to the theatre in London with John and Mary. Sometimes he was invited by members of the Household. A note from Ponsonby written on 6 December 1889, suggests that Reid 'throw Physic to the Winds and come and see Barnum. I have got a box and a place for you in it.'

Another time, after a year of exhausting tiffs with the Queen about the Munshi which had succeeded in undermining his health, Carington,[1] Legge[2] and Davidson[3] decided that Reid needed a little light diversion, and entertained him to dinner at the Hotel Cecil, after which they all went to a play, then to supper at the Savoy, followed by a fancy dress ball at Covent Garden. Marcus Beresford, renowned for his wit and sense of fun, had been invited to join the party to enliven the proceedings. Fritz Ponsonby, Sir Henry Ponsonby's son Frederick, who had recently become an Equerry, recalls an amusing incident which occurred.

After the play was over they decided to walk the short way down the Strand to the Savoy for supper. Reid and Beresford came last of the party, and as they passed another theatre which the audience was leaving, there was a smart brougham drawn up at the door with a beautiful woman in it, waiting for her husband. Beresford seized Reid before he understood what was happening, pushed him into the brougham, slammed the door, and said 'Right' to the coachman, who drove away. Of course Reid was furious, and after he was finally released told everyone that the beautiful lady had said to him, 'You ought to be ashamed of yourself. You're drunk.' What with hammering at the window to stop the coachman, and the lady shouting at him, he had no opportunity of explaining his case. However,

[1] Sir William H. P. Carington. Groom-in-Waiting and later Equerry to Queen Victoria, 1880-1901; Comptroller to the Prince of Wales, 1901-10; Keeper of the Privy Purse to George V from 1910.

[2] Sir Harry Legge. Equerry-in-Waiting to Queen Victoria, King Edward VII and George V, 1893-1915; Paymaster to the King's Household, 1915-20.

[3] Col. Sir Arthur Davidson. Groom-in-Waiting to Queen Victoria and later Equerry-in-Waiting, 1895-1901; Equerry, Assistant Keeper of the Privy Purse and Assistant Private Secretary to King Edward VII, 1901-10; Extra Equerry to King George V and Equerry to Queen Alexandra from 1910.

the husband, to whom he apologised, had seen the incident and roared with laughter.

The usual country pursuits enjoyed at Balmoral, such as fishing, shooting and stalking, did not interest Reid. He was more interested in new inventions, which never failed to intrigue him. He was the first person at Court to possess a phonograph – the earliest form of gramophone – which he took great pride in showing off to keen observers, including the Queen, who had a message to the Emperor Menelik recorded and sent out to Abyssinia. He was also invited to the Duke and Duchess of York's rooms to demonstrate his phonograph, and he enjoyed attending rehearsals of the Queen's private band and getting them to play into his instrument.

Bridge became fashionable in the 1890s, having been introduced into the Portland Club by Lord Brougham, who had learnt to play it in Cairo. The game appealed to Reid, who was frequently asked to make up a four with Ministers in Attendance, members of the Household, and visiting royalty.

Being doctor to a fresh air fanatic like Queen Victoria, Reid could not ignore the virtues of regular exercise. Apart from walking, which he enjoyed, he would on occasions play ice hockey at Osborne with members of the Household and royal guests. The Queen did not approve of this activity. She thought it undignified for the Princesses to be seen in a heap on the ice, revealing their petticoats. The hockey turned quickly into figure skating when it was thought that Her Majesty was in the vicinity. As well as ice hockey, Reid occasionally played golf.

In the summer and autumn of 1895, he was gripped by the current craze of bicycling. Every possible spare moment was allotted to it, and when he was not practising this new pastime himself he was busy repairing the wounds of others who had been over-enthusiastic. Prince Henry of Prussia (the Kaiser's brother) sprained his knee by a fall from his bicycle, and was 'fomented and bandaged and sent to bed'. Arthur Bigge and Fritz Ponsonby were Reid's chief cycling companions, their instructor being Acland, the Empress Eugénie's footman. Each afternoon Reid would walk from Balmoral to Abergeldie Castle, where the Empress stayed as a guest of the Queen, and spend an hour or two learning to ride his bicycle, under the guidance of Acland. The lessons were followed by tea with the Empress who was always an hospitable and friendly hostess. She loved to talk, and Reid was a sympathetic listener.

By now the Empress treated Reid as she would an old friend. He had been her doctor for many years and she felt able to talk freely with him on all manner of subjects, knowing that she could rely upon his discretion. On one of these occasions the Empress unburdened herself to him on the subject of her dramatic flight from France in 1870 (see Appendix III). He had visited her on various occasions at Farnborough, where she had proudly shown him round her house and garden, including the relics of the Emperor and her son, the Prince Imperial. When in Nice with the Queen Reid was invariably invited to Villa Cyrnos, where the Empress went each spring, and once or twice he went sailing with her at Cowes, where she stayed on board her yacht, the *Thistle*. Reid's simplicity and kindliness appealed to her, and she felt confidence in his medical skill.

The innovation of the bicycle resolved the problem of distance. Reid became highly proficient at cycling, and soon acquired a bicycle of his own. From then on his daily walks became daily bicycle rides, and he thought nothing of cycling from Balmoral to Birkhall, if the Empress was staying there instead of at Abergeldie Castle, or even from Windsor to Maidenhead and back. By March 1898 his cyclometer registered 3196 miles. Already in 1896 bicycles had become so popular at Court that it was necessary to construct 'a home for them' at Balmoral. There followed similar constructions at Osborne and Windsor.

Another person of Imperial status with whom Reid came into contact from time to time was the young Kaiser Wilhelm. His was a complex personality. He had inherited his mother's quick intellect but, although he had a powerful memory and could express his ideas with clarity, his knowledge was superficial. He was full of his own importance, impatient of difference of opinion and susceptible to flattery. Like his uncle, the Prince of Wales, he was restless and easily bored. As a result of having been born with a withered arm he suffered from a feeling of inadequacy which he tried to cover up by appearing in public as the 'epitome of customary masculinity'. He was, it has since been suggested, a latent homosexual. The Kaiser's character was such that he managed to effect a complete reversal in the British attitude to Germany – a change from friendliness to hostility.

Queen Victoria, who had in the past doted on her eldest grandchild, began to dread Wilhelm's annual visits to Cowes. Shortly after his father's death and his accession to the throne, the Queen inveighed against the Kaiser during one of her nocturnal conversations with Reid. 'He is so unreliable and shows such a want of knowledge of what he ought to do that no one can tell what can happen at any minute. It seems as if someone was constantly stirring him up against his relations, and for a young man of twenty-nine to behave as he does is disgraceful.' The Queen's intuition had not failed her, for while these words were spoken, the Kaiser was indeed being 'stirred up' – by Bismarck. (Though even after the redoubtable old statesman had been dismissed, hostility towards England continued as before.)

In August 1889 Reid attributed the Queen's general malaise and spell of sleeplessness to her dread of the German visit. The Kaiser and his Suite arrived to 'take over' Cowes on 2 August. Everywhere was crammed full. 'In fact, it is more like a German Colony than England. The Queen does not like it, and will be glad when it is over,' Reid reported to Mama. The day for the review was abominable but, far from minding, the Queen was gratified. 'I could not help seeing when H.M. was speaking about it, she is rather pleased it is so!!' Reid remarked to Jenner.

Reid's relations with the Kaiser were always most cordial, however, and on this particular visit he was presented by Wilhelm with a diamond and pearl scarf-pin as a reward for entertaining his Suite. Dr Leuthold, the Kaiser's personal physician, became a friend of long standing and, as Reid always enjoyed an opportunity for practising his German, these annual visits to Cowes were welcomed on that account, as well as for enlarging his circle of friends. He was one of the few members of the Household who could speak German fluently, and was therefore in constant demand, looking forward to renewing his acquaintance with the Kaiser's Suite on the Queen's visits to Germany.

In October 1894 a letter arrived from the Kaiser's adjutant, General Hans von Plessen, together with a silver cup – a gift from members of the Kaiser's Suite. All their names were engraved on it. Reid proudly showed it off in the smoking room, where 'Prince Henry of Prussia filled it with whisky and drained it to my health.'

The Kaiser invited himself to Cowes for the last time in 1895. As usual, the Queen was nervous and agitated, and her grandson did not always behave tactfully – on more than one occasion keeping the Queen waiting for dinner. He no longer stayed at Osborne House, but remained on his large white yacht where Reid saw and spoke with him on several occasions, and arranged and accompanied an expedition to Winchester with the German Suite. The annual visits to Cowes ceased after 1895 as a result of the Kaiser's exultant but inept telegram sent to President Kruger after the Jameson raid.[4] The Queen administered a gentle rebuke to her grandson and made it clear that he was no longer welcome in England.

It was not until the autumn of 1899 that she saw fit to invite him again, though William, who had the greatest regard for his grandmother, arranged with Reid that he should be kept privately informed about the Queen's health in the meantime, and that her doctor should be the first to warn him in the event of illness or her sudden death.

In September 1896 the Queen's granddaughter and goddaughter, Princess Alice of Hesse – known as 'Alicky' – now Czarina of Russia, came with her husband Czar Nicholas II and baby daughter, the Grand Duchess Olga, to stay at Balmoral. The visit was somewhat marred by appalling weather. 'All the decorations at Ballater [erected in honour of the Imperial visit] looked sadly lashed by rain,' Reid told his mother. He had had to curtail his holiday in Ellon and return to Balmoral 'to look after Profeit in case of his getting drunk' – something which had occurred previously on the occasion of the visit of the King of Portugal, to the consternation of all present. Profeit was now a confirmed alcoholic and Reid was given the unenviable task of telling him that the Queen wished him to resign. In addition he was suffering from haematemesis and had to be visited regularly. His retirement was short-lived, for he died only a few months later.

But Reid had a more illustrious patient to attend to than Profeit. On 30 September 'at 9.30 a.m. I was sent for by the Czar, whose left cheek was much swollen from irritation at the stump of a decayed molar. I examined his mouth with my finger and applied Tinct. Iodi to be repeated frequently over the gum of the 2nd left lower molar.' The following day Reid found the Czar better, the swelling having subsided.

From the political[5] and sporting point of view the Imperial visit may

[4] Under the command of Dr Jameson, the British Administrator of Rhodesia, a few hundred mounted police made a midnight dash into the Transvaal to raise a revolution against President Kruger. The Jameson raid was brought to an ignominious end by the Boers, who surrounded the raiders on 4 January 1896. From captured papers a British conspiracy was uncovered to reoccupy the Transvaal, involving Cecil Rhodes and his South African Company and, to some extent, *The Times*, the Colonial Office and the Secretary of State, Joseph Chamberlain himself. After his failure, Jameson returned to London to attend his trial at Bow Street Magistrates Court for breach of the eleventh clause of the Foreign Enlistment Act. He was sentenced to fifteen months' imprisonment.

[5] Lord Salisbury had suggested to the Queen that she might invite the Czar and Czarina to Balmoral to persuade them 'to sweeten the rest of Europe towards British exertions in the Sudan'. See Elizabeth Longford, *Victoria R.I.*, Weidenfeld & Nicolson, 1965 (p. 545)

have been a dismal failure, but Reid enjoyed it. He was invited to the royal dinners, and in the more informal atmosphere which existed at Balmoral, where everyone was packed together like sardines, he had several opportunities of talking with the Czar and Czarina. He went to the nursery to see the ten-month-old baby Olga having her bath. 'A beautiful child – Empress playing with her – a pretty sight.' This charming picture presents a striking contrast to the accepted view of the Czarina as aloof, cold and hard. Her haughty exterior, in reality, masked an unconquerable shyness. In his diary Reid also noted: 'In forenoon weighed the Grand Duchess Olga – aged 10 and a half months, 30 and a half lbs. less clothes 3 and a half lbs.'

On the day of their departure he wrote: 'At 7.0 p.m. I was sent for to the Library by the Emperor of Russia, who talked with me some time and presented me with a gold cigarette case with his Imperial arms in gold and diamonds in the corner, as a souvenir of his visit, and on my having attended him on the 30th and 1st. He spoke about his visit here, his child, and about his return next year.'

The Czar had enjoyed the relative informality and the freedom from intrigue which the Queen's Highland home offered; for Alicky it was like returning home, a reminder of her childhood days when, after her mother's untimely death, the Queen had opened her house to the desolate widower and his large family.

The Queen entertained many other interesting guests from all walks of life, besides visiting royalty. Among them was Rudolf Slatin, whom she invited to stay at Balmoral in October 1895. Born in 1857 of a well known Viennese family, he was known as Pasha, a title given him by the Khedive of Egypt. He became a professional soldier and went to the Sudan to take up service with the Egyptian Government under General Gordon's direction. In 1881 he was appointed Governor-General of the Egyptian Province of Darfur. Two years later he became nominally a Muslim, believing that it was the only way to hold the loyalty of his troops against the rise of that fanatic religious ascetic, the Mahdi. In December 1883 he was forced to surrender to the Mahdi, and was held prisoner by him and his successor, the Khalifa, until February 1895, when he escaped to Cairo.

The Queen recorded her view of Slatin as a 'charming, modest little man, whom no one could think had gone through such vicissitudes, for he looks so well; but there are lines in his face which betoken mental suffering. His final escape was quite miraculous. He had been eleven years in captivity and nine months in irons. While he was in prison they brought him General Gordon's head to look at.' As Slatin could speak no English and very little French, Reid's knowledge of German once more came into its own, and he was selected to look after him. 'As he is Viennese he fraternises much with me,' Reid reported to Mama. He found Slatin a refreshing and interesting companion, whose exploits offered a stimulating contrast to those of a staid courtier. They formed a friendship which was to last for many years.

Another person whom Reid met whose exploits had caused a great stir was Dr Jameson. While Jameson was awaiting his trial in London, a mutual friend, Dr William Gowers, 'arranged a quiet dinner with no one else present'. After the dinner, Reid informed his mother, 'I had a most interesting evening with Dr Jameson. He is a very fine fellow, and impresses one greatly. He told me all about his raid, and what led up to it, and that it was not his fault it was not a success. I trust he may be acquitted, but it is uncertain.' A week later Joseph Chamberlain, then Colonial Secretary, came to Windsor and after dinner he and Reid repaired to the smoking room and 'had a long talk about Jameson and the Transvaal'.

Reid often talked with Joseph Chamberlain in the smoking room at Windsor. He was interested in politics and affairs of state and, although he was a Tory – as were most of the permanent courtiers, with the exception of the Ponsonby family – he was not in the least bigoted. Indeed, the Minister with whom he had the greatest rapport was Lord Rosebery, the Liberal Prime Minister. Rosebery's character was complex. He had achieved success at an early age too easily, and with too little effort. He was handsome, rich and aristocratic, as well as being highly intelligent. He had had three great ambitions in life: to marry an heiress; to become Prime Minister; and to win the Derby. All three were realised. Lord Esher, who knew him well, wrote of him:

> His rapid and early growth into manhood, with the aloofness entailed by it, and that necessary element of what is called 'pose' in everyone who is a man at that age when others are boys, fitted him for oligarchic rule, but not to be Chief of a Democracy. He is curiously inexperienced in the subtler forms of happiness which come from giving more than one gets. He has been satiated with the sweets of life; and the long process has left him longing for affection, universal approval, omnipotent authority.

Nevertheless, he enjoyed social bonhomie, and when Reid was absent during one of Rosebery's visits to Balmoral, he complained to Ponsonby, who in turn wrote to Reid: 'Rosebery asks why you were away when he comes here. Russell Reynolds [President of the Royal College of Physicians] is an excellent man, but he don't make noisy jokes, and is sober and staid.' Reid's sense of humour was a passport to friendship. The statesman and the doctor were frequently seen setting off on long walks together at Balmoral. After the death of his wife, Hannah Rothschild, Rosebery suffered from great loneliness and he would from time to time ask Reid to dine with him *tête-à-tête* at his house in Berkeley Square.

In March 1894 the aged Gladstone was forced to retire from political life as a result of failing eyesight and increasing deafness. The Queen was determined that Rosebery should succeed him, and used Reid as a pawn to achieve her aim. Anxious to settle matters quickly before leaving for Florence, she claimed that she was '*urgently* pressed by her physicians to go to the south for a month before going to Coburg for her grandchildren's marriage'. She commanded Reid to write to Rosebery to 'urge him to take office as Prime Minister on the grounds of saving the Queen's health'. The following day Reid learnt that 'Lord Rosebery accepted office as P.M., being in great measure influenced thereto, as he told Ponsonby who informed the Queen, by my letter to him of yesterday.'

Having acquired Rosebery as her new Prime Minister, the Queen was immediately upset by his proposals in the Queen's Speech for Welsh and Scottish Disestablishment, and spoke to Reid about it, who wrote at once to Rosebery. Reid saw him the following day at Windsor, and told him how upset the Queen was. Rosebery, who was devoted to the old lady, left Windsor 'greatly distressed about the Queen. Pray send me a line to say how she is.' By the time Rosebery had received Reid's reply, the Queen was on her way to Florence where political worries were superseded by domestic troubles caused by an Indian servant.

8

Indian Affairs – Munshimania

On May Day 1876, after the Royal Titles Bill's turbulent passage through Parliament which 'shocked and surprised' the Queen, Victoria had been declared Empress of India. Ever since the transfer of India to the Crown in 1858 the idea of becoming an Empress had been in her mind. The question of precedence had made it imperative that the idea should become a reality. She had been indignant that the emperor of Germany had considered that his son should take precedence over her son. She had to put herself upon an equal footing with the Emperors of Russia and Germany. Moreover, the timing was perfect, for the Prince of Wales was nearing the end of his triumphal tour of India where he had succeeded in captivating the inhabitants by his ebullience and charm. From then on the Queen-Empress, who always signed herself V.R.I. (Victoria, *Regina, Imperatrix*), became deeply attached to India.

Ten years after she had become Empress, Victoria opened the Indian and Colonial Exhibition at the Royal Albert Hall, and the following year, at the time of the Golden Jubilee, decided to employ Indian servants at her various royal homes.

At the end of June 1887 the Queen engaged the first two, Abdul Karim and Mahomet Buksh: the former was twenty-four years old, slim and handsome; the latter was plump and smiling. They were both Muhammedans and *Khidmutgars* (male waiters), who were suitably decorative for the purpose of waiting at table. Major-General Dennehy, who had been political agent in Rajputana and was subsequently appointed extra groom-in-waiting, was placed in charge of the Indian servants. At first the Queen was merely excited about them as a child might be with a new toy. Tutors were engaged to teach them English, their wives were invited, and Sir Henry Ponsonby wrote, 'She has given me a Hindu vocabulary to study', while on 3 August the Queen wrote in her Journal: 'I am learning a few words of Hindustani to speak to my servants. It is a great interest to me for both the language and the people. I have naturally never come into real contact with it before.'

Reid found, all too soon, that he came into real contact with the Indians, and it was not long before he was put in charge of their total welfare, not merely their health, Dennehy having proved himself to be useless. On 20 August, whilst still at Osborne, the Queen sent him a memorandum, 'Rules for Scotland':

> Mahomet Buksh and Abdul Karim should wear in the *morning out of doors* at breakfast when they wait, their *new* dark blue dress and always at lunch with any 'Pageri' [pagri] (Turban) and sash *they like*, only not the *Gold Ones*. The Red dress and gold and white turban (or Pageri) and sash to be always worn *at dinner in the evening*. If it is wet or cold the breakfast is *in doors* when they should of course always attend. I may take the tea in doors (and of course later on always) and then they should attend. As I often, *before* the days get too short take the tea out with me in the carriage, they might do some extra waiting instead, either *before* I go out, or when I come in. Better before I go out, stopping half an hour longer and should wait *upstairs* to answer a handbell. They should come in and out and bring boxes, letters, etc: *instead* of the *maids*. In the same way they would alternately or *both* according to the number at tea, wait at my tea *instead* of the *maids*. *Indoors if they choose* at breakfast time they may wear some of their own thicker clothing. They should not put on the thickest underclothes at once, but gradually a warm Tweed dress and trousers can be got for them at Balmoral to go about in, when off duty in their own room. But it must be made in Indian fashion and the Pageri always be worn. The woollen stockings and socks and gloves, as well as thick shoes for walking can be got at Balmoral. When the days shorten and it becomes cold then the tea will always be taken *indoors*. And when the days become short (in seven or eight weeks or two months time) they better wait after tea to answer the bell as there will be no time after luncheon.

These higgledy-piggledy instructions were rewritten clearly and precisely in a more coherent form by Reid, and shown to Major-General Dennehy. The Queen always did her utmost to make her Indians feel at home in England but she never wanted them to lose their exotic flavour, hence the Indian cut to the Balmoral tweeds, and she even ventured to eat curries cooked for her by Abdul.

What to do with her Indians after meals worried the Queen, and an anxious note on the subject, written in pencil, was received by Reid a few days after they had arrived at Balmoral.

> It seems to me that they need not hurry away after meals to their rooms, and may stay either in the corridor below or above, or with anyone if they like, for, from living out of the house they are out of reach. At Osborne and at Windsor this will not be the case as here I mean to build some rooms for them. At Osborne I am building some which will communicate with the house.

The question of their position in the Household hierarchy bothered the Queen too. Unlike most of her contemporaries she was totally free from racial prejudice and was determined that her Indians were to be given a suitable position in the Household, and were to be treated with the respect that she thought was owed to them; Reid was to see to it.

Pray take care that my good Indian people get one of the *Upper Servants places* which Hyam knows is their proper position and they are *not* put far from our saloons, also that they have every comfort so that they are warm *at night*. They must be near. To put them at the very end would be too bad. If there is no room Morris should go with them, otherwise he better go on 1st and some one else be specially told to look after them. I *hope* Francie [Francie Clark, the Queen's Highland attendant] has had no hand in the arrangement for he is very prejudiced and was not inclined to be kind.

Very soon Abdul became too big for his boots and there were signs that the Queen and Reid were having differences. In a reassuring letter Jenner, who had obviously been consulted, wrote to Reid: 'The Queen will think all the better of you for having said what you did about the Indians after a while. I am rather surprised that Abdul occupies John Brown's room. I don't believe in the ghosts of those long dead or I should expect one in that room.'

However, the Indians went from strength to strength. Abdul was created the Queen's Munshi (literally, teacher) in 1889 and given the grand title of Munshi Hafiz Abdul Karim. In other words, he became the Queen's official Indian Secretary and as-such was relieved of all his domestic duties, and as Elizabeth Longford aptly puts it, 'rapidly graduated from blotting the Queen's letters to assisting her in their composition'. Apart from giving the Queen lessons in Hindustani he instructed her in religion and social customs and looked after all her boxes. She also handed over to him petitions from India merely acquiring a formal refusal, little realising how illiterate he was. He was even painted by Joachim von Angeli against a background of gold.

A firm lengthy order from the Queen, written on 13 May 1889, clarified the Munshi's position in relation to the other Indian servants, whose numbers had rapidly increased since their first introduction into the Queen's Household.

The Queen wishes to repeat in strong terms her desire that Dr Reid should *never* allow Ahmed Hussain to complain and speak against the Munshi Hafiz Abdul Karim who *is* the *first*, and from the position his family have always held, and his superior education holds a position *now*, and this he was *from the first* entitled to, which is equal to that of Clerk in her Privy Purse and with this addition that Karim is *Personal Indian Clerk to the Queen*. He looks after the accounts of all the Indians, orders them clothes and is *the* person, who besides looks after the Queen's boxes, letters, papers. And it has been the Queen's object to wish that the others should look to him for advice and help in every way. Abdul has shown them every reason of pride in his promotion and has always wished to do what the others like and has objected to nothing. But he disapproves with right of any extravagance and likes the Queen's *written* orders to be strictly *adhered to*. He knows Ahmed Hussain thoroughly and his wish to be the 1st or at least equal in every thing, which will *not* do. The Queen is greatly shocked at Ahmed's conduct behind Abdul's back and Dr Reid must on no account listen to or encourage his complaints which are extremely wrong. This is very wrong that he shld. behave as he does as she likes him personally.

The Queen was being unreasonable since it was she who had asked Reid to find out why Ahmed Hussain was depressed. When he told her that the cause of Ahmed's melancholy was the Munshi's high-handed and dictatorial behaviour, she accused him of listening to complaints.

A month after the Queen's reprimand an incident occurred which confirmed Reid's suspicions regarding the Munshi's character. The story is related in his own words:

At Balmoral one afternoon in June 1889, the Queen on getting into her carriage, after having tea in the cottage, missed a brooch that had been given her by the Grand Duke of Hesse, and which had been put in H.M.'s shawl by the dresser on duty that day, and sent out to the cottage for H.M. to use on her drive. When she returned the Queen found fault with the dresser for not sending it, and was very angry and reluctant to believe the assurance that it had been sent. Search was made at the cottage and the gravel turned over without result. Rankin [the footman], who was on duty that day in the place of Clark, who had got a holiday, privately expressed his conviction that Hourmet Ali (Abdul Karim's brother-in-law) who was hanging about after waiting at tea, had stolen it: but of course this could not be told to the Queen. Weeks passed without any word of the missing brooch, and during this time the Queen made frequent recriminations to the dresser for having lost it.

On the 27th July, on the way back from the Earl of Fife's wedding, Mahomet while on the yacht *Alberta* told Mrs M. and Mrs T. [Mrs MacDonald and Mrs Tuck, the Queen's dressers] that Hourmet Ali had sold the brooch to Wagland, the jeweller in Windsor, for 6/-, that he did not know where Hourmet had got the brooch, but he did not think it belonged to him.

Next day (Sunday) Mrs T. wrote to Wagland asking him to send her at once the brooch that he bought from the Indian servant. On Tuesday morning she received the missing brooch, with a letter from Wagland saying the *Indian had* sold it to him, representing it to him as his own property, that he had come to his shop constantly, often many times in a day, till he bought it off him to save himself further annoyance, that he had no suspicion that it did not belong to the man, as he was the Queen's servant; but that he had often come offering to sell him things, though he had never bought anything but this brooch.

Mrs T. took the brooch and the letter to the Queen. H.M. at first was much surprised, but immediately became furious with Mrs T. and Wagland for insinuating that Hourmet had done or could do anything wrong. 'That is what you English call justice,' she shouted, and was dreadfully angry. After a conference with Abdul she told Mrs T. that 'not a word of it was to be mentioned to Rankin or Miss Dittweiler [housekeeper at Balmoral], or a single soul; but that Hourmet was a model of honesty and uprightness and would never dream of stealing anything, that Abdul said that he had picked it up, and that it was an Indian custom to keep anything one found and say nothing about it, and that he was only acting up to the customs of his country!!' Abdul said that he had picked it up at the policeman's box, but on the day it was lost, the Queen had not been in that direction at all, but driving from the house up by Donald Stewart's and back the same way.

So the theft, though proved absolutely, was ignored and even made a virtue of for the sake no doubt of Abdul about whom the Queen seems off her head.

This illustrates how illogical the Queen could be in her behaviour, particularly when compromised by her Indian servants. She was like a mother hen shielding her defenceless chicks. To those not involved there is something almost endearing about it, though to the Household it must have appeared outrageous, and only served to exacerbate a growing tension caused by what they saw as the Indian intruders.

Reid's sense of humour enabled him for a time to accept the Queen's vagaries over her beloved Munshi. In a light-hearted vein he wrote to Jenner from Osborne in July 1889: 'I am in my new room, which is very nice and comfortable. I hear the Queen has given Abdul not only my old room but also the large central sitting room off it, which she declined to give me last year, and then only under conditions and restrictions! I am not grumbling at all, but merely mention the fact to show you the relative estimation in which Abdul and I are held!!'

After her State visit to North Wales in August the Queen and her Court moved on to Balmoral by train. Reid wrote to Jenner after they arrived. 'General Dennehy is here and he and the Queen are engrossed in *Indian Affairs*. There has been a row between Abdul and one of the others and the latter is to be packed off to India next week!!' But that was not all the news Reid had for Jenner for, on 17 October, he wrote: 'The Queen is off today to Glassalt[1] Shiel to stay there till tomorrow. She has not done this since 1882, having given it up when Brown died, and said she would never sleep there again. However, she has changed her mind and has taken Abdul with her!' Is this all humour or is there a twinge of jealousy? It would have been natural for the Queen's favouritism to have aroused envy, and the Munshi seems to have been as much disliked by her family and Household as John Brown had been, but whereas Brown's worst enemy could not have accused him of disloyalty the Munshi was highly suspect. The Queen, who trusted him absolutely, even showed him secret dispatches from India from which leaks appeared, through contacts he had there.

In February 1890, whilst at Windsor, the indispensable Abdul became ill. Having recently recovered from scabies, he was suffering from a carbuncle on his neck. The Queen, greatly concerned, wrote to Reid on 21 February:

> The Queen is much troubled about her excellent Abdul, who is so invaluable to her, and who has hitherto been so strong and well. She trusts Dr Reid is not anxious about him? He has always been so strong and well that she feels troubled at his swelling. She is always very anxious about them *all*, lest the climate should not agree as they are so useful to me and I was happy to think that they were well and did *not* suffer. Abdul is excellent, so superior in every sense of the word that she feels *particularly* troubled about anything being the matter with him.

It is interesting to note that the Queen lapses from third to first person within the same letter.

Reid poulticed regularly and gave Abdul opiates, while the Queen visited him in his room several times daily and 'stroked his hand'. On 1 March, when he was still no better, Reid noted in his diary: 'Queen visiting Abdul twice daily, in his room taking Hindustani lessons, signing her boxes, examining his neck, smoothing his pillows, etc.'

The Queen always showed concern when any of her servants were ill but they never experienced treatment such as the Munshi received,

[1] Glassalt Shiel, on Loch Muick, was a small lodge Queen Victoria had built in 1868 to retreat to when the cares of the world became to heavy a burden. Once, when approached with a problem which required the Queen's attention, Sir Henry Ponsonby replied: 'She has gone to the Glassalt and there is an end to all arguments.'

with the exception of John Brown, of course. Some would say that this behaviour was undignified and unbefitting a Queen, but to her the Munshi was more than a servant; he was, as it were, an adopted child who was far from home and needed love and attention.

By the beginning of March the Queen was wondering whether a second opinion was necessary in Abdul's case. Her note to Reid on the subject is a masterpiece of tact and delicacy:

> Do you think you are quite sure you wd. not like to have Sir J. Fayrer's opinion as to the cutting of Abdul's neck, on account of the difference of Indian constitutions. I *don't* wish it, I only ask what you wd. like yourself. Of course he could be telegraphed for, but if you are not alarmed or anxious of course it is unnecessary. I am a little over-anxious for I feel a sort of responsibility about this dear good young man, and about them all indeed away from all their own.

Reid did not need Sir Joseph Fayrer's opinion, but on 8 March Dr Ellison came from Windsor and assisted him in opening the abscess on Abdul's neck, after which his recovery was rapid.

Abdul was not the only Indian to give the Queen cause for anxiety. Yussuf fractured his right arm while tricycling at Osborne, and Reid set it with splints and a starch bandage. But it was not long before a third Indian became ill. On 25 March the Queen and her Suite set off for their spring holiday in Aix-les-Bains, where she took up residence at Maison Mottet. No sooner had they arrived than Ahmed Hussain caught a cough with an accompanying temperature of 101°. The Queen enquired after him constantly and wanted to know exactly what his temperature was.

There was also a further contretemps on the vexed problem of Ahmed Hussain's 'complaints and insinuations'. The unfortunate Reid was put in an impossible position. As a doctor he was obliged to question his patient. On 12 April, just before Ahmed was to return to India for a long holiday, a strident note reached him:

> Though I have just been speaking to you upon this subject, I wish to say a few words with reference to what you told me on several occasions of Ahmed Hussain's complaints and insinuations, I think that you should *at once* have told the Munshi Abdul Karim of them and to have ascertained what reasons there were, or were not for complaints. I of course told the Munshi of the complaints and especially with respect to the cook. He is *naturally* most deeply hurt at them and I must say I have *also been*, and I must confess I am *much* annoyed at your *always seeming* to believe Ahmed's complaints and not to ask explanation from the *responsible* person, whose greatly superior education, very high character, and confidential position

Voyage de Madame la Comtesse de Balmoral

MARCHE-ROUTE

D'AIX-LES-BAINS A DARMSTADT

STATIONS	HEURES d'arrivée	TEMPS d'arrêt	HEURES de départ	STATIONS	HEURES d'arrivée	TEMPS d'arrêt	HEURES de départ
	h. m.	m.	h. m.		h. m.	m.	h. m.
Le Mardi 22 Avril 1890.					matin		matin
Aix-les-Bains....... *Départ.*	soir	....	4 »	Tavannes..................	Minuit 48	1	Minuit 49
Culoz......................	4.27	5	4.32	Delémont.................	1.40	5	1.45
Bellegarde.................	5.10	1	5.11	Bâle.......................	2.35	15	2.50
Genève....................	5.54 (Heure de Paris)	10	6.30 (Heure de Berne)	Bâle (gare badoise).......:...	3. 1	9	3.10 (Heure de Carlsruhe)
Lausanne (Dîner)............	7.54	1.21	9.15	Fribourg	—	—	4.14
Cossonay...................	9.36	1	9.37	Offenburg.................	5. 5	4	5. 9
Yverdon....................	10.10	3	10.13	Carlsruhe.................	6.17	4	6.21
Neuchâtel..................	11.10	3	11.13	Heidelberg...............	7.16	9	7.25
Bienne.....................	11.53	5	11.58	**Darmstadt**......... *Arrivée.*	8.45	.....	matin
Soncebo z	Minuit 28 matin	3	Minuit 31 matin	*Le Mercredi 23 Avril 1890.*			

Imp. A. MEULDE et Cie

An itinerary for Madame la Comtesse de Balmoral, 1890.

about me, *warrant* implicit credence being given to what he says. The Munshi feels this behaviour of Ahmed Hussain, to whom he has been invariably most kind, doing all he wished and liked, *very* deeply. You I think, always for the future, [must] at once ask him when complaints are made and it would be better even now to ask the Munshi about the cooking.

I am much pained and hurt at your always speaking against *him* and thinking ill of a person *whom* I *know* so thoroughly and who is in every way such a high minded and excellent young man. But I am, and we all [are] *very* much distressed about poor Ahmed Hussain as I like him very much. He has unfortunately neglected his health and been restless. We must hope however that India will set him up again rapidly.

Reid replied to this missive respectfully, but leaving the Queen in no doubt as to his view of his position in relation to the Indians:

With reference to Ahmed Hussain's complaints and insinuations, Dr Reid hoped Your Majesty had understood from him that Ahmed *volunteered* no complaint and no insinuation. Seeing that Ahmed was evidently unhappy, and knowing well how favourable to the insidious onset of a disease like phthisis such a mental condition is, Dr Reid as a professional matter bearing directly on Ahmed's physical condition tried to elicit from him what was the cause of his despondency. Ahmed did not say a word on the subject until Dr Reid asked him to say what was the matter.

Having discovered this Dr Reid conceived it to be his duty not to conceal it from Your Majesty when directly questioned by Your Majesty regarding Ahmed's condition. He would on no account have mentioned it had he been aware that Your Majesty would disapprove of his confiding to Your Majesty what he thought was a factor in Ahmed's illness and therefore within Dr Reid's province. He deeply regrets that he should in any way be brought into a matter affecting the personal relations of the Indians, more especially as his action has caused Your Majesty pain. This would not of course have happened but for Ahmed's unfortunate illness, and Dr Reid feels sure that Your Majesty will recognise that he would not be fulfilling his professional responsibilities were he to disregard, in the consideration of the case, those fixed ideas which, even though imaginary on Ahmed's part, do not on that account react less on his bodily condition.

Your Majesty says it was Dr Reid's duty to have gone at once to the Munshi Abdul Karim on the subject; but Dr Reid has a written order from Your Majesty dated May 1889, forbidding him for the future to take any cognisance of any complaints Ahmed might make. Accordingly Dr Reid treated Ahmed's statements and mentioned them to Your Majesty, not as a complaint on Ahmed's part, but exclusively as showing a mental condition directly affecting his health.

Dr Reid begs most humbly and respectfully to assure Your Majesty that it is his aim to confine himself entirely to matters within his own province.

The Queen, though slightly mollified, was still not entirely convinced that Reid thought the Munshi blameless. In her reply to his
rather formal and cumbersome letter she wrote more simply, in the
first person: 'I have to thank you for your letter and will not allude to
what has passed. But I *never wish anything* to be *concealed from me*. I
certainly *did not* wish you to receive complaints but if they come and
complain you shd. *at once* ask for an explanation w. wld. clear it up
directly and I hope that you will not again think that the Munshi is to
blame, when *I tell* you *I know* it is a fact *not* to be so.'

There was no end to the Munshi's demands. He even had
the audacity to ask Reid for certain drugs to be sent to his father
whom the Munshi always alleged was a Surgeon General in the Indian
Army. He had succeeded in convincing the Queen that this was so,
when in reality he was merely the apothecary at Agra gaol. Reid wrote
an exasperated note on the subject to Jenner:

> The Munshi came to me a day or two ago with a long list of drugs which
> his father has written to ask for; and he said the Queen wished me to get
> them for him. The list is too long to trouble you with; but it contains about
> 60 articles, and the quantities he asks for are enormous. For example he
> asks for 6lbs of Chloral Hydrate, 6oz Morphine, 12oz of Nitrate of Silver,
> 3lbs of Chlorodyne, 6lbs of Laudanum, 2lbs Tinct. of Belladonna, 2oz of
> pure Strychnine, 6lbs Paregoric, 6lbs tincture Iodo, 8oz Croton Oil, and
> so on. There are many other poisons besides those I have named, which
> he asks for in like quantities, and other drugs in correspondingly larger
> amounts. On thinking it over, I came to the conclusion that I could not
> take the dangerous responsibility of ordering in *my* name poisons (which
> I have calculated are amply sufficient to kill *12,000* or *15,000* full grown
> men or an enormously larger number of children) for a man I don't know,
> and whom I know not to be legally qualified in our sense of the word.
>
> H.M. has agreed to my suggestion that I should write to Sir J. Tyler in
> India to get for the 'Doctor' what is required from some English Chemist
> there, and send the bill here. The Queen says the Munshi must not in
> any way be annoyed or put about on the subject: so Dennehy is coming
> on Saturday to explain matters to him in a conciliatory way!!!

In May 1892, when Sir John Tyler came to Windsor, Reid had the
opportunity of finding out the truth about the Munshi's father for
himself. He was told that he held no medical diploma, was not
'qualified' in the English sense, and could not be put on the medical
register. He had received instruction at the Agra Medical School for
which he held a certificate, and was qualified as a 'Hospital Assistant'.
In India such men were called 'native doctors'. Tyler told Reid: 'I
make a great deal of him now on account of the high position Her

137

Majesty has raised his son, and because the Munshi has "The Queen's ear". But for this he is not a man with whom I should have any social intercourse, nor would he have ever emerged from his former obscure position. He is anxious to have his position raised, now that his son is such a great man and made so much of by the Queen.'

In June the Munshi's father arrived in England, and the Queen arranged for Abdul to accompany him on a visit to Edinburgh. Arthur Bigge wrote from Balmoral to Reid, who was on holiday in Ellon, about the proposed trip. 'The A.B. [Father] and Sohn [Munshi] went off this morning to Edinboro' and are going to visit the Infirmary, University and Jail to the authorities of which Dennehy has written saying exactly who and what the Oriental visitors are. They are to be put up at the Balmoral Hotel *coûte que coûte*. I am in hopes that they may find a happy and lasting retreat in the Jail!'

But Bigge hoped in vain, for the Munshi, far from losing ground, was continually strengthening his position with the Queen, who became more and more stubborn each day. Sir Henry Ponsonby summed up the situation with his usual aptitude: 'The advance of the Black Brigade is a serious nuisance. I was afraid that opposition would intensify her desire to advance further. Progression by antagonism.'

By 1894 the Munshi Hafiz Abdul Karim had become insufferable, his name appeared in the Court Circular and in the official ceremonial at public functions, and published attacks on him began to appear in the newspapers. In April, when the Queen went to stay in Florence at the Villa Fabricotti, the Munshi presented Dosse, the Queen's courier, with an autograph manuscript which he ordered him to publish in the *Florence Gazette*. The following is a verbatim copy of what the Munshi wrote.

The Munshi Mohammed Abdul Karim son of Haji Dr Mohammed Wazirudin an inhabitant of Agra the Cheef City of NWP who left his office in India, and came to England in the service of the Queen Victoria Empress of India in the year 1887.

He was appointed first for some time as Her Majestys Munshi and Indian Clerk. From 1892 he was appointed as her M's Indian Secretary. He is belonging to a good and highly respectful Famiely. All is Famiely has been in Govt. Service with high position. His father is still in the service of the Govn. 36 years ago. One brother of his is a city Collector. All the Indian attendants of the Queen are under him and he also wholes different duties to perfirm in Her Majesty's Service.

This was to be published together with a copy of a photograph of himself, with all his decorations and his sword, in which the head was to be made 'thinner and less dark'! Fortunately for the Munshi his version was edited but it gave the readers a false impression of his background.

Whilst he was in Florence, Reid wrote down all the things about the Munshi which had annoyed him. As he was not in the least petty by nature he must have been sorely tried by this odious Indian to have prepared such a dossier, or maybe he realised that the time would come when he would be forced to present a case to the Queen. Whatever his motives may have been the notes reflect not only the Munshi's character, but also illustrate how unpopular he was with everyone around him, including his own countrymen.

1. Complaint on arrival to Q. of position of his railway carriage from Bologna.
2. Proposal by H.M. to Ponsonby that he should drive with the gentlemen of the Household on occasions.
3. Visit to Rome for one night, £22.
4. Refusal to allow other Indians in any part of the same railway carriage as himself.
5. Deprived H.M.'s maids of bathroom and W.C. and insisted on having it entirely reserved for himself.
6. What the Nurse and Mrs Boyd and Mrs Keith said about his wife and mother-in-law. 'More degraded and dirty than the lowest labourers in England; spitting all over the carpets. Performing functions in sitting room, etc.'
7. In Broge's shop window with large crowds looking at it –. A large frame for 10 cabinet photos, of these, 9 various photos of the Queen and the 10th the Munshi in the centre! After a few days Col. Clerk got vice consul Placci to go to Broge and have the M.'s photo removed. The Italians say he is a 'Principe Indiano' with whom the Q. is in love and this accounts for the photo being put where it was.
8. Bigge overheard conversation about him in the English Club, remarking on his low appearance and that he was a man who in India would have no place anywhere but with menials. Much astonished at his being with the Queen and surmises as to the meaning of it and who was responsible.
9. He complained to Dosse that the newspapers took too little notice of him; also to the Q. who sent Mrs MacDonald to Dosse to say that he was to see that the newspapers took notice of and mentioned the Munshi more frequently!

Snobbishness and racial prejudice apart, the contents of these notes do indicate what an unusually tactless, pushing and high-handed man the Munshi was. That he was dangerous *per se* is doubtful, but of his pernicious effect upon the Queen there can be no question.

From Florence the Queen and her Suite travelled to Coburg to attend the marriage of Victoria Melita of Saxe-Coburg-Gotha (known as Ducky) to Grand Duke Ernest Ludwig of Hesse. Both bride and bridegroom were grandchildren of Queen Victoria, but alas the marriage so dear to their grandmother ended in divorce in 1901. Once again the Munshi misbehaved himself. Here, related in Reid's words, was what happened at Coburg:

> The Duke of Coburg, through Monson [his equerry], told Ponsonby that nothing would induce him to allow the Munshi to come into the chapel with the Q's Suite for the wedding, and that he was to tell H.M. so, putting it on the ground of his religion, if he wished for any reason to assign other than the real one. This Ponsonby did and H.M. was most indignant, and did all she could to get him put with us. The most of the day preceding the wedding till very late, and the next forenoon itself were almost entirely occupied by her writing to Ponsonby and seeing him about it. (She would *not* speak to her son the Duke about it!) The Duke remained firm; and at last it was arranged that he was to be taken to a gallery in the church by the son of one of the Duke's gentlemen, the Queen specially saying there must be no servants there! But on being conducted to his place, the Munshi recognised among his neighbours some of the grooms, and was so furious that after waiting a few minutes he left without seeing the ceremony. He at once wrote an indignant letter to the Queen, wh. was given her after the couple left. She was greatly distressed and cried a great deal! All the servants about her knew and were talking about this, and even Dosse spoke to me about it in terms of glee at the M.'s discomfiture but of shame of H.M.! After this the Queen took the management of the Munshi's position out of Ponsonby's hands and gave it to Condie Stephen [Duke of Coburg's Private Secretary], to whom she herself spoke about it. After this the Munshi drove every day in a royal carriage with a footman on the box, and often with Bambridge sitting on his left! He was also invited to the State concerts etc., and was escorted in by Bambridge, but everyone avoided him.

The whole incident seen from both sides seems petty in the extreme, but one cannot help but admire the Queen for her dogged persistence in defending her Munshi against what amounted to united resistance on the part not only of her Household but also her family. She and the Munshi apparently triumphed over them all. Ponsonby, who had borne the brunt of the Munshi's arrogance and the Queen's tears, wrote with feeling to Reid when, for a short time, he was relieved from his responsibilities: 'I hope you like your holiday. I do very much and I have been able to forget the Munshi entirely.'

Whilst at Balmoral Reid heard from Dr Profeit that the Munshi was threatening to publish his life in two volumes early in the new year. This piece of news caused great consternation all round and Reid and Harriet Phipps agreed that it must somehow be prevented. Since no volumes were forthcoming they presumably succeeded in persuading both the Queen and the Munshi against publication.

After Sir Henry Ponsonby's serious illness in January 1895 Arthur Bigge, his successor, had to share the 'Injun' problem with Reid. He had neither Ponsonby's detachment nor his tolerance towards the Munshi, and his relations with the Queen started on the wrong foot by his objecting to her proposal that the Munshi should drive with the Gentlemen of the Household. Nor did the Household feel any happier when they opened the Nice newspaper, *The Galignani Messenger*, on 22 March to read:

> By telegraphic error it was made to appear that the Munshi assisted the Queen from her carriage on her arrival at Nice, which was of course not the case, as Her Majesty is always assisted by an Indian servant. The Munshi, as a learned man and the Queen's Indian Secretary and preceptor in Hindustani, is one of the most important personages '*auprès de la Reine*' having several men under him, and being often privileged to dine with his Royal Mistress and pupil.

Reid wrote off in haste to Lord Rosebery, enclosing the offending article, and he replied sympathetically. 'I well understand the anguish of mind with which you sent me that marked paragraph in the Nice paper.'

The anguish was not eased by a conversation which Reid had with Sir John Tyler in June. By this time the Munshi had been decorated with the Companion of the Order of the Indian Empire, in spite of opposition from all sides. Reid was told by Tyler:

> The Queen had made a vital mistake in giving the Munshi the C.I.E.; that he is a man of very low origin and of no education, that he was never anything but a 'Khitmagar' in wh. capacity he was sent here; and that the idea of his being considered a gentleman is most ludicrous to those who know him; that the accounts of him published by Raffiudin Ahmed in *Black and White* and other magazines were false in almost every particular, and that Raffiudin Ahmed is a clever but unscrupulous and dangerous man who ought never under any pretext to be admitted into any of the Queen's houses; that he uses the Munshi as a tool for his own purposes; and that when it will serve his purpose, he will be the first man to expose him and turn him into ridicule with the public, wh. he will have no difficulty in doing.

Raffiudin Ahmed was a friend of the Munshi's involved with the Muslim Patriotic League. Three years earlier the Munshi had approached the Queen to use her influence in assisting Raffiudin Ahmed in his career at the bar, and Ponsonby had received orders to introduce the Munshi to the Lord Chancellor with this in mind. It was Raffiudin Ahmed who was suspected of being responsible for the leaks from secret dispatches which had been shown to the Munshi by the Queen. More intelligent than the Munshi, he was potentially a far greater danger, but the Queen, naïve as she was about her Indians, continued to further his cause.

Tyler, who was well acquainted with the Munshi's relatives, also told Reid that he 'had constantly seen the Munshi's wife and female relations in India, as they were never shut up there from public gaze, belonging as they do to quite a low class, and that the idea of their being in purdah was never dreamt of until they came to England to pose as ladies, and that this has excited much amusement among those who knew them in India'.

In November Sir Henry Ponsonby died. The Queen wrote to his daughter Magdalen:

> There is one person who feels your beloved Father's loss more than anyone, and whose *gratitude* to him is *very deep*, and that is my good Munshi Abdul Karim. Your dear father was kinder to him than anyone, always befriending him, and the loss to him is, as he says, that of 'a *second* Father'. He could not well go to the funeral tomorrow to his regret, but sends a wreath, and I enclose what he wrote on it as I fear in the multitude of similar wreaths this tribute of gratitude might be overlooked.

Magdalen wrote a note to Reid, enclosing the Queen's letter, asking: 'If you think I ought to write to the Moonshi [sic], of course I will if you think it is expected of me, and that the Q. wishes it. I don't want to start him as a brother.' Reid's answer was definite. He both wired and wrote no, adding that 'the wreath was made in the Gardens by H.M.'s special command, and she dictated to the Munshi what he was to write on it'.

For Reid, 1897 was to be 'the year of the Munshi'. In January he and his friend Randall Davidson, Bishop of Winchester, had frequent discussions on the subject of the Queen and the Munshi, 'his view being that Her Majesty is off her head on this point'. Since December Reid had been treating Abdul for gleet and on 20 February he 'told the Queen about the Munshi having a relapse of venereal disease and had an interesting talk with her'.[2] Gleet or no gleet, the Queen was

---

[2] The content of this talk was written down in a green notebook, which was burnt after Reid's death on his instruction.

determined to take the Munshi with her to Cimiez, which would necessitate his dining with the Household. There were strong objections to this from the Gentlemen, who deputed Harriet Phipps to break the news to the Queen that she must choose between the Munshi or the Household. The Queen, in a rage, swept all the paraphernalia from her crowded desk on to the floor. This was an impasse from which there seemed to be no way out. The Queen would not be dictated to by the Household, and the Household would not associate with the Munshi.

It was at Cimiez that the real trouble started. The Prince of Wales sent for Reid and had an interview with him 'about the Munshi and the crisis which the Queen's treatment of, and relations with him is bringing on. I told H.R.H. much that I knew, and how serious I think it. He was much impressed, and promised to support us in any action we may take.' Was this a serious crisis, or was it merely a storm in a teacup? To the Gentlemen of the Household it must have been important since they were willing to make a firm, united stand against the Queen, and, if necessary, were prepared to go on strike, or resign in a body. To the Queen the issue was vital since she was afraid of losing face and did not want to appear to be ruled by her Household.

The final straw was the uninvited arrival of Raffiudin Ahmed at Cimiez. This was too much for the Gentlemen to endure, and at the insistence of Arthur Bigge, who was appalled at the sudden appearance of this disreputable political suspect, Raffiudin was sent packing soon after his arrival. The Queen hoped that with Raffiudin safely out of the way the Household would calm down. But in this she was wrong for, having successfully disposed of Raffiudin, the Gentlemen were determined to put the Munshi firmly in his place. By 27 March matters were coming to a head. Prince Louis of Battenberg, who acted as liaison between the Queen and the Household, had been sent by the Queen to Arthur Davidson, the groom-in-waiting, to say that the Gentlemen were to associate more with the Munshi. The Household were up in arms and 'all agreed to stand together and to resign if H.M. presses the matter'. The following day there were 'many conferences with Bigge, Carington and Davidson about the Munshi row, and a long one in the evening with Prince Louis of Battenberg who has been charged by the Queen to find out our objections to him. At 11.30 I went to the Queen and stayed an hour. Told her *all* I knew about the Munshi.'

Reid's painstaking efforts to write down everything he had heard and knew about the Munshi now came into their own. The case which he presented to the Queen was foolproof and unanswerable, and never for one moment did he flinch from what he considered to be his duty. The Queen was anxious that Reid should tell Prince Louis all that he had told her and on 30 March he was 'sent for many times during the day about the Munshi affair, H.M. admitting she had been foolish in acceding to his constant requests for advancement but yet trying to shield him. Told him again about the comments outside and by her family and that I had been questioned as to her sanity.' On 1 and 2 April there were more interviews and discussions with the Queen about the Munshi, which carried on intermittently throughout the day, and Prince Louis also had a long talk with Reid, and seemed to share Randall Davidson's view. 'He thinks the Q. mad on this point.' Reid also told the Queen about a letter he had received himself from the Chief of Police for London, Sir Edward Bradford, warning him of the Munshi's complicity in Muslim Patriotic League affairs. 'H.M. quite caved in. In the evening, before dinner the Queen quite broke down to me, admitted she had played the fool about the Munshi; cried and said she knew what people were saying about her; begged piteously to be "let down easily" and promised to do all we wanted only not abruptly for fear of scandal.' On 4 April Reid had a 'very excited interview with the Queen', in which he did not mince his words:

> It seems to me that Your Majesty is only thinking of the Munshi's feelings: but that is of infinitesimal importance compared with the gravity of the situation as regards Your Majesty. As I said to Your Majesty before, there are people in high places, who know Your Majesty well, who say to me that the only charitable explanation that can be given is that Your Majesty is not sane, and that the time will come when to save Your Majesty's memory and reputation it will be necessary for me to come forward and say so: and that is a nice position for me to be in. I have seen the Prince of Wales yesterday and he again spoke to me very seriously on the subject. He says he has quite made up his mind to come forward if necessary, because quite apart from all the consequences to the Queen, it affects *himself* most vitally ... Because it affects the throne.

On the following day there was a 'very painful interview in the morning with the Queen, who got into a most violent passion and said we had all behaved disgracefully. I replied to her in such terms that she was obliged to ask me not to repeat what she had said!' All through these quarrels Reid had the constant backing of the Prince of Wales, who thanked him for all he had done, knowing that there was no one else who would have had the audacity to speak to the Queen in such a way.

Having confronted the Queen, with some success, Reid now tackled the Munshi.

By your presumption and arrogance you have created for yourself a situation that can no longer be permitted to exist. The Queen has believed all the lies you have told her and in her kindness has given you all that you have asked for up to now; but she is beginning to find out what everyone in England and India knows, viz., that you are an impostor. On the subject of your origin we have a certificate from India about your Father, your wife and yourself.[3] You are from a very low class and *never* can be a gentleman. Your education is nil. To be called 'Secretary' is perfectly ridiculous; you could not write either an English or an Indian letter that would not disgrace the name of Secretary. You have a double face, one which you show to the Queen, and another when you leave her room. The Queen says she finds you humble and 'honest' and kind to everybody! What is the reality? The Queen says the other Indians like and respect you. What do they tell me? And what would they say if they were not afraid of you and the old ones were brought back to give evidence? You have been deceiving the Queen in other ways . . . You have told the Queen that in India no receipts are given for money, and therefore you ought not to give any to Sir F. Edwards [Keeper of the Privy Purse]. This is a lie and means that you wish to *cheat* the Queen. The Police know this and other things. The Queen's letters in your possession are asked for by H.M. Where are they? Why have you not given them up at once? You had better do so now or it will be the worse for you. If the Queen were to die and any letters of hers were found in your possession no mercy will be shown you. The Queen does not know *all* I have told you because it would shock her greatly to know how completely you have deceived her and what a scoundrel you are, and she hopes it may be possible for you to stay with her still. But this can only be if your 'position' is altogether taken away. No one of the Queen's Gentlemen can recognise you in any way whatever. But if it be necessary to tell the Queen all about how you have deceived the Queen then it will be impossible for you to remain in England. Prince Louis was to have been sent by the Queen to speak to you but that would be much more serious than *my* coming. But he will come next if it be

---

[3] Information had just been received from the Viceroy of India, in cypher, on the subject of the Munshi's background. 'Munshi's Father Sheykh Mohammed Wazirudin in Subordinate Medical Service as Hospital Assistant; pay 60 rupees a month, reported respectable and trustworthy. Native of Agra. No record of ancestry but his position of family humble. Eldest son served in gaol department, promoted Tahsildar 1893 at H.M.'s wish. Four daughters married husbands in gaol department or Constables. One of them Hurmat formerly in Queen's service. There are other relations but no mark of education. Munshi was a Mohurrur or vernacular clerk in Agra Gaol at 10 rupees a month till he left India to become Household servant to the Queen. No information about wife or there being more than one.'

necessary. The Queen says you tell her you are in great distress and can't
sleep or eat and Her Majesty in her great kindness is sorry to hear it. But
if you do this again, and try to humbug the Queen, the Q. will be told
everything about you, and then her pity will be turned to anger when she
finds out how you have deceived her and you will only hasten your ruin.

The Munshi was to a certain degree chastened after this diatribe,
but some time was to pass before he accepted his true place in the
Household. Before leaving Cimiez the Queen issued a memorandum
to the Gentlemen on how the Munshi should be treated, and wished
they 'should not go on talking about this painful subject either amongst
themselves, or with outsiders, and not *combine* with the Household
against the person'. So while the Queen had been left in no doubt as
to the feelings of both her family and Household, her defence of the
Munshi against them continued as blindly as ever. As for the Munshi,
his putting down by the Household had done nothing to quench his
desire for titles.

Reid recorded in his diary, 'When he was last in India he wrote to
the Queen and asked her to make him a *Nawab*, a title which Dennehy
tells me implies *regal* dignity. The Queen wrote to Dennehy to ask
him what he thought, and when Dennehy explained to H.M. what it
meant, she said it could not be done.'

The Munshi had also been bullying the Queen about giving him
the M.V.O. (Member of the Royal Victorian Order) as a Jubilee
honour, and Reid took it upon himself to remonstrate with Abdul
about his conduct to Her Majesty. There was also an 'unpleasant talk
with the Queen about her intention of giving the Munshi the M.V.O.',
and the Queen was further incensed by a letter she had received from
Sir Fleetwood Edwards on the subject.

Sir James Reid tells him that he has placed Your Majesty in possession
of Sir Fleetwood Edwards' views as regards giving the Order to the
Munshi. He has only of course to carry out Your Majesty's commands as
regards the Order, but he has earnestly hoped Your Majesty could have
adhered to the former decision that the Munshi was not to have it, as
otherwise he is convinced the results will be most unfortunate.

She wrote to Reid in a frenzy:

I must own that I am very indignant at this unnecessary letter from Sir F.
Edwards. He threatens me in such a way that he almost makes it impossible
for me to do what I feel in not doing I should break my written word.
This set at me makes my position a very painful and cruel one, and I never
shall get over it with the Gentlemen or the pain wh. it caused the poor

Munshi. I am crushed and annoyed at Sir Fleetwood's letter. This hatred and determination to treat a man whom I have no reason not to trust is yielding to a shameful unjust interference.

At a garden party held at Buckingham Palace Reid was ordered by the Queen to talk to Lord Salisbury who, as Prime Minister, was the dispenser of honours. He spoke to him at length, and also to Lord Rosebery and Lord Rowton,[4] 'all three deprecating Her Majesty's proposal' that the Munshi should be given the M.V.O. That evening Reid received a second note from the Queen. 'Pray take care that Sir F. Edwards knows that it is *not* because he wrote that rather impertinent letter that she does not *at present* include the Munshi amongst those who are to receive the order, but on Lord Salisbury's advice.' Lord Salisbury, with his usual wiliness, had pointed out to the Queen that it would not be advisable at this stage to promote the Munshi, for it might arouse Hindu jealousy and look as though she favoured her Muhammedan subjects. (The Queen was inclined to think that all animosity towards the Munshi from her Indian subjects amounted to Hindu jealousy.)

On 5 July, on the East Lawn of Windsor Castle, Her Majesty inspected the officers of her Imperial Service Troops and Indian Cavalry Corps detailed to serve as a Guard of Honour during the Jubilee celebrations. Princes and Maharajahs were present in all their splendour, and the Indian officers looked magnificent in their highly coloured uniforms. It was a great occasion and one which the Queen relished, for of all her Imperial Dominions India held a special place in her affections. The event was marred on the following day when the Queen saw in the Court Circular that the Munshi was omitted from the list of grand names. As usual Reid became embroiled in all the ensuing rows between the Queen and the Master of the Household, Lord Edward Pelham Clinton.

It was not only the Household that the Queen had to contend with. The Indian officers, too, were up in arms against the Munshi. Risking the royal displeasure yet again, Reid sought an explanation from Ahmed Hussain who, as ever, was very ready to unburden himself on the subject of the Munshi, revealing the startling information that the Munshi was reputed to have had 100,000 rupees off the Queen. He also offered his former fellow servant some sensible advice:

---

[4] Baron Montagu Corry Rowton. Formerly Private Secretary to Disraeli, whose advice was often sought by the Queen.

Munshi always wants more, and every day ask Queen plenty thing. Queen give him too much and plenty present and too much money. India Rajah very angry Munshi get C.I.E. when Rajah and big Indian man not get, and Munshi very little man like Queen footman, and some Queen footman better man. He tell me all Englishmen cross, but he say I fight all and Queen always help me. I tell Munshi much better you quiet. You only 10 year servant, very little man in India, and your Father very little doctor, and brother and sister husband very little servant man and policemans. Queen give you plenty money and everything plenty give. Queen never give so much English servant or English Gentleman. Plenty English servant and English Gentleman with Queen 15, 20 years and get nothing, not English custom. But Queen give you very much money, and recommendation for the brother and sister husband, and big house, and the land. You better quiet and not always ask Queen and want be big officer.

Meanwhile, further accusations against the Munshi were brought to the Queen's notice. She poured out her troubles to Reid in a long letter written intermittently over several days.

You say it is of no importance, but the feeling that the poor M. is distracted and anything can be invented against him and that he is suspected by jealous people of being dishonest is extremely trying and painful to me. She [the Queen] has known him for 10 years intimately and certainly has never had any reason to suspect or doubt him. The fact of its being believed that he was the cause of the footman Bagley not being promoted shows how ready everyone is to injure him. The M. never mentioned Bagley's name or ever mentioned any one of the footmen or of my other servants. But he is kind in trying to help others in trouble. The Queen has constantly, long before the M. came, chosen people herself on enquiry, but these Gentlemen wish to have it all in their own hands, and in their hatred of the unfortunate Munshi, put all down to him. It is very offensive that I should always be supposed to be *made* to do things.

On the afternoon of 18 July Reid 'had three quarters of an hour of very unpleasant talk with the Queen about the Munshi who had been bullying her, and offered to take him to task but H.M. would not sanction it'. He was just recovering from this altercation when he received a sixteen-page letter from the Queen:

I began this letter some days ago but go on today after the very painful conversation I had with you this afternoon. I must go on. If people believe the story about Bagley which is *completely false* may they not believe any painful story brought against this poor defenceless man.

Orientals invent and are of the most unbounded jealousy. The hatred of Hindu against Muhammedan only adds to this. They talk to the Officers,

A.D.C.s and Anglo-Indians who readily believe and retail everything. I do think it very shameful of people connected with the Govt. or the Court to give ready credence to these stories of a person in my service. The position of *doubt* is becoming quite intolerable to me.

I *must* have it out with my poor friend. If there have been imprudences and faults it may, I should hope, be possible to put a stop to this, and so let the poor M. redeem his character. It is impossible for me not to feel the position as most offensive towards me. I can't bear it.

The poor Queen had got into a muddle from which she found it difficult to extricate herself. Her only defence was to close her mind to the possibility that the Munshi was deceitful and dishonest and fight on. In her blindness she worked herself into a frenzy and became totally unreasonable. For Reid, who was above everything a rational man, the Queen's behaviour was extremely tiresome and tried his patience beyond endurance. Eventually, the daily storms were to undermine his health.

The whole of the autumn visit to Balmoral was marred by what had now become known as the 'Munshi crisis'. Reid was attacked from all sides and was expected to turn a deaf ear to every plea and complaint. On 8 September, in spite of having seen the Queen at least twice on that day, he nevertheless received a letter from her.

I would sincerely ask you *not* to give heed to all you hear and this extends especially to the shamefully persecuted Munshi. It is wicked to listen to idle stories which are distorted and exaggerated. You *must* not allow such stories to be told to you. It is so injurious and ungenerous to a man who is totally different to us, and whose life is a very dreary one thanks to the treatment of those whom I will *not* mention but who must be suppressed. I *do* feel indignant.

Reid felt equally indignant and firmly told the Queen the next day that 'the tendency is at once to think of the M.'s influence in *every*thing that happens in the house, for there is a very general belief not only in Y.M.'s family and Household, but also among all the servants that Y.M. is entirely under the influence of the M. and that he knows it.' This was bold talk from a courtier to a Queen, but Reid had never been afraid to say what he thought, and the Queen respected him for his honesty.

The Munshi was threatening to leave and return to India, hoping that by giving in his notice he would stir up further trouble in the Household and that the Queen would champion his cause with even greater fervour. On 10 September Reid received yet another letter from the Queen, who had once again been aroused to indignation.

I am much troubled at the M.'s expressed determination or rather decided wish *not* to remain beyond this year. He says everything can be enquired and looked to, and that all receipts will be forthcoming but that he is not of the nature to endure such treatment which he has experienced. Of course I feel and understand what his feelings must be, for I feel *deeply* hurt at what has occurred since *March* and it has *always been present* in my mind. I told him I cd. not let him go, and that it besides would do him and me much harm. He wd. appear to admit the accusation and I to have yielded to very shameful pressure.

The Queen was always, quite understandably, afraid of losing face. Her defence of the Munshi had become second nature to her and it was difficult at this stage to appear to change in her attitude either towards him or to her Household, however much she might have wanted to. It is impossible to imagine that she really believed beyond all doubt that the Munshi was unimpeachable.

In the middle of September Dr Thomas Barlow arrived at Balmoral to take Reid's place so that he could enjoy a well-earned rest in Ellon. Once at home with his mother, and enjoying his favourite pursuits of gardening and bicycling, Reid's greatest wish was that there would be a respite from the Munshi and all his attendant problems. This was a forlorn hope, for he had been at Ellon for only a few days when a long letter arrived from the Queen who was, as usual, 'worried and anxious' about the Munshi.

Then, when he returned to Balmoral, the Munshi saga, which Reid earnestly hoped had died down during his absence, blew up with additional ferocity. From his good friend Arthur Davidson he received a letter supporting him in any action he might take. Davidson had on more than one occasion threatened to resign his position as groom-in-waiting on account of the Queen's behaviour towards him over the Munshi and her refusal to communicate with him directly.

The climax, after months of stormy interviews, rows and tears, was reached on 16 October as a result of the publication in the *Daily Graphic* of a large photograph of the Queen, sitting at her table with her dog at her feet, signing documents. There is a hint of a smile on her face. The Munshi, now no longer lithe and handsome but obese and opulent looking, holds one of these papers and stares out with an expression both smug and supercilious. He seems to be saying to the world, 'I am King of the Castle'. Under the photograph is written 'The Queen's Life in the Highlands, Her Majesty receiving a lesson in Hindustani from the Munshi Hafiz Abdul Karim C.I.E.'

The same day Reid had a talk with the Queen about the offending photograph and 'made her rather uncomfortable'. Two days later he cycled to Ballater and saw Milne, the photographer, 'who told me that the Munshi had on the 16th June at Ballater station ordered him to have the photograph of the Queen and him published in the Jubilee number of the *Graphic*. Told the Queen all that Milne had said and had three painful interviews.' There followed a note from the distraught Queen early on the morning of 20 October. 'Pray do not see Milne if he comes. The Munshi tells me he has written to Milne and wants to see him. There is a great deal of indignation about your going to see and question him, which is most unfortunate and you should not have done it *without* telling me, as now it may produce very painful consequences for me as the Munshi looks on you as his bitter enemy.'

The Queen was beginning to be afraid of the enraged Munshi, and felt that Reid had let her down, though she did concede that she had made a grave mistake. In the afternoon a fourteen-page letter reached Reid, in which she unburdened herself freely.

I am terribly annoyed and upset by all this stupid business which unfortunately I am to blame for, and regret extremely. I ought never to have allowed the publication of *that* [picture], and had it been stopped nothing would have been said or talked about and the present very painful position for me wd. have been avoided. I don't know what to do. You don't see this and don't put yourself into that cruel position of doubting a person against whom I personally cannot after 10 years service say to him I disbelieve you and believe others. I feel continually aggrieved at my Gentlemen wishing to spy upon and interfere with one of my people whom I have no personal reason or proof of doubting and I am greatly distressed at what has happened. I have suffered enough from having suspicions put into my mind and if I am put into a still further difficulty I shall be unable to talk as I did before even to you whose kindness I shd. most gratefully acknowledge. I quite dread seeing him this evening, for I fear more trouble and mischief. If you think you must see Mr Milne it ought to be to say merely there has [been] some great misunderstanding which it is however needless to investigate further now and 'The Queen' will exonerate him in this very annoying business. I shall take care to clear up and watch everything and any order I give the Munshi for the future and see letters.

He is so furious against you all that I do not advise any interview at present. I fear however Milne will say one thing to you and another to him. You say there is no intention or wish to drive him away, but how painful it will be for me to have a person whose veracity is disbelieved. I am feeling dreadfully nervous. I thought you stood between me and the others and now I feel you also chime in with the rest. Better put an end to this story and don't try to bring about a possible scandal. I shall see him now and see how matters stand. But my peace of mind is terribly upset. I fear I have made great blunders in this business. I should not have repeated anything to the Munshi that night. I can't read this through and would beg you to burn it as well as my letter this morning.

Poor Queen Victoria, isolated by her position, had too much time to brood on all the 'tittle-tattle' which surrounded her. She imagined that she was being persecuted by her Household but, in reality, she was being harassed by the Munshi and had fallen a victim to her own folly and blindness to the Munshi's manifold failings. The Queen may have been worried but poor Reid was driven to despair. He passed a sleepless night, partly from pain due to a boil on his right thigh, and partly from worrying about the 'Munshi business and the Queen's giving me away to him'. At five a.m. he wrote a letter of resignation, which he did not send as Her Majesty changed her attitude towards him and 'was very gracious and nice'. Reid was too precious to lose and the Queen had the sense to realise it in the nick of time.

Reid retreated to Ellon again, thoroughly run down by all the unpleasantness of the past nine months. He became seriously ill with a severe carbuncle on his thigh and six boils on his neck. The risk of succumbing to septicaemia was considerable. He retired to bed, where he was tenderly cared for by his devoted mother. A few days later an anxious letter arrived from the Queen:

> I must write a line to say how distressed I am at your getting unwell (as I well know) from the worry I caused you the last few months and especially the last week which might *all* have been prevented but for my senselessness and want of thought. Pray now *don't* think at all of it and let nothing be talked or written to you. I also will not allow anything more to be said at all. I hope to hear you are better; I fear your poor mother will be worried.

This letter shows the Queen at her very best and most endearing; while she might be blind to others' faults she recognised her own, and showed a humility unusual in a person in her position. The great devotion which she engendered from those closest to her is easily understood after reading these words. The Munshi rows may have undermined Reid's health, but they had served to bind his relationship with the Queen more firmly than ever. She realised that in her doctor she had not only a dependable servant, but also a true friend, who was not afraid of telling her the truth about herself and about others, when by doing so he was serving her cause.

By 10 November, fully recovered, Reid was back at Balmoral and informed his mother that he 'had a long and pleasant interview with the Queen this evening'. On the surface it appeared that the Munshi discussions had died down, but underneath the apparent calm the cauldron still bubbled. The Bishop of Winchester, as well as Princess Louise, was constantly seeking him out for talks on the vexed question and there was no doubt but that the poor Queen was still being pestered by Abdul. Three days before Christmas Reid had the unpleasant task of having to inform the Queen about the Munshi's gonorrhoea, and how bad it was, and 'H.M. was greatly taken aback'. Then on Christmas Day he had a most stormy talk for three quarters of an hour. 'H.M. was quite mad with rage, but I stood my ground firmly.'

Before Christmas the Prince of Wales had written to Reid inviting him to visit Sandringham in January. The Queen did not approve of this invitation and wrote to Reid on Boxing Day firmly ordering him to decline.

> Mrs Mallet[5] told me that the Prince of Wales has asked you down to Sandringham, which I do not particularly like as I fear mischief, attempts at interference, more stories and gossip. If it shld. be on medical grounds about Prs. Victoria of course it would be different. But otherwise I wd. much dislike your going there; in fact it gave me quite a shock when I heard it, and I will not tolerate any more stories, and exaggerations and more inventions. I would wish you to say how much honoured you are but I could not spare you for more than 10 days and you require rest. I can also say the same myself to the Prince. Nothing is easier than civilly to decline temporarily this invitation.

To the Prince of Wales she wrote:

> I heard that you very kindly asked Sir J. Reid to come, but I have said however you will kindly excuse his not accepting this kind invitation for I can only spare him for not longer than 10 days, and he has an engagement with a friend wh. he could not well give up and he must besides be quiet and take rest, wh. he will be able to do with his (only) brother. He is writing to express his regret and gratitude but I thought I would just also explain his view.

Reid succumbed to the whims of the old lady with good grace and even found that the incident appealed to his sense of humour. He had a 'long consultation with Davidson and Bigge as to the terms of my letter to the Prince of Wales asking him to excuse my not going to Sandringham, as H.M. wished me not to go. Agreed to not give away the Queen.'

[5] Née Adeane, Maid-of-Honour to Queen Victoria before her marriage, then Extra Woman of the Bedchamber from 1895 and Social Secretary to the Queen.

If only the Queen had realised how magnanimous her Gentlemen were she would have saved herself much worry and anxiety.

In January 1898 Reid left for a holiday in London, but he had to curtail it 'as the Queen was out of sorts, and also was missing me for other things'. No doubt the Munshi was playing her up yet again, and certainly he was upsetting his fellow Indians in the Household. Mustapha told Reid that the reason 'for his leaving the Queen is not his health or his family, but the Munshi's ill treatment and tyranny. "The Queen want me to stay longer, but it is quite impossible me to stay longer with Munshi. He very bad man. If you send that debbel away we stop."'

On 3 February Reid wrote in his diary: 'The Queen was very absent-minded in the morning and forgot my having painted her throat a minute after. Hear from Mrs Tuck that she had had a box from Lord Salisbury in the morning and that she seemed upset, and that after lunch the Munshi had had the most violent row with her and had shouted at her. Later she wrote him a long letter.' The cause of the hullabaloo this time was Raffiudin Ahmed and the Munshi's determination to take him as a companion to Cimiez in March. The Queen attempted to avoid a recurrence of the previous year's fracas by refusing the Munshi's demands, but the Munshi's bullying behaviour caused her to waver. Reid appealed to Lord Salisbury, drawing his attention to the views of Sir Edward Bradford, the Head of Police, who had warned Reid about Raffiudin the previous year.

On 18 February Lord Salisbury came to Windsor to see the Queen, and strongly advised her not to take Raffiudin to Cimiez, though he could not make her believe that he was associated with the Muslim Patriotic League. However, he prevailed on another front, telling Reid, 'I told the Queen that it would be most unfortunate if the French press got hold of anything and turned her into ridicule, and that was an additional reason for not having Raffiudin there. She quite saw this, and seemed impressed by it, and I am quite sure that this is the argument to use with her.'

The crafty old statesman had saved the day once again and Raffiudin remained behind, although the Munshi still continued to torment the Queen. Lord Salisbury, when told by Reid about the Munshi's bullying, said he did not think much of this 'as she could always get rid of him, but that he believes she really likes the emotional excitement, as being the only form of excitement she can have'. He had penetrated right to the core of the Queen's relations with the Munshi. In her position as Queen there was no necessity to tolerate such insolence and live in dread and fear of such a low, cunning and otherwise insignificant Oriental. She had created for him and herself a position which was untenable but her pride prevented her from dismissing him. It is difficult to imagine that she could have been fond of him; but maybe she was. A far more likely explanation was her masochistic enjoyment of the rows revolving round this singular individual, who provided a welcome respite from the affairs of State, which after more than fifty years of daily toil had become an intolerable burden to her.

On 12 March the Queen and her entourage set off for Cimiez again. The Munshi had been left behind, much to the Household's delight, but before many days had passed he turned up 'to the despair of the poor Gentlemen', not least Reid himself who was once more charged with interpreting the Queen's provisions for her protégé's arrival at her Household. To forestall any possible rupture when the Munshi arrived she had sent Reid a memorandum 'which is *only* to be used if there should be any *symptom* of a *return* of the *very slightest* kind of what happened last year. I may mention that the person *will have* his carriage as he always had, the objection to which Lord Rowton and Lord Salisbury considered most preposterous. His arrival will also be mentioned without title, when he arrives. Burn this now.' Another note reminded Reid that there was to be no gossip amongst the Gentlemen. 'Though I deem that *all* that passed here at Cimiez last year should be *buried in oblivion, all* be as it was before the lamentable and unnecessary occurrence, still I think it right that I *cannot* allow any remarks *about* my people being made by my Gentlemen, or any gossip and reports or stories being listened to by them; but [they] are at once to be stopped.'

In the main, the 1898 spring holiday was much more peaceful than the previous year had been. The Queen, now beginning to age, had become calmer in her attitude to the Munshi and his relations with the Household. She was gradually beginning to accept their terms, although there were still occasions when she saw fit to reprimand the Gentlemen.

On his return to Windsor Reid became deeply involved in discussions with Sir Edward Bradford concerning measures to be taken to secure all the Queen's letters to the Munshi, in the event of her death. It was natural that the Chief of Police should consult her doctor as he would be the one nearest to her at the time of her dying, and Reid was the man who had had the closest dealings with the Munshi and knew him better than any other member of the Household did. In the event, no drastic measures were resorted to, but after the Queen's death a bonfire of the Munshi's papers was made by order of King Edward VII, in the presence of Queen Alexandra and Princess Beatrice.

As far as the Household was concerned there was no further trouble from the Munshi, who continued to serve the Queen living quietly at one of his three homes: Frogmore Cottage at Windsor; Arthur Cottage at Osborne; and Karim Cottage at Balmoral. After the Queen's death he retired to Agra to live at yet another Karim Cottage, from where the Prince of Wales, later King George V, wrote to his father when he visited him in 1905: 'He has not grown more beautiful and is getting fat ... I must say he was most civil and humble and pleased to see us. I am told he lives quietly and gives no trouble at all.' He died in 1909 when there was a further burning of papers, though Mrs Karim was permitted to keep a few letters in Queen Victoria's handwriting.

The blame for 'Queen Victoria's last exotic friendship' does not lie entirely with the Queen. It is true that she raised a humble Oriental to a position which was above his station both socially and intellectually, but then it was within her power to do so. She was unwise to be so ostentatious in lavishing her attention and worldly goods upon so mean a character and she remained stubbornly blind to his faults, even when they could be proved beyond all doubt; but this was part of her nature. The more she was attacked the more staunchly would she defend; never mind if the person under her unyielding protection were not worth a straw. Being an Indian the Munshi was a romantic symbol of the land of her dreams over which she ruled but which she had never seen.

Though the Munshi greatly fostered her natural interest in India, he seems to have given her a bias in favour of Muslims which, during a period of increasingly serious Hindu–Muslim riots, was dangerous. As her favourite he was disliked, as persons in that position usually are, but the feeling of repugnance with which he was regarded by the Household was in all probability based upon snobbery and racial prejudice, although his character did nothing to mitigate these sentiments. In late Victorian times few English people would sit down at table with an Indian unless he were a Prince. The Queen, ahead of her time on this point, was remarkably free from racial prejudice, and felt exasperated by her Household's attitude. Reid, knowing what he did about the Munshi, had one object in mind, and that was to protect the Queen from the Munshi's bullying and deceit. He, more than anyone else, spoke his mind to the Queen, and was prepared to go to the utmost lengths, even to the point of resigning, for what he believed to be right. He was a snob, and no doubt he was racially prejudiced, too, but his firm stand against the Munshi stemmed from his knowledge of the Indian's evil character and his pernicious influence upon the Sovereign. He knew that if the Queen continued to behave as she was she would, eventually, lose the respect of her subjects, and, in an effort to save her, he risked having to relinquish his position in the Household. In the end he triumphed, and the Queen came to rely upon his common sense and good judgment all the more on countless matters outside the scope of his profession, the Munshi crisis having clearly shown that he was no mere sycophant but a loyal and dependable adviser, thereby cementing a relationship that had grown over the years.

Emperor Frederick III of Germany in 1888.

Sir Morell Mackenzie in 1887.

The Empress Frederick and Queen Victoria holding a photograph of the late Emperor, January 1889.

The Empress Eugénie in 1882.

The Kaiser's brother, Prince Henry of Prussia.

The Empress of Russia, the Queen's granddaughter, 1896.

Princess Christian (Helena) of Schleswig-Holstein, 1883.

Prince Christian of Schleswig-Holstein, 1883.

Princess Victoria Melita of Saxe-Coburg-Gotha and Duke Ernst Ludwig of Hesse at the time of their marriage in 1894.

Francis Clark, the Queen's Chief Highland Attendant, 1895.

Hermann Sahl, the Queen's German Secretary, sports Highland dress.

Royal dressers and servants: standing fourth from left, Mrs Tuck, and seated centre, Annie MacDonald

The Countess of Erroll, Lady-in-Waiting to the Queen, 1881.

Lady Churchill, Lady-in-Waiting to the Queen, 1885.

A rare smile: The Queen with Princess Henry (Beatrice) of Battenberg, Princess Louis (Victoria) of Battenberg, and her baby, Princess Alice, future mother of HRH Prince Philip, Duke of Edinburgh, in 1886.

l to r: Rev. George Peter, Beatrice Reid, John and Mary Reid, Reid's brother and sister-in-law, 1887.

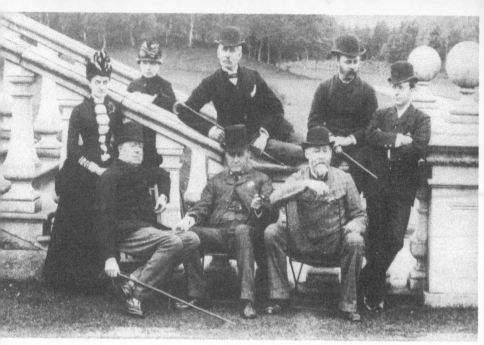

Household group at Balmoral, 1886, behind, l to r: Miss Rosa Hood, Miss Bauer, Major Fleetwood Edwards, Reid, Dr Francis Laking; seated, Lord Bridport, Lord Cranbrook, Sir Henry Ponsonby.

Hosehold group at Osborne, 1888, standing, l to r: Sir John Cowell, Hon. Harriet Phipps, Miss Minnie Cochrane, Herr M. Mutter, Sir William Jenner; seated, Reid, Hon. Alex Yorke, Sir Henry Ponsonby, Major Arthur Bigge, Hon. Marie Adeane.

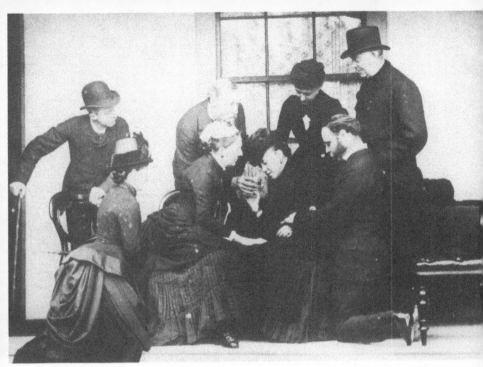

A household mime, 1885, standing l to r: Major S. Waller, Sir Henry Ponsonby, Hon. Evelyn Moore, Lord Bridport; in front, Mlle Norèle, Dowager Duchess of Roxburghe, Hon. Horatia Stopford, Reid.

Household dramatics, *Used Up*, and adaptation by Charles Matthews of the comedy *L'Homme Blasé*, performed in 1889. Major Arthur Bigge, centre, played Ironbrace a blacksmith; Reid, second from right, played Fennel, a lawyer. Seated, Princess Beatrice (Lady Clutterbuck) and Prince Henry.

Munshi Hafiz Abdul Karim in 1890.

Ahmed Hussain whose 'complaints and insinuations' aroused the Queen's indignation, 1890.

Sir Edward Bradford, Chief of the Metropolitan
Police, 1890.

Magdalen (Maggie) Ponsonby with her father,
Sir Henry, in 1890.

The offending photograph, 1897.

The Munshi Abdul Karim going out for a drive at Cimiez, 1898. 'I may mention that the person will have his carriage as he always had.'

9

A Position of Pre-eminence

With Jenner's declining health his visits to Windsor and Osborne became less and less frequent until finally they ceased altogether in May 1893, although he did not officially retire until January 1894. As early as 1889 Reid had been left in sole charge of Prince Leopold of Battenberg when, at the age of seven months, he suffered a severe attack of bronchitis. Sir William had been unable to attend the case on account of his own illness, but neither he nor the Queen was in the least hesitant in leaving it in Reid's capable hands. 'I am glad the Queen showed her confidence in you; if it had been one of my own I should have left the child in your charge only,' Jenner wrote to Reid, while Reid confided to his mother, revealing his ambitious nature: 'I have had all the responsibility and anxiety myself. If the infant recovers, which I now think is likely, it will be just as well that I had no one else.'

From 1889 on, therefore, Reid was, in effect, in sole charge of the Queen's health. In August 1891 Jenner had intimated his wish to retire in a letter to Reid, who replied: 'As to your remark about retiring, I am convinced that such an idea has never occurred to H.M. When all is well she certainly seems to forget what is your position and what a debt of gratitude she owes you for the many years of devoted service you have rendered her. But this is her nature, and I think that she can't be measured by the same standard as ordinary people.' In the last remark lies the kernel of Reid's whole relationship with and understanding of the Queen, and it helped him to forgive what otherwise might seem unforgivable.

Although she may have appeared ungrateful and inconsiderate to persons of high rank, to her servants the Queen was tolerant and kind, even lax at times. Reid noted:

> It is quite astonishing how lenient the Queen is to drunkenness among her servants. When any of the constantly recurring cases comes to her knowledge she always tells me I am on no account to breathe a hint of it to anyone 'especially the Gentlemen and Sir H. Ponsonby and Sir J. Cowell', and she often thus fancies no one knows anything of it, while in reality there is hardly a soul in the house who does not know. Any other offence is never overlooked.

When Hugh Brown, John Brown's brother, died in 1896 Reid was 'commanded by the Queen on no account to tell the Ladies and

Gentlemen that Hugh Brown had died of alcoholic poisóning!!' There was the case, too, of Mrs Chapman, who was in charge of the linen room, being constantly intoxicated so that at night she was bordering on delirium tremens. As she was so particular on all other matters regarding behaviour this quirk of the Queen's is somewhat curious. It can perhaps be attributed to her persistent championship of the underdog. She thought that the lot of a servant was hard, and that they needed an outlet; in consequence she felt concern for, rather than contempt of, the inebriate. This feeling, of course, did not extend to those better placed in society.

A typical example of the Queen's concern was shown in the case of her footman Rankin. At the Queen's wish Reid 'saw Rankin and found him violently maniacal from the effects of drink. Told H.M. he was dangerous and must not be near her, but must go away as soon as possible.' Rankin's brother duly arrived at Osborne to remove him. Although he recovered temporarily and was reinstated, there was a relapse in June 1899, which Reid records in his diary: 'Saw the Queen repeatedly and also Rankin regarding the mental and physical condition of the latter, the result of renewed drinking habits. Very difficult and diplomatic business. H.M. was much concerned about him and saw me at midnight.' The following day Reid had a long interview with Rankin who left in the afternoon. 'Queen much exercised about him and rather sympathetic.'

In the spring of 1891 the Queen, for the first and only time, went to Grasse. In spite of its being 'the prettiest of the places we have been to', for Reid the visit was not a success. Royalty, Household and servants all succumbed to bouts of illness, and there was a smallpox scare which necessitated vaccinations all round. To begin with Prince Henry 'had measles rather badly – had to be with him constantly' and so there was 'no time to enjoy myself'. Then Reid received the unhappy news that 'young Hoffmeister of Cowes, who sometimes comes in my place at Balmoral, was thrown from his horse last Tuesday, and got concussion of the brain. I think,' he confided to his mother, 'something of the sort would have been my fate sooner or later had not Providence taken me away from my former drudgery at Ellon. I am always thankful to be where I am.' Later, when Hoffmeister was dying, Reid wrote to her: 'It is a most melancholy affair and almost consoles me for not having a horse to ride!'

A week later he wrote that 'all the Suite and ten of the servants have been ill'. The chief cook had diphtheria, the Queen had a bad cold, and even Reid had had a sore throat and cold. 'Our party have all taken a dislike to Grasse in consequence of every one being ill.'

But this had not been all. Elizabeth Reynolds, the Queen's personal housemaid, became 'dangerously ill with blood poisoning of the hand and arm from the prick of a needle, and I have been with her day and night. Today I had to get the French surgeon here (a very nice man) to come and help me to chloroform and operate, cutting down on the bones of the hand and arm.'

In spite of all Reid's efforts, Lizzie died a few days later at the age of thirty-eight. The Queen, who on such occasions was at her most understanding, wrote Reid a sympathetic note:

> I am most anxious to express my very warm thanks to you for all the care and attention you have shown to my poor good Elizabeth during this terrible week of intense fatigue, which I fear you will feel. The end has been a very sad one which really till Sunday evening, or rather Monday, did *not* seem likely. It is very hard for a Doctor to be unable to save life. But there is a higher Power who orders all for the best, and tho' we cannot see this *now* we must submit. I thought she looked so peaceful and humdrum lying there, and one felt thankful the poor spirit was at rest after so much dreadful suffering as she knew from Wednesday to Monday, when it ceased. In fact, on Friday, after the severe operation, she seemed much easier. Such a thing never happened before in our midst as it were, and seemed to bring it home to us all.

Reid had to arrange Elizabeth's burial and the problem of dealing with the corpse, as always, occupied a great deal of the Queen's attention. Reid received an anguished note from her on the subject which no one can fail to be moved by, irrational as it is.

> I hope you will never often think me fastidious, but I have in my drive this *afternoon* to Peymeiran twice passed the cemetery, and I *cannot bear* the thought that my poor Elizabeth should be put for two whole *nights* in that *dreary* place *out* by herself all alone – so far away. And I must ask that she should be *taken* to the Church nearby. The objection to the funeral being there in the middle of the day should be abolished by her being taken *quite quietly*, say at 6 or even 5 in the morning to the cemetery and *then* let her funeral be at any hour there, at 10.30 or 11, or 12, or when most convenient, but I cannot let her be taken there *tonight*. No, my *whole* soul and body revolt against it.

The same evening at ten p.m. in the Grand Hotel there was a funeral service for Elizabeth before the Queen and royal family, Suite and servants; 'rather a weird business', Reid informed his mother. At one thirty a.m. the body was removed to the English Church, and two days later was taken to the cemetery where there was a further service.

Francis Clark, the Chief Highland Attendant, was another servant whose illness caused great concern to the Queen. In 1895 he developed cancer of the throat and tongue, and when Reid informed the Queen of his and the surgeon's diagnosis she 'was much upset and cried'. An operation, according to medical opinion, afforded the only chance of recovery for Clark, but the risk was grave. He agreed to go to Buckingham Palace where the operation was to be undertaken. At first it appeared to have been a success, and the day after the case looked hopeful. The Queen insisted that Reid should go to Buckingham Palace daily in order to follow the case closely. For the first five days there seemed to be progress, but then the unfortunate Clark 'developed septic pneumonia, ptosis and hemiplegia, evidently from a right cerebral thrombosis. Oxygen inhalation was given steadily and he was fed by tube.' Reid was up all night on 7 July, in the middle of which Clark died, and the following day, very tired, he returned to Windsor to make arrangements for the funeral. In the meantime he had received a touching telegram from the Queen: 'Deeply, deeply grieved, but thankful he is free from suffering. Most grateful for the kind care and attention bestowed on my good faithful friend, and very sorry for you all.'

The Queen may have been an exacting, demanding mistress, but she was generous in her feelings towards her servants. Francis Clark had obviously been popular for there was a large gathering of doctors, nurses, members of the Household and many servants present at the funeral service, which was held in the Bow Room at Buckingham Palace. 'Very impressive', Reid noted, and even Lord Rosebery showed concern by writing, 'Please if not too busy send me a line as to the terribly sudden end of Francis Clark.'

There were times when some of her servants did not come up to the Queen's expectations, however. Donald Brown, another of John Brown's brothers, was as truculent as his elder brother, it appears, and annoyed the Queen by refusing to do his duties as porter. Moreover, he quarrelled with his neighbours. The Queen made his position quite clear to Reid:

I am greatly disappointed and shocked to hear of Donald Brown's most extraordinary and improper conduct. He wished to leave Osborne as he could not agree with anyone there when everything had been done to suit his wishes. He has been placed at the principal gate at Windsor Castle, where the duties are very slight, and where his predecessors have always lived, contented and satisfied. But he does nothing but complain, and to my astonishment and great displeasure I hear that he disobeys orders, interferes with the guard, and refuses to open the gates on the terrace, which all the other porters at that gate, where he is, have done. He should feel that it was *entirely out of regard* to his *excellent* eldest brother John that he got the place of Extra Porter, and then, after some years, of Regular Porter. He has been more indulged, and more has been done for him than for any other person in his position, and yet he is never satisfied. This is extremely ungrateful, and besides sets a very bad example to the other servants in a similar position. He must be told *plainly* and *decidedly* that if he does not obey orders which are now conveyed by Lord Edward Clinton, as Master of the Household, I shall be obliged to pension him which, for the sake of his brother, I should regret, but he must promise in writing to do what are *his duties*: if he refuses to do so he *must be pensioned.*

Once again Reid acted as a liaison between the angry Queen and the unhappy servant. Why, one asks, did the Queen refer to Reid rather than to Lord Edward Clinton over a matter which was strictly within the latter's province? The answer is that more and more the Queen relied on her doctor. He was readily at hand, and the servants found him approachable. Her Majesty had recently tended to ignore the male members of her Household to such an extent that the Master of the Household was forced to complain to Reid 'about the impossibility of checking abuses unless H.M. gives him full powers'.

Meanwhile, the Queen's overworked secretary, Sir Henry Ponsonby, was beginning to irritate her and to give her cause for anxiety, though it was some months before he became seriously ill. Her Majesty, whose sight was rapidly deteriorating, complained that his handwriting was illegible, and that he was forgetful. She expressed herself forcibly to Reid at Balmoral in September 1893. 'I have no confidence in the present government. Then Sir Henry gives me no help in such matters. He has no backbone, is always placid and easily talked over by anybody. He has no courage, but agrees with me, and then is talked over by others and agrees with them. He agrees with everybody.' Ponsonby was a diplomat who valued peace above all things and, though a strong Liberal, he exhibited great impartiality in his dealings with the Queen, who did not always show the gratitude which years of virtual slavery justfied.

On 7 January 1895, Sir Henry suffered a paralytic stroke at Osborne, from which there was little hope of recovery. He had been the linchpin in the Household for so long, since 1870, that the Queen and her entourage felt his loss deeply, both personally and professionally. Reid wrote to his mother: 'Sir H. Ponsonby is *very* ill – paralysed and unconscious. I have to go four times daily to Ponsonby's house. I fear if he recovers he will, at best, be a wreck.' Sir Henry's right arm and leg were paralysed, and when he recovered consciousness his speech was affected. Walter Gibson from the Privy Purse Office had foreseen what would happen. 'And so the *inevitable* has befallen poor Sir Henry at last. I *am deeply* sorry for him; but his work had long been too much for *any* one man – and *beyond* him.'

Telegrams arrived for the Queen from the Kaiser, Empress Eugénie, the Empress Frederick, the Princess of Wales and many others, all of them finding their way to Her Majesty via Reid. For days on end the Queen constantly consulted him about the respective merits and capabilities of Edwards and Bigge, with a view to one of them succeeding Ponsonby. He was pestered, too, by the Princesses Christian and Louise with their opinions on the subject. A letter of a most confidential nature from Walter Gibson reached Reid.

> I want just to give you my opinions and reasons, for what they may be *worth* as to what *might* be done, and would, as far as I can see, work well:
>
> | | |
> |---|---|
> | Make Sir F. Edwards Keeper of the Privy Purse | at £1500 p.a. |
> | Make Col. Bigge Private Secretary | at £1500 p.a. |
> | Make myself Assistant Keeper and Secretary of the Privy Purse | at £1000 p.a. |
> | Make Engelbach Assistant Secretary of the Privy Purse | at £ 500 p.a. |
>
> Burn it at once if you think best and *note* what you think well to note.

It might seem strange that such confidential information about matters totally unrelated to medicine should be put before Reid who was, after all, only the Queen's doctor, but Gibson found that the only way in which to filter information and suggestions to the Queen was through him. Bigge and Edwards, who were promoted to succeed Ponsonby, at first temporarily and then permanently, were denied access to the Queen. Bigge wrote to Reid that he had grave doubts as to the possibility of carrying out the duties of Private Secretary as the Queen 'finds it inconvenient to see me' and therefore his only communication was through written messages. He found it 'impossible to do the job properly under these circumstances'. Reid intervened, and during one of his late-night chats succeeded in persuading the Queen of the necessity for seeing her Private Secretary regularly.

Reid had become indispensable now, not only to the Queen, but to her Household, too, as being the only male member who had a ready approach to her. His importance as a liaison between the Queen and the outside world was inestimable.

Meanwhile, by the middle of February 1895, Ponsonby was no better 'and is still wrong in the head'. Arthur Bigge wrote to Arthur Ponsonby, Sir Henry's other son, 'Reid has, they all say, been capital. It is so fortunate that Sir H. always liked Dr R. as evidently his frequent visits are a pleasure to him, and Reid has now a power over him which perhaps no outside man could have acquired as Sir H. would not have known him.' But Reid had to leave Osborne when the Queen moved to Windsor and was sadly missed, not only by Henry Ponsonby, but by his wife, Mary, too.

> If I were to begin to say all I feel about your absence, and what my gratitude is for your friendly and affectionate care of my dear husband in this terrible time of trouble, I should not know where to stop. Dr Thompson [Surgeon Apothecary to the Queen at Osborne] is most careful and attentive, and I think we are very fortunate to get his services, although I need not say that the blank of your absence is in no wise filled up.

With this letter was sent 'a writing box in which to stow away some of your letters' as a mark of Mary's gratitude.

On 9 March Reid visited Ponsonby at Osborne and found the patient better than expected, 'but not so well as last time, intellect duller, lung condition unsatisfactory, but no immediate danger as yet', he telegraphed to the Queen. In May Reid informed the Queen that 'there was little or no material restoration of intellect' although, according to Magdalen Ponsonby, 'he always brightens up at any conversation about you or *Sir* Arthur Bigge, and seemed quite amused when I said I should find it difficult to call him Sir Arthur.' (Bigge had been made a KCB on the Queen's birthday.)

While he was at Osborne, Reid helped Mary Ponsonby prepare Sir Henry's letter of resignation, and discussed with her her future plans. Sir Henry lingered on, enjoying very few lucid moments, until 21 November, when the Queen received a telegram from Mary Ponsonby informing her of his death. As always she was ready with her sympathy. 'My heart bleeds for you and your children, and I feel deeply the loss of so faithful and devoted a friend. May God support you in the hour of deep affliction.' The Kaiser sent his condolences to his grandmother, saying that he was 'deeply affected by poor Sir Henry's death. You have lost a most devoted and trustful [sic] servant and we all a most cherished friend.'

The funeral service, which took place at Whippingham Church, was conducted by his friend Randall Davidson, now Bishop of Winchester. The Queen remained at Windsor, being represented by the Duke of Connaught. Reid was present and afterwards went to see Mary and

LOST COURTESY TO THE QUEEN: A DRESS REHEARSAL AT WINDSOR BEFORE THE ROYAL RECEPTION OF "QUEEN VICTORIA'S NURSES."

Reid teaching the nurses to curtsey. He found himself burdened with 'so many things to do quite apart from medical work'.

Magdalen Ponsonby at Osborne Cottage. The meeting was 'very painful'.

'There had been immense crowds at the funeral, and great feeling was shown,' the Queen noted in her Journal after Reid had returned from Osborne with his report of the occasion.

Both the Queen and Reid had lost a true friend, but Ponsonby's absence made the Queen rely more than ever on her doctor, to the extent that he was prompted to complain to his mother that he was given 'so many things to do quite apart from medical work'. Since Ponsonby's illness earlier in the year, Reid had become the Queen's foremost courtier, the one to whom others turned for advice when they needed the Queen's ear.

Within a few months of Ponsonby's death an even greater tragedy occurred to the Queen. Prince Henry, who for ten years had meekly fulfilled his duties as husband to Princess Beatrice, and son-in-law to a demanding old lady, felt stifled by the inactivity and monotonous routine of life at Queen Victoria's Court. He wanted some action, and he wanted to serve his adopted country. He was determined to join the expeditionary force which was being sent out to the Ashanti region of West Africa to enforce order and demand that King Prempeh should adhere to the terms of the 1874 Treaty made with the British Government. The Queen had consented to Princess Christian's eldest son, Prince Christian Victor, serving there, but for Prince Henry to leave her side was another matter, and would never do. However, the Queen had not reckoned with Princess Beatrice who, sympathising with her husband, firmly backed him in his enterprise. United resistance was too much for the Queen to withstand, and reluctantly she granted permission. She appealed to Reid to impress upon them the dangers of contracting fever and he was sent to London to see the Chief of the Medical Department, Sir William Mackinnon, and Dr Taylor, P.M.O. of the Ashanti expedition, to find out about the risks involved in undertaking such a journey. He had to 'tell them about Prince Henry's health, and also (by Queen's order) that if he were to die, either there or at sea, his body must be preserved and brought back'.

Where death was concerned, the Queen was never unprepared. In this case she was right, for hardly more than a month after he had set sail from the Royal Albert Dock in the *Coromandel* Prince Henry had contracted malaria, 'Ashanti Fever' as it was known, and although reluctant to leave African soil until Kumasi was occupied, he was persuaded to board H.M.S. *Blonde* on its journey back to England. He rallied for a short while, but then, after a relapse, he died quietly on the evening of Monday 20 January 1896, off the coast of Sierra Leone. That same day King Prempeh surrendered to the Governor of Cape Coast. News did not reach Osborne until two days later. The Queen and Princess Beatrice had imagined from earlier telegrams that Prince Henry was on the way to recovery, and the Princess was preparing to go to Madeira to meet her husband, so that the shock was all the greater. The nation was so concerned for the Queen and Princess that Reid was obliged to issue bulletins to reassure them, and ironically, since his death was hardly the result of gallantry in war, Prince Henry was made into a hero by the very people who had formerly despised him.

It was a 'very busy and very trying' time for Reid with 'H.M. crying and sobbing much'. As usual, he had to arrange about the coffins and 'sent off a crucifix from Princess Beatrice to be put in the Prince's hands'. He had to deal with the press, too, as he wrote hastily to his mother, 'There was a panic in London about the Queen, and one evening they had her "dying" and even "dead"!! The Queen and all her family take much of my time, and all the Household people want me constantly. H.M. doesn't see any of them yet but Miss Phipps and me, so that a great deal of business has to pass through me.'

The Queen still refused to see Bigge and Edwards and she also insisted that Reid write to the Prime Minister, Lord Salisbury: 'Owing to her sorrow and consequent need for rest and recuperation, she proposes to start for Cimiez the first week in March. The Queen hopes you will understand that she cannot for some time do all that she would otherwise have done (such as the March Drawing Rooms).'

Reid spent the morning of 25 January with Hertslet from the Lord Chamberlain's office, who was

> starting in the afternoon for Madeira with the undertakers, and gave him instructions as to the Prince's body. He was to be dressed in Ashanti uniform, his rings left on, also a locket around his neck with Princess Beatrice's hair – the crucifix to be put in his hand with a piece of ivy, of white heather, of myrtle from the Princess's wedding bouquet, and a small photo of the Princess attached to it. There were to be three coffins, shell, lead, and oak.

The body had to travel a long way in equatorial heat, and the problem was how to conserve it until it could be put in a coffin at Madeira. The solution was found by placing it in a tank made up out of biscuit tins and filled with rum. It had been necessary, so Reid learned from the Prince's doctor, Hilliard, 'to remove the intestines before the body was preserved in rum, and drop them overboard'. At

Madeira, Prince Henry's body was transferred from the *Blonde* to the *Blenheim*, which reached Portsmouth on the morning of 4 February.

On 26 January Reid noted that the 'Queen and Princess were getting much more composed' but on 1 February they became distraught because the Princess had lost several pages of Prince Henry's diary which had arrived two days previously by post. They searched and searched, but feared that they had accidentally found their way into the wastepaper basket and 'been burned by the coal porter'.

The preparations for the funeral were elaborate and kept the Queen, her doctor and her Household busy. On 5 February a short service, conducted by the Bishop of Winchester and the naval chaplain, was held on the *Blenheim* in the Captain's cabin before the coffin was transferred to the *Alberta* for Prince Henry's final journey to the Isle of Wight and his burial at Whippingham Church. Although invited to attend the service, Reid watched the funeral procession from Osborne Cottage, together with Mary and Magdalen Ponsonby, instead of going to the church. He declared it to be an 'imposing sight'.

A year later, in 1897, Reid had the responsibility for steering the Queen through her Jubilee celebrations, this time her Diamond Jubilee, without mishap. Two weeks before, she had written to Reid from Balmoral: 'I am feeling tired and somewhat depressed, and not as well as usual here in the spring. I don't sleep badly, but I have so much to do, so many questions to answer, that I know no rest.' Poor Queen Victoria, no wonder she was anxious, for she was about to embark on the most exacting programme of events and festivities in the whole of her reign, at the age of seventy-eight.

On 18 June Reid wrote to his mother from Windsor that 'the Jubilee bustle has fairly begun. I'm glad that you are not come up for the Jubilee for the squash and confusion everywhere will be terrific.'

Although the Queen's health was his first concern, and he watched her vigilantly on the day of the Thanksgiving Service at St George's Chapel, he had other royalties to attend to besides the Queen. He was 'sent for by the Grand Duchess Serge to remove a small red spot from her face (used Nitric Acid)'. Formerly Princess Elizabeth (Ella) of Hesse, the Grand Duchess was reputed to be the most beautiful royal in Europe, even lovelier than her sister the Czarina of Russia, so it was understandable that no spot, however small, should be allowed to mar her perfection.

The Queen had recovered from her depression and was buoyed up by the nation's enthusiasm for her. The evening before the Jubilee Procession Reid attended a grand reception held by the Queen for foreign and Colonial dignitaries, and noted that 'H.M. was not much tired at night'. The following day, he wrote to his mother, 'At the last moment I was put in the procession (in the 6th carriage) instead of Lord Kintore, for fear of anything going wrong with the Queen, so I saw the whole affair splendidly, and it really was a most wonderful experience.' It was a far cry from the days when Reid had trudged through the snow on horseback, tending his father's practice in the remote north. He had come a long way and had taken only sixteen years to achieve his present position. But the day was to be memorable for another reason: 'At 11.10 p.m. was sent for by the Queen who told me, in the kindest way, that she had given me a Baronetcy, and showed me Lord Salisbury's letter formally submitting it.'

Before the news was reported in the papers Reid had informed his mother of his baronetcy and told her: 'The Queen said a lot of nice complimentary things to me. It is a great step up for me, and I have now got all I should ever care to have. It will be more marked than if she had put it in the general list with the common herd!' Then there was a change of tone, Reid clearly showing Jubilee strain: 'Every day there is something and I wish it were all over; for I am getting dead tired! Still, I must not complain, considering what I am getting, and really my luck since I came to the Queen has been extraordinary.' It had indeed, but as the shoals of letters that poured in from all quarters testified, his success was not solely due to luck. Sir Thomas Barlow declared:

> No honour will compensate you for your ceaseless and tireless work and anxiety, and I am especially glad for the sake of our profession, for this will give you a still more commanding influence than before and enable you to act with still more effect in all matters that concern the relations of our craft and the Court. I am confident that it has been a good thing for medicine in England that you have been able to take old Jenner's mantle, and some day our brethren will realise it.

Reid's new position gave him more confidence at Court and his voice more weight in matters relating to his profession and, as he replied to Barlow: 'Now I mean to lay down the law about professional matters in a more commanding, and I hope more successful, tone than hitherto!'

Once it was realised that Reid had such ready access to the Queen (in her later years he saw her between four and eight times a day), he became involved in numerous requests and applications for titles and appointments, particularly from medical men. Whenever the Birthday or New Year Honours List was drawn up his advice on medical appointments was sought both by the Queen's Private Secretary and by the Prime Minister. The Queen, when applied to, simply answered: 'Ask Sir James Reid first, who knows what the faculty feel, and then let me know.' So while Reid was denied scope for introducing innovative medicine himself, he had the power, albeit indirectly, to reward those who had achieved distinction in one branch or another within the profession.

In December 1898 Lord Salisbury sought Reid's advice on an appropriate honour for Sir Joseph Lister, whose introduction of antiseptic methods into surgery had revolutionised medicine. He was a man who deserved a higher title than those normally bestowed upon medical men. No doctor had previously received a peerage, but Reid considered that Lister was more than worthy of such an honour, and said so to Lord Salisbury. His word was acted upon, and Joseph Lister became the first medical man to take his seat in the House of Lords. In a letter of acknowledgment to Reid, Lister thanked him 'for his kind expressions, and for the share you have yourself had in bringing about the event'.

Reid had always been ruthless in his dismissal of the claims of those who put themselves forward for recognition. Lady Granby had been requested by Dr Hood to apply to him to use his influence in securing the position of Physician Extraordinary to the Queen which had recently become vacant. Reid's reply was strictly to the point. 'My own experience in the matter of medical appointments at Court is that it tells against a man to make any application, either directly or indirectly; and I recollect Sir William Jenner's writing in reply to such an application that "it points to a defect in his character medically considered".'

In the event the position was given to Thomas Barlow, who wrote to thank Reid for his part in the appointment. Reid considered that he was in no way entitled to Barlow's gratitude.

> I feel that in the position in which accident has placed me, it is my moral duty, in helping the Queen with medical appointments, to recommend those I believe to be the most worthy both professionally and otherwise, and the best fitted for the duty, quite irrespective of personal regard or friendship. In your case I did not depart from my principle, nor should I do so for any of my friends, so you are under no obligation whatever to me; but all the same, I rejoice that the man who has been selected solely on his merits is one of my most valued friends.

When Prince Alfred, Duke of Coburg, put forward Dr William Playfair's name for a baronetcy, Reid persuaded the Queen against his promotion, and was amply supported by Sir Russell Reynolds and

Sir James Paget, the Presidents of the Royal College of Physicians and Surgeons respectively. They declared that: 'Dr Playfair's professional position in no way entitled him to the honours of a baronetcy. His obstetric practice appears almost to have ceased, and he is now, as Sir R. Reynolds expressed it, only an "hotel keeper" for hysterical women whom he subjects to massage and starvation.' Needless to say, Dr William Playfair received no baronetcy.

In 1897, when Sir William MacCormac, the new President of the Royal College of Surgeons, applied for a baronetcy – to which, being in that position, he had a strong claim – Reid once again resisted, replying to Fleetwood Edwards:

> He is a good touter, and on the last two occasions of vacancies in the Queen's surgical staff he has not only applied in writing for the post, but has canvassed members of the Royal Family, and numbers of the 'nobility and gentry' and ladies to write for him to people about Court, which is, 'medically speaking', very bad form and is never done by men of the highest order. He has already got a knighthood. The man who before MacCormac ought to get a baronetcy is the President of the Royal College of Physicians, Dr Samuel Wilks. *He* will never ask for it, or tout in any way whatever.

Wilks was made a baronet, MacCormac was not.

Fleetwood Edwards submitted the whole list of proposed Jubilee medical honours for Reid's perusal and comment, which he readily gave. 'You may quote my opinions, if you please, to the Queen or to Lord Salisbury. I know all the men: they are more or less friends of my own, but in such matter right and justice ought to stand above friendship.'

In the case where a surgeon waived his fee after the performance of an operation on a member of the royal family, in the expectation of receiving recognition in the form of a title in lieu of a fee, Reid was equally positive in expressing his opinion. Herbert Allingham had operated twice upon the Duchess of Teck for strangulated umbilical hernia, both times successfully, although on the second occasion the patient died from heart failure a few hours after the operation. When asked for a statement of his fee he declined to offer it, but was anxious that an honour should be bestowed upon him instead. The Duchess of Teck's brother, the Duke of Cambridge, applied to the Queen on behalf of Allingham, and she, as was her wont, referred to Reid. Reid thought 'that it would be wrong, and, as a precedent very awkward indeed, to admit the principle that a medical man may deprecate taking a fee from a member of the Royal Family on the ground clearly implied that he may thereby lay claim, as compensation, to a titular honour'. On hearing this, the Queen gave orders to Fleetwood Edwards that Allingham's request 'should be declined civilly for the reasons given by Sir J. Reid'.

Self-seekers were not to Reid's taste and he was understandably incensed when he thought one of them was trying to prescribe for the Queen's rheumatism, writing to Jenner: 'I don't think the Queen will use anything he may send without telling me, but I can't feel certain; and if he begins that sort of thing, there is no saying where it may end.' In fact the unfortunate doctor in question, Sir Oscar Clayton, foresaw the professional elephant trap into which he was being zealously urged by his own satisfied patient, Princess Louise, and backed off in a hasty disclaimer to Reid, but it so happened that Clayton was not free from taint in Reid's eyes. In 1889 he had applied for a baronetcy in return for services to the Duchess of Cambridge, and his probity was questionable on another matter too. The Duke of Edinburgh had been suffering from 'Maltese Fever'. The Queen made the most of the illness because the Admiralty wished to have him examined in a Court of Enquiry over the loss of H.M.S. *Sultan* and, naturally enough, the Queen and the Duke wished to avoid that.

> Consequently Sir Oscar Clayton, who the Queen says 'understands him better than anyone else' (which I fancy means that he will do or say whatever he thinks will please!!) is sent down to Portsmouth to go and meet the Duke at Spithead, and report to H.M. and the Admiralty on his condition and say whether he does not think the Duke unfit for travel to London, or for business of any kind. Perhaps Sir Oscar may so manipulate the service as to further his claim above mentioned.

Perhaps this was a little harsh on the hapless Sir Oscar Clayton.

By the end of the nineteenth century the social position of medical men was becoming more assured, and surreptitiously they had crept from 'below' to 'above' the salt. Even Queen Victoria was beginning to accept their new status, though occasionally she had a lapse, sending the following note to the Master of the Household: 'The Gentlemen and Sir James Reid are to come this evening to the Drawing Room.' Reid, needless to say, was highly amused.

In his letter congratulating Reid on his baronetcy, Sir Douglas Powell attributed the change in status of medical men in some measure to Reid. 'All in the profession know how strenuously and successfully you have maintained and advanced the dignity of medicine in high quarters, and how skilfully you have guided and safeguarded Her Majesty in health matters.' By the nature of his position Reid was deprived from making any scientific advance in medicine, but a letter such as this one went a long way towards consoling him for what he had missed.

Happy Marriage

Reid was approaching fifty and still there were no signs of marriage in sight. He was constantly being chaffed by members of the Household and his Viennese friend, Slatin Pasha, who taunted him with memories of the beautiful girls in his native city. There was another Austrian, too, who reminded him that it was high time he found himself a wife whom he could grace with the prefix 'Lady', and that was Karl Lodron, his pupil of former days who was now a high-ranking officer in the Austrian army. His mother was also anxious that her successful son should come home to The Chesnuts one day with 'a good true wife'.

Reid was not averse to women; on the contrary he enjoyed their company and they found him an amusing, lively companion. However, not being an emotional man, his head ruled his heart. He realised that if he were to carry out his duties as resident physician to the Queen successfully, and to her entire satisfaction, there was no room for another woman in his life. Sir Henry Ponsonby had suffered deeply from enforced long absences from his wife, and both Sir Arthur Bigge and Sir Fleetwood Edwards had complained that they were rarely permitted to dine at home. It is curious that Queen Victoria, who herself had had such a close relationship with her husband, and could not bear to be parted from him for a moment, appeared not to notice the suffering she inflicted upon her gentlemen- and ladies-in-waiting. Husbands and wives were constantly left behind to fend for themselves as best they could while the Queen with her accompanying entourage travelled all over Europe, to Balmoral, and to Osborne. On the other hand, the courtiers must have realised what they had undertaken, and have been prepared to suffer the consequences for a monarch whom they adored, in spite of all her foibles.

During the eighteen years which Reid had spent with the Queen he had been perfectly content with his way of life; 'it fits me to a T', he had written on several occasions to his mother. From a medical point of view the work cannot be said to have been either innovative or riveting, but there were many compensations. Reid, who enjoyed his comforts, lived in the lap of luxury and was constantly able to mix and converse with the most distinguished persons in all spheres of life, from Emperors to actresses. As a highly intelligent man he was in a position to keep his finger on the current pulse, politically, scientifically and socially. In his relations with women, however, there had been a problem as far as marriage was concerned. Being of humble origin, Reid was from a different social background from the rest of the Queen's Household, and while they all found him irresistible as a companion the ladies would not have contemplated marrying him. It would have been a *mésalliance*; besides which he would not have been in a position to support them in the way in which they had been accustomed to live. Since he left the Court rarely, and then usually to spend a few quiet weeks in Ellon with his mother, where would Reid have found a suitable woman to marry? Life at Court had spoiled him for an ordinary wife.

But by the beginning of 1899 his baronetcy had swept aside all social obstacles, and his financial position was adequate after many years of saving. Furthermore, he was able to provide a sizeable and well-equipped country home for any prospective spouse. He was not handsome, but he had more enduring qualities such as intelligence, charm and a sense of humour, and, in addition, he was eminent and successful.

The first mention of Reid's future bride occurs on 9 December 1898, when his diary records 'went to tea in Miss Bulteel's room to meet Misses Baring, Ponsonby and Biddulph'. At Christmas Reid and Susan Baring exchanged cards and he received a photograph of her with the following words written underneath: 'One of ze Queen's Maids-of-Honour. *Also* not handsome and *also* so old!' This humorous allusion is to Prince Christian's constant sigh and complaint about the women surrounding the Queen being old and ugly. It is true to say that not even Susan's dearest friend would have called her beautiful, but she was only twenty-nine years old. Her father, the first Lord Revelstoke and senior partner of Baring Brothers, the merchant banking firm, had died from diabetes at the age of sixty-nine, one year before Susan was appointed a maid-of-honour to the Queen. Her mother, Louisa Emily Bulteel, a sister to Mary Ponsonby and a granddaughter of Lord Grey of the Reform Bill, had died in 1892 at the age of fifty-six, worn out by the Baring crash and the financial worries resulting from it.[1] Fortunately for Susan she was one of a large family of exceptional ability, and although she had little money of her own she had two older married sisters who were only too eager to welcome her into their folds. The elder, Elizabeth, was married to

---

[1] The boom of 1886-90 was largely based on investment in South America, with which Barings had been involved to a great extent, and when the boom broke Barings were gravely threatened. In a celebrated episode of financial history they were rescued by the direct intervention of the Bank of England and by Rothchilds.

Viscount Castlerosse, who later became Earl of Kenmare, and lived at Killarney. Margaret was married to the Hon. Robert Spencer, half-brother and heir to Earl Spencer, and lived at Dallington in Northamptonshire. The three sisters were devoted to each other but Margaret and Susan were particularly close since they shared a common interest in music, at which they both excelled, There were five brothers, each of them distinguished in his way, and Maurice was to become famous as a writer and a poet of unusual talent. He was much sought after in society, being both quixotic and a daredevil, and he and his eldest brother, John, the second Lord Revelstoke, were connected with the Souls, a glittering group of friends renowned for their intellectual and artistic interests. They included Lord Curzon and Margot Asquith. In their correspondence and conversation the Souls used an exclusive and elaborate vocabulary, much of which originated from the Baring family.

Shortly after her father's death, while she was studying pianoforte and singing at the Royal College of Music, Susan received a letter from Louisa, Duchess of Buccleuch, the Mistress of the Robes, inviting her to become maid-of-honour to Queen Victoria. This was an opportunity not to be missed and Susan accepted with alacrity. She was delighted to have found a niche for herself and to be independent, at least to a certain extent, for in her new position she would receive £300 per annum. The Queen's maid-of-honour was expected to be both accomplished and versatile, and to be able to speak, read and write French and German with proficiency. She might also be called upon at any moment to play or sing and had to be able to do so readily at sight. It was taken for granted that she could sketch, do needlework and be conversant with the usual indoor games (such as backgammon, *vingt-et-un* and bridge). Discretion, too, was important for a maid-of-honour. She was not permitted to keep a diary (though some did), and her lips had to remain sealed where the private life of the royal Household was concerned. Each day before dinner the maid-of-honour had to stand in the corridor outside the Queen's private apartments. In her hand she held a bouquet which, on entering the dining room, she laid at the right hand of the Queen's plate. When no royal visitors were present, the maid-of-honour sat at dinner next to the gentleman on the Queen's right; it was necessary, therefore, that she should be a good conversationalist and well informed on current events.

Susan's first waiting was at Osborne in August 1898. The house was 'too hot for words' because of the hot water pipes which surrounded her room. Fortunately, much of the time was spent sitting under the beautiful cedar tree in the garden. To her sister Margaret Spencer she wrote giving an amusing insight into her new life. (Susan's letters are full not only of humour, but also of 'Baringisms' which, to the uninitiated, are incomprehensible. In order to be accepted into the Baring fold it would be essential for Susan's future husband to learn the family language.)

> Yesterday at 6 I went out driving with the Queen for the first time, rather curled [shy] – however she was most nice and easy to relevé [gossip] with. 'And you work a great deal at the Royal Academy.' The Royal *College*, Ma'am, from me. 'That is what I mean of course.' I tried to talk about Sir Hubert Parry but got on to Arthur and Dolly (Ponsonby) instead. We drove for nearly two hours, 4 horses, and fast which was nice. Princess Thora [Princess Helena Victoria of Schleswig-Holstein] was the third, very nice and talks better than Princess Beatrice. 'Ze' evenings are trying. Church this morning was rather a strain, thankful none of la famille near me as it would have been a prize moment for *fou rire*! Lady Lytton golden [very kind] to me and I have got the greatest culte [liking] for her. Fanny Drummond (the other maid-of-honour) most kind and easy and knowing archives so tells me, but prize dank house [dull] as a releveuse [gossip].

In a second letter to her sister Susan writes:

> We had a ladies' dinner with the Queen two nights ago, rather amusing, the Queen doing puppets of the German ladies too killing!! They talked about Chaminade,[2] and a ringing voice across the table from the Queen: 'Susan, have you heard her?' Janotha came to play after dinner. She played far fetched things by Chopin, a long fugue that had never been played, the Queen rather lasséed, 'Fugues are very difficult to play!!' was all she said, and Janotha quite mad knelt in front of the Queen who was rather nervous as to what she would do next.

In spite of her great age and heavy responsibilities the Queen was able to relax at times and enjoy herself, especially in the company of her ladies.

Reid recorded in his diary on 3 January 1899 that Miss Baring had been present in the Durbar Room when the private band was practising and he had got the bassoon and cornet to play into his phonograph –

---

[2] Cécile Louise Stéphanie Chaminade was a French composer, born in Paris, and was best known for her piano pieces which she frequently performed in England. Madame Natalia Janotha, of German origin, child prodigy and pupil of Clara Schumann.

his prize possession. In February, for the first time, he called on 'Miss Baring at West Halkin Street', where she shared a house with her youngest brother Hugo. 'Had tea with her and Miss Ponsonby and Countess Valda Gleichen.'

In March when Reid was on the annual visit to Cimiez he received a letter from Susan in reply to a telegram he had sent her. 'Your "Télégramme" is quite the nicest thing I have ever seen! and I am *delighted* with it! I wish one's messages were always answered in that sort of way! I hope you will remember your way to the saddler's shop when you come to London for a Drawing Room in May, as I shall be longing to hear your "Impressions de Voyage". With very many thanks from ze Old Maid-of-Honour (also *not* handsome.)'

Reid was not disappointed when he returned to Windsor to find that Susan was there to resume her waiting upon the Queen. On 8 May he noted in his diary, 'Miss Baring came to my room to be weighed', and on the following day in the evening he 'called on Miss Baring and gave her Nice talismans to select from'. On 15 May Reid went with the Household to attend the Queen's Drawing Room at Buckingham Palace, after which he 'had tea with Miss Baring' at her house and saw her maid, who had phlebitis of the left leg. Thereafter he visited Susan daily for a week on the pretext of tending her maid. Then for two months their meetings ceased. Reid went to Balmoral, and to Ellon for two weeks' holiday, while Susan remained in London and attended the Royal College of Music.

They met again at Osborne on 22 July when Reid 'had tea with the ladies (Lady Erroll, Mrs Mallet, Misses Lambart, Baring and Bauer) under the cedar tree in front of the house. Began to rain so could not go cycling but had a talk with Miss Baring in the house.' The following day he 'had a nice talk with Miss Baring before dinner in the Ladies' Drawing Room'. On 24 July Reid describes in his diary how they became engaged. 'Cycled with Miss Baring by Barton, King's Quay and Brock's Lodge. Back by the sea. Halted to rest by the tree at the foot of Swiss Cottage Road and asked her to be my wife, which she consented to. Jolly ride home together. So happy.'

They had been skilful in escaping unnoticed from such a closely knit circle as existed at Osborne but, happy as they were together, their plans for the future were not without problems; for until the Queen was informed of their intentions they were not free to broadcast their engagement as ecstatic couples long to do, but had to appear to the world as though nothing extraordinary had occurred. They met surreptitiously, but they were rarely together on their own, which must have been extremely frustrating for them.

The day after his engagement Reid wrote to his mother:

> I am actually engaged to be married! to Susan Baring, one of our
> Maids-of-Honour, sister of Lord Revelstoke. Look up the *Peerage* under
> Revelstoke, and you will see exactly who she is and about her family. She
> is not very pretty, nor has she much money; but she is clever, accomplished
> and sensible to a degree, and she likes *me* which is the chief point! She
> does not care for riches or gaiety, and is just the woman to be a real
> companion to me. We are not to tell anyone here until she has gone out
> of waiting a week or two hence: but she is to tell her two sisters, and I
> have written to tell John and Mary. No one else will know it for the
> present, so keep it to yourself. When it will come off, and how we will
> manage with my being with the Queen has all to be thought over yet by
> us: but. in any case, you I hope will be pleased with the news!

Wise as usual, Reid was not blind in his love, and had made a
decision which he was never at any time for the rest of his life for one
moment to regret. His devoted brother John wrote:

> I am simply delighted that you have at last awoke to the happiness of
> running in double harness. I cannot affect great surprise myself because
> one afternoon I was with you when you drove around to see Miss Baring's
> maid; worldly knowledge whispered the visit might not be entirely in the
> pursuit of medical science! Mama, too, will have her wish gratified: she
> was lamenting to me in quiet on your seeming determination to remain a
> bachelor: she evidently thought it great folly if not an actual sin!

After John had met Susan a few times he informed his mother of
his own 'unbiased' opinion on her new daughter.

> Jamie has evidently, as usual, had his wits about him, and I am sure is to
> be congratulated on his selection. Miss Baring is quite a little woman
> about Mary's height I should say, with very dark brown hair, and I should
> call her well looking rather than pretty. She looks old for her years, but I
> believe she was the good Samaritan of the family, nursing and trying to
> keep cheery her father and mother, after the Baring Smash, for some ten
> years till they both died, and I suppose their troubles have left their mark
> on her. She seems a sensible kind-hearted little woman and much more
> of a domestic than a society lady. She is exceedingly clever, but very
> modest and unassuming, and has an open natural manner which is very
> taking. In half an hour you will feel almost as much at home with her as
> you do with this rascal. There can be no doubt of its being a love
> attachment, and I am sure their married life will be exceedingly happy.
> Jamie is radiant, and I have never seen him looking better.

This was indeed a reassuring letter for a future mother-in-law to receive, for John's description of Susan was both perceptive and accurate. Between daughter and mother-in-law a relationship was to flourish which was warm, loving, and respectful.

Soon they confided their secret to Randall Davidson. Reid told his mother, 'The Bishop of Winchester who is here just now and is an old friend of mine is *quite delighted* and is to marry us when the time comes! We will tell the Queen on the 8th [August].'

Another person whom they let into their confidence was Arthur Davidson, who was asked to be best man. He wrote to Reid:

> For the last dozen years I have always declined being anyone's best man, but I shall be only too pleased and proud to be yours, and am very proud and flattered at being asked. The only selfish regret I have is that it will, I fear, take you to a great extent away from us and we shall be in perpetual depression, instead of only those fortnightly lapses when you go off from Balmoral. You will of course have a toughish time of it with H.M. but that cannot be helped and *it's worth it*!

Surprisingly enough there was no adverse reaction to the match from any member of Susan's family. Reid was, after all, twenty years older than his intended bride, and he came from a background which was poles apart from the Baring milieu. Lord Revelstoke, Susan's brother, who acted *in loco parentis*, wrote to Reid expressing satisfaction at their engagement. This said a great deal for Reid since Revelstoke was a notorious snob. Susan's Uncle Mina – Lord Cromer, Consul General of Egypt and a statesman held in high esteem – also approved of the match. Susan reported to Reid: 'He said he had had a talk with you at Osborne and liked you and thought you so clever.' The Barings, unlike many aristocratic families who were suspicious of 'clever' men, tended to be intellectual and therefore appreciated Reid's intelligence and enjoyed his sense of humour.

Winning the approbation of Susan's family was one thing, but establishing his position with the Queen was another, and one which Reid dreaded. Two weeks after their engagement he enlisted the help of Harriet Phipps. On 8 August he wrote: 'In the forenoon went over with Susan my letter to Miss Phipps for her to read to the Queen. At 1.30 Miss Phipps told us she had seen H.M. and told her and read our letters and that all was received better than expected. The Queen was dumbfounded at first, but later on reconciled. Saw H.M. at 11.00 p.m. who was very gracious but did not say a word about our engagement.'

Although Reid saw the Queen daily as usual she never mentioned the painful subject, but kept him continually in suspense. Any developments were conveyed by Miss Phipps and relayed by Reid to his mother:

> H.M. was very much astonished, and of course she does not quite like it, as she always very much dislikes any of the Gentlemen about her getting married! But she is much less ferocious about it than we expected: and I am quite sure she will be quite reconciled in a day or two. She has told the Princesses today, but no one else knows it yet; and she wishes us to abstain from announcing it, or from telling any of the Household here, for a few days longer, until she has quite digested it, and thought it all out!

Susan left Osborne and stayed on her brother's yacht at Cowes before leaving for London. She was informed by Reid that the Princesses, having been told, 'are without exception, very nice about it, but considerably *amused*! The idea of the youngest Maid-of-Honour, who has only been a year in the Household, marrying the *one* man whom nobody ever imagined capable of such audacity, has been a source of much mirth to them, which is an excellent thing, as it makes them well disposed all round!' Although Susan was no longer at Osborne, Reid continued to take tea under the cedar tree which meant so much to both of them, 'as I thought it would look a bit suspicious if I absented myself now that you are gone, as I should prefer to do'. He also kept Susan in the picture about the Queen's reactions to Harriet Phipps' negotiations:

> H.M., seeing we are not dictating to her, is actually looking on us with favour, and beginning to arrange our plans for us! Isn't that nice? I have all my life been lucky, and now that my supreme piece of luck capturing a human angel, has come, I believe we are going to be doubly lucky in the future! Miss P. is writing you that H.M. wishes you to come to Balmoral for a farewell waiting of a fortnight on the 15th September, while I am *away*. That is hard, but we had better not say a word of remonstrance, as we can afford now to give in to the Queen's whims, and it will make it all the smoother for us. Miss P. says H.M. proposes we should be married in November, when she returns to Windsor! That *is* an advance on her part, isn't it? Miss P. has managed, and is managing, for us with consummate skill, and we must be grateful to her.

To Susan Harriet Phipps wrote: 'Of course she does not like his marrying but she has been very nice and kind throughout, and I feel you will get him home to dinner sometimes! H.M. is very anxious your engagement should not be known for some little time longer by *anyone*. I will let you know as soon as it may be divulged.'

Another week passed and the Queen still showed no signs of allowing them to announce their engagement. Reid was becoming very impatient, but 'Miss Phipps counsels patience'. In despair he wrote to Susan to say:

Domestique [Miss Phipps] was defeated last night by Bipps [Queen Victoria], who said that she and Princess Christian thought it would be soon enough to announce when we left here!! This is quite monstrous, and I told Domestique that I am getting dangerously near 'breaking out'. So after talking it over with her I went, by her advice, to Princess C. and pointed out to her how important in many ways it was for us to speak out *at once*, and begged her to *befriend* us, and get H.M. to give us the permission. Though inwardly in a whirlwind, I managed to keep outwardly placid! She saw it quickly, and has promised me to speak to the Queen on the very first opportunity.

He wrote again on the same day, 'It is very annoying, and rather irritates me, but it does not make me *really* angry, because not even Bipps can take you away from me, and, knowing that we irrevocably belong to each other, I look on everything else as of secondary importance. If I hear nothing from Princess C. before evening, I shall go to her again.'

As far as Susan's friends were concerned the cat was out of the bag already, and she had received many congratulatory letters which she posted on to Reid. For the first time there is more than a hint that he realised his presumption in asking Susan to marry him. '*All* your friends, who know as yet, are pleased you are going to marry *me*, and think I am good enough for you. I never expected *that*: indeed, had I known months ago what I do now, I might have saved myself many disquieting doubts, and many a torturing fear that my visions of happiness were presumptuous folly on my part, and would be dispelled in a moment by a word or a look from my darling! But all that only adds to my happiness *now*.' Then there is another burst of anger. 'It is *ridiculous* to have to submit to be treated as if we were children about all these things which are only *our own* business. So ridiculous indeed that it rather *amuses* as well as *irritates*, me!! Of course we need not do it unless we liked; and therefore I think we deserve great credit for being so good-natured! But it is a farce, like most things here!'

Susan had told her friends and Reid wanted the freedom to tell his. He already felt the footmen were 'eyeing me with unwonted curiosity'. He confessed to Susan:

I have just told Bigge! He leaves at 7 tomorrow morning for Scotland, and I felt I could not allow *him* to learn it from the newspapers, just after he had seen me and been with me here. So I threw aside the *padlock* [secret] for *him*; he is quite delighted, but told me he had seen it all the time, and felt sure of it, and had been constantly telling his wife in his letters that it was coming! So *you* were right, you clever little puss, when you said you thought *he* suspected. He *thought* that it was all settled the day that you left: but *since then*, he has been thinking that it must be 'off' for a time, because all is so quiet, and the Queen in such good humour, whereas if we *were* going to get married, he felt sure H.M. wd. be *furious* and that things would be *very hot* here!

Having committed Reid and Susan to secrecy, the Queen herself confided in her 'old friend' Lord Rowton. A few days later he met Reid for 'a private talk about the Queen'. Neither of them broached the subject of the engagement, and Reid reported the conversation with relish to Susan:

Lord Rowton told me that I must never think of leaving her under any circumstances, as he knew she would not live 6 months afterwards (of course that is a gross exaggeration on his part, but I *knew* why he was saying this, after what Domestique had told him about us). He said that were I ever to speak of leaving H.M. he felt certain that the strongest pressure would be brought to bear on me by Lord Salisbury and others, in addition to the Queen's family, to make me remain with her. I replied that I was *not* going to leave the Queen, though by a strange coincidence circumstances *had* arisen lately which *had* made me contemplate the step, though only for a short time. It amused me to play with him knowing that '*he* did not know that *I* knew that *he* knew', as Sir John Cowell used to say!

It was now a few weeks after their engagement and the Queen, though gracious in her manner towards Reid, still would not sanction an announcement, nor would she mention his betrothal. For once in her life perhaps Queen Victoria was nonplussed. The Duchess of York, who was staying at Osborne, wrote to her husband the Duke on 21 August:

Grandmama told me in *profound* secret that Susan Baring was engaged to Sir J. Reid, she does not approve and did not wish it to be announced, she told me that hardly any of the Household knew of it, and she only told me as I was leaving Osborne. Gdmama does not like the idea of Sir James being married, and she is sorry to lose Susan, so that altogether it came as rather a shock to Gdmama. Oddly enough when I was driving with Gdmama one day we met these two bicycling, and she asked who they were and I told her and she said 'Dear me, how odd.'

To the Empress Frederick the Queen was more explosive in expressing her views.

> I must tell you of a marriage (wh. annoyes me vy. much) wh. [will] surprise you gtly. Sir J. Reid!!! and my late M. of H. Susan Baring!! It is incredible. How she cld. accept him I cannot understand! If I had been younger I wld. have let him go rather – but at my age it wld. be hazardous and disagreeable and so he remains living in my House wherever we are!! And she quite consents to it. But it is too tiresome and I can't conceal my annoyance. I have never said a word to her yet. It is a gt. mésalliance for her, but he has money of his own.

The Queen was without doubt angry at the inconvenience which this marriage would cause, but her snobbish attitude towards it was inexcusable since it was a trait which she so despised in others and, in fairness to her, it was not normally something she was prone to.

Before leaving for Balmoral the Queen dictated to Harriet Phipps some regulations which were to be observed by Reid and Susan after their marriage. Fortunately he had been forewarned by Harriet Phipps, and wrote to Susan: 'Domestique *quite* nice, but full of fuss! She says Bipps is writing me a paper, laying down all the conditions we have to observe when we are married! I expect it will be a rather interesting and unique document worthy of being handed down as an heirloom! You shall have it as soon as I get it: but D. says it may take some time, as Bipps is bestowing much thought and attention on all the clauses!!' The Queen's regulations, mercifully written out in Harriet Phipps' handwriting, were as follows:

> I think it absolutely necessary that Sir J. Reid and Miss Baring should know exactly what their position will be when they are married. Sir James knows that considering my age, I cannot well allow him to leave his present post. This will entail that he must continue living in the House *wherever* we are, excepting for a fortnight and two or three days holiday in the spring, and five weeks (divided) in the autumn when he has his holiday. He must always, as now, come round after breakfast to see what I should want, and then be back before luncheon. He must also in the afternoon, before he goes out, do the same. Of course as the days shorten and in the winter, he would go out earlier and come back earlier. Sir James should always ask if he wishes to go out for longer, or to dine out, returning by eleven or half past eleven. His wife should not come up to his room here, nor to the Corridor, where some of the Royal Children live. At Windsor she might occasionally come to his room but this must not interfere with his other duties. It is absolutely necessary that they should be fully aware of these conditions so that they cannot complain afterwards.

Once again it is difficult to believe that the Queen was addressing adults, let alone an eminent physician approaching his half century. There was no alternative but to treat these regulations light-heartedly and with a sense of humour. Reid posted 'The Queen's Regulations' off to Susan in London who 'was very much *amused* by the Dossier; it is very funny and I think most harmless and much less violent than expected. Of course you would go to her as usual after breakfast, etc: She evidently had a panic that I should be "Madame Moi-Aussi" and come too, to feel her pulse!'

The regulations concerning their marriage had been issued, but by 22 August when Randall Davidson wrote to Reid there was still no announcement of the engagement: 'I wish the shackles that restrain you from telling your friends at Osborne were removed. I am sure you are wise in not letting H.M. know that I was in the secret. It is far better that she should think that she was the first to know. There is a pathos as well as a comicality in what you tell me as to the conditions she lays down for you!' At last, however, on 24 August, exactly a month after Reid had asked Susan to be his wife, the Queen relented. 'Domestique has just told me that Bipps says I may *now* tell the *men* here "in a quiet way, and ask them not to talk much about it!"' But this was impossible. Once the news was out there was

No caution as to reticence. At luncheon Brocklehurst [the new equerry] told Misses Hughes and Majendie, who were on each side of him, and it went round the table like lightning. After we got up, I was surrounded and mobbed by everybody and my hand nearly shaken off. Miss Hughes says she is to hug me the first time she catches me alone, and even Miss Bauer is now satisfied! I told her that I had heard that she was shocked at *our* ongoings, and that we had taken it so much to heart that we felt we *must* get married, to put it all right! I have to promise to go to the ladies' tea under the cedar tree.

Letters poured in from all quarters after the engagement had been announced in the newspapers. Sir Henry Ponsonby's wife Mary, who was Susan's aunt, and her daughter Magdalen (Maggie), were overjoyed and Magdalen wrote: 'Mama and I have been so much thinking how delighted Papa would have been.' Lord Pembroke's [Lord Steward of the Household] only fear was, 'that the Queen may have instantly sent for the Lord High Executioner, and that you may have lost your head before receiving this!' Lord Rosebery wrote, 'I never thought of you as a marrying man, but you were too wise not, sooner or later, to embrace that prospect of happiness.' Prince Charles of Denmark shared Lord Rosebery's view but the Queen's equerry,

William Carington, wrote to Reid in a more jocular vein: 'A reformed
rake makes the best husband so you are bound to be all right. Muther
is now the only "*célibataire*" on the permanent staff, what a devil of a
fellow he will be! L'affaire Reid has quite snuffed out L'affaire
Dreyfus[3] as far as I am concerned.' From Princess Louise Reid
received a sympathetic letter sixteen pages long and marked
'*private*'.

> I only hope your life won't be made too difficult, and it grieves me to think
> that it has not been easy so far for you. But with time these difficulties
> will let us hope pass when H.M. has got used to the fact of looking upon
> you as a married man. Since hearing from you, in a letter the Queen wrote
> on some business she informed me of your engagement, from which I
> gather she did not quite like it. How trying for you, and I must say unkind
> of the Queen not to have spoken to you on the subject all these weeks
> when you have served her *so* loyally and unselfishly; it was such a charming
> opportunity of showing her gratitude. But I am sure when left to herself
> and others no longer speak to her on the subject she will come round.

On 31 August, the day that the Court was moving to Balmoral,
Reid received a letter from the Queen, her first recognition of his
proposed marriage. For five weeks since his engagement he had seen
the Queen daily, and sometimes – as on 17 August – as many as six
times during the day, and yet she had said nothing to him on the
subject which was so close to his heart. The tone of her letter was
formal and stiff and for the first time in several years she wrote in the
third person.

> Before leaving Osborne the Queen is anxious to express to Sir James Reid
> her sincere good wishes for his happiness in his intended marriage with
> Miss Susan Baring. The Queen cannot deny that she thinks their position
> will present many difficulties, but she feels sure that they will both do
> their utmost to lessen as much as possible the unavoidable inconvenience
> to the Queen and that Sir James will still faithfully devote himself to his
> duties as in the past.

Reid was both delighted and relieved at long last to have had his
betrothal acknowledged and replied to the Queen in a manner which
her own behaviour barely justified.

---

[3] Alfred Dreyfus was a victim of virulent anti-Semitism. A Jewish officer in the
French army, he was falsely accused and convicted of treachery in 1893. The case
was reopened in 1899, but it was not until 1906 that his innocence was proved and
the verdict reversed.

It is the earnest desire of Miss Baring, no less than of himself, that whatever inconvenience may arise from their marriage shall be felt by themselves alone, and that Your Majesty shall find no difference, and experience no inconvenience, from their union. Miss Baring has repeatedly expressed herself strongly in this sense; and it is the firm purpose of both to carry it out. Sir J. Reid's devotion to Your Majesty is as absolute as is his gratitude for all the favours shown to him, and the confidence reposed in him, by Your Majesty during these long years: and these feelings on his part nothing can ever shake or alter. Your Majesty may, under all circumstances, rely implicitly on his fidelity and honour: and neither his marriage nor anything else will ever make the slightest difference in his discharge, both in the letter and in the spirit, of the duties pertaining to the position of trust that it is his proudest privilege to occupy with Your Majesty.

On his journey from Osborne to Balmoral Reid was fêted both by the ship's officers and by the attendants and guards on the train, many of whom he had known ever since he had joined the Household. He was immediately busy at Balmoral when Mrs Tuck became seriously ill for many days with a nervous breakdown. Being the Queen's chief dresser was no easy matter, and now that Her Majesty's sight had deteriorated she was becoming more demanding than ever. Reid was in constant attendance both upon the Queen and Mrs Tuck, but eventually he was released and went to Ellon with Susan, whom he had met at Aberdeen. There for the first time she met his mother, his brother and sister-in-law, John and Mary, and their daughter, Meta, at The Chesnuts. It was to be a brief but happy meeting, 'Susan accommodating herself beautifully to her surroundings,' Reid confided happily to his diary.

All too soon it was time for her to go into waiting at Balmoral during his absence. Susan had written to him when he was at Balmoral, 'I have fearful curling toes at the thoughts of my waiting. I do dread it rather; I feel green from shyness! and I *shall* be so bored without you.' But she was not to be without her fiancé for long, for soon after she had arrived at Balmoral Sir Douglas Powell, Reid's locum and Physician-in-Ordinary to Queen Victoria, became ill and Harriet Phipps telegraphed to Reid to come at once. He needed no second bidding and within a few hours had reached the Castle, to find that Powell, on the previous night, had fallen down in a faint in Her Majesty's Drawing Room and bruised his face, but was feeling better by the time Reid saw him. Susan and he made the most of their time together, talking and walking by the river. Balmoral was, as usual, bulging at the seams and the housekeeper was obliged to put Reid in the stables, much to the annoyance of the Queen when she discovered this later.

Powell's recovery was all too rapid and Reid had to leave Susan and return to Ellon. This must have been the only occasion when he was reluctant to go home. But Susan kept him informed of all that was happening at Balmoral.

Yesterday we had the Carriage shut, and I had to read the newspapers, which I didn't like much! it was so dark and shaky and difficult to read. The Queen laughed when I told her Maggie was most amused about my engagement! She said 'we were all very much *amused*! We didn't know he was so dangerous!' That broke the ice and really she was more than nice. Now it is all over I am bird [happy], and she said nothing about our life, or difficulties, or *position* or commandments! so all is well I think.

Another time, while driving with the Queen and Princess Beatrice, Susan had a discussion about wedding presents.

Bipps was nice to me and they both talked a good deal about my wedding presents. Bétrave [Princess Beatrice] said she would like to give us a breakfast service. I didn't like to say it was the one thing we didn't want as I thought it would sound ungrateful, but I am going to make Domestique say we have got one. I am sure she would choose such an ugly one! Bipps was very funny saying to me, '*I* shall not give my present till nearer the time. I never do, as it is so awkward sometimes when they have to be sent *back*! not that I mean it would be so in your case, but sometimes marriages *are* broken off.' We all laughed very much! Perhaps she has a dim hope that you may get tired of me before November!

By the middle of October the Queen had still not quite recovered from the shock of Reid's and Susan's intended marriage. In a letter to Susan her cousin Elizabeth Bulteel describes a conversation she had with the Queen while they were out on their daily drive at Balmoral. 'The Queen said, "My dear Bessie, weren't you astonished when you heard it?" Of course I had to say "Yes", and asked her if she hadn't been. "I'm afraid I was more than astonished. I was rather *angry*. I did not expect to have my Maid-of-Honour snapped up before *my very nose*!"' Susan had already left Balmoral and returned to London to make preparations for the wedding, but Reid was there on duty. Bessie 'was glad to see Sir James, I can't call him Jamie; I feel he is another man if I do, but I daresay I shall get used to it in time!' The young maids-of-honour, nearly all of whom were cousins of Susan, found it difficult to become familiar with the Queen's revered doctor, too. In time Reid was to suffer indigestion from a surfeit of Susan's relations: the ubiquitous Barings, Bulteels and Ponsonbys. There always seemed to be either a christening, wedding, or funeral to attend.

Their wedding was arranged for the end of November at St Paul's, Knightsbridge; 'but you will certainly be suffered to have adopted advanced High Church opinions under the glamour of your new prospects', wrote Randall Davidson, who was to marry them. 'Had you better not fix St Andrew's Day (Thurs. Nov. 30) so as to emphasise your Caledonian loyalty?' Reid disregarded this suggestion and 28 November was the chosen day.

A week before the wedding the German Emperor and Empress came to Windsor Castle on a State visit and Reid, in Levée dress, was present at their arrival. Both royal families and their respective Suites lunched and dined in great splendour in the Waterloo Room. After dinner the Kaiser spoke to Reid and chaffed him about his marriage. Before his departure to Sandringham the Kaiser presented him with the Royal Prussian Order of the Crown (2nd Class), an honour which gave him special pleasure to receive just before his wedding, as also did his present from the Queen, a magnificent box of silver knives, forks and spoons with the family crest engraved upon them. Susan was given a diamond brooch, bearing the royal cypher 'V.R.I.', an Indian shawl, and a signed photograph of the Queen, as wedding presents.

The day after the wedding Mary Reid wrote to her mother-in-law about it.

It was an ideal day for a wedding, clear bright sunshine and as warm as Summer. The church was beautifully decorated with palms and white lilies and chrysanthemums, and the music was exquisite. Everyone remarked on how happy Jamie looked and I never saw him look better. He wore such a pretty fawn coloured waistcoat and white silk tie and was so well turned out. The bride was very punctual and came up the aisle preceded by the choir boys singing and conducted by Lord Revelstoke. She looked sweet but very white, and for a moment seemed as if she were going to faint, but recovered and was alright for the rest of the time. I think she was just over-tired and naturally a little nervous. She had a lovely wedding dress of soft white satin and lovely old lace which suited her well. The little page boys [Jack and Cecil Spencer] were sweet in their white sailor costumes; they walked next to the bride, then the two youngest bridesmaids [Delia Spencer and Cecily Browne] and last Lady Castlerosse's eldest girl and Meta who are about the same height. The dresses were very pretty in pink and white and the hats quite lovely.

The church was crowded and the guests of honour were Queen Victoria's three daughters, the Princesses Helena, Louise and Beatrice. So many of the royal Household and staff had attended the wedding that the Queen was heard to say in an anxious voice beforehand, 'And who shall bring me my tea?' She need not have worried for, 'at the end of the service, Princess Beatrice had kissed Susan so affectionately and said she was sorry she could not come to the reception afterwards as Mama was alone and she must go back to Windsor. We then went on to Lord Northbrook's house in Hamilton Place where there was a great crush, but everything splendidly managed. When we had all finished tea Princess Louise proposed the Bride and Bridegroom's health and then we all went to see them start and shower rice on them.'

From Paddington the bridal couple took the train to Maidenhead and drove to Taplow Court, the Grenfell family home, where they spent the first few days of their honeymoon. The Grenfells were away and so they were spared the glittering galaxy of Souls who normally inhabited the vast, spacious house. Peaceful as it was, they were not left entirely to their own devices, for not many days had passed before a letter arrived from the Queen. 'I am anxious to know if you would come over for an hour or two on Wednesday as I have to speak to you about Rankin who seems to [have] delusions and is again quarrelsome. I think we must come to some decision.' Her shoulder was aching and she was suffering from flatulence and indigestion. The Boer War was also worrying. 'I think it is the anxiety. My appetite is not very good.' Poor Reid, even his honeymoon was not sacrosanct, and Susan learnt early on in her married life that the Queen was most definitely 'Madame Moi-Aussi'.

Reid sent a reply saying that he would come to Windsor on the appointed day, but a second letter from the Queen forestalled him. 'I find on enquiring that poor Rankin is really trying to behave himself, and that tho' he is full of suspicions nothing should warrant his being pensioned as yet. So I *will* not require you to come over. I have gone through so much anxiety that I am not surprised I shld. get bilious. The bowels are acting fully.' The newly married couple were relieved and delighted to be left in peace to enjoy the rest of their honeymoon at the Stud House, Hampton Court, and at Sandown, on the Isle of Wight, where they stayed in the Royal Suite of the Ocean Hotel.

11

The End of an Era

Whilst luxuriating in the comfort of the Royal Suite at Sandown, Reid and his wife began to look for a small house where Susan could live while he was on duty at Osborne. It was essential to find a place within easy walking distance of Osborne House so that, when he was free, he could spend as much time as possible with Susan, and she could walk up to the garden and meet him under the cedar tree. They found a small, undistinguished, semi-detached house, The Warren, in East Cowes which would tide them over until something better should turn up. Just as they were getting it in order for Christmas, by which time Reid had to resume his duties, a telegram arrived from Windsor to say that the Queen would not be coming to Osborne for Christmas as usual, but would require Reid at Windsor. This was, as Susan's sister, Margaret Spencer, wrote a 'bouleversement', and the newly married couple had to pack up yet again and move to Windsor, where Davidson had found lodgings for Susan at the White Hart Hotel. At Windsor Reid had a great reception at the Household dinner, after which he went and saw the Queen, his first audience with her as a married man.

Busy as he was with all the 'ailing in house' he still managed to find time to see Susan once or twice a day, and life was made easier by the fact that she was allowed to visit him in his room at Windsor, although strictly forbidden to do so at Osborne and Balmoral. They spent Christmas Eve with the Bigges and their children in the Norman Tower, and on Christmas Day they dined *à deux* at the White Hart Hotel, Reid returning to the Castle by eleven p.m. on both days.

On 28 December the Court moved to Osborne and Susan settled down in The Warren. Early in the new year the Queen caught a feverish cold and cough and Reid was much in demand, his bicycle being in constant use as he whizzed from Osborne to The Warren and back again at least twice a day and sometimes more. Life for Susan was at times lonely, living as she did in a furnished house, but she livened up the afternoons with a series of tea parties, and on occasions she was invited to dine with the Queen at Osborne.

The Queen, meanwhile, was thinking of changing her usual routine for her Continental holiday and going to Bordighera instead of to Cimiez, but when Reid heard how insanitary the Hotel Angst at Bordighera was he decided that the arrangements for the holiday must

191

be altered. The Duke of Connaught thought that the Queen should not go abroad at all on account of the criticism from the Continent of Britain's role in the Boer War and, when approached, the Queen herself admitted to having been thinking of giving up her foreign trip and going to Ireland for three weeks instead. She needed little persuading from Reid, who had accompanied her to see the sick and the wounded at Netley Hospital, many of whom were Irish troops. The troubles caused by the war weighed heavily upon her and we have seen how they had begun to take their toll on her health. She knew, too, that it would be unpatriotic of her to go abroad to France at a time when her presence was needed at home, both at her desk and with her wounded soldiers. She was never one to shirk her duty in moments of crisis.

Reid's own health was not quite as it should have been either, although he presented to the world his usual sanguine disposition. He had been to London with Susan to see Douglas Powell, who had 'overhauled' him and found that he was not 100 per cent fit. He smoked too much and he had been plagued yet again by boils on his neck, similar to those from which he had suffered during the period of 'Munshimania'. The responsibility for the Queen's health which, in her eighty-first year, was rapidly deteriorating and becoming a worry to him, was beginning to affect him and, in addition, his married life was far from ideal, living as he did in a separate establishment from his wife. He reported Powell's opinion of his health to Princess Beatrice, not wishing to concern the Queen about it.

On 2 April 1900 the Queen set out for Ireland on what was to be her last journey in her old yacht the *Victoria and Albert*. She had not crossed St George's Channel since 1861, and now she was going to thank the Irish in person for all the gallantry their troops had shown in the war. Reid described the crossing as 'smooth but rainy' and Susan, who had travelled separately, wrote in a letter to his mother: 'It was very pretty coming into Kingstown Harbour to see the Fleet and the Queen's Yacht all decorated with flags; they had arrived a few hours before I did, so Jamie came out in a little launch and met me and put me into my train.' Before dinner the channel fleet was illuminated and a procession of boats from the warships, also illuminated, sailed round the *Victoria and Albert* and cheered Her Majesty. Reid dined on board with the Queen and several naval officers.

At eleven thirty on the following morning, in Levée dress, Reid rode in the Queen's procession from the Victoria Wharf to the Viceregal Lodge. Susan saw him embark upon his journey. 'Jamie was in the first carriage and I saw him very well but he was not able to make me out as there were so many people waving handkerchiefs! Poor Queen looked rather tired but she said she was *not* and was able to go for her drive as usual in the afternoon.' In her Journal the Queen describes the journey.

> We three wore bunches of real shamrocks, and my silver bonnet and parasol were embroidered with silver shamrocks. On entering my carriage, in which I sat alone, Lenchen [Princess Christian] and Beatrice opposite me, an Address was presented from the Chairman and Councillors of Kingstown, and I said a few words in handing my reply. The procession, consisting of four carriages, then started, mine coming last. Arthur [Connaught] rode near my carriage all the way, and I had a travelling escort of the King's Dragoon Guards. The whole route from Kingstown to Dublin was much crowded, all the people cheering loudly, and the decorations were beautiful.
>
> The drive lasted two hours and a half. We went all along the quays in the poorer parts of the town, where thousands had gathered together and gave me a wildly enthusiastic greeting. At Trinity College the students sang 'God Save the Queen', and shouted themselves hoarse. The cheers and often almost screams were quite deafening. Even the Nationalists in front of the City Hall seemed to forget their politics and cheered and waved their hats. It was really a wonderful reception I got and most gratifying.
>
> Lord and Lady Cadogan received and welcomed me at the door of the Viceregal Lodge. I recognised the outside of the building, but not the inside. I was rolled a good way to the staircase, up which I was carried, as there was no lift. I have very comfortable rooms.

Reid also 'got a nice room at the Lodge', but, having been party to the Queen's tumultuous welcome in the morning, was delighted to be able to walk alone in Phoenix Park and in the private grounds of the Viceregal Lodge in the afternoon.

Susan's letter to her mother-in-law continued: 'Jamie is very well and seems to enjoy the novelty of being in Ireland! He has to go to Dublin today to be received as Honorary Fellow of the Royal College of Physicians. He hoped he would not have to make a speech!' Making speeches was not a pastime which Reid enjoyed, and whenever possible he tried to avoid it. Not only was he made an Honorary Fellow of the Royal College of Physicians, but he was also granted an Honorary M.D. by the University of Ireland, much to his amazement. 'I am rather overwhelmed by the doctors, who seem rather a nice lot, and inundate me with invitations!' he wrote to his mother. 'The Irish people make much more noise than we are accustomed to!'

What with attending all the functions arranged for the Queen, amongst them the inspection of 40,000 Irish children in Phoenix Park, the musical party given by the Connaughts, the State banquet given at Dublin Castle, and military and naval reviews, as well as the numerous calls upon his attention by the Irish doctors, Reid was kept busy in a round of social activity. He did, however, manage to visit the Adelaide and Mater Misericordiae Hospitals with Princess Christian, and he also made a tour of the Meath Hospital. He vaccinated Prince Drino, eldest son of Princess Beatrice, preparatory to his going to Wellington College for the summer term, and he attended Prince Arthur Connaught, who went down with German measles. He had, too, to look after Dosse, the Queen's courier, who became seriously ill with pulmonary congestion and had to be left in the care of another doctor when Reid returned to Windsor. Otherwise his medical duties were limited. The Queen, buoyed up by the excitement and novelty of the Irish visit, was in remarkably good health although, hardly surprising at her age, she did get tired from time to time. Her ailments were always worse at home where there was less distraction from them.

On 26 April the Queen left Ireland, greatly moved by the warmth of a reception which had far exceeded her expectations, and in her gratitude to the Irish people she wrote them an effusive letter, which ended, as *The Times* reported, with the words: 'The Queen earnestly prays that goodwill and harmony may prevail amongst all her people, and that they may be happy and prosperous.' Alas, her hopes remained unfulfilled and although the Irish people united briefly in the warmth of their welcome for this little old lady, within less than two decades they were to become embroiled in the horrors of a civil war, thus denying themselves all that the Queen had prayed for.

On her way back to Windsor the Queen received a great reception at Chester and at Wolverhampton, but apart from a visit to Wellington College in May, where she saw her grandson, this was Queen Victoria's last journey away from her three royal residences. It was also one of the happiest excursions of her later years.

Reid returned to Windsor to find that Susan was ill with a threatened miscarriage, known in the Baring family as a 'mademoiselle voiture'. This drollery could not disguise Susan's low state of health and spirits when, despite the best attentions of the royal gynaecologist, Sir John Williams, she lost her baby. On recovering enough to travel, Susan went to Ellon while Reid was on duty at Balmoral, where in the middle of June he received the welcome news that the Queen was to lend Susan May Cottage during their time at Osborne. This was a great improvement on The Warren and more than he had hoped for.

On 11 July the Queen held a Garden Party at Buckingham Palace which both Susan and Reid attended. There were 5,000 guests assembled on a brilliant hot and sunny day, and as they roamed over the beautifully kept green lawns beside the lake they presented a dazzling sight in their coloured uniforms, picture hats, and long floating muslin dresses. In the centre was the Queen, sitting in her carriage pulled by two grey horses, and behind her came her family: the Prince of Wales, the Duke and Duchess of York, the old Duke of Cambridge and Princess Beatrice with Princess Ena. The Queen's customary black accoutrements were relieved by white feathers and a rose in her bonnet, there were pearls around her neck and she carried a white parasol. Sadly, this great day proved to be her swansong and her last grand public occasion, though she still reserved some energy for inspecting her troops when they returned from the Boer War.

Her health was beginning to decline and others started noticing. Reid received a letter from Sir Francis Laking, the Prince of Wales' doctor, saying: 'The Prince of Wales does not think the Queen is looking well and that he is afraid the Queen is dieting herself too strongly and not taking sufficient food and wine to keep herself up.' She had lost weight and was sleeping badly. Her memory, which formerly had always served her well, was letting her down, and she was forced to exert additional mental effort which tired her. Her failing sight did not make life any easier for her as she had to rely entirely upon Princess Beatrice and her maids-of-honour to read to her. Nevertheless, she still travelled to Osborne in July, to Balmoral in September, and to Windsor in November.

At Osborne Susan installed herself at May Cottage, and renewed her series of tea parties. Perhaps she became a little too sociable for Reid, who noted in his diary on 3 August that he was 'rather upset at not seeing Susan alone all day!' Several times he went on board the *Thistle* to see the Empress Eugénie, who was ailing. Then the news of the assassination of King Humbert of Italy broke the peace at Osborne, and was followed closely by the arrival of a telegram for the Queen which announced the death of Prince Alfred, Duke of Coburg, from cancer. Reid was, quite naturally, worried about the effect that this family tragedy would have upon the Queen's health, but she behaved with great fortitude and bore it well. Although she demanded to see him constantly, he wrote in his diary that she had 'a good night and was as well as could be expected'. The Kaiser was concerned for his grandmother, and sent the following telegram to Reid: 'Should be grateful for news from Grandmama. I hope the sad facts have not harmed her constitution. Leave for Coburg tonight. W.I.R.'

On 1 September the Court moved to Balmoral for the last time during Queen Victoria's reign. Once again, Slatin Pasha stayed there, and Reid and he had much to talk over in the Smoking Room until the early hours of the morning, together with Prince Henry of Prussia. But he was required urgently elsewhere, for an anxious Susan, who thought she might be pregnant again, wired him from Ellon to say that she needed him as Dr Fowler was ill, and she was afraid of not being within reach of medical aid should she once again suffer a miscarriage. With the Queen's permission Sir Douglas Powell was sent for and Reid got leave to go to Ellon. He found Susan well enough, but confined to her bed where, on Sir John Williams' orders, she was compelled to remain for several weeks. On 25 September Reid returned to Balmoral where he saw the Queen for a long time as, during his absence, she had been suffering from acute dyspepsia. After a week she began to improve, but Reid thought that she was eating more than she could digest and told her so. He had a lively discussion with her on the subject but, as he said, 'She disagrees in toto with my views!'

There were bad reports from Germany about the Empress Frederick, who was suffering acutely from cancer of the spine. The Kaiser sent Reid five telegrams giving a detailed account of his mother's condition, but he would not succumb to the Queen's repeated offers to send Laking to see his mother. 'I won't have a repetition of the confounded Mackenzie business, as public feeling would be seriously affected here.' As it was, Empress Frederick rallied and outlived her mother by six months. Courageous to the last, she died at Friedrichshof, after a long agonising illness, on 5 August 1901.

By the middle of October it was clear that Susan was pregnant and Reid wished the Queen to be informed of her condition. Once again he invited Harriet Phipps to be his ambassador and she 'mentioned it to the Queen in the drawing room after dinner'. Her Majesty's reactions are not recorded, but Susan remained at Ellon while Reid was on duty at Balmoral.

On 29 October Reid received a telegram from Dr Bankart informing him that Prince Christian Victor of Schleswig-Holstein, Princess Christian's elder son, had died at Pretoria of enteric fever – yet another victim of the Boer War, but closer to home this time. The death of her young grandson in the prime of life affected the Queen deeply and she wrote to Reid, 'I feel quite crushed.' She could not sleep and her normal interest in food vanished. Reid noted that she was 'most depressed, and cried much', when he saw her. On 6 November, a dark and gloomy day, the Queen left Balmoral for Windsor for the last time. Normally the long autumn sojourn in her Scottish home strengthened and revived her, enabling her to face the rigours of her political and social life in the south with renewed energy. This time it was different; her insomnia and general wretchedness had left her weak and apathetic.

When Reid returned to Windsor on 10 November, after a week's holiday in Ellon, he 'found the Queen looking and feeling far from well. Foul tongue, no appetite, digestion very bad, much emaciated, bad nights, etc.' He was 'disquieted and anxious about her'. For several nights he was up attending to her and he gave her Dover's Powder to settle her. On the evening of 17 November he 'had a long interview with the Prince of Wales in his room about H.M.'. Although her appetite had returned the Queen was still 'very nervous, and always talking and thinking about her ailment'. However, by the end of the month she was decidedly better, and was able to review the Canadian Contingent from South Africa in the Quadrangle at Windsor, and also to attend a luncheon with the officers afterwards.

On 2 December Reid decided that he should send a report on the Queen's general condition to the Prince of Wales, realising that the Prince did not appreciate fully the extent of the Queen's deterioration.

Since Your Royal Highness was here, the Queen's condition has materially improved in all essential respects, but still she is not what she was before, and I begin to fear that her health may remain permanently on a lower plane than hitherto. She is sleeping and eating better, though not yet satisfactorily, and the bodily functions are in a better state. But her digestion is not at all vigorous, she is feebler generally than she used to be, her voice is weaker, and her nervous system is a good deal shaken. I am very doubtful whether, at her age, they may regain their former level.

Two days ago, with the Queen's consent, I asked Dr Barlow [Physician Extraordinary] to come and see Her Majesty with me; and, as he has repeatedly been in attendance at Balmoral, and knows her well, and is one of the most eminent authorities, I was very glad to have a consultation with him. He quite concurs in what I have stated above; and although, like myself he sees no evidence of organic disease, he thinks the Queen has gone down-hill since he last saw her over a year ago. In the course of nature this must be progressive, though with constant care and attention I trust it may be slow. Of course there is, in addition, always present the risk of some sudden illness which would be very serious at the Queen's age, and in her enfeebled state.

Dr Barlow, whom I questioned as to his opinion on the Queen's going abroad, said he considered that it would not be unattended with risk, and that it was a matter demanding serious consideration before being determined on. This, however, is a question which, I think, need not be decided immediately, until we see how Her Majesty is a few weeks hence.

The Prince of Wales replied: 'I truly understand and appreciate everything you have written. The Queen has much extraordinary vitality and pluck that I hope that the present shock and the indisposition from which she has suffered may keep away.' His Royal Highness 'thought Barlow an excellent man, but I wish you could induce the Queen to see our friend Laking'. Reid did not share the Prince's confidence in Sir Francis Laking but, complying with His Royal Highness's wishes, Laking was sent for on 9 December, but the Queen refused to see him, and became 'nervous after dinner'. On 16 December the Queen had a bad night, and Reid was called to her at five a.m. and gave her twelve grains of Trional, which acted at once. She woke up in time to attend the service in the morning, 'but slept from 3.30–5.30 p.m., and was much better, and very angry about it!' he recorded in his diary. After dinner the same evening he had a talk with Lord Salisbury about the Queen's health but, in spite of Reid's views, Lord Salisbury wanted the Queen to go abroad as usual.

In addition to the anxiety caused by the Queen's declining health, Reid had to solve the problem of where he and Susan should live while he was at Windsor. Susan could not go on for ever staying in rented rooms, especially when her child was born. Princess Louise, always a great support in times of difficulty, spoke to the Queen about their getting a house at the Castle, and the Queen agreed to give them the Small Tower next to Lady Biddulph. Reid went to see the Tower, his comment on it being 'very small, but will do'. He was relieved to have found a home, at last, and also to learn that the Queen was reconciled to his becoming a father. In a letter to Susan he wrote:

When I got in I found I had been sent for and was wanted at once by

1. Bipps
2. The Duchess of Connaught
3. Domestique!

Each of them told me *exactly* what I was to say to Bipps, and each something different! So I took my own way, and got through it far better than I expected. Bipps knows everything, and is quite composed.

On 18 December Reid left with the Queen for Osborne. 'Her Majesty stood the journey well, but was very tired, and had a long fit of nerve restlessness and depression after our arrival till she went to sleep. Was with her very often.' From this time onwards, until her death, the Queen did not go down to the dining room for her meals but had her food taken to her room and was to all intents and purposes an invalid. Reid was in regular contact with the Prince of Wales who, as he did not live with the Queen, failed to grasp the gravity of her condition and thought that the return of Christmas would 'occupy her mind and take her, I hope, out of herself'. She managed to go to the Durbar Room on Christmas Eve, as usual, and was present at the *'Bescherung'* [distribution of presents] but, as Princess Beatrice wrote to her sister, the Empress Frederick, 'She was very depressed, and generally weak, her sight is so very bad and she could hardly see all her pretty presents.' Even Christmas was unable to restore her spirits, though she still insisted on driving out daily as she had always done.

On Christmas morning, just after seven o'clock, Reid was woken and told to go to see Lady Churchill. When he got to her room he found her dead in her bed, 'having apparently died in her sleep some hours before of syncope from heart disease'. He had the unenviable task of breaking the news to the Queen that her dear friend and Lady of the Bedchamber, who had been closely associated with her for fifty years, was dead. Though much upset the Queen 'took it well and was none the worse'. She had borne so much tragedy during the past months that her feelings had become quite numb. Death, it seemed, was part of her daily life and she was growing accustomed to it, but with the demise of Lady Churchill the Queen's own will to live diminished. She existed now mostly on a diet of broth, warm milk and Benger's Food, but on 29 December she noted in her Journal that she 'managed to eat a little cold beef, which is the first I have had for weeks, and I really enjoyed [it]'.

On New Year's Day 1901 the Queen's Journal began on a gloomy note. 'Another year begun, and I am feeling so weak and unwell that I enter upon it sadly.' For Reid it was an anxious time, but he was encouraged by a letter from Princess Louise, written from Sandringham. 'I am so truly sorry for you in all this extra worry and fuss. The dear Lady [Lady Churchill] how she would *hate* causing any disturbance. The Prince has just come into the room and bids me say again what a comfort your letters and telegrams are to him, and he has such confidence in your judgment.'

On 5 January Sir Francis Laking arrived to relieve Reid for a week. Susan had her own views on the subject.

Laking's visit at Osborne is a great fraud! and does not relieve Jamie of any of his work! and all our beautiful hopes of a rest and Jamie living at May Cottage (while Laking was at Osborne) have been dashed to the ground. The Queen will not see him! at least not about her health, and she can hardly bear Jamie out of her sight! She is no worse, but has ups and downs and gets very easily over tired, and when so, she gets into a nervous depressed hopeless state. However, she sleeps and eats well and Jamie says that is all one can expect just now, but her family and Miss Phipps will insist (in spite of Jamie's opinion!!) on thinking her much better than she is and it is all he can do to prevent them overtiring her, by too much talking. The only difference Laking's visit has made is that Jamie was able to dine here twice. Last night he was to do so again but the Queen was in a nervous mood, so he gave it up, and she was so pleased and so grateful!! She does depend on him entirely now, and happily he is *very well*. I am quite pleased with his looks, and he is able to sleep well, *now* he is not disturbed at night. As things are at present Jamie thinks it is out of the question that the Queen should go abroad, and all the men of the Household are of that opinion. However, the family and Miss Phipps are still in favour of it, but I think gradually they will see for themselves that it is impossible.

This letter of 12 January is interesting in illustrating how little understanding those close to the Queen had of the gravity of her condition. Reid was the only one who realised that the monarch whom he had served for twenty years was rapidly declining, but it is doubtful whether even he imagined that within ten days of Susan's letter being written the Queen would be dead. Although she had rallied as far as eating and sleeping were concerned, Reid noted on 13 January that the 'Queen was rather childish and apathetic'. On the following day she received Lord Roberts, and this was her last official duty as Queen of England. On 15 January Pagenstecher examined the Queen's eyes, and told Reid the 'cataract was little worse but [he] confirmed my opinion (for many weeks) of cerebral degeneration. He told the Princesses Christian and Beatrice. During the past few days the Queen's disposition had quite altered; nothing annoyed her and she took apathetically things that formerly would have irritated her. When she woke from sleep in her room she was not able for some time to realise where she was.'

During the period of Queen Victoria's final illness and death Reid wrote a minutely detailed account of all that occurred. As he was with the Queen constantly, hour by hour, day and night, tending to her every need, he, more than anyone else, was in a position to record accurately the events which took place. The diary which he kept during these days is a unique historic document and, as such, justifies being quoted in full.

16 January
The Queen had rather a disturbed night, but was very drowsy all forenoon, and disinclined to get up, although she kept saying in a semi-confused way that she must get up. I saw her asleep in bed in the forenoon, as I was rather anxious about her, and the maids said she was too drowsy to notice me. This was the first time I had ever seen the Queen when she was in bed. She was lying on her right side huddled up and I was struck by how small she appeared. She looked well and her breathing was quiet and normal. She did not get up till 6 p.m. when she had a dress loosely fastened round her and was wheeled into the sitting room. At 7.30 I saw her and found her complexion good, but she was dazed, confused, and aphasic.

I asked her to see Laking, as he was going away next day, and she said yes, and I got the maids to remind her. Accordingly at 8 he was sent for, I having told him about the Q's dazed condition. And at 8.45 as I was going down to dinner I met him coming back, and to my surprise he told me the Queen was all right, that she had been speaking to him for ¾ hour on a great many topics and was quite herself, in fact that he did not believe she was as bad as I thought. I told him it was only an instance of how wonderfully she could pull herself together when she saw anyone but her maids or me, and that I should not wonder if she were quite confused again after he had left. 10 minutes later I was sent for by the maids and found H.M. quite exhausted and as confused as ever. She went back to bed at once. I wrote tonight to the Prince of Wales, and told him exactly what I thought about the Queen. I felt now so anxious about the Queen that I told Miss Phipps I should so much like to get Sir D. Powell to come and see H.M. with me, the difficulty being how to tell the Queen without frightening her. Miss Phipps suggested that I might say he had come to see Susan who was ailing, and I thought the idea a good one. I had already written *privately* to Powell this morning telling him I was very anxious and might want him on short notice, and that he was to be ready to come at once.

It is astonishing to note that after twenty years of looking after the Queen Reid had never seen her in bed, until this moment. The various draughts and potions that he had prepared for her, at all hours of the night, over many years, must have been administered to her by one of her maids or dressers.

17 January
The Queen had a quiet night, but in the morning was, when I saw her in bed, very confused, aphasic and drowsy. I did not at all like her condition,

and thought she might be getting comatose, and might in fact die within a few days. I at once saw Princess Beatrice and Princess Christian, and told them I was very anxious and that I wanted Powell at once, to which they consented, and I wired asking him to come by the first train he could catch. When I told Laking what I had done, he said he would like to stay another day to 'help' me. The Queen was fairly quiet all the afternoon but staid in bed till 7 p.m. when she got out of bed, and was wheeled to her sitting room, dressed as last night. She asked the Princesses if people were beginning to be frightened about her, as she had not been out for 2 days, and when Princess Christian said the weather had been so bad that people would not be surprised, she replied that the people knew she always went out in rain! She also said it was 'very odd' and 'so foreign' for the Bishop of London to be buried so quickly after his death. In the evening I was rung up specially on the telephone by Mrs Tuck, who said the 'Q. wanted to know how I was, as she was afraid I would break down and be ill, and that I must have help, and I must not be allowed to break down, as "he is the only one that understands me"'. Being so anxious to prepare the public for what I feared was coming, and also thinking that her condition was too serious for it to be kept longer from the public, I thought a statement ought to be made in the Court Circular, and accordingly Bigge and I drew up a paragraph which we wished to be put in tomorrow's Circular, and in it we mentioned that I had sent for Sir D. Powell. Before sending it off, Bigge telephoned it to Marlboro' House for the P. of W.'s approval, but got a reply saying H.R.H. wished no statement whatever to be made, so we were obliged to cancel it. Powell arrived at 7.30, and I told the Queen that he was in the island and had called to see me, and, as he was in the house, I hoped she would see him. She expressed no surprise (as she would have done in her usual condition) and said certainly. So at 8.15 he saw H.M. with me for a few minutes. She was rather apathetic and did not pull herself together at all (for the first time) on seeing a stranger. She said nothing to him, except to answer rather incoherently the few questions he put to her. On leaving the room Powell said to me there could be no possible doubt as to her having cerebral degeneration, and that her condition was precarious but not hopeless. H.M. later on asked if Sir Douglas was going back 'by the afternoon boat' (!); and the maids told her I should like him to stay a little and help me, to which she at once said certainly.

During these days when Reid was busy with the Queen, Susan saw little of him. However, on 17 January she managed to meet him 'for a minute' in the bicycle house, when he told her how seriously ill he thought the Queen was. Susan informed Reid's mother that:

Laking is no good. Last night he saw the Queen and thought her wonderfully well!!! and Jamie saw her after he did and thought her all wrong. By what Jamie said this morning (though I saw him so hurriedly) I fear there is not much hope. I know how much you feel for Jamie. It is wonderful what he has been to her all these years, and now, if the end comes, I know it will be a wrench to him, and what a sensation in the world! the only consolation is that I don't think one could wish her to live in a state of childishness, which from the present state of her brain seems inevitable.

Susan saw the chances of her living at Windsor receding. 'I wonder if we shall live in the little Windsor Tower! I fear not.'

On the same day Reid scribbled a note to Susan in which he said: 'Princess B. *volunteered* to say that you are to come up here as much as you like, as I can't go to you. She says you can have the room next to the Council Room to sit in, if there isn't time to come all the way to mine.'

18 January
Queen had a fair night; little change from yesterday. She remained in bed all day until 8 p.m. and I saw her at frequent intervals. Respiration 23, pulse 72, rather tense. She took food well, mostly in liquid form. Her mind was fairly clear but there was some aphasia and the articulation was bad. The right side of her face was rather flat, and the left side drooping. She slept much and was very weak. In the afternoon, knowing that the Kaiser relied on me to let him know if his grandmother was very ill, I sent him this telegram: 'Disquieting symptoms have developed which cause considerable anxiety. This is private. Reid.' No one knew I had sent it, as I knew the Princesses would disapprove. Laking left for London at 1 o'clock to my great relief, as he took up so much of my time by talking, and was no help to me. I did not take Powell to see H.M. during the day, as I did not know how she might take it, but at 7 p.m. I took him to see her in bed, after asking if I might do so. He saw her again with me at 8.45 when she had been wheeled into the sitting room, while her bed was made. He did not think her better. I thought her intellectually rather worse, but not vegetatively. In the afternoon she said to me, 'Is there anyone in the house?' I did not know what she meant, but she at once added, 'Is the Prince of Wales here?' I said no, but that he could come if she would like to see him, and she replied 'I do not advise it at present.'

In the evening 8.15 I got, to my great surprise, a telegram from Laking who had just seen the Prince of Wales, saying, 'Everything considered quite satisfactory. He hopes to go to the country until Monday', meaning Sandringham where he was to receive guests, Laking evidently not yet realising the gravity of the situation, or at all events not having impressed the Prince with it. Bigge telephoned to Marlborough House that he was overwhelmed with telegraphic and other enquiries regarding the Queen's health about which alarming reports were already in circulation, and that he thought some statement must be published; and the Prince of Wales then consented to the publication tomorrow of a modification by him of the statement we had wished to publish this morning, omitting the most alarming part of it as well as the fact that Powell had been summoned to Osborne.

It is generally thought that the Kaiser learnt of the Queen's condition from the Duke of Connaught, who happened to be staying in Berlin at the time. This is unlikely since the Princesses and the Prince of Wales had played down the Queen's illness. Reid had always maintained close contact with the Kaiser on matters concerning the Queen's health, and it was undeniably the telegram quoted above which prompted the Kaiser to come to England immediately.

19 January

The Queen passed a fair night, but was rather worse in the morning, being very weak, wandering, and incoherent, taking food well but in an automatic way; tongue furred. Princess Christian, who was sending daily telegraphic reports to the Prince of Wales, still took a sanguine view and wrote a favourable report this morning, saying 'the Queen had passed a good night, was taking food well, and that she felt happier about her', but ignoring all the essential and unfavourable points. In the meantime I happened to go to Bigge's room just as he was in telephonic communication with Sir Francis Knollys at Marlborough House, who was asking him for the Prince of Wales how the Queen was, and whether he should go to Sandringham as arranged. Seeing me come in, Bigge asked Knollys to wait a minute, as I had just come in and he would get my opinion, which I gave as follows: 'Tell the Prince of Wales that in my opinion he ought not to go to Sandringham but to remain in London ready to come here at a moment's notice; that I consider the Queen's condition is a most serious one, and that I think it quite possible she might be dead within a few days.' After this had been done, Princess Christian's message, above quoted, was sent by her for Bigge to cypher, and Bigge, struck by its tenor so contradictory to mine, went up to see the Princess and point this out to her before sending it. She sent for me at once, while Bigge was there, and rather angrily upbraided me for sending such a report in contradiction to hers. (She did not want the Prince to come, and for some days had been telling me how undesirable it would be for the Prince and Princess of Wales to come.) I replied that I had told the Prince of Wales my exact opinion, that I considered the Queen was worse, and in a very dangerous state, whereas anyone getting *her* telegrams would naturally conclude that H.M. was going on satisfactorily and form an opinion of her progress the reverse of the truth: but that when I was asked *my* opinion I gave it. She was much annoyed at first, but she soon calmed down, and said, 'Then the Prince had better come', and accordingly she substituted that for her other telegram, and the Prince arrived at 5 p.m., the Princess of Wales coming from Sandringham late in the evening. Powell saw the Queen with me repeatedly during the day, and we issued our first bulletin in the forenoon. 'The Queen is suffering from great physical prostration accompanied by symptoms that cause anxiety.' Before luncheon I met the Princesses Christian and Beatrice who had just heard that the Kaiser was starting today for England with the Duke of Connaught (who was in Germany for the Anniversary of something and had been telegraphed for to return). They were most excited about it and said the Kaiser must be stopped at all hazards, and that they had telegraphed to the Duke of Connaught to do so. This rather startled me as I had no doubt the Kaiser was coming on account of my secret telegram to him, which they knew nothing about, and I thought I might get into a pretty row if it came out I had sent it. I had still more misgivings, as the Queen in the afternoon and evening became clearer in intellect, and I feared that this being so, the agitation of the Kaiser's coming, if she realised it, might give her the impression that we considered her dying, and help to turn the scale in the wrong direction. I thought of telegraphing to Flushing to stop the Kaiser (who had actually started), or, at all events, to warn him that if he came he could not see his grandmother at present, but Bigge informed me that the Government had already sent a ship to meet and escort him: so I gave up the idea.

About 6 o'clock, when I was seeing the Queen, she was clear and talked to me coherently though with difficulty. Among other things she said to me, 'Am I better? I have been very ill.' I said, 'Yes, Y.M. has been very ill but you are now better.' She added, 'You must be very tired, but you must not break down, you ought to have help.' I told her Sir Richard [Douglas Powell] was with me and was a great help, which seemed to please her. Then she said, 'There is much better news from South Africa today', evidently referring to some telegram which the Princesses had mentioned to her, and showing how even then she had got the war in her mind. She next said, 'I think the Prince of Wales should be told I have been very ill, as I am sure he would feel it.' I replied 'H.R.H. does know as I have reported to him all that I think Y.M. would wish me to tell him, and Sir F. Laking who went back yesterday has also told him. He is most concerned and is anxious to come as soon as Your Majesty would like to see him. Would Y.M. like him to come now?' She replied 'Certainly, but he needn't stay.' (The Prince was already in the house.) All this made me think the Queen was really better, and I again became hopeful that she might still pull through after all, though of course still most anxious and feeling that a day or two would decide one way or the other. Later on when I went to see her with Powell, she said to Mrs Tuck, 'I want everybody to go out except Sir James', and so they all went out leaving me alone with her. When I told her that everybody had gone out, she looked in my face and said, 'I should like to live a little longer, as I have still a few things to settle. I have arranged most things, but there are still some left, and I want to live a little longer.' She appealed to me in this pathetic way with great

205

trust as if she thought *I* could make her live. In the evening we issued a rather more favourable bulletin: Osborne, January 19th, 6 p.m. 'The Queen's strength has been fairly maintained throughout the day, and there are indications of slight improvement in the symptoms this evening.'

During the afternoon and evening I had several interviews with the Prince of Wales who was very nice, and quite agreed that it was better the Queen should not know he was in the house. I gathered however from the Princesses that, as H.M. was rather better, the Prince of Wales thought he had been brought down rather on false pretences and to some extent 'made a fool of', as they put it. He did not however say this to me, but only that my message in the morning had greatly surprised him, after Laking's report and Princess Christian's telegrams. I asked him to see Powell with me, that he might hear that he (Powell) took an equally serious view with me, which he did.

The Prince of Wales took up the view of the Princesses as to the inadvisability of the Kaiser's visit, and said the only thing he could now do was to go up to London tomorrow to meet him and keep him at Buckingham Palace, on the grounds that he could not be allowed to see the Queen at present, and this also made the Prince of Wales decline my offer to let him see the Queen from the door of her bedroom (without her knowledge), as he said he wished to be able to give the Kaiser his word of honour that not even *he* (the Prince of Wales) had been allowed to see her. He then definitely settled to go up tomorrow and intercept the Kaiser.

At night the Queen was not so well again, and very weak.

Reid not only had the anxiety and responsibility of caring for the Queen these last days of her life, but he also had to contend with opposition from the Queen's children, who still refused to believe that their indomitable mother might die. Princess Louise was at first more cooperative than the others, and sent a telegram saying, 'Could I be of any help to you, ready for anything.' But after her arrival at Osborne Reid wrote to Susan: 'Louise is as usual, much down on her sisters. Hope she won't stay long, or she will do mischief!' Susan, who kept Reid's mother in the picture, admitted that 'Jamie is privately astonished at Princess Beatrice not being more concerned and upset about her Mother's condition. She takes it all very calmly, and was *out* yesterday when the Queen sent to say she would see her!! I think Princess Christian has more feeling. She has shut her eyes wilfully to the truth for so long, that now it is a shock.'

20 January
Was up all night with the Queen, and fetched Powell repeatedly, as she was very confused and restless and evidently worse. We, for the first time, began giving her oxygen during the night. As she was now quite unable

to do anything for herself it was most difficult for the nurse and her maids to manage her in the large double bed: so in the morning we decided to try to move her onto a smaller bed. Woodford and his two men brought a screen, which the maids and I put round her bed, so that the men could not see her while they brought in and fitted together the small bed, which was in parts. They then went out, and the maids and I removing the screen wheeled the small bed close to the Queen's, and after a good deal of difficulty we together lifted her on to it. During this operation she seemed but vaguely conscious of what we were doing, though her face at times expressed discomfort. We then wheeled the small bed on which we had moved her into the corner, and put up the screen round it, while Woodford and his two men came in again and pushed the big bed out of the way towards the fireplace. This being done they retired, and we wheeled the Queen back into the position her large bed had occupied. This change we found a very great advantage during the next two days. During the day she took food fairly well, but was very apathetic and aphasic, and hardly ever intelligible. Pulse 100, respiration 28. Powell and I were again most anxious. During the day we kept reporting by telephone to the Prince of Wales who had left in the morning for London. In the evening the Queen was almost quite unconscious and had much difficulty in swallowing. I told all the Princesses that they might go and see the Queen now without any fear of doing harm. This they did, but she recognised none of them. As the condition was so bad, I telegraphed to Barlow, asking him to come and join Powell and me tomorrow morning by the 7.55 train, reaching Cowes at 12.10: but later on fearing this might be too late, I again telegraphed asking him to start if possible by the 5.40 a.m. train, reaching Cowes at 9.30. I had already two days before written to him explaining matters, and that I should probably want him to be ready to start. This I did in accordance with the Queen's private written instructions to me for the event of her serious illness.

On 12 February 1898 the Queen had spoken to Reid about what she wished to be done in case of her serious illness or death. At the same time she had handed him two memoranda on the subject, her 'private written instructions', the first in her own hand, and the second in Sir William Jenner's handwriting. The first was written when she was staying at the Glassalt Shiel, possibly in 1875.

In case of the Queen's death she wishes that her faithful and devoted personal attendant (and true friend) Brown should be in the room and near at hand, and that he should watch over her earthly remains and place it in the coffin, with Löhlein [Prince Albert's valet] or, failing him, one who may be most generally in personal attendance on her. This her Physicians are to explain in case of necessity to those of her children who may be there.

The second memorandum was written at Windsor Castle on 6 December 1875.

The Queen wishes Sir William Jenner to understand that it is her *command* that in case of serious illness she should only be attended by her own Doctors who always attend her, only calling in, after consultation with Princess Beatrice (supposing she was too ill to be herself consulted), any such Doctor or Surgeon whom her own professional Physicians *knew* the Queen *liked*, or *thought fit* to consult, or who was *not* a total stranger to herself, and *not* to yield to the pressure of any one of her other children, or any of her Ministers, for *any* one *they* might wish to name.

The Queen's daughters Princess Helena, Princess Louise and Princess Beatrice are fully aware of her wishes on the subject. She wishes to add (which they likewise know) that she *absolutely forbids anyone* but her *own four* female attendants to nurse her and take care of her, as well as her faithful *Personal Attendant, John Brown*, whose strength, care, handiness, and gentleness make him invaluable at *all* times, and most *peculiarly* so in illness, and who was of such use and comfort to her during her long illness in 1871, in lifting and carrying and leading her, and who knows how to suggest anything for her comfort and convenience.

The Queen wishes *no* one therefore but J. Brown, whose faithfulness, tact and discretion are not to be exceeded, to help her female attendants in anything which may be required for her. *In case* he should require assistance, Löhlein, her other personal attendant, and failing him any one person who Brown can entirely rely on, should give it. Princess Beatrice, from living always with the Queen, is *the one* who is to *be applied to* for all that is to be done. If it is necessary to send for anyone of the rest of the family, it is *on the express understanding* that *her wishes expressed* in this memorandum should be *strictly adhered to*, and *in no way departed from*.

Her Physician should likewise inform the Prince and Princess of Wales, and any of her sons should they be there, of these her wishes, especially regarding the calling in of any additional medical man. Her Privy Purse and Private Secretary should also be made aware of the Queen's orders on *this* point, so that *they* can *resist* the interference of any Minister. The Queen wishes never to be deceived as to her real state. This is to remain in force till such time as the Queen asks for this Memorandum.

It is curious that the Queen should have given these obsolete instructions to Reid, for John Brown, by 1898, had been dead for fifteen years and Löhlein had also died. In the event Reid fulfilled Brown's role without the assistance of a male attendant, and with the addition of superior knowledge of the Queen's circumstances. As far as calling in physicians was concerned her decrees were still relevant in 1901, and were adhered to. Reid never deceived the Queen as to her real state until she was within a few hours of dying, when he succumbed to telling white lies. On 19 January, when the Queen had said to him, 'Am I better? I have been very ill,' and Reid had replied, 'Yes, Your Majesty has been very ill, but you are now better,' he was, at the time, 'hopeful that she might pull through after all'.

20 January (continued)
In the evening we also advised the Prince of Wales to accelerate his return to Osborne and bring the Kaiser with him; we even thought, that, in the uncertainty as to how soon anything might happen, they might have to travel at night: however it was finally decided that they should start at 8 a.m. instead of at a later hour as originally thought of.

The Sunday bulletins on the Queen's health were:

January 20th, 11 a.m.
The Queen has passed a somewhat restless night. There is no material change in her condition since the last report.

January 20th, 4.30 p.m.
Her Majesty's strength has been fairly maintained throughout the day. Although no fresh developments have taken place, the symptoms continue to cause anxiety.

21 January
Was up all night with the Queen, Powell was with me, and we gave her oxygen frequently. We thought she was perhaps going to die quickly, but we did not fetch any of the Princesses, who never came to enquire at night. Towards morning however she rallied, and got stronger though was still almost unconscious until late in the morning, when she became more clear headed, and was able to speak and to swallow better. Barlow arrived at 10, and at once saw the Queen with Powell and me, but could do nothing more, though we were very glad to have him with us. In the forenoon the Queen suddenly asked for her favourite little dog 'Turi' (Italian Spitz), but unfortunately he was out for exercise and not to be found. However when he returned he was taken and put on the Queen's bed, who patted him and seemed pleased to have him beside her.

The Prince of Wales, the Kaiser, the Duke of Connaught and the Duke of York arrived in the forenoon, and I took them all in separately to look at the Queen from the foot of the bed, but I did not then think it advisable for any of them to speak to her or to rouse her. The Queen's eyesight had for some time been so bad that there was no fear of her seeing them, even if she opened her eyes. In the afternoon I saw the Kaiser who was most anxious to know about his grandmother, and thanked me for my telegram which he said had at once decided him to come. I told him that I was anxious he should see the Queen alone, and talk to her, and promised to do my best to manage it, for which he thanked me, as it was the one thing he desired, saying he had a good report to her of his mother, etc., and that he would say nothing to excite her.

In the evening I took the Prince of Wales to see the Queen and to speak to her. After the Prince of Wales left the Queen, Mrs Tuck and I went to her bedside, and H.M. took my hand and repeatedly kissed it. She evidently in her semi-conscious state did not realise the Prince had gone, and thought it was *his* hand she was kissing. Mrs Tuck, realising this, asked her if she still wanted the Prince of Wales, and she said 'yes'. The Prince returned to her bedside and spoke to her and she said to him 'Kiss my face'.

Later on I took the Princess of Wales to see the Queen and left them together for a short time.

On the same day Reid scribbled a note to Susan: 'Bipps was very bad last night, and we thought she was going to bat [Baringism for 'die']: but she has rallied and is rather better again! but is almost unconscious. Come up to the bicycle house about *12.45* and I'll come to you.' How quaint these semi-clandestine meetings were, but Susan did not want to become entangled with the royal family at this time, and thought it more tactful to stay away from the proximity of the sick room.

22 January

Was up all night; I fetched Powell and Barlow repeatedly, but remained myself the whole time. The Queen was semi-conscious, her swallowing was difficult and tracheal rales were beginning. Her cough was efficient at first, but getting weaker and ineffective towards morning. I gave oxygen repeatedly. She took a little fluid food occasionally, with difficulty in swallowing. She knew and asked for me frequently. About 9.30 a.m., when I had gone to my room for a short time to wash and change my clothes, and had asked Powell to go and take my place, he rushed up to my room, and asked me to hurry back as she looked like dying. All the family were summoned, and the Bishop of Winchester said prayers for the dying while I kept plying her with oxygen. The Princesses Christian, Louise, and Beatrice kept telling her who was beside her (the Queen for long too blind to see), mentioning each other's names and those of all the rest of the family present, but omitting the name of the Kaiser who was standing at her bedside. I whispered to the Prince of Wales, 'Wouldn't it be well to tell her that her grandson the Emperor is here too.' The Prince turned and said to me, 'No it would excite her too much', so it was not done. Later she rallied, and Powell and Barlow said her vitality was phenomenal. I sent out all the family to let her rest. She began to take food again, talked better and got clearer in her head, and I could not help admiring her clarity.

In the forenoon I went to tell the Kaiser I meant to take him to see the Queen when none of the family was there. He was very grateful and said, 'Did you notice this morning that everybody's name in the room was mentioned to her except mine.' I replied, '*yes*, and that is one reason why *I* specially wish to take you there.' For about three hours she was left comparatively alone with the maids and nurse, I looking in and out occasionally. During this time she asked for Mr Smith of Whippingham, who was sent for and waited in the house. She often smiled when she heard my voice and said, when I asked her to take food, 'Anything you like'. I helped to lift and move her when necessary, as the maids said she liked me to do it. In the forenoon I went to the Prince of Wales to report about the Queen, and said I would like to take the Kaiser to see her. He replied, 'Certainly, and tell him the Prince of Wales wishes it.' I took the Kaiser to see her, and sent all the maids out and took him up to the bedside, and said, 'Your Majesty, your grandson the Emperor is here; he has come to see you as you are so ill', and she smiled and understood. I went out and left him with her five minutes alone. She said to me afterwards, 'The Emperor is very kind.'

At one thirty p.m. Reid wrote to Susan: 'She does not look like dying just now; and I can't help admiring her determination not to give up the struggle while she can. I hardly dare to hope she may yet win, though she deserves to.' For a brief moment Reid was optimistic. 'She often smiles when she hears my voice, and says she will do "anything I like". The whole thing is most pathetic, and rather gives me a lump in the throat vulgarly called a "ridge"!'[1]

22 January (continued)
She was again getting weaker, and at about 1.45 she got very bad again, and at 3 we summoned the family once more who stayed in and about the room. The Bishop and Mr Smith kept alternately reciting prayers and verses of Scripture, but she still lingered on, and, after a time, as it was necessary to make her comfortable, I asked the family to go out again at about 4, the Princesses going to her sitting room, and the Prince of Wales and Princes, into the Prince Consort's room to write telegrams and talk. During this time after talking with Powell on the subject I asked the Prince of Wales whether it would not be better to suspend the prayers until the Queen was actually dying, as it was otherwise so painful, and he said, 'Certainly, tell him not to come into the room until I send for him.' I explained this to the Bishop who approved. At this time we sent the 4 p.m. bulletin: 'The Queen is sinking.' I returned to her room after five

---

[1] To have a ridge is to suffer in Baring vocabulary.

minutes' absence, and did not leave till she died at 6.30 p.m. The family returned soon after me, and kept going in and out, but the Kaiser remained the whole time, standing on the opposite side to me, as did the Princess of Wales. The Queen kept looking at me, and frequently gasped 'Sir James', and 'I'm very ill', and *I* each time replied, 'Your Majesty will soon be better.' A few minutes before she died her eyes turned fixedly to the right and gazed on the picture of Christ in the 'Entombment of Christ' over the fireplace. Her pulse kept beating well till the end when she died with my arm round her. I gently removed it, let her down on the pillow, and kissed her hand before I got up. When she died at 6.30, I had for the last hour been kneeling at her right side with my right hand on her right pulse all this time, my left arm supporting her in a semi upright position, helped by the Kaiser who knelt on the opposite side of the bed. The Prince of Wales was sitting behind me at the end, and Princess Louise kneeling on my right. All the rest were round about, Nurse Soal sitting on the bed at the top, and Mrs Tuck standing beside her. The Bishop of Winchester was saying prayers. The Queen kept looking at me and saying 'Sir James' frequently. When all was over most of the family shook hands with me and thanked me by the bedside, and the Kaiser also squeezed my hand in silence. I told the Prince of Wales to close her eyes. Later the Prince and Princess of Wales sent for me and thanked me together in their room, and the Prince said, 'You are an honest straightforward Scotchman', and 'I shall never forget all you did for the Queen'. The Princess cried much, shook hands and thanked me.

Later in the evening I went to see the Prince of Wales to remind him about the Queen's coffin. I found him in Edwards' room with the rest of the family, reading the Queen's written instructions about her funeral and other allied matters. It so happened that she mentioned that she wished her coffin to be made on the model of those in the Royal Vault at Windsor Castle (St George's Chapel), and on my telling the Prince that this was in the Lord Chamberlain's department, he told me to speak to Lord Clarendon, who was at Osborne (at East Cowes Castle) and fire the necessary orders. Accordingly, I wrote to Clarendon telling him that the coffin must be at Osborne on Thursday morning [the Queen died on Tuesday evening], so that the Queen's body might be put in it that day.

I was very busy and tired. I was sent for, and left the dinner table to help the maids and nurse to arrange the Queen's body and to lift it to her usual bed, and replace the latter in its normal position. (She had a ventral hernia and a prolapse of the uterus.) I left them to dress her, and saw her later, looking beautiful, surrounded by loose flowers and palms strewn on the bed.

What is astounding is that Reid observed for the first time that his patient had a ventral hernia and a prolapse of the uterus, not uncommon conditions for a woman who had borne nine children. Although he had been attending Queen Victoria for twenty years, he had obviously never examined her. Certainly, when he was away, his locum was always warned never to use a stethoscope as the Queen had a great aversion to it, but it is extraordinary that her own doctor had to treat her purely through verbal communication, especially as her natural inhibitions should have been broken down after so many childbirths.

Susan wrote simply, but with great pride, to Reid's mother:

> *Everyone* thinks it is wonderful what he has been to her all these years, and to know how she depended and clung to him to the last is so touching. When it was all over all the family came, one after the other, to Jamie to thank him for all he had done for his Queen. He said it was *very* touching. I fear the reaction after this great strain will be very trying and Jamie will feel his life so empty. I saw him for a few moments late last night. He was very exhausted and worn out with the emotions of the day, but not harassed by thinking anything more could have been done. He has all the Queen's last wishes written down by her, so of course there is still much to do.

It was typical that the Queen, even in her last hours, should not forget to include Canon Clement Smith, the vicar of Whippingham, in the reading of prayers and verses from the Bible. She would not wish him to feel left out.

The final bulletin issued on the evening of 22 January announced that 'Her Majesty the Queen breathed Her last at 6.30 p.m., surrounded by Her Children and Grandchildren.' Her oldest grandchild, the Kaiser, showed his deep attachment to his grandmother throughout. He, more than her own children, displayed finer feelings, behaving impeccably, and with a gentleness and selflessness uncharacteristic of him. His behaviour went some way towards mitigating previous misdemeanours and, as a result of it, he enjoyed a brief popularity throughout the country. It was sad that his dying mother was never to receive the same loving attention seven months later.

23 January
In the morning I saw the Queen's body and that all was nicely arranged. I took Powell and Barlow to the room to see her. I was busy in the forenoon with Powell and Barlow drawing up the report (see Appendix V). At two o'clock I cycled to May Cottage for five minutes to see Susan and Margaret [Spencer] whom I took to see the Queen. I had tea in my room with Powell and Barlow who left at 5. Susan and Margaret staid till 6.40, when I went to the Queen's room with Fuchs[2] who came

---

[2] Viennese painter and sculptor who worked in Berlin.

to make sketches. He was to have made a plaster cast of her face by the Kaiser's orders, but the Princesses were all against it and said the Queen would not have liked it. I left him at 8.10, and told the maids that he was not to be left alone with the body, but that one of them must always be there unless I was. Pfyffer[3] was hanging about there too on the pretext of having charge of Fuchs. I told the maids that my order applied to him also. The Prince of Wales[4] had left for London in the morning, so the Princess telephoned to him and got him to rescind the order for the cast.

Susan's impressions of the Queen are recorded in a letter to her sister-in-law, Mary Reid. 'I was allowed to see her on Wednesday, lying on her bed – it was so beautiful. Her face like a lovely marble statue, no sign of illness or age, and she still looked *"the Queen"*, her wedding veil over her face and a few loose flowers on her bed – all so simple and grand. I shall never forget it!' But anxiety about the future is evident already. 'Poor Jamie is exhausted in body and mind – there is still much to do and to think of – we know nothing as to our future plans! or whether Jamie will have to look out for a place!! He hopes I may be allowed to stay on here a little longer, and he would like to come back here, after the Funeral and just *rest*.'

24 January
In the morning I was in and out of the Queen's room. Fuchs and Herkomer[5] (who had just arrived to make a sketch) were at work.

The Queen's shell had not arrived from London as ordered, but instead a man from Bantings London came to measure the body. As this would have caused considerable delay, we decided that the shell must be made at once in Cowes (under the direction of Bantings' man) and brought to Osborne by 7.30 tonight, so that the body could be lifted in before dinner. I arranged this with the Princess of Wales. I then went to measure the body with Bantings' man, the Kaiser coming with us, and also the Bishop of Winchester whom we met in the passage, and who seemed to think he ought to be there, and who made himself prominent in giving directions. The Kaiser rather resented this interference, and said to me when we came out of the room 'If I were dead and my pastor came in the room like that he would be hauled out by the neck and shot in the Courtyard!'

At one o'clock I cycled to May Cottage for half an hour to see Susan and Margaret. In the afternoon the King returned from London, and

---

[3] Herr Pfyffer, secretary to the Kaiser.

[4] It took Reid another day to think of the Prince of Wales as Edward VII. The Princess of Wales would not accept her position as Queen until after Queen Victoria's funeral.

[5] Sir Hubert von Herkomer was born in Bavaria and emigrated to England, where he became a successful portrait painter.

there was a service beside the body. I had a talk with Mrs Tuck who, the night before, had read me the Queen's instructions about what the Queen had ordered her to put in the coffin, some of which none of the family were to see, and as she could not carry out Her Majesty's wishes without my help, she asked me to cooperate. Later I helped her and the nurse to put a satin dressing gown and garter ribbon and star, etc., on the Queen. We cut off her hair and rearranged the flowers. I was very busy in the evening and could not get out so Susan came up and saw me for a few minutes.

The shell came up too late for the body to be put in till tomorrow. I saw the King repeatedly about this and other matters. The Queen [Alexandra] begged me for the body to be left till the morning – 'no smell' ('Georgie ill'). After dinner we were all received by the King and kissed hands. After this I went to meet the Queen's shell and superintended its being carried into her room and being placed by the bed, on the other side from where she was lying. The bluejackets, under Lieutenant Pelly of the *Victoria and Albert*, having come up to carry the coffin downstairs were kept waiting all evening, and then were allowed to file past the body and were sent back with orders to return at ten tomorrow morning. The Duke of York came back from Marlborough House ailing – feverish – cough – and lumber pain. I sent him to bed.

This was to develop into an attack of German measles. The next day Susan wrote to her mother-in-law:

All is rather in a state of chaos here at present and everyone still fearfully busy. Jamie is the mainstay at the house! and is wanted and consulted by all, and has everything to arrange and settle. Jamie has to carry out all her last wishes as to what she wears, and photographs of the Prince Consort and her children are to be put in, also a garment worked by Princess Alice. She is to be in a white silk robe and the Order of the Garter on. I fear it will be a very sad moment for our Jamie to feel that after that, there will be nothing more he can do for *Her*. These last days he has not left the house, except for a few minutes, as he felt she was still his charge. She wished to have no lying in State and therefore embalming was not necessary, and she is to have a Military Funeral as Head of the Army. She left very minute directions as to all she wants done, which is a comfort, as it saves all discussions!

The care of the Queen's person was Reid's responsibility until the final moment when the coffin was sealed. The 'Instructions', written on 9 December 1897, 'for my Dressers to be opened directly after my death and to be always taken about and kept by the one who may be travelling with me', were strictly adhered to by Reid, who took upon himself the task of carrying them out. To be placed in the coffin were

215

rings, chains, bracelets, lockets, photographs, shawls, handkerchiefs, casts of hands – all souvenirs from her life – early, middle, and late. No friend or servant was forgotten, and each member of her family was remembered. It was truly a burial worthy of a Queen and Empress. As she had been meticulous over the funeral arrangements of her family and even her pet dog, so she was in her instructions for her own burial. In keeping with her character the arrangements for her departure from this world combined simplicity with grandeur.

25 January
At nine I saw the Duke of York in bed with a feverish attack. At 9.30 I went to the Queen's room, and arranged with Mrs Tuck and Miss Stewart to put on the floor of the Queen's coffin over the layer of charcoal 1½ inches thick the various things (dressing gown of Prince Consort, cloak of his own embroidered by Princess Alice, the Prince Consort's plaster hand, numerous photographs, etc.) which Her Majesty had left instructions with them to put in. Over these was laid the quilted cushion made to fit the shape of the coffin, so that it looked as if nothing had been put in. I then got Woodford and his men to move the shell round to the side of the Queen and on the same level as the bed on which she was lying. I sent them out into the adjoining dressing room. The Princess of Wales [the Queen] came, and she and the King remained a few minutes alone in the room, and the Queen laid some flowers on the body. Then I brought in the Emperor of Germany (the Queen having gone out), the Duke of Connaught, Prince Arthur of Connaught, Mrs Tuck, Misses Stewart and Ticking, Woodford, Scott and Spenser. We lifted the Queen into the coffin (Mrs Tuck and I taking the head, Misses Stewart and Ticking the feet, the King and Duke of Connaught, the Emperor and Prince Arthur the straps (laid under the body) on the left, over the coffin, and Woodford, Scott and Spenser, on the bed on the right side of the body). Then all the Royalties went out, leaving Mrs Tuck, Misses Stewart and Ticking with me, and they rearranged the Queen's dressing gown, the veil and the lace. Then I packed the sides with bags of charcoal in muslin and put in the Queen's left hand the photo of Brown and his hair in a case (according to her private instructions), which I wrapped in tissue paper, and covered with Queen Alexandra's flowers. After all was done I asked White, Shooter, Brown and Gordon who were nearby to come and see the Queen and then went to the drawing room and asked the Royal ladies there to come and have a last look. They all came, the Princess of Wales, the Duchess of Coburg and her daughter Beatrice, the Duchess of Connaught, and her two daughters, the Duchess of Albany, and her daughter; the Duchess of York, the Princesses Christian and Thora, Princess Beatrice, Princess Louise, and Princess Ena. When they went out I asked the King to let Miss Phipps come, which she did, with Miss Knollys. Then I got from him leave for Clinton, Edwards, Bigge, McNeill, Carington and Fritz to

come and look, which they did. The King sent for the Munshi to come. Then all went out, and in the presence of the King, the Emperor, the Duke of Connaught, Prince Arthur, the Duke of Coburg and myself, Woodford and his two men came in and screwed down the lid, and carried the coffin, covered with a white pall, into the passage at the top of the stairs, whence a party of bluejackets from the yacht carried it downstairs into the dining room which had been prepared as Chapelle Ardente, where soldiers now mounted guard, and my duties were over with the Queen after twenty years' service!

It was hardly surprising that after this lengthy ordeal Reid wrote in his diary: 'Feeling quite exhausted.' He had remained calm and decisive throughout, while those around him were often bewildered and at a loss as to what should be done.

Reid's services to the Queen did not go unrecognised. The Kaiser presented him with a photograph of himself with a note attached to it: 'In remembrance of dear Grandmama's last hours. Osborne 22 Jan, 1901.' Douglas Powell wrote, 'Your accuracy of judgment and your devotion in your sad and arduous task invited my warmest admiration and it gave me great satisfaction to do my best in helping you.' Lord Rosebery expressed his sympathy with characteristic eloquence. 'I cannot help thinking of you at this sad time, for everyone who has ever seen anything of the Queen must realise all that those who loved Her owed to you, and your vigilant and unceasing care of Her. It has been your lifework so far, anxious and absorbing beyond description. But, whatever fate may have in store for you, you must always feel proud of the service you rendered to the Queen, and so to your Country. I hope that you have not overtaxed yourself.'

Arrangements for the funeral were progressing rapidly, but as so many years had passed since the death of a Sovereign no one knew quite what to do, and there was an air of bewildered activity and anxiety regarding the correct procedure. Old staff hesitated to give up their duties, and new staff to take them on. In the midst of all these arrangements the Kaiser had his forty-second birthday on 27 January and Reid went to the Council Room with the Household to congratulate him.

On 31 January, the day before the funeral, Susan wrote to her mother-in-law from May Cottage:

Jamie leaves with the Funeral Procession in full dress Levée clothes. I am staying here as Jamie thought it best I should *not* go to the Funeral. I shall see the Procession here from the grounds. He may be kept several days next week at Windsor so I have got 'Cherie', my old governess, coming

217

GREAT · WESTERN · RAILWAY.

— FUNERAL OF —

Her · Late · Most · Gracious · Majesty · the · Queen.

— ARRANGEMENT OF ROYAL TRAIN. —

Paddington to Windsor 1.32 p.m. Saturday 2nd Feby 1901.

here on Saturday so I shall not be *alone*! The Duchess of York's Lady-in-Waiting does not arrive till tomorrow, – so till then I am to take her place! but they promised Jamie to be careful about the infection of measles, so I am not allowed to go to her rooms.

In daily letters to Susan Reid described the various phases of the Queen's final journey from Osborne on her way to join her beloved husband in the sanctuary which she had created for them at Frogmore.

1 February, Friday. Royal Yacht, *Osborne*, Portsmouth.
Here I am on board the *Osborne* feeling rather tired, but happily with nothing to do except write to my Pussy! Everything went off most satisfactorily, and it was fortunate the day was so fine – 'Queen's weather'! The walk from Osborne to Trinity Pier was very slow, and I was glad when it was over. We *all* crossed to Portsmouth on the *Victoria and Albert*, all Royalties and Suites, the *Alberta* in front with the Queen's coffin and a few of her people. Next to us the *Osborne* and last the *Hohenzollern*. It was a wonderful sight and most impressive. I tried to see you on the beach at Osborne, but could not make you out: however, the crowds of people on steamboats and along Southsea beach were *wonderful*, more than I have ever seen here before, and the miles of warships firing minute guns were most imposing. On arriving here about 4.45 (we came very slowly), the *Osborne* lot left the *Victoria and Albert* and came on board here; Edwards, Bigge, Fritz, Domestique, Lady Lytton, Gleichen, etc.

2 February, Saturday. Windsor Castle.
My last journey with Bipps is over, and I feel rather sad. After being with her so many years, I liked to be beside her today, though it was a rather trying experience, and my eyes got a little dim now and again! At 8.15, again in full dress we went on board the *Alberta* at Clarence Yard. There was a short service by Lang,[6] and all the family were present round the coffin, which was then put in the train. We started at 8.45 from Gosport in pouring rain which looked like lasting all day: but half way to London it cleared off, and the weather was fine up to the last.

There was an imposing assemblage at Victoria Station, and a little confusion until the Procession was arranged and started. I walked on the left side of the gun carriage behind the aides-de-camp, and just in front of Davidson – a very slow march – two hours I think till we reached Paddington, immense crowds all the way, and no end of purple cloth stuck up on balconies, stands, etc., as mourning; not much black. Not a sound anywhere as we passed, and everybody in the crowds looking woebegone. A quick run from Paddington to Windsor, and then a similar procession through the gates at the end of the Long Walk, under my window, through the Quadrangle, and round by Bigge's house to St Georges. At the Station

6 Cosmo Gordon Lang was Vicar of Portsea and later Archbishop of Canterbury.

the horses of the gun carriage got frightened and kicked and broke the traces: so the team was taken out, and 100 bluejackets, who were there as a guard of honour, dragged the gun carriage all the way. They did it beautifully and I think it was better than the horses.

I marched up the inside of St George's beside the coffin with the equerries, and stood close by during the service. The Chapel was *crammed* with notabilities of all sorts, but I hardly noticed them. It was not over till 4, and then there was luncheon in St George's Hall, but I did not go, preferring to have tea with John and Mary in my room.

Although 'too tired for anything', Reid gathered enough strength to write a letter of thanks to the King for the unusual honour which had been granted to him. He was the first doctor to have stood beside the coffin at a Sovereign's funeral.

I beg to express my heartfelt gratitude to Your Majesty for being allowed to accompany the remains of the Queen on their last sad journey and to take part in the funeral throughout. Your Majesty could have granted me no greater privilege than that of being to the last near Her whom, during long years of close attendance I had come to regard with feelings not only of the truest loyalty and veneration, but also of the deepest affection. I know well that it is to Your Majesty's gracious appreciation of these relations that I owe the exceptional privilege accorded me, which I can never forget, and which has offered me a melancholy satisfaction that will end only with my life.

On 4 February the coffin was borne from St George's Chapel to the Mausoleum at Frogmore where Reid saw 'the Sarcophagus opened for the Queen's reception, and also the Prince Consort's coffin'. His letter to his wife continued:

The last act of the drama is over. All went well. No rain. The Procession was rather pathetic, all the Royalties (men and women) walking. The Service in the Mausoleum was most impressive. I send a few flowers from the 'grave', if it can be called so.

The King saw us all tonight and gave us the Victorian Order, Clinton, Edwards, Bigge, McNeill, and I got the 1st Class. So I am now G.C.V.O. (Promise!)

The Kaiser has given me the star of my blue order [Star of Crown Order] which I had not got before, so now I have three stars!

The King was very nice but said nothing about a pension! It will be so nice to be really with you and quite free.

There is a note of relief in that last sentence. Sad as the Queen's death had been for Reid, and great as the upheaval it caused would be, it nevertheless came at just the right moment for the Reids. The combination of married life and the position of royal physician in constant attendance upon the Queen had been far from ideal, and had imposed a great strain upon him and, although Susan had accepted the situation, unselfish as she was, there were times when the demands had taxed even her good nature.

Now all that remained was the sad business of packing, and sorting out his letters and papers, many of which he burnt. The Kaiser spoke to Reid before he took his leave on 5 February, and the following day Reid 'dined for the last time in Windsor Castle and went to the smoking room afterwards'. On 7 February he was sent for by the new Queen, 'who took leave of me very nicely, and gave me sleeve-links of red enamel with V.R.I. and the Crown on them. At lunch I said Goodbye to all. At 3 I was at the door to see the King off to London, and was taken leave of by him. In the afternoon I was sent for by Princesses Louise and Beatrice to say Goodbye and they gave me one of the Queen's walking sticks, used by her.' So ended twenty years of life in Queen Victoria's Household.

One of ze Queen's
Maids of Honour –
also not handsome
& also to old!

Christmas card sent by Susan Baring
to Reid in 1898.

Hon. Harriet Phipps, a sympathetic
intermediary between Reid and the
Queen at the time of his engagement.

Reid in his Household uniform, 1897.

Suasan Baring on the day of her
engagement to Reid, 24 July 1899.

Reid outside The Warren, February
1900.

Rudolf Carl Slatin, known as Pasha, a title given him by the Khedive of Egypt in 1899.

Lord Salisbury on the terrace at Hatfield House, 1902.

Household group outside Viceregal Lodge during the Queen's visit to Ireland in 1900, l to r: Sir Fleetwood Edwards, Col William Carington, Capt Frederick (Fritz) Ponsonby, Reid, Lord William Cecil.

The Kaiser, Wilhelm II, gave Reid this photograph at Highcliffe in 1907.

The Prince of Wales in 1899.

The Queen on her deathbed, 'looking beautiful, surrounded by loose flowers and palms strewn on the bed', 22 January 1901.

Reid in his consulting room at 72 Grosvenor Street in 1906.

Back to back with Edward VII outside a wine shop in Biarritz, 1910.

The King inspecting M. Bleriot's aeroplane on his visit to the Biarritz–Bayonne Aerodrome in March 1910. Reid is second to the right of the King.

Lord Rosebery at Balmoral, photograph taken by Reid in September 1910.

Reid and Lord Spencer (Bobbie) enjoying a joke at Lord Althorp's (Jack's) coming-of-age in 1913

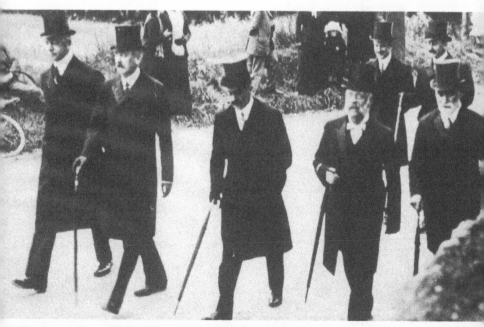

The press captioned this the 'King's Ministers walking out from Balmoral'. Reid is second from the right.

The Doctors whose reports the whole Empire watched.

The medical men who attended King Edward during his last illness.

1 Sir Francis H. Laking, Bt., G.C.V.O., M.D., Physician-in-Ordinary to the late King.

2 Sir James Reid, Bt., G.C.V.O, K.C.B., M.D., Physician-in-Ordinary to the late King.

3 Sir R. Douglas Powell, Bt., K.C.V.O., M.D., F.R.C.P., Physician-in-Ordinary to the late King.

4 Dr. Bertrand Dawson, M.D., F.R.C.P., Physician-Extraordinary to the late King.

5 Dr. St. Clair Thomson, M.D., F.R.C.P., F.R.C.S., the eminent specialist in diseases of the throat and nose.

The Reid family at The Chestnuts, Ellon, in August 1909,
l to r: Peter, Ned, Beatrice, Jamie, Margaret, Susan, Victoria.

Reids and Spencers at Althorp, taken by Reid, Christmas 1911, l to r: Jack, George, Delia,
Margaret Reid, Margaret, Victoria Reid, Peter Reid, Susan, Lavinia, Ned Reid.

Queen Alexandra in 1906 at the age of sixty-two.

Queen Mary at Balmoral in September 1913.

King George V and Queen Mary at the Garter Ceremony at Windsor, June 1912, with Ned, right, as a page.

12

Starting Again

The death of Queen Victoria opened a chasm in Reid's life. He was jobless, to all intents and purposes, homeless, and about to become a father. The King granted him a pension of £1000 per annum for life, and he had, in addition, the sum of £210 paid to him in an occasional consultative capacity as Physician-in-Ordinary. Edward VII did not employ a resident physician, and his own personal doctor, Sir Francis Laking, was a man of whom we have seen Reid did not have a high opinion. Nor did Fritz Ponsonby who had become Equerry and Assistant Private Secretary to the King. He wrote to Reid, 'I do hope you are going to be about with us again later on, instead of that charlatan Laking, otherwise we shall degenerate into a dull prosy lot.'

Arthur Bigge expressed the feelings of many of the old Queen's courtiers. He had become Private Secretary to the Duke of York and, accompanying the Duke and Duchess on their Royal Colonial Tour, wrote wistfully to Reid from the HMS *Ophir*: 'It is exactly eight weeks ago today since the Queen died – and how we are scattered to the winds – McNeill nearly in Ceylon! You taking your "*otium cum dignitate*", I in an utterly new position and on the briny ocean. I miss all my pals most terribly, for tho' everyone is very kind, still one can't be on the same terms of intimacy as with the friends of twenty years.'

Thomas Barlow, who had recommended a nurse for Susan's baby, soon to be born, sympathised with Reid's predicament and offered encouragement: 'Dear old Queen, with all her goodness she had mis-conceptions about some things. I expect she thought nothing could be simpler for you than just to settle down in practice immediately. But I feel confident that things will come right.'

On 3 April, restored after his rest at Kent House, Osborne, lent him by Princess Louise, Reid moved to 28 St James's Place, which he and Susan were to share with Margaret and Bobbie Spencer. He and Bobbie were to rent it from Lady Sarah Spencer, Earl Spencer's sister, 'for a *small* rent which we can easily afford'. This charming house, which was once lived in by William Huskisson, lies next to the grander Spencer House overlooking Green Park, where Bobbie's much older half-brother lived, the fifth Earl Spencer (known as the Red Earl on account of his long red beard). Susan was delighted to have the chance of seeing so much of her sister and the two brothers-in-law became the closest of friends. Reid, now free to start a medical practice, was immediately engaged by Bobbie and Margaret to become their family doctor.

On 20 April, after a prolonged labour during which both her sisters were present, Susan gave birth to a son. Reid, a father for the first time at the age of fifty-one, was overjoyed. Fritz Ponsonby sent congratulations from the King, adding that he only hoped 'your son will not take after his father. Is it true that his name is to be Karim Reid?' Reid's brush with the Munshi was still savoured in Court circles. A few days later a letter arrived from Sir Francis Knollys saying that it would give the King 'very great pleasure to propose being Godfather to your boy', and that he wished the baby to be called Edward, as he was to be his first godson since he became King. On 7 May the christening took place in King Edward's presence in the Chapel Royal, St James's Palace. Reid must have wondered what the old Queen's reactions would have been had she been alive. She had never become accustomed to her doctor being a married man, let alone a father.

Now that there was an addition to the family Reid felt it was high time for them to have a home of their own. Sir Samuel Wilks was looking for a buyer for his house at 72 Grosvenor Street. Reid went with Susan to look round it and considered it ideal for their purposes, the perfect place from which to set up practice, and they agreed to take it over.

In December he was appointed Physician-in-Ordinary to the Prince of Wales (formerly the Duke of York), which carried with it prestige, but little money. Building up a practice became a priority, but first he persuaded colleagues to take him for days to the main London hospitals so that he could give himself a refresher course in developments that might have passed him by while he had been cut off from the mainstream of his profession. With Powell he saw the farm at Bishop's Stortford where tuberculosis experiments were being undertaken, and at St Thomas's he watched typhoid tests with Dr Sharkey. He was also free now to attend all the meetings of the Royal College of Physicians, and at the Medical and Chirurgical Society, which he did assiduously for the rest of his life, becoming a great 'club' man, attending numerous dinners. He enjoyed home life, too, though at times he found the endless comings and goings of Susan's infinite number of relations trying. Hence his retreat to a male world of clubs and committees.

Nevertheless, he had not entirely lost his connections with his royal friends of former days. Princesses Christian, Louise and Beatrice all visited him and Susan at 72 Grosvenor Street from time to time, and

Reid drove to Kensington Palace regularly to see Mrs Tuck, who was both friend and patient. Each year during King Edward's reign, on 22 January, he was invited to attend the Memorial Service for the old Queen at the Mausoleum at Frogmore. He travelled by special train to Windsor with his old friends, Bigge, Davidson, and Rosebery. The service was taken by Randall Davidson, Bishop of Winchester, and followed by a luncheon at the Castle, which was for him something of a reunion. Rosebery thought Windsor 'seemed haunted', while Lord Esher declared that 'the Corridor and Palace looked much the same – but the atmosphere was all changed. It may be my imagination, but the sanctity of the throne has disappeared. The King is kind and debonnaire, and not undignified – but too *human*!' Reid left no comment of his views.

He was to receive his own sign of the changing times in the most professionally galling way in June 1902. His notably equable temperament must have taken a severe jolt when he discovered at second-hand about a royal illness severe enough to postpone the Coronation. Laking had diagnosed appendicitis. When peritonitis set in the King still refused to postpone the ceremony. Eventually the surgeon, Sir Frederick Treves, was called in and a room at Buckingham Palace prepared for operating. After much resistance the King, who was laid out on a billiard table, finally gave way and the anaesthetic was administered, Queen Alexandra and three strong men helping to hold him down as he struggled and threw his arms about, growing black in the face. The operation was completed in forty minutes, and so successful was it that on the following day he was sitting up in bed smoking a cigar.

But neither Reid nor Sir William Broadbent, both Physicians-in-Ordinary to the King, had been informed, let alone consulted. Susan, mad with indignation on Jamie's behalf, wrote to her mother-in-law:

> The German Emperor telegraphed to his Embassy to say that he wished *Jamie* to keep him informed constantly as to the King's condition. Jamie had to say he knew nothing (which was thought most odd!). Still Count Metternich [German Ambassador] insisted on Jamie getting the information, so the result was that Laking asked him to have luncheon at Buckingham Palace with the Doctors, and they explained the whole case to Jamie. They were very nice to him, and rather apologetic! James does not think that Barlow likes the whole thing very much, but he is too *weak* to assert himself. Laking and Treves are the masters of the situation. Sir T. Smith told Jamie privately that they had behaved very badly to Lord Lister and himself. Though they went to sign the bulletins every day, they were never allowed to see the King, and never examined the wound after

the operation. They both now mean to get out of it and not go again. They are great men in their profession and won't stand being treated like that! Happily the King is going on as well as possible and everyone is much relieved. Jamie is very well and I don't think he worries.

As always, Reid was able to accept set-backs with equanimity, his sanguine temperament being a great boon to him during these difficult times of readjustment. To make up for his original omission from the case he was invited regularly to lunch at Buckingham Palace with Treves, Barlow and Laking.

On 29 July Sir Frederick Treves wrote to Reid from H.M.S. *Victoria and Albert*, where the King was convalescing: 'The King is doing well in every respect. The wound is now equal in length (on the surface) to the diameter of a two shilling piece, and its depth is just equal to the diameter of a sixpenny piece. He walked today for the first time and did marvellously well.'

The King recovered so well that the Coronation was able to take place on 9 August, almost seven weeks to the day after his operation.

On 8 September Reid left for Balmoral to relieve Laking who was taking a month's holiday. At dinner he sat opposite the King 'who spoke to me across the table'. The atmosphere at Balmoral had changed with the new regime; Reid thought for the better.

We do not all go from the table together as we used to at the old Queen's dinners, but the men remain to smoke – so last night I was left next to the King. He eats far too much, and drinks to match! In the drawing room the Queen came and spoke to me *all* the time. She was most nice and kind, and also full of fun. She was very funny about the old Queen not allowing smoking for so long, and the 'stiffness' which used to prevail around her, and told me she always felt 'frightened' when she came to stay with the Queen. It is a wonderful contrast to the way in which V.R.I. spoke to us, and makes all the difference. In fact, life here is pleasant in every way.

He also regaled Susan with gossip about the other visitors to Balmoral: 'We were 20 at dinner last night. I had lots of talk with Rosebery. Balfour [A.J.] also is an old friend of mine, and is very cordial. Winston Churchill looks like a young girl, and seems pleasant, at least he was to me, but they say he is very conceited and egotistical!' On further acquaintance he adds: 'Churchill is rather clever and smart with his tongue.' But there were two of the King's guests about whom Reid was less than complimentary: 'Sassoon [Reuben] is a good-natured beast, rather stupid – and his raison d'être seems to be made the object of jokes and to lose money at bridge, which he seems to do very regularly. Paget [General Sir Arthur] is a "terrible" fellow to talk – he knows about *everything* far better than anyone else! If he stays on I shall ask him for some hints in medicine!'

Reid returned to London in the autumn to find that Laking was busy trying to enlist the support of the King and Knollys (now Lord Knollys) to secure his election as a Fellow of the Royal College of Physicians. Bigge broached the subject with Reid who reported the substance of his conversation to his colleagues Barlow, Powell and Sir William Church – who was President of the Royal College of Physicians – all of whom were unfavourable to the suggestion. Not even the King could persuade them, and Laking failed to achieve the coveted accolade for, despite his position, there were limits to promotion if it were palpably undeserved.

Early in the new year of 1903 Reid administered chloroform to Susan during the birth of her second son. Princess Louise agreed to be his godmother, and in her honour he was christened John Peter Lorne. Reid's household was rapidly increasing and it was, therefore, essential for him to build up his practice accordingly to meet the cost. As a physician to the King it was also necessary for him to maintain a certain standard of living. When the Reids moved into 72 Grosvenor Street they employed seven servants, and as the number of children increased, so did the number of servants. If it had not been for his pension from the King, and the small income from the investments he had made during his time with the Queen, the family could not have survived, for it took a number of years to build up a practice of any size, and even then, without a prestigious hospital position, it was impossible to make a fortune. While his colleagues were able to think in terms of tens of thousands, Reid worked on the basis of hundreds of pounds. He was fortunate in his choice of wife, for Susan was thrifty and undemanding, and she had generous brothers and uncles who helped her from time to time by giving her gifts of money and lavish presents for her children. Furthermore, the Spencers, and many of the Barings, employed Reid as their doctor and refrained from taking advantage of their relationship to him by omitting to pay fees. At the beginning they formed the nucleus of his practice.

In November 1903 Reid received his first appointment as a consultant physician. King Edward, disregarding his mother's will, which provided for Osborne House to be kept in the family, and having offered it to each member in turn, without success, presented the place to the nation. The State apartments were opened to the public, the private rooms were kept closed by bronze gates, the rest of the rooms were used as a convalescent home for army and naval officers, and as a Royal Naval College. Reid had been approached by Sir Frederick Treves to be one of the consulting staff at the Convalescent Home, and he accepted with alacrity. The following February he went round Osborne with the King, feeling 'rather sad at seeing the old place and all the changes'. Once he had overcome his feeling of nostalgia Reid enjoyed his new job, and looked forward to his regular visits to the Isle of Wight.

In September 1904 Reid was asked to Balmoral once again. This time it was only for a week, and he enjoyed himself thoroughly, knowing that he was not forfeiting too much of his Ellon holiday. But he was suddenly called back by Lord Knollys at the end of the month as the King wished to see him on an urgent matter. George Profeit was threatening to blackmail Edward VII over the late Queen's letters written to his father, Dr Profeit, about John Brown. Reid was asked by the King to retrieve them from George Profeit, which was not an easy task, or one which he relished.

In November Reid had tea with Princess Beatrice at Kensington Palace, and talked with her about the problem. A few days later George Profeit came to see Reid to negotiate about the letters and Reid informed Lord Knollys of what had taken place. There followed

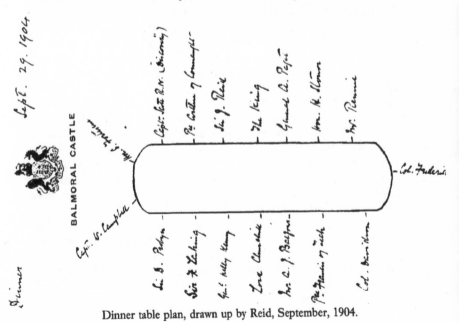

Dinner table plan, drawn up by Reid, September, 1904.

several similar visits. Then, on 8 May 1905, there is a triumphant entry in his diary: 'At 3 p.m. George Profeit came and delivered over to me a tin box full of the late Queen's letters to his father about John Brown, for which he has blackmailed the King. He left 4.15.' Reid handed them over to a grateful monarch in person. There were over 300 of them, many, as he noted in his diary, 'most compromising'.

Three queries immediately spring to mind. First, what does Reid mean by 'compromising'? Second, what sum of money did the King have to pay in order to retrieve the letters? And third, what happened to the letters? The first two questions will in all probability remain unanswered for ever. To the third question there is a simple answer. It is highly unlikely that the letters still exist as Edward VII was a great destroyer of papers and, in loyalty to his mother, he would not have allowed 'compromising' evidence to remain for future generations to exhume.

At the same time Reid was immersed in his own financial problems. He had always been interested in gambling on the Stock Exchange in a small way, but as the years went by his social elevation and his marriage involved him in a more expensive way of life, with the result that he became more adventurous. Reid had first met Whitaker Wright a high flier, who promised to help him, in April 1896, by which time the latter had made, lost, and remade a fortune. Wright acquired great publicity through his exotic and flamboyant life-style at his country house at Lea Park, Witley, where Reid went to stay in January 1898. In January 1897 Reid had received a cheque for £500 from Whitaker Wright for Lake View shares which Wright had bought and sold for him.

Wright also succeeded in persuading Reid to get a loan from the bank so that he was in a position to underwrite the Le Roi Mining Company which 'W.W.' (as he was generally known) was setting up. This Reid agreed to do, thereby involving himself in a highly speculative venture. At the time of his engagement at Osborne, in July 1899, he was invited on to W.W.'s yacht, the *Sybarite*, which had the distinction of having beaten the German Emperor's *Meteor* before the aloof but admiring gaze of the Royal Yacht Squadron. Here, in the sunshine, with a glass of punch in his hand, Reid 'had long talks with Whitaker Wright about shares, etc., and he promised to do all he could to help me'. In return, Reid agreed to become W.W.'s wife's trustee, an undertaking he was eventually deeply to regret. But in the meantime he communicated regularly with W.W. and went down to Lea Park to talk over affairs with Mrs Wright.

By December 1900 Wright had overreached himself by his manipulation of the Stock Exchange, and the London and Globe Finance Corporation, which was the central company through which all his other ventures were promoted, collapsed. A panic followed. No less than thirty members were hammered on the Stock Exchange and many of the subsidiary companies were forced into liquidation. Thousands of small investors found themselves ruined overnight. While not ruined, Reid was certainly affected by this fiasco, but Lord Edward Pelham Clinton, who had first introduced Reid to Wright, lost a good deal. Reid recorded in his diary on 30 December: 'Clinton much upset.'

Nothing further happened until February 1903, when Mr George Lambert moved a motion in the House of Commons calling attention to the fact that no proceedings had been taken against the Directors of the London and Globe Finance Corporation. On reading the speech in the paper, Whitaker Wright immediately fled to the United States via France. A demand for his extradition was addressed to the United States Government, and after much resistance Wright surrendered and returned to England. His trial began in the King's Bench Division of the High Court on 11 January 1904. It was found that though he could not be prosecuted under existing Company Law, he could be prosecuted under the Larceny Act of 1861. The prosecution was brilliantly conducted by Rufus Isaacs, and the defence, with almost equal brilliance, by Lawson Walton. In his summing up Lord Mersey was ruthless and W.W. received a sentence of seven years' penal servitude. Leaving the courtroom he requested that he might retire to the adjoining lavatory for a few moments. When he returned to the room where Sir George Lewis, his solicitor, was waiting for him it was observed that he was swaying a little and clutching his thighs. It was put down to the emotion of the moment. He tried to reach the armchair, but collapsed in agony on the carpet. It was found at the inquest that he had swallowed a capsule of cyanide of potassium.

Shortly after his death, in February, Reid received a demand from Sir George Lewis, acting for Mrs Wright, for £9,000 for negligence in the conduct of her affairs. In July Mr J. M. Williams, Reid's solicitor, informed him that 'Mrs Wright's action had collapsed for the present, the Judge refusing order for immediate judgment.' Reid was able to enjoy his holiday that year with a certain sense of relief, though all was by no means over.

Since he was so closely connected with the royal family there must be no hint of scandal of any description. He therefore felt compelled to confide in Lord Knollys, who arranged to see Mr Williams. Lord Knollys also offered to meet Sir George Lewis and as a result of his visit Lewis suggested a compromise. The case was settled out of court,

Williams agreeing, on Reid's behalf, to pay Mrs Wright £5,000.

While Reid's relief was immense, there still remained the problem of where to find the money. His stalwart brother, John, came to his rescue, and with his help and the backing of Susan's brother, Lord Revelstoke, Reid was able to clear his debt. His diary entry for 6 January 1905, reads: 'At 2.30 went to the city to see Mr Williams, solicitor, who has paid up the £5,000 to Sir G. Lewis for Mrs Wright and got from him my letters and the cheque for £9,000, all of which I burned with Mr Williams. The case now finally settled.' Reid had been caught up in an alien world, about which he had no real understanding, and for the rest of his life he was to pay for his ignorance and folly by never being free from financial worry.

The near scandal in no way set him back professionally or socially, however. His practice was gradually expanding. He was unanimously elected a member of the Council of the Royal Medical and Chirurgical Society, and nominated a Director of the Clerical, Medical and General Life Assurance Society. He served on the visiting committee of King Edward's Hospital Fund, and he became a consulting physician to the Tottenham Hospital. He opened new hospital wings with Princess Louise.

At home there was another addition to the household. On Christmas Day 1904, Susan gave birth to a fine healthy girl, who was christened Margaret Cecilia, and aptly so, for she was to become an able musician. Then there were three royal weddings, one after another. Reid had been present at the birth of each of the brides, and now he was to join in their matrimonial celebrations. Princess Alice of Albany married the Princess of Wales's brother, Prince Alexander of Teck, at Windsor. Princess Margaret of Connaught married Prince Gustavus Adolphus of Sweden in St George's Chapel, Windsor, after which there was a State luncheon at the Castle. But perhaps most important of all, as he had attended her throughout her life, was the wedding of Princess Ena to King Alfonso of Spain. While the Reids did not travel to Madrid for the wedding ceremony, they joined in the pre-nuptial festivities which were held in England. There was also a convivial dinner with Randall Davidson, now the Archbishop of Canterbury, and his wife, at which the Reids were the only guests and were able to talk freely of old times. Then there were State balls, and society balls, and medical dinners by the score. Social life, far from diminishing, became more hectic than ever. Edwardian exuberance had replaced Victorian staidness.

In 1904 Reid had been present at the death of his old friend Sir John McNeill, whose hospitality at Colonsay he had enjoyed in the '80s and '90s. But it was the tragic death of Susan's sister, Margaret

Spencer, which dealt a severe and unexpected blow to the family. On 4 July 1906, at three thirty a.m., she was delivered of a baby girl by Dr Blacker who, being anxious about the mother, sent immediately for Reid. He wrote to his mother that

> On going into the room I found poor Margaret looking as if she were dying – we did all we could with strong remedies, oxygen, etc., but she never revived and died quietly at 6. It was heart failure, and I think an attack of influenza she had a month ago, which lasted three weeks, had left her heart in a weakened condition. Susan came in just before she died, and Margaret recognised her and said 'my boys', meaning that Susan would look after them. Poor Susan has had a terrible day. She was devoted to Margaret, and they were always together.

A stunned Bobbie had been left to cope with six children, ranging from the ages of seventeen to new-born. The three boys were Jack, who became the seventh Earl Spencer, Cecil and George. Inevitably he turned to Susan, his wife's sister and closest friend, and the burden of holding the family together fell upon her. She was ably supported by Delia, the eldest daughter, who undertook to run the household and oversee the younger children. But she always turned to her aunt for advice and help and, remembering Margaret's deathbed plea, Susan took on the responsibility of their upbringing, which involved frequent visits to Dallington, their country home in Northamptonshire, and later, when Bobbie became Earl Spencer, to Althorp. Always in a delicate state of health, Bobbie never completely recovered from his wife's death and remained a widower for the rest of his life.

During the autumns of 1905 and 1906 Reid was again called to Balmoral but to his delight Susan joined him on both occasions. The first time they were invited by Queen Alexandra from 'Saturday to Monday' and were present as guests, although Reid did go to Abergeldie Castle to see the Prince of Wales, 'who has his right pupil dilated from cocaine (?)'. Reid played bridge with the Queen, and they lost twelve shillings to their opponents. Queen Alexandra had the gift of making others enjoy themselves, and Reid describes a 'lively time' he had sitting between her and Princess Victoria at dinner. She was a keen photographer, and took snapshots of the Reids when they went on a picnic excursion together.

The following year the King offered Abergeldie Mains to the Reid family for a month, thinking that 'perhaps the change might be good for Lady Reid'. (Susan was recovering from another miscarriage.) Reid hired a pony and trap for the children, to their great excitement, and he and Susan bicycled along beside it each afternoon. The King came to see his godchild and, having given him a sovereign, sat with his father smoking a cigar. On Susan's birthday the Queen and Princess Victoria spent the afternoon at Abergeldie Mains playing with the children, who sang and danced for them and were each given a shilling for their pains. There were return visits to Balmoral for dinner and bridge, and once they lunched alone in the library with the Queen and Princess Victoria. They were joined later by Ned and Peter, who were 'very wild when playing'. Queen Alexandra thought otherwise. 'Those delightful and most charming little children of yours did enjoy that afternoon at Balmoral to the full content of their little hearts in spite of their dear and anxious parents' remonstrances!!'

At the end of October Reid left Ellon for London with what now amounted to a large entourage akin to a royal progress. A whole carriage containing several compartments had to be taken to accommodate his mother, himself and Susan, the children, their nurses and all the servants. His friendship with the Superintendent of Railways stood him in good stead on such occasions, for he was always assured of comfortable travelling conditions.

Reid was frequently selected by the King to accompany him on his spring visits to Biarritz. Unlike Queen Victoria, King Edward took a small Suite with him, and travelled relatively simply. Life followed a regular pattern in which medical duties could hardly be described as arduous. Reid did, however, have responsibility for the King's welfare, for which he was paid the not very princely sum of £5 per day. The King ate, smoked, and, on occasion, drank too much; and, in addition, was bronchitic; but he was in no way a hypochondriac. Quite the reverse was the case, for there were times when he pretended that there was nothing wrong with him, when patently there was. As far as the King was concerned, there was no social stigma attached to doctors either. Reid was treated as a friend, and was to be seen striding out daily with the monarch along the esplanade. On their morning constitutional walk they invariably met Mrs George Keppel and Mrs Cassel,[1] at which point they parted company, the King strolling with Mrs Keppel, while Reid walked with Mrs Cassel round the Rocher de la Vierge. ('Two miles by my pedometer,' he noted with his usual precision.)

Abergeldie Mains was offered to the family again in 1907 during the King's sojourn at Balmoral. Immediately on his arrival the King

[1] Alice Keppel (the Hon. Mrs George Keppel), Edward VII's favourite mistress. Wilhelmina Schönbrunn Cassel, sister to Sir Ernest Cassel, a Jew of German origin, who was in charge of the King's private investments and an intimate personal friend.

complained that he was 'feeling out of sorts'; he looked 'rather grey and drawn, foul tongue, some crepitations at both bases – would not have temperature taken, cough troublesome,' Reid noted, 'and applied Radium to his nose for twenty minutes', a remedy he repeated on several occasions. To us such treatment would appear drastic, and rather haphazard. But in 1907 both the King and his doctor, satisfied by the rapid cure which it effected, were ignorant of the risks that had been taken.

The younger Wales children, Henry and George (later the Dukes of Gloucester and Kent), came to play with Ned and Peter, and the Reids were invited to dine at Abergeldie Castle with the Prince and Princess of Wales, and to attend a servants' ball afterwards. The night before his departure, Reid sat next to the King at one of the all-male dinner parties which became a feature of the royal visits to Balmoral.

In October Reid was summoned to Buckingham Palace by Knollys, who 'told me the King had lost confidence in Laking, who he says is not what he was, and that he (Knollys) and Treves want *me* to look after H.M., while trying to make it easy for Laking.' The following day Treves called on Reid at home and 'had a long talk with me about Laking's dazed condition and my looking after the King in his place'. The situation required tactful handling. Reid had never held a high opinion of Laking but, at the same time, he realised that Laking had been personal physician to the King for many years, and it was not easy simply to oust him. A system was devised whereby Laking was left to deal with the King's minor ailments, but where it was suspected that anything of a more serious nature might crop up, Reid was to be sent for at once.

Reid was also involved in Kaiser Wilhelm's State visit. On 6 November 1907 Count Metternich, the German Ambassador, invited Reid to the Embassy 'to discuss whether the Kaiser should go to the Isle of Wight, or to Bournemouth for his catarrh'. Reid advised the latter. Preparations for the State visit, which was due to begin on 11 November, had been supervised in detail by King Edward, who had been astonished to receive a most extraordinary telegram at the end of October announcing that his nephew was feeling tired and weak after 'bronchitis and acute cough effect of a virulent attack of influenza', and that he had decided not to come at all. There were reasons for what was believed by all to be a diplomatic illness, but whatever they were, the strongest possible pressure was applied to the Emperor by the King and the British Government, as well as by the German Foreign Office, with the result that the Emperor and Empress disembarked as planned from the Imperial yacht *Hohenzollern* at

Portsmouth on the appointed day. Superficially the visit was a success, and the Emperor was impressed by the grandeur of the celebrations in his honour, but he failed to impress British Ministers, and appeared to have little grasp of major political issues. The Empress returned to Germany after a week's stay at Windsor, but the Emperor caused dismay by insisting upon remaining privately in England for another month at Highcliffe Castle, near Bournemouth. On 6 December Reid stayed the night. 'Sat on Emperor's left at dinner and had long private talk with him afterwards. Bed 11.30,' he recorded in his diary. He was up at 8 o'clock the following morning, and 'sat on the Emperor's left again (Metternich on his right as last night). Had lively talk with him.'

Sadly, he made no comment on the content of these conversations from which it can be deduced that he was neither shocked nor surprised by what Wilhelm had to say. Accounts of the fantastic Imperial table-talk at Bournemouth had reached London clubs and drawing rooms. Besides claiming much of the credit for the British conquest of the Boer republics, the Emperor alleged that he had sacrificed the political interest of Germany on the altar of his English family affections by vetoing proposals for an anti-British Continental coalition at the start of the Boer War; that he alone was capable of holding in check the anti-British sentiments of a majority of his subjects; and that he was cruelly misunderstood. Such irresponsible chatter would certainly have been recorded by Reid who had been fortunate all along in seeing only the more favourable side of what can only be described as an unbalanced character.

The last event of any significance in 1907 was a meeting of the Comitia of the Royal College of Physicians to discuss the admission of women to College examinations. Reid's attitude to women's entry into the medical profession had not changed since his student days in Vienna, and he voted against the motion. In many ways a tolerant and liberal man, his views as regards women's rights remained reactionary all his life. He was strongly opposed to the Suffragette movement, and actively espoused the cause of his uncle by marriage, Lord Cromer, in vetoing any attempts of the opposite sex to improve their position in society. His view of women as second-class citizens may, partly, have accounted for his down-to-earth and outspoken behaviour to Queen Victoria. There is no instance of his chiding Edward VII, or of his telling him that he was eating and smoking more than was good for him. Their man-to-man relationship forbade it, besides which the King did not listen to what he did not want to hear – any more than his mother had.

January 1908 saw the birth of Reid's fourth and last child, Victoria Susan Beatrice. Once again the King gave permission for the family christening to take place in the Chapel Royal, his daughter Princess Victoria acting as chief godmother. Reid's customary luck had not run out. He had been blessed late in life with two sons, followed by two daughters, this feat of organisation being enhanced by the fact that each one proved to be gifted and capable.

Early in March Reid accompanied the King once more to Biarritz. While they were there on 8 April Herbert Asquith came to kiss hands as Prime Minister. The inconvenience caused to the House of Commons by the new premier's journey to Biarritz, and to Ministers by the King's delay in returning home, provoked widespread criticism and papers accused him, for the only time in his life, of a dereliction of duty. This was the first time a British Prime Minister had been sworn in on foreign soil, and on that day Reid enjoyed an informal luncheon at the hotel with the King, Asquith, Fritz Ponsonby and Arthur Davidson.

In the autumn Reid was required again at Balmoral. The King wrote to Sir Dighton Probyn, Queen Alexandra's Comptroller: 'I expect to have a good many guests, so it is better to have a good doctor in the house.' This time Susan and the children did not accompany him, and Reid lived at the Castle. His friends Slatin Pasha and General Sir Reginald Wingate were there, and Bobbie Spencer arrived later. There were picnics with the King and his party who were 'deer running' at which Reid took endless snapshots; and more bicycling with the cyclometer – which now registered 6141 miles. Sir Arthur Davidson had to have a pellet removed from his left cheek, but the King, and the Wales, Connaught and Teck families all remained in good health. Reid's services were only required to attend Pew, the King's loader, whom he declared unfit for further work, and Donald Stewart, Queen Victoria's old servant, who suffered from a 'hemiplegic stroke'.

Death of the King

In 1909 Reid was invited to join the royal Suite for the State visit to Berlin in February. The King's decision to visit Germany was prompted by a desire to improve the strained relations between the two countries, but at the same time he feared that his efforts would be to no avail. Thus, he departed with the Queen on 8 February in a pessimistic mood. Furthermore, he was not in good health. Three days before his departure Reid had been called to Buckingham Palace in the morning and found him full of 'bronchial wheezing'. He visited him again in the evening, and twice daily before he left for Berlin.

He was accompanied by a large Suite which, besides Reid, consisted of: Lady Antrim, Lady-in-Waiting; Miss Charlotte Knollys, Woman of the Bedchamber; Lord Crewe, Secretary of State for the Colonies and Minister in Attendance; the Lord Chamberlain, Bobbie Spencer, now Lord Althorp; Lord Howe, Lord Chamberlain to the Queen; Sir Charles Hardinge, representing the Foreign Office; Field Marshal Lord Grenfell; Admiral Sir Day Bosanquet; Lord Granville, Lord-in-Waiting; Commander C. E. F. Cunninghame-Graham, Groom-in-Waiting; Colonel Streatfield, Equerry; and Fritz Ponsonby. They had a fine crossing in the *Alexandra*, and a special train conveyed them from Calais to Berlin via Brussels and Cologne. During dinner the train lurched, and a footman upset some quails on Queen Alexandra, actually leaving one hanging on to her hair much to everyone's amusement – especially when she announced that she would arrive in Berlin *coiffées de cailles*.

The following morning they reached Berlin where, as Reid related to Susan:

> There was a tremendous reception at the station and all along the route to the Palace. The horses of the carriage in which were the Queen & Empress stopped at a certain point, and would not go on, and they had to get out and go in another carriage! Reischach, who is 'Master of the Horse', is rather in a way about it. The Kaiser was very gushing to me: and I have had a talk with the Empress. The King is fairly well, but not *quite* the thing; however I think that he will get through it all right. After our arrival here and our reception by the Kaiser, we got out of our uniforms, and went to luncheon in frock coats, except the soldiers. It was a big affair with a lot of ladies. I have just got the 1st Class ('Grand Cordon') of the Crown. It is not so good as the 1st Class of the Red Eagle

(I believe), but it is a pretty ribbon like the Garter, and I am quite satisfied! I shall have to wear my new blue ribbon tonight, instead of my Victorian Order ribbon. Bobbie is all right – very fussy, but quite in his element and delights in it all.

A second letter described a gala dinner:

Which was a very imposing affair, and impressed me more than any of the similar banquets I have seen at Windsor. The Kaiser and the King's speeches to each other were thrilling. [King Edward, fearing what the Kaiser might say, had insisted on both speeches being seen by the other beforehand.] Before dinner I had another talk with the Kaiser and thanked him for my new order, which I find *is* a bomb after all and almost as good as the Eagle ribbon, and much *prettier*. Granville and I are the only two who have got it, and Streatfield has got the 3rd class of it only. So I am after all delighted with it. I had a very good place at dinner, and saw no end of old friends near me; so I had to do a lot of health drinking, but did *not* get knurd [drunk]. I was *very* careful with my eating: but *had* to taste various wines that one has a chance of only once or so in a lifetime! I have most luxurious quarters here. 3 rooms, a salon, a bedroom and a dressing room 'en suite'. The Kaiser said he hoped I was comfortable.

Reid enjoyed the round of lavish celebrations, but had his anxious moments. At luncheon at the British Embassy the King, wearing a tight-fitting Prussian uniform and smoking a huge cigar, collapsed in a choking fit and fainted while chatting to the elegant and beautiful Princess Daisy of Pless. Reid was fetched at once, and everyone was asked to withdraw; but the King recovered immediately when Queen Alexandra unfastened his collar. A quarter of an hour later the guests were asked to return, and Reid, who had been firmly instructed by the King to play down the incident, appeared to treat the matter in a casual manner. His loyalty to the King cost him some professional prestige, for those who did not realise his position considered him to have been negligent, and Hardinge even went as far as to write to Knollys expressing fears for the King, and doubts about the doctor. Princess Daisy must have shared Hardinge's misgivings over the King's doctor, for she sent Dr Lowenberg, famed for his treatment of operatic singers, to see the King. The Kaiser was enraged at this breach of medical etiquette, as Reid records. 'In the forenoon I was sent for by the Kaiser who spoke to me about H.M. for 20 minutes, and especially about Lowenberg, being furious at the episode and especially angry with Princess Pless; was *most* nice to me.'

During this interview the Kaiser presented Reid with a telegraphic code, 'with a request that I should use it as a private cypher to his

Imperial Majesty in the event of the King's serious illness any time'.

Code composed and written out by the German Emperor about Radium
I. Radium most interesting in its effect. (H.M. *seriously* ill)
II. Radium cures can be reconed [sic] with. (*Please come* at once)
III. Institute of Radium cures great success. (H.M. rapidly sinking)

It is interesting to ponder what Edward VII might have thought about this code, and whether or not he would have approved of it. There was no love lost between uncle and nephew, but in the event of death, blood is thicker than water and the Kaiser, for all his faults, paid homage to family connections especially where funerals were concerned. The code is revealing as an illustration of the bond between the Kaiser and Reid. These two men, so different from one another, had been drawn together by their mutual devotion to Queen Victoria, and the role they had played at her deathbed.

Hardly had he returned to London and settled in, when Reid had to prepare for another journey to Biarritz. After dinner at the Hotel Bristol in Paris the royal party went to the Théâtre des Variétés and saw *Le Roi qui s'amuse*. The British Ambassador, Sir Francis Bertie, recalls:

His Majesty had ordered a box without telling his 'gentlemen' to what theatre he was going; they were rather scandalised when they learned that it was to see the play in which figured 'Le Roi Edouard'. At dinner His Majesty consulted his doctor, Sir James Reid, as to his food and drink. H.M. was not to have champagne, but instead, some 'nice light hock' – which the waiter interpreted by producing some very strong Rudersheimer – no cognac, and, instead of coffee, 'some warm milk'! His Majesty coughed a good deal, and in the automobile he insisted on having the front windows open; it was a bitterly cold night. When, in the course of the play, the stage King visits the lady and sees, instead of his own portrait, the photograph of King Edward he exclaims, 'Le Roi Edouard!' The spectators turned their eyes on H.M., who was as much amused as they.

Reid noted that 'at the end of the second act, the audience rose, cheered and waved to the King as we left'.

From Biarritz they made an excursion to Pau, where they enjoyed the spectacle of Wilbur Wright flying his aeroplane. Reid noted, 'Wright can go with the aeroplane in the air at a speed of 30-40 miles an hour, and as high or low as he likes, rising and sinking also as he pleases. We are all thrilled with the performance as we have never seen anything like it. The King was *most* interested.'

In January 1910, to his great delight, Reid was elected a Councillor of the Royal College of Physicians. Three months later he became a member of the Athenaeum and told Susan: 'It is a very exclusive Club, and no end of men are blackballed after waiting for 20 years. So it looks as if my reputation is *good* – at least among the people who do *not* know me!' During the same week he was elected to the Royal Institution of Britain.[1]

The King made his annual spring visit to Biarritz where his health gave Reid increasing anxiety. When he arrived he 'was not quite well'. He had a heavy cold and was coughing and wheezing, and Reid did not dare to let him venture outside. He refused to remain in bed but received only very few visitors, who included Mrs Keppel and the Portuguese Minister in London, Marquis de Soveral. On 14 March 'in the afternoon H.M. had a slight rigor, his temperature went up to 101.4 pulse 84, respiration 3, much cough and expectoration. Feeling and looking very ill. He dined alone with Mrs G.K. I sat up all night in the next room to the King.' Reid had cause for anxiety for, although slightly better the next day, the King remained in his bed. Two days later Nurse Fletcher arrived to relieve Reid from his vigil; the temperature had not gone down, and Reid records that 'Mrs G.K. was much alarmed.' Then, gradually, the King began to improve, his appetite revived, and he was 'smoking big cigars again'.

Within two weeks of his illness, the King was in San Sebastian watching the Easter bull fight. It was an unusually cold spring, which did not do the King's bronchitis any good but, nevertheless, he insisted upon throwing himself into his usual activities, which included watching pelota, and the newly discovered aviation.

Three days after his return from Biarritz the King went down to Sandringham for the weekend. In a piercing east wind he inspected the home farm and his pedigree stock. Coughing and wheezing, he returned to Buckingham Palace on Monday 2 May, in time to dine quietly with Miss Keyser[2] in Grosvenor Crescent. That evening the Reids were dining with Lord and Lady Mount Stephen when a

---

[1] One of the first scientific research centres in Britain, the Royal Institution was founded in 1799 by Benjamin Thompson, Count Rumford, in Albemarle Street, London, and received a royal charter the following year. In its constitution it was described as: 'A Public Institution for diffusing the knowledge and facilitating the general introduction of useful mechanical Inventions and Improvements, and for teaching by Courses of Philosophical Lectures and Experts the Applications of Science to the common Purposes of Life.'

[2] Miss Agnes Keyser was the founder of King Edward's Hospital for Officers at 17 Grosvenor Crescent, which she ran as matron with the help of her younger sister. She became a great friend of Edward VII, and frequently entertained him to dinner when he wanted to relax in an informal and domestic way.

messenger arrived with a note from Agnes Keyser, written in pencil. 'The King is dining here. He would like to see you tonight at Buckingham Palace at 11.15, if you would kindly go there, as he has a cold, and a little cough, and the Nurse is not there.'

On arriving at the Palace I found H.M. sitting in his dressing gown in an easy chair, breathing very fast, 36 per minute. Temp. 100.2, Pulse 92 and bounding. Cough and purulent expectoration, and complaining of dyspnoea. Loud crepitation at both bases behind, and a little sporadic rhonchus. As the nurse was away, I made two linseed and mustard poultices and applied them on the chest and back for three quarters of an hour, replacing them with a thick layer of cotton wool. Gave H.M. 15 mil. Tr. Chlor. et Morph. B.P. 1885 with his red linctus to take at night if necessary. Wrote to Sir F. Laking reporting all that had occurred, and asked him to meet me to see the King next morning at 9.o'clock.

When Reid returned to Susan at one a.m. he replied to her enquiry, 'The King may recover, as he did at Biarritz but if not he will be dead in three days.'

At 9 o'clock the following morning, Reid went to Buckingham Palace and 'saw the King with Laking'. He continues:

H.M. had had a bad night, but was feeling rather better. Temp. *normal*. Pulse 84. Respiration 32. Still complaining of dyspnoea. Cough and expectoration as before, and also the chest signs. Bowels had acted once, but the last two days they had been well moved with a blue and rhubarb pill on two successive evenings. We gave H.M. an effervescing expectorant with Carbonate of Ammonia and tincture of ipecacuanha to take every four hours, and he agreed to remain upstairs. At 10 I saw him again with the dentist, Mr Hern, for half an hour. We saw H.M. again at 7 p.m. He was sitting at his writing table, and complained of malaise and dyspnoea. Temp. 99.6, pulse 84, regular. Respiration 32. He had seen a number of people. Gave him a draught at bedtime of liquor ammon.citrates paregoric etc: The poulticing as last night. Also 15 drops of his favourite chlorodyne draught like last night, to take in the night.

Reid did not sleep at the Palace, but returned the following morning at 9.30. 'Went to see the King with Laking, and we then sent for Dr St Clair Thomson, who saw him with us. Temp. 99.2, pulse 80, regular when I took it twice, but Thomson found it wobbly.' Later that day, 4 May, Reid discussed the King's condition with the Prince of Wales. 'At 6.30 p.m. saw the King with Laking, Douglas Powell and St Clair Thomson. Temp. normal, pulse 84, regular and fairly full. Resp. 34. Lung crepitation as before, but very little rhonchus.

H.M. had several fits of acute dyspnoea during the day, but the amyl nitrate had not much effect.'

Next morning, 5 May:

H.M. seemed to me worse, with much dyspnoea, and some cyanosis. He had had a restless night. Temp. 99. Pulse 84 regular and fairly full; respiration 36. The oxygen and amyl nitrate gave temporary relief only. To go on as before, the mixture slightly changed, and twice a day to have an hypodermic of strychnine. Returned at 12, having called on the way to see Mrs Keppel. Found the King worse, and remained there with Laking. Saw the King repeatedly, Mrs G.K. with him. At 5 the Queen arrived from the Continent. Saw her alone. At 6 consultation and first bulletin issued. Had dinner alone at the Palace. Came back at 9.0 p.m., calling on Mrs G.K. on the way. Put on evening dress. Saw Bobbie. Back to the Palace for the night. Remained up till 4.0 a.m., going out and in to the King, who sat up all the night with more or less dyspnoea, but no more cardiac attacks. Got him a better chair. At 4 went up and reported to Laking, who came down and joined me for a little, and then at 4.50 I went up to bed and rested till 7, when I got up. Went down and found Laking gone up to shave, etc. Saw the King and thought him worse, (but Laking had been reporting him as much better), and went to tell this to Davidson. Consultation at 10 with Powell, Laking, Dawson and Thomson, and *all* signed the bulletin. Laking and I remained all day on duty, H.M. gradually getting worse and kept going by oxygen, which for the last half of the day was almost continuous, and frequent hypodermics of strychnine, alternated with Tyramine. He sat in a chair all day, the Queen and Princess Victoria with him; towards afternoon he gradually became quite unconscious, and at 5 barely recognised Mrs G.K., who came to see him, and did so in the presence of the Queen and Princess Victoria. Consultation at 5 p.m. 'Critical' bulletin issued, signed by Powell, Laking, Dawson and self. From 5 p.m. Dawson remained with us, as Powell had been from 1, when the King had had an alarming cardiac failure after moving to another chair, and for a time we thought he was dead. Towards evening things got worse, and we were all with the King more or less continuously. Had snap dinner in the waiting room at about 9.30 p.m. After this in constant attendance, and at about 11 p.m., with the greatest difficulty, the King was lifted into bed, being partially revived by ether and strychnine hypodermics, and oxygen; *quite* unconscious, but *no* stertor. At 11.45 he died as per bulletin. The Archbishop of Canterbury was present, and gave the blessing. Remained up with Laking till 1.30. Powell went home about 12.45, and Dawson soon after. Thanked by the new King for all I had done.

Throughout his fatal illness the King displayed exemplary courage and, although confined to his rooms, continued to attend to his duties as Sovereign: giving audiences, receiving the Grand Duke Michael for luncheon, and signing papers. Even on the morning of his death he indignantly rejected the informal clothes which his valets had laid out, insisting upon a frock coat before receiving Francis Knollys, who found him very feeble in voice, but not in mind. Until the end he remained lucid during intervals of consciousness. On that same morning Susan wrote to Beatrice Reid: 'By the time you get this letter I am afraid the poor King may be dead – it is really too sad! Jamie has just telephoned to me that he thinks things are as bad as possible and that he has given up hope – he thinks it may be all over this afternoon. The poor Queen is quite broken-hearted. I feel *so* sorry for Jamie, as he will have lost a good friend in the King.'

Reid's duties did not end with the King's death. He took upon himself the responsibility for drawing up the reports on the King's illness for the *British Medical Journal* and *The Lancet*, as well as sending an official statement on the King's death to the Kaiser, rather to the annoyance of Laking. On 7 May the official warrant was issued of his appointment as 'one of the Physicians-in-Ordinary to His Majesty, George V', making him the first doctor to hold the position of Physician-in-Ordinary to three monarchs.

The day after the King's death Nurse Fletcher took Reid and Susan 'to see the dead King'. On 10 May Reid writes: 'Susan and I went by Queen Alexandra's wish to Buckingham Palace and knelt together by the dead King. Queen Alexandra sent word to us not to go away, and took us in again to see the King, and talked. We left a bunch of lilies of the valley from Ned.' In the evening Reid 'went to the Palace to see the King put in his coffin, but the Queen postponed it. Dined with the Household.' A day later, at precisely the same time, Reid went to Buckingham Palace again, and after dining with the Household he 'saw the King's body put into the coffin (from the bed) in its silk nightgown'.

A touching letter from Princess Victoria testifies to the gratitude felt by the royal family for the part Reid played in his endeavour to keep his sovereign alive.

I must send you one tiny line of *deep* gratitude for all your kindness to my beloved Father, which can never be forgotten by me. Those last hours of agony we all passed through, and your never failing perseverance and energy to keep this precious life – there are no words to express the misery now. I only just wished to say '*thank you*', which I feel you will understand. He *was* grateful too for all you did for him at Biarritz. May God bless you and yours, from his broken hearted daughter Victoria.

A week after her husband's death, and with characteristic generosity, Queen Alexandra sent Reid a cheque for 200 guineas, 'that you may know Her Majesty fully appreciated your kind and willing services during King Edward's illness, and sad death last week'. Needless to say, the much needed money was gratefully received.

Owing to Queen Alexandra's extreme reluctance to part with the body, the funeral was not held until a fortnight after the King's death. On 17 May Reid, 'in full dress with trousers, walked in the procession with the King's body from Buckingham Palace to Westminster Hall, and to the service there'. A quarter of a million people filed silently through Westminster Hall, where the body lay in State upon a catafalque from 17-19 May, and vast crowds watched the funeral procession through the streets of London to Paddington Station in superb weather on 20 May. Immediately behind the gun carriage, which bore the coffin, walked King Edward's disconsolate fox-terrier Caesar, followed by the German Emperor and eight kings. The Reids saw the procession from Lord Revelstoke's house in Carlton House Terrace, and then, hurrying to Paddington Station, they 'went by 11 a.m. special to Windsor, and were in the nave of St George's Chapel for the King's funeral service'. Afterwards they lunched in St George's Hall, where they saw many of their old friends.

On 23 May the Kaiser, who was still staying at Buckingham Palace, telephoned to Reid to come and see him. 'Went and waited outside while the Kaiser was dictating to his secretary. Then at 10.20 a.m. he joined me, and we walked till 11 in the garden, talking about the King's illness and death and Mrs G.K. He told me that Mrs G.K. had asked to see him on his arrival, and he had refused.' Although he saw the Kaiser again on official occasions, this was the last time that Reid conversed alone with him. The rapport which had built up over the years was to be broken, inevitably and irrevocably, by future political events, and the horrors of the Great War.

14

Last Years

The new reign opened with some good news, imparted to Reid by his old friend Arthur Bigge, King George V's Private Secretary. 'The King desires me to write to you on his birthday, to say that it gives him great pleasure to have your son Edward to succeed to the vacancy which will occur among the Pages of Honour by the superannuation of Lord Knollys' son on July 16th. 1911.' Not only was this a much coveted honour, but it carried with it financial reward (£230 per annum) which more than covered the cost of Ned's school fees and was, therefore, a heaven-sent bonus for Reid. His advice was also sought over the new medical list of appointments, and he went to Marlborough House with Laking to discuss the names with the King before they were submitted to the *London Gazette*.

In July Reid went to Althorp with Susan, where he was called upon to examine the old Lord Spencer, 'who did not know me, and could not be made to understand anything, and evidently had softening of the brain, although he walks well and drives out. He came to dinner with us, but understood nothing, and after dinner put on hat and coat and said he must go home to Althorp! Great difficulty in getting him to go to his room and to bed.' The following day Doctors Buzzard and Churchouse joined Reid in drawing up and signing a certificate, in the presence of Lord Spencer, to say that he was incapable of transacting business or managing his affairs. He died on 13 August, when Bobbie inherited the earldom and moved from Dallington to Althorp.

A new era began for the young Spencer family, in which the Reids inevitably became involved. They spent each Christmas at Althorp, where they threw themselves into theatricals, their performances normally being conducted in French, and held in the Long Library before an audience comprising family and servants. The cousins enjoyed themselves skating, tobogganing and tumbling about in the snow, and when the weather permitted, they went to the meet on Boxing Day, where Reid took photographs of the three eldest Spencers, Delia, Jack, and Cecil, on their amounts. At new year there was a servants' ball at which Susan, Ned and Peter danced energetically, and the boys were allowed to stay up for supper at midnight. Reid, now well into his sixties, enjoyed the quieter pleasures of conversation, and inspecting the magnificent paintings and treasures at Althorp. These happy carefree holidays are all recorded in a series of photographs taken by Reid, who never missed a chance of marking an appropriate occasion, or capturing a ludicrous situation.

Bobbie, who was still Lord Chamberlain and had necessarily to spend a great part of his life in London, divided his time between Spencer House and Althorp. On 2 April 1911, there was an urgent telephone call for Reid from Spencer House requesting him to come by at once, as Bobbie was seriously ill. Reid found that he had 'acute colic suggestive of appendicitis'. Ten days later, after much consultation, it was decided that an operation was unavoidable. For an hour Bobbie was on the operating table, but the result was successful, although he was left very weak. Not naturally robust, Bobbie took a long time to recover, and was never able to resume his duties as Lord Chamberlain. Thereafter he spent more and more time at Althorp, away from the rigours of London life.

At this time Reid was anxious to acquire an augmentation to his arms. All his life he had penalised those doctors who angled for place or honour, but this is a dignified petition for something that would add pleasure rather than career prospects from a man with a fair sense of his own merit. He wrote to his cousin by marriage, Fritz Ponsonby, George V's Assistant Private Secretary, on the subject.

The Honourable Augmentation that I mentioned, and which I should very greatly prize, is a distinction that has sometimes been conferred by Sovereigns on their doctors (and on others), and it was last given in 1907 by King Edward to Treves and Laking. By Royal Warrant His Majesty granted them an 'honourable augmentation' to their arms, this augmentation consisting of the addition to their shields of one of the lions from the Royal Arms, such augmentation to be borne by their descendants. I can't help thinking that, if the King knew how greatly I should value this distinction, perhaps His Majesty might be graciously pleased to have it acceded to me. For my services to Queen Victoria I was handsomely rewarded, but for my services to King Edward I have never received any recognition. Besides my attendances on His Majesty at Balmoral and in London, I was five times abroad with him: and at Berlin in 1909, and at Biarritz last year, I had very great responsibility and anxiety, which was out of all proportion to the remuneration I received. I was also the first doctor he sent for in his last illness, and was with him, as you know, until the end. In view of these facts, I believe that, in recognition of services to his Father, the King might be disposed to accord me this 'honourable augmentation'. I should be proud to have it, to mark the association of three British Sovereigns, which it has been my privilege to enjoy, and to keep it in the remembrance of my descendants.

245

Reid's request was complied with immediately, and he became one of the select few to be allowed a royal lion in his coat of arms, the official Warrant of Augmentation being signed by Winston Churchill, then the Home Secretary. The announcement was made in the *London Gazette*, just before the Coronation.

Each autumn Reid was summoned to Balmoral by George V. In September 1910, he was required to replace Laking, and he remained there for five weeks, ample time to become acquainted with the new Sovereign and his wife at home. Lord Esher, who was there at the same time, observed that:

> It is altogether different here from former years. There is no longer the old atmosphere about the house – that curious electric element which pervaded the surroundings of King Edward. Yet everything is very charming and wholesome, and sweet. The house is a home for children – six of them at luncheon – the youngest running round the table all the while. The Queen knits of an evening. The King sat on the sofa talking with me until bed-time. Everything is very 'easy'. That does not imply licence – only the perfect ease of English home life.

Slatin Pasha, Wingate, Lloyd George and Balfour arrived to enliven the party, and then a few days later Susan and Delia Spencer settled at Abergeldie Castle, where they stayed with Lord and Lady Carrington. Queen Mary saw in Reid exactly the person she needed to help her with the tenants and cottages on the Balmoral Estate. Reid had known the families for nigh on thirty years; he was a local inhabitant, and spoke their language. Furthermore, he had on several occasions tended them when they were sick. The Queen was by nature shy, and tended to be formal and stiff. She needed an escort who had the light touch and understood the Deeside mentality. Reid was pressed into service without delay, and records that on 10 September, 'at 3 walked with the Queen, Princess Mary, the Prince of Wales and Prince Albert, as their guide and introducer, to call on twelve of the cottages in and near the village. Also to the shop. We all went to tea at Michies.' The ice had been broken, but nevertheless, on subsequent occasions, Queen Mary took Reid with her when visiting tenantry whenever she could. Sometimes they walked, sometimes they drove, but either way he was indispensable, as is illustrated in a letter written by Queen Mary to Lady Mount Stephen after Reid's death. 'I don't know what I shall do at Balmoral without Sir James. We used to go off *tête-à-tête*, and he helped me so with all the Scotch people, and we had such delightful talks, and he was such fun, and such a friend.'

A week after Reid's guided tour of the tenantry, the Queen sent

for him and asked him 'to try and get back a ring with George III's
hair, that had been given to Sir John McNeill, as a souvenir of
Queen Victoria, after her death'. This he succeeded in doing almost
immediately, by writing to McNeill's son, who, it appears, had no
option but to do what was requested of him. Queen Mary's acquisitive
propensities are renowned. What she saw and liked she desired
to possess, and she would stick at nothing to achieve her purpose –
especially if it had royal connections. For this, one of her less charming
characteristics, the nation must be thankful today.

At Christmas 1911, Reid's mother had a fall and fractured the neck
of her femur. He hastened north from Althorp to Ellon, where he
found her quite cheerful and suffering no pain 'except when the leg
is moved', and he stayed with her into the new year when he was sure
that she was on the mend. A week later he received a telegram to say
his mother had died of heart failure. She was eighty-six years old.
There followed several days of agonising remorse when Reid convinced himself that he should have stayed in Ellon at his mother's
bedside instead of returning to London. For fifty years his mother
had been the only woman in his life – devoted, affectionate, and
undemanding – and she had never shown the slightest hint of jealousy
when Susan appeared on the scene, but had embraced her with open
arms. By general consent she was a grand old lady.

For three days before her funeral Reid spent long hours contemplat-
ing her in her coffin, laying fresh bunches of lilies of the valley on her
breast, 'feeling very miserable and unhappy'. After the burial he spent
'a bad night, with vain regrets at not having returned to Mama', and
a 'very bad day' looking 'at Mama's grave covered with wreaths'. John
'paid the accounts for Mama's nursing and funeral'. Reid returned to
London to find 'Susan and the children at the door to meet me, all
well, but Susan looking haggard and worn'.

Life resumed its normal course, Reid rushing from patient to
committee and from committee to lecture. He became President of
the Finance Committee of the Royal College of Physicians, Vice-
President of the Royal Institution of Great Britain, and a member of
the Council of the Royal Society of Medicine. He also served on the
Reception Committee at the International Medical Congress which
was held in London in 1913. In addition, he made great efforts to
keep up to date with all new techniques in surgery and innovations in
medicine, by reading papers and frequently attending seminars and
lectures. Always present at royal openings of new medical centres and
hospital extensions, he took an active part in presenting members of
the medical profession to the royal visitor. He, rather than Laking,

who was not highly esteemed by the medical fraternity, acted as liaison between the royal family and the profession. It was he who was asked to represent the King at Lord Lister's funeral, and he retained his connection with Queen Alexandra through his activity on the Council of the Queen Alexandra Sanatorium at Davos.

On 28 February 1912, he attended a huge anti-women's-suffrage meeting at the Albert Hall, presided over by Susan's uncle, Lord Cromer, and he and Susan were given places on the platform, being among those whom Millicent Fawcett described as 'extinct volcanoes'. A couple of months before the meeting Lord Cromer had written to Reid urging him to attend, as he wanted 'the medical profession to be well represented'. The issue of women's suffrage was strictly non-party and the vast gathering of 10,000 was treated to the rhetoric of Lord Loreburn, the Liberal Lord Chancellor, on the one hand, and Lord Curzon, a staunch Tory, on the other. These were but two out of many great names who declaimed their views to an excited public. That Reid should deny female opportunities in the professions is perhaps understandable, but for Susan actively to deprive herself of a voice in the country's affairs, educated as she was, is curious.

During his stay at Balmoral in 1912 Reid had the task of 'cutting the Queen's corns' and attending to her knee, which she had sprained while out walking. She was anxious about the Prince of Wales, too, who, at the age of eighteen, was small and thin, and only weighed seven stone two pounds. Reid was asked to 'overhaul' him, but apart from his puniness could find nothing wrong with him.

Serghei Dmitrievich Sazonov, the Russian Foreign Minister, was also staying at Balmoral.

> This evening after dinner I talked to Sazonov, sitting on a sofa in the drawing room for over half an hour. The King was sitting talking to Aberdeen, the Queen to Matthews and John [Revelstoke], Benckendorff, Farquhar, and Gray were playing bridge in the little drawing room. Hence it was that Sazonov fell to me to entertain, and I was glad to have the chance of being able to form an opinion of him. He told me the Empress has something wrong with her heart and is very ill, and that she is always in terror of her boy being ill or dying, especially as he is not robust. [The Czarevich suffered from haemophilia]

Reid also enjoyed the company of Arthur Balfour. 'I sat next to Mr Balfour at dinner last night and we had a very pleasant and lively conversation. He and Salisbury were much interested in hearing my account of the burning in effigy of Lloyd George at Turiff a fortnight or so ago.' Balfour thought that, 'for a Radical politician to be burnt in Radical Aberdeenshire certainly has its humorous side!'

Although a notoriously reluctant traveller, King George V was obliged to make the occasional journey to the Continent. As was to be expected, Reid was selected to accompany him to Berlin in May 1913, where the King and Queen were to attend the marriage between Princess Victoria Louise of Prussia and Prince Ernest, son of the Duke of Cumberland. This was not a State visit involving long and tiring ceremonial but a family gathering, at which George V and his cousins, the Kaiser, and the Czar of Russia, met for the last time before the combined calamities of the Great War and the Russian Revolution were to change the structure of European politics and society. For Reid the visit was both notable and enjoyable since the Kaiser awarded him the Order of the Red Eagle, First Class, and he had the chance of meeting all his old friends.

The following year on a State visit to France, Reid was able to add the Insignia of the Commander de la Légion d'Honneur to his honours, a consolation for having to nurse a duodenal ulcer on Benger's Food which he had so frequently prescribed for Queen Victoria. One wonders if an element of sour grapes crept into his comments on the indifferent catering at the Hôtel de Ville. Certainly, the royal party noted that French ceremonial was less well organised than the Kaiser's. But the warmth of the Parisian welcome for the royal couple buoyed the King with much needed self-confidence and consolidated the entente cordiale inspired by his more genial father. In less than four months the two nations were allies in war.

On his return from Paris Reid took to his bed with phlebitis in his left leg. He had just recovered when he learned the news of Laking's death and immediately rushed round to Buckingham Palace, to find 'that Treves was already with the King about it'.

Sir Bertrand Dawson was the man selected to succeed Laking as the King's Physician-in-Ordinary, and being a younger man, and highly able, he became the doctor whom the King consulted most frequently. Now that Laking was out of the way and the King had found confidence in his new young doctor, Reid's role as medical adviser to the royal family slowly diminished, until it finally ceased to exist, although he still officially held the position of Physician-in-Ordinary and remained, until his death, a friend of the family.

Three weeks after the outbreak of war Reid received a telegram from Sir Frederick Treves, telling him 'to go to Wick to meet Prince

Albert[1] who has appendicitis and is to be landed there from the *Collingwood* tomorrow'. He hastened dutifully to Wick.

> Met at the station by a coast guardsman, and at the hotel by the ship's officer, who took me off in a pinnace to the hospital ship, *Rohilla*, where I saw Prince Albert with Fleet Surgeon Lomas. We decided that it was not quite safe to move him, and that I was to remain on board. At 6 we sailed in a fog for Scapa Flow, Orkney, arriving 8 p.m. On the way we passed eight battleships, and twelve destroyers with them, all cleared for action. We were escorted from Wick by two destroyers.

Within a few days, Prince Albert showed a marked improvement. Meanwhile Reid was as close to the war in action as he was ever to be. As he records in his diary, he 'spent the forenoon on the deck watching the warships of all kinds round us coaling, etc. Had an interview with the C. in C. Sir J. Jellicoe, who came on board re Prince Albert. Wrote to the King. At 6 saw the squadron of battleships and destoyers go out with Jellicoe on the *Iron Duke*. Lights out 9.15.'

The following morning brought 'another lovely day. Prince Albert still better. In the forenoon watched the thrilling scene round us, and went over the engine room and refrigerating chambers with the Chief Engineer. At 5 we sailed for Aberdeen. Stayed on deck till 7 to see the islands and ships we passed, and the Caithness coast, and went on deck after dinner. Ships lights all on tonight.' The Aberdeenshire coast was sighted at four a.m. and at five the *Rohilla*, being too big to enter the harbour, anchored outside the breakwater. Shortly after six, '45 invalids and the Prince were disembarked in cots by crane into tugs, and we went ashore in them.'

Whilst playing his minor role in the war effort, Reid was receiving news of a more serious nature from Susan. '2000 British casualties makes one shiver,' she wrote. 'Poor Elizabeth had no idea of *that* when she wrote yesterday, and now she will be dreadfully anxious.' Written less than a month after war broke out, this gives but a small foretaste of the slaughter which was to follow over the next four years. The Reids, whose children were too young to engage in the war, escaped the immediate personal tragedy which affected so many of their family and friends. Susan's sister, Elizabeth, lost her son Dermot in action, and their brother Hugo was wounded, as was Jack Spencer, now Viscount Althorp, though neither of them was seriously incapacitated. Apart from the tragic loss of life at the front, the First World

---

[1] Later George VI, serving then as a midshipman.

War had less effect upon civilians than the Second and life carried on much as before, though with less emphasis on social frivolity. Reid, who continued to keep his diary daily, barely even mentions the war.

On 9 September 1914 Prince Albert had his appendix removed by Professor Marnock, Professor of Surgery at Aberdeen University. Reid was present and reported to the King by telephone, and also wrote the bulletin. There were no complications, and the Prince recovered rapidly. During his convalescence he went to The Chesnuts, where he spent a couple of afternoons relaxing in the garden and taking tea.

Two years later, however, Prince Albert was suffering from abdominal pains again, and once more Reid was asked by the King to attend him, this time in Rosyth, where the Prince was still serving on the *Collingwood*. After a few days Prince Albert's mysterious abdominal trouble cleared up, and he was allowed to return home to Windsor where he was ordered to convalesce. While at Ellon Reid received a letter of thanks from Prince Albert, and one from Arthur Bigge, now Lord Stamfordham, writing on behalf of the King, which could not have failed to please him.

> His Majesty feels that in you he has an old friend of the family to whom he can always turn in confidence, and I know that it was a real joy to Prince Albert to see you at his side again. The King was sorry to disturb you in your short holiday spent in the bosom of the family, and to entail upon you a tedious journey – but it was a great comfort to Their Majesties to know you were there with the Prince, of whose previous illness and operation you had complete knowledge, and to receive your daily letters and telegrams.

On the subject of Prince Albert's health and his future Lord Stamfordham expresses doubts: 'It is mysterious and unsatisfactory, especially in the light of the future, that there are these recurrences – and one sometimes doubts whether he will be able to continue in the navy.' But continue he did, and in spite of the fact that gastric troubles recurred intermittently, disrupting his war career, the Prince behaved throughout with great courage, rising from his sick bed to resume his duties in a gun turret on the *Collingwood* during the Battle of Jutland, as a result of which he was mentioned in dispatches.

In 1915 Stamfordham had lost his only son, John Bigge, on active service. In an affectionate letter to Reid he exhibits his customary selflessness.

251

Thank you, my dear old friend, with all my heart, and a very aching one I can assure you! You knew the dear boy since his birth, and can appreciate our loss. Life without him seems at present unbearable, but one has to ask why should he be spared more than others. He was so devoted to parents, sisters and home; and it was only for his sake that I had my ambition in the world. Some day I shall be able to talk of it all to you.

Broken-hearted as he was, Stamfordham continued stoically to dedicate his life in the service of the King.

But the death that affected Reid most was that of his brother John. Reid was still in Scotland and able to attend to his last hours. 'John passed a quiet night opening his eyes at times, and showing momentary consciousness. He told me he had no pain or worry. Pulse in the morning 140, very weak. Temperature 102.5, respiration 30, taking very little nourishment, but taking his strychnine regularly.' During the night of 19 September 1916 John died peacefully, with his brother, his wife Mary, and his daughter Meta at his bedside. For the rest of the night Reid slept fitfully; 'woke at 5 and thought much of John and the days of our boyhood, and all his great goodness to me since.' John, less ambitious than his elder brother, was patient and gentle with children, and generous to a fault. Though socially less successful than Reid, his merchanting business in Japan had flourished, and he had been able to bail his brother out of the financial difficulties into which his career with the royal family, and his marriage into the aristocracy, had plunged him. The brothers had been devoted to one another.

At home, Reid could take satisfaction in watching Ned and Peter emulating his own youthful academic successes. Ned, having previously won a scholarship to Eton, left King's College, Cambridge, with a First in Classics, and the additional accolade of being awarded the Browne Medal for his rendering of an epigram in Greek, a prize he was to receive for three successive years. Peter passed out first at Dartmouth, earning a generous tribute from King George, Lord Stamfordham writing, 'I am commanded by the King to congratulate you and Lady Reid upon Peter's brilliant success, and to say that unfortunately His Majesty's own son [Prince George] occupied the opposite pole!! but His Majesty is so glad that tho' so far separated intellectually they are closely associated as friends!'

The two girls, Margaret and Victoria, who were never given the same opportunities as their brothers, showed themselves to be able musicians. After many years of being closeted with a governess, they were sent to St Paul's School for Girls, where they flourished under the tutelage of Gustav Holst. Margaret was offered a place at Newnham

College, Cambridge, which was turned down because her male chauvinist father considered that she was needed at home. Inhibited by genteel poverty, and kept back because they were girls, their childhood and early teenage – according to Victoria – was dreary in the extreme. Had it not been for the generosity of Uncle Bobbie and their Baring uncles, John Revelstoke and Cecil, who invited them to stay at their houses in the country, and for Aunt Maude, Cecil's beautiful, sympathetic and unconventional American wife, who understood the needs of children and whose own girls, Daphne and Calypso, became their firm friends, they would have had little contact with the world outside 72 Grosvenor Street. Once at St Paul's, rebelling from high society, they became caught up in a world which revolved around music and art. Imogen Holst became their special friend, and through their brother Peter, who was in the navy with Casper, they became acquainted with the exotic family of Augustus John. Since they had neither money nor impeccable lineage, they found their niches among those with whom talent counted for more than social position.

Now in his seventies, Reid had not completely lost his connection with the Court, though his visits were less frequent. In January 1916 he was sent for by Queen Alexandra, who had shingles, and in 1920, at Princess Victoria's request, he went to see the ageing Queen again, who was by this time not only deaf, but blind as well, and deeply depressed. Reid noted: 'Sat with H.M. for over half an hour and tried to cheer her up.' His annual visits to Balmoral were now purely social. Sometimes he was consulted about medical honours, but other times not, for his inflexible views were well known. The case of Sir Frederick Hewett's K.C.V.O. illustrates that then as now the honours system could cause much agonising and recrimination. In January 1921 Fritz Ponsonby wrote from York Cottage, Sandringham:

The old Romans refused to consult the oracle when they feared it would be unfavourable, so the King refused to allow me to consult you when Hewett's knighthood was contemplated. This was very much pressed by Queen Alexandra, Princess Victoria and Sir Dighton, and I was opposed to it on the grounds of age. I thought Hewett was not old enough and had not been long enough at his job for a K.C.V.O.

The King thought first I should write adversely on this theme, and secondly that you would knock it on the head. As a compromise H.M. suggested I should write to Dawson, and I did so. Dawson threw cold water on the proposal, but added 'although I admit that a knighthood is more of use to a man when he is young'. The King seized on this, and pushed the thing through, but I still think there was no hurry and Hewett could have been given the C.V.O. Fairbank pressed very hard for an ordinary knighthood on the grounds that he was Mayor of Windsor when the Prince of Wales received the freedom of the town. Downing Street, however, refused even to consider this and eventually he was given a C.V.O. This requires no answer, I only thought you would be amused to hear what had happened about their honours.

Needless to say, Reid did answer and put forward his views forcibly:

I maintain that a Knighthood ought to be given as a recognition of proved preeminent merit, and of an established position and reputation, *not* as a lever to push and advertise a man 'in the making'. I constantly hear men that I come in contact with say (and I rather agree with them) that present day honours are as a rule not given to the men who really deserve them, but to men on a lower level who, directly or indirectly, tout and intrigue for them, which the good men will not do. The result is that in the main medical honours are not now regarded in the Profession as a hallmark of distinction, but as a brand of successful intrigue! Indeed, a very distinguished F.R.S. said to me the other day that the Medical Honours nowadays are a 'scandal'. Poor old Fairbank! I think they should have made him a 'KNT' for being Mayor of Windsor, considering who have been some of the recipients. Even in my day they knighted a Mayor of Windsor, who kept a shop. If Fairbank could have sung or preached in Welsh, he might have got it.

On his seventy-third and last birthday, Reid received a letter from Princess Louise, who had always shown great interest in her godson Peter's progress at school and in the navy, and who had maintained regular contact with the family. Two days previously Reid's best man and Queen Alexandra's devoted equerry, Arthur Davidson, had died. Princess Louise, warm-hearted and emotional as she was, expressed her sympathy over his loss.

I know you will feel dear Colonel Davidson's death. You know well how to appreciate his splendid character; he was such a noble man in every way. I am always so proud that through me he came to the Queen. My thoughts have been so often turning towards you that I could not help writing these few lines. I am feeling very much that some of my family would be glad if I were out of the way. It's always been so, but I am not as strong as I was and I cannot throw it off so easily though it will never disturb me. One can live above minding, and I try to. I remember when you were in trouble years ago you used to write to me; so now in my loneliness I cannot help having a talk on paper with you. Pray excuse, and *please burn* this when *read*.

What awful sorrows are surrounding our Country! It will take a long time to right itself. An angry and bitter fighting opposition will also be a trouble and hamper the country. Why can't there be selfless politicians who love their country more than themselves!

In her last letter to Reid Princess Louise reveals not only the intimacy of their relationship, but also a deep pathetic sadness. She had inherited her mother's emotional instability, but not her common sense.

The last royal event which Reid attended, on 26 April 1923, was the wedding of Prince Albert, Duke of York, to Lady Elizabeth Bowes-Lyon at Westminster Abbey. A month later he had an acute attack of phlebitis from which he never recovered. For more than five weeks he lay in bed restless, depressed and suffering from breathlessness and severe pains in the chest, caused by a failing heart. Three doctors saw him frequently each day, and Susan was with him constantly watching over him as he grew weaker by the hour. In the middle of it all, Peter arrived back from Malta after two and a half years away at sea, just in time for Reid to catch a glimpse of him. On 27 June Susan wrote in her diary: 'Jamie now eats nothing and he just knew me.' The following morning, 'after a very restless night my dearest Jamie died at 7.0 a.m. He became unconscious and slipped away. Ned and Peter and I were with him at the last.' His funeral, held in his home town of Ellon, was fittingly simple and as he would have wished it – no hearse with nodding plumes for him. The coffin, which was conveyed from The Chesnuts to the parish church, and thence to the cemetery, on an open cart drawn by two horses, was embedded among beautiful wreaths, one of which bore the inscription: 'For our dear old friend, Sir James Reid, from Alexandra'.

Tributes from two of his closest surviving friends perhaps serve more aptly than anything else to illustrate his personality and summarise his achievements. In the words of Fritz Ponsonby:

He was always so pointful, and his keen sense of humour made him such a delightful companion. He occupied such a unique position in Queen Victoria's reign that I think she was guided more by him than anyone else, and statesmen like old Lord Salisbury always said he was by far the most interesting of the Household. So many trips we took together abroad, and his absence of Royal Culte and delightful way of stripping the leaves from the trees and putting things in a blunt way was always a pleasure to me.

On 23 July, 1923, Lord Stamfordham wrote in *The Times*:

The honesty which shone in his face was the reflex of his heart. His innate straightness and integrity of purpose scorned all intrigue or self-seeking;

his shrewd Scotch common sense and fearless spirit successfully coped with difficulties, great and small, which might have daunted a more pedantic and less elastic mind. Beloved and respected by the medical hierarchy, he stood in their estimation for all that is honourable, independent and true.

Appendix I

Sir James Reid's Notes on Professor Pagenstecher's Visit to the Queen, 24 August 1896

He came with Nettleship and I met them at Cowes at 12.10 and we drove up together. We talked in my room till 1.30, when we three lunched together, and then went to arrange the tables, lamps, etc., in the Prince Consort's room, returning to mine till the Queen was ready. During this time I was several times sent for by H.M., who wished to know about Pagenstecher, what was to be done, etc. About 3.30 we were summoned to the Queen in the Prince's room, Princess Beatrice being with her throughout. Pagenstecher examined her eyes for 20 minutes or so, and Nettleship for three or four minutes. Then I dropped Homatropine into the eyes, and we withdrew. At about 4.20, when the pupils were well dilated (I saw H.M. in the interval and repeated the Homatropine), the Queen returned to the Prince's room and we were again summoned. Pagenstecher then completed his examination and Nettleship also had a look with the ophthalmoscope. The Queen then conversed with Pagenstecher, after which (about 4.45) we returned to my room, where Pagenstecher wrote a statement of the result of his examination, which is in my possession. At 5.15 we drove to Trinity Pier, and I saw them off at West Cowes.

During the day I had much conversation with Pagenstecher, who was very agreeable and frank, and gave me the impression of being 'straight'.

Among other things I told him of the many reports I had heard here of his curing cases that had baffled English oculists, and of his rectifying their mistakes. He said that he was very sorry that people made such statements, as they were quite untrue. I mentioned having been told by Princess Christian and others that he could cure cataract by 'absorption' without an operation. He said that this was absurd, and that if I heard such a story again I might contradict it on his authority. That there were cases of liquid turbidity, where he used Iodide of Potassium ointment and thought it sometimes did good; but that in cases of real cataract it was useless, and that there was nothing to hope for but by operation. Then I asked him about Miss Stopford [a lady-in-waiting], who had told me that her eyes were very seriously affected at one time, and that no one in England could do her any good whatsoever, so she went to Pagenstecher, who cured her. He replied that in reality there was little or nothing the matter with her eyes, and that it was entirely a case of nerves – in fact a form of hysteria, which he treated on general principles, giving her, as a placebo, applications for the eyes.

I mentioned to him Lady Lytton's [a lady-in-waiting] having told me about her sister, Lady Loch, having very bad eyes, that the English oculist had made a great mistake, so she went to Pagenstecher who found it out and told her 'the nerve was twisted'. When I told him this he roared with laughter, said he had no recollection of Lady Loch, but that this was the first time he had ever heard of such an affection! We all made very merry over this story.

Then as to Princess Christian having been almost blind and been cured by him, he said that there was absolutely nothing the matter with her eyes, that her symptoms were simply the result of her nerves being for the time shattered by stimulants and narcotics, and ceased when these were for the time being cut off from her. No doubt he had given her applications for her eyes to please her, and to work on her imagination, but for nothing else. He gave her a spirit lotion to rub in, which is neither good nor bad for anything. (This lotion the Princess had great faith in, and she got some bottles of it for the Queen to use at Cimiez).

Pagenstecher told me that I must know quite well that all these stories of his cures where English oculists had failed were untrue. I replied that of course I did, but that my opinion was of no value whatever, as there were so many non-medical people here who know far more of medical subjects, and of 'cures' than I do! – and we all three laughed heartily over it.

With regard to his general treatment of patients, he told us that, in his opinion, the most important thing is to tranquillise the patient's mind, whatever may be the matter, and that, in order to do this, he considers it right and justifiable not to tell them anything, or even to adhere strictly to facts, if by so doing he can make them feel satisfied and happy when they would otherwise be miserable and live in constant unhappiness. For instance, he often does not tell patients that they may have cataract, as he finds so many have a horror of this, and of an operation looming in the distance, but he simply tells them that they have a little opacity in the eye, which very many people get as they grow older, that it may not get worse, but if it does, it can be removed, without saying how. If they ask direct whether it be cataract he says *No* (as he does not call it by that name until it is advanced). By doing so he leaves the patient happy and contented, and they live with an easy mind. As so in other cases he often finds it best not to destroy the beliefs of patients as to their eyes being bad, but to humour them and work on their imagination, all for their own good and peace of mind. If he worked according to rigid rules, he would have no success in practice. I saw that Nettleship did not approve of this principle of tampering with facts in dealing with patients, and he said, 'Well, Pagenstecher, as to what one says to a patient, every man must judge for himself what he considers right.' Pagenstecher was quite frank and open in telling us the principle on which he acts, and he, I am sure, does so because *he* considers it right. But I cannot help thinking that this principle may be carried too far, and that he has perhaps insensibly and gradually got into the way of doing so, and that this may to some extent account for the wonderful confidence he inspires in non-medical patients, and for his reputation among them for extraordinary cures, a reputation quite out of proportion to his professional reputation not only in England, but in Germany, and which I believe he himself would honestly repudiate.

The Queen was delighted with him. He has a very pleasant sympathetic manner, and while he was examining her eyes, he kept saying (in German), half to himself and half to her as it were, such words as 'good', 'very good', 'quite healthy', 'not at all as bad as I should have thought', and so on, which reassured Her Majesty greatly, though his real opinion, as written out by him afterwards, could hardly be squared with such expressions. Nettleship, on the other hand, though at the very least as able an oculist as Pagenstecher (his professional reputation is higher) is a man of few words, plain spoken, and will not deviate from the strict facts for anybody, consequently he did not use similar expressions to the Queen, and the result is that Her Majesty thinks him cold, harsh, abrupt and unsympathetic, and compares him very unfavourably with Pagenstecher. No doubt Pagenstecher's manner and system are what exactly suit the Queen, and Her Majesty is much relieved and satisfied with his visit, though in reality we are exactly where we were, and Pagenstecher could suggest no change of treatment whatever, and said we could only go on ringing the changes with glasses and temporising.

My belief is that Pagenstecher is a straightforward man, and that acting on the principles above enunciated, he does so with the honest conviction he is right. And it may be so, though I can't myself believe it to the extent he does. And I cannot help being convinced that it accounts for the wonderful things one hears of him from patients and their friends, stories which he himself utterly repudiates, and is annoyed about. In fact it is a case of 'Save me from my friends'.

Appendix II

Morell Mackenzie and
the German Doctors, 1887–9

On 9 November 1887 Professor von Schrötter from Vienna, and Dr Krause from Berlin arrived in San Remo, and were joined a day later by Dr Moritz Schmidt who had been sent by the Emperor. They had been summoned to examine the throat of the Imperial Crown Prince Frederick. Schrötter affirmed that the disease was cancer and recommended excision of the whole larynx. Krause considered that the disease was a 'malignant neoplasm', but thought it wise to give potassium iodide first in order to make sure that it was not syphilis. Schmidt agreed with Krause and urged that large doses of potassium iodide should be given before embarking on the more serious course of an operation, on the ground that syphilitic infection might exist dating from many years back. In 1869, on the occasion of the opening of the Suez Canal by the Empress Eugénie, the Crown Prince had fallen prey to a beautiful Spanish woman Dolores Cada. Evidence of syphilis appeared a short time later and had been treated by the Khedive's physician. Mackenzie, as has been seen, thought it best to wait until the swelling of the larynx had subsided and then remove a small piece of new growth for microscopic inspection. At this stage there was still a tiny glimmer of hope that a past indiscretion of the Crown Prince might be the cause of his malady rather than the fatal disease which at heart all the medical men suspected.

Meanwhile, in a letter to Reid written on 10 November Mackenzie had referred to the 'kill or cure' policy of the Germans. Reid's reaction to this comment was that it was not 'quite fair, seeing that his own plan does not include even the ghost of a "cure", which theirs does'. Reid, it must be remembered, was not in possession of all the facts of the case, as is illustrated in a letter from Lady Ponsonby to her husband written from San Remo. 'I don't think Mackenzie has entered into all the details with Reid,' she writes and goes on to make an interesting comment about the Queen: 'I think she has been "envenimée" against M. Mackenzie by Uncle [Ernest, Duke of Saxe-Coburg-Gotha], who is in charge of his nephew William, and thinks and says the English doctor is only trying to feather his nest.' In fact it was Reid's arguments which influenced her, rather than the Duke's.

Early in February 1888 a tracheotomy was performed by Dr

Bramann, but on 16 February there were complications and Mackenzie told Reid of incompetence on the part of the German doctors.

> After a day or two it was evident that the tubes did not fit. They were
> repeatedly changed but they all caused irritation, nevertheless the surgeons
> would not try my tube. At last they had to ask me to put in *my* tube! This
> I did, and the Crown Prince has since been much better. Had my tube
> been put in from the first, no unpleasant symptoms would have arisen,
> but we must still expect some trouble, as the German tubes have caused
> so much *tracheal* irritation, that it will take some days for it to go down.
> Last night all was going on well at 9 o'clock but it was the turn of Dr
> Schrader to come on duty. I asked him to allow Mr Hovell to take his
> place, as I was sure he would make a muddle with the tubes. He, however,
> declined to give way. In the middle of the night Dr Schrader was obliged
> to call upon Mr Hovell, because he could not insert the inner tube. He
> had drawn the outer tube slightly out, and the end was cutting into the
> flesh and causing haemorrhage. Mr Hovell put it back directly, but this
> will throw the Crown Prince back several days. At last they have consented
> that we shall attend to the tube for the future. Having got the patient into
> a bad condition, the surgeons propose now to withdraw and I shall not
> stand in their way.

After reading this letter it is easier to understand the Crown Princess's
determination to cling to Mackenzie. The English doctors not only
offered hope for the future but were, unquestionably, mechanically
more adept than the German doctors. It is worth mentioning that the
German physicians and surgeons involved, although eminent in their
profession were not laryngologists, with the exception of Schrötter
and Tobold who were only consulted briefly and did not follow the
case throughout its course. This may be one reason for Mackenzie's
attitude of superiority which aroused the German doctors' enmity.

In Berlin on 12 April, the Emperor, as he had now become, was
seized by a severe attack of coughing which slight adjustments of the
cannula usually relieved. Mackenzie decided to try a cannula of a
new pattern, and invited von Bergmann to witness the change. Von
Bergmann, Mackenzie and Hovell went into the Emperor's room and
the unfortunate patient was then submitted to a great deal of rough
handling by von Bergmann, who bungled the fitting of the new
cannula. The tube had to be withdrawn, whereupon a violent fit
of coughing and haemorrhage followed. He tried a second time, and
again the tube had to be withdrawn, and with its removal there
followed renewed coughing and haemorrhage. Then von Bergmann
sent for Bramann who succeeded in passing the cannula into the
trachea with the greatest of ease, but it was hours before the coughing

and bleeding subsided. According to Mark Hovell von Bergmann had been drinking, and he swayed from side to side as he tried to insert the cannula.

Certainly the Emperor would never allow von Bergmann near him again, and considered that he had been 'ill treated' by him. Von Bergmann retired from the case on 30 April, which occasioned further vitriolic outbursts in the German newspapers against Mackenzie and the Crown Princess. Mackenzie wrote to Reid giving him an account of what had occurred on 12 April, in no way exaggerating the incident, and informed him that the patient had 'tracheitis which I fear may travel down and cause bronchitis'.

The death of Emperor Frederick III, far from ending the wrangling between the doctors, started a fresh battle. Mackenzie injudiciously spoke freely to a reporter of a Dutch newspaper giving his account of the case. This in turn was published in Bismarck's semi-official newspaper, the *Norddeutsche Allgemeine Zeitung*, and not only infuriated the Germans but also brought down the wrath of Colonel Leopold Swaine, upon Mackenzie. In a venomous letter to Sir Henry Ponsonby he gave his opinion of the English doctor.

If Dr Mackenzie really spoke in this sense to the reporter of a newspaper in Holland then nothing is bad enough for him. His behaviour all through this too, too sad case has been such that it will be almost an impossibility, however much Dr M. may deny it, to induce people to believe he is an injured individual. If it is true – I have it from very good authority that it is so – that the English medical profession are exasperated against Dr M.'s actions towards the German doctors associated with him, it would have a surprising effect here and, although this may seem almost impossible, tend greatly to cement the good feeling between the two nations, if the English medical profession gave some public expression of their feeling in that respect. At present it is only natural that everyone here thoroughly believes Dr Mackenzie to be backed up in England by all his colleagues, and the condemnation of the present condition of the Medical Science in England is therefore severely criticised. I should like Dr Reid to know this.

On 24 July, Sir Edward Malet, the British Ambassador in Berlin, was staying at Osborne where Reid had the chance of talking with him in the billiard room after dinner. Malet's views, as noted by Reid, are worth recording as they reflect not only the German attitude to Mackenzie, but also that of all the British living in Berlin:

In spite of all her cleverness, anyone can get round the Empress Victoria who fawns upon her, hence it is always the blackguards who get hold of her, and this has been a great misfortune. This he said with reference not only to Mackenzie but also generally. Malet thought Mackenzie a most unprincipled and designing man, and said he had done no end of mischief, political and otherwise. He pestered the Emperor continually for his knighthood and for his order. His conduct with newspaper reporters was notorious. He was continually seeing reporters, and he selected the reporters of lower Radical papers.

In Berlin the German doctors had their own answer to all Mackenzie's newspaper reporting activity. Issued from the Imperial Press on 11 July, was a black-bordered pamphlet 62 pages long, entitled *'Die Krankheit Kaiser Friedrich des Dritten'* (The Illness of Frederick III). Instead of it being, as expected by the medical profession, a plain scientific statement of facts, the report turned out to be a biased account of the case, vehemently attacking Mackenzie who was accused not only of raising false hopes which led to the postponement of an operation which would have cured the disease, but also of actual malpractice. The seriousness of the operation was played down. The whole trend of the report was to show that the sagacious, experienced and high-minded German professors had always been right and the ignorant, clumsy and untrustworthy English doctors always wrong.

Mackenzie's reply was in the form of a book published on 15 October containing 244 pages, entitled *The Fatal Illness of Frederick the Noble*, in which he states the case from his viewpoint, from time to time condemning the German doctors, and producing statistics unfavourable to the removal of the larynx to justify his refusal to allow an operation. The book which was injudicious, to say the least, shocked the English-speaking world who were ignorant of the vilification and vituperation which had been heaped upon him by the German physicians and surgeons. The medical profession, in particular, was critical of Mackenzie and said that he had violated the secrets of the sick room.

In England 100,000 copies were sold in a fortnight and an American edition and French translation were published simultaneously. A further 100,000 copies of *Frederick the Noble* were distributed throughout the German Empire, but on the day of publication the German police confiscated every copy of the book at the instigation of the young Emperor, Wilhelm II. Mackenzie, in his turn, met the English translation of the German pamphlet by instructing Messrs Lewis & Lewis, his solicitors, to send telegrams to all publishing firms in London: 'If translation of German pamphlet is published by you we have instructions from Sir Morell Mackenzie to commence an action of libel against you and claim heavy damages.' The pamphlets were immediately withdrawn from circulation, but one copy at least slipped through the net into Reid's possession, and remains amongst the Reid papers to this day.

As far as Reid was concerned this was not the end of the matter. On Christmas Day 1888 he was asked by Ponsonby to write to Sir James Paget, the Queen's Sergeant Surgeon, about a resolution that was to be brought up at the Royal College of Surgeons concerning Mackenzie's book and his professional conduct, a step which he strongly disapproved taking. The letter illustrates how scheming Mackenzie was in the way in which he took advantage of the Empress's good nature and gullibility, using her to protect himself. On learning of the resolution, Mackenzie, as Reid relates to Paget,

> went to Miss Green (an old English governess, who has long been with the Empress Frederick, and has just left them and settled in London) and told her this resolution is aimed not so much at him as at the Empress Frederick herself, and that it will do her great harm both in England and, especially, in Germany ... This Miss Green writes to the Empress, who has gone to Sir Henry and asked him to do something to avert 'this terrible blow that is aimed at her'. Mackenzie's conduct in this is, you will see, on a par with his usual course of action. I have told him [Ponsonby] plainly, and he quite understands it, that nothing he could say, or even the Empress, would in the slightest degree influence the President and Council of the College in the discharge of their duty; and that for him or the Empress to interfere would be in the highest degree improper. He quite agrees with me, and asks me to explain to you that all he wants is a private note from you, telling him that in whatever is done no insult or disrespect is intended or will be shown to the Empress, and that the matter is purely a technical and professional one relating exclusively to Mackenzie. The Empress is of course under a misapprehension on the subject, Mackenzie having produced this in the way above stated.

Sir Henry Ponsonby who always found it difficult to say No to a request, however unreasonable, had landed himself in deep water and Reid accused him of being 'very weak'. Where principle was at stake Reid never allowed kindness to overrule his judgment of what was right and proper.

Early in the new year of 1889 Reid had reason to write to Sir James Paget again on the same subject. Princess Christian who was staying at Osborne 'opened fire on me yesterday on behalf of the Empress in regard to the resolution to be discussed tomorrow at your College. She is not a very satisfactory person to understand reason or logic; but I think I made it clear to her that the Council can't evade its duty.' Another and final letter to Paget indicates how energetic Reid was in furnishing material which would ensure the passing of the resolution. It appears that on 15 July Mackenzie had written a letter to the Queen in which she was misrepresented. Reid now asked her whether she would sanction its contents being telegraphed to the Royal College of Surgeons. 'Her Majesty consented without the slightest hesitation, and quite approved of the course you proposed to take. She said to tell you she regretted the Mackenzie affair was coming up again, but that if it must come up (as I explained was the case), of course she would not have her name misused and facts misrepresented by Sir Morell. I trust the letter was telegraphed correctly, and that it strengthened your hands, and I hope the resolution has been passed.'

Although his case was never formally discussed at any meeting of the Royal College of Physicians, Mackenzie nonetheless resigned his fellowship of the College in November 1888. On 10 January 1889, at a meeting of the members and fellows of the Royal College of Surgeons, Mackenzie's book was discussed and general regret was expressed both at its publication and at his professional conduct.

Nevertheless, ignoring Mackenzie's behaviour towards his colleagues, and his repeated indiscretions to newspaper reporters, his treatment of the case was the more correct of the two courses open to the unfortunate patient in 1887. Statistics show that an operation would almost certainly have been fatal, and had it by some extraordinary chance proved otherwise, the Crown Prince would have been left voiceless and in a miserable state from which death would have been a mercy. It is true that Mackenzie relied too implicitly on the result of microscopic examination, but his insistence on biopsy was well in advance of his time. All along he felt that there was a fair chance that the Crown Prince had syphilis of the larynx, and although he admitted the possibility of cancer, he claimed that it could not be proved. At the time, his perseverance in the use of palliative treatment was the kindest and wisest course open to him, and one in which the patient concurred. Reid, to whom Mackenzie was anathema, cautioned Ponsonby that 'at the bottom of all Mackenzie's arguments was self'; but that explanation is neither quite fair nor complete. Mackenzie's flamboyance and indiscretion, and at times his inconsistency, blinded Reid to his medical skill. However that may be, Reid's influence, not only upon the Queen, but also upon the Presidents of the Royal Colleges of medicine by presenting unfavourable reports of Mackenzie was to a great extent responsible for Mackenzie's decline and disgrace.

Appendix III

Sir James Reid's Account of the Empress Eugénie's Flight from Paris in 1870

The following was told me at Abergeldie Castle on October 10th, 1895, by the Empress Eugénie in the presence of Madame de Arcos. Her Majesty seemed much affected by the recollections, and at the story of the Station Master she stood up, saluted, and was quite dramatic in her talk and gestures. I never saw her like this before; she seemed to forget I was there, and it was most affecting and deeply interesting.

[*The Empress's narrative*] When the flag was pulled down, and the mob was already invading the Tuileries, they told me I must leave; but we found it was impossible to escape from the Tuileries by the front, and therefore we went along the passage leading to the back entrance – there we found the doors locked, and we had to wait a long time till the key was got. While we were waiting there, Prince Metternich left me, saying he was to get a carriage, and I never saw him again. Count Nigra also left me, and I was alone with Madame le Breton.

Eventually we got out into the street and were quite alone. We got into a cab, and for half an hour we drove at a foot's pace through the mob, and how I was not recognised I do not know. I felt that if I were to be taken it was my 'sort' and I was indifferent to what happened.

Madame le Breton and I consulted as to where I should go. I said I would not go to any 'friend's' house as it might be the cause of ruin to them, and that we must go to Dr Evans, the dentist, as he was an American, and therefore not amenable to French resentment.

It took us four days to get from Paris to Trouville, and several times I thought it was all over. Sometimes we travelled by rail, sometimes by carriage and sometimes on foot. At one place the driver of a fiacre asked if we had come from Paris: 'Oh no, but from –', mentioning another place. The driver then said, 'I hear a revolution has broken out in Paris – Oh! if I could but catch the Empress,' clenching his fists. We got rid of him and his carriage as soon as we could by saying we were going to an hotel close at hand, instead of to a railway station.

At another station I had to wait in the *salon d'attente* along with a

267

crowd of people, and Dr Evans told me to read a newspaper, and I sat reading it with the people all around me. When the train came up, the Station Master came in and began to push me out roughly, saying, 'Be quick, the train is here, get in, and don't loaf about here.' I was alarmed at his rudeness and roughness, and hurried out and got into a compartment, and was surprised that he seemed to keep strangers from getting in beside me. As the train moved off, he drew himself up at my carriage window and saluted respectfully. I then saw that he had recognised me, and helped me, and I kissed my hand to him. So everybody was not bad!

When we arrived at Trouville, Dr Evans went to find out if there was any English ship in the harbour, and found there was Sir John Burgoyne's yacht, with himself and Lady Burgoyne on board, and Sir John agreed to take me.

It was at first decided we were to start next day, but a train came in from Paris, and Dr Evans heard the people talking of arresting Princess Mathilde [Prince Napoleon's sister], and he considered it was not safe to stay overnight, so we went and arranged with Sir John Burgoyne that I was to go on board the same evening. It was not safe for us to go together: so Madame le Breton and Dr Evans went together a round way by the suburbs, and I went all alone through the town to the *plage*, where it was arranged Sir John Burgoyne was to meet me. He did not know me, nor I him, so it had been settled that in order to recognise each other he was to say to me: 'Is that you, Lizzie?' or some such name. I said 'Yes', and then we walked on together, he talking and laughing in a chaffy way, so as to disarm the suspicion of anyone we met and make it appear we were enjoying ourselves. Then when we got on board his yacht, he knelt down and kissed my hand. We started at three, and it took twenty-four hours to get to Ryde. The storm was dreadful, and we all thought we might be lost. I felt I did not care, no one would have known what had become of us. We had all to go below, and the hatches were fastened down to let the sea go over the deck. The men were tied to their posts, and the Captain had only his head out of his place to give the orders. They all risked their lives to take me. It was the same night the *Captain* was lost.

During all those days I wore simply a veil with black spots on it, and refused to disguise myself with a wig, or painting or any other way. I said, 'No, I will not do anything ridiculous of that sort. If I am not to escape without that, I must be taken, and it is my fate.'

People talk of anxiety and grief and sorrow killing you, or driving you mad – but they do not. If your health is unsound, they may kill you. If your brain is weak, they may drive you mad. But if your mind and body are sound, they do none of these things; you do not die or go mad. If anxiety and sorrow could kill or drive mad a sound body and mind, I should have been dead or mad long ago.

[On asking her if she had kept a Diary]

It is far better I did not keep a Diary. There are things I could not have written down. For example, could I have written down what occurred in these last bitter days when I had to leave Paris; how very few friends were with me of all I had before, and how alone I was? Could I have written down how all these friends gradually came back to me afterwards? No, I could not, and it is better so.

Pindaric Epithalamium by Lord Rosebery on the Marriage of Sir James Reid, 28 November 1899

I
    Arise, Aberdonian Muse, and sound
    Thy Bagpipes o'er thy classic ground:
    (Let it not be said she tarried
    When her darling son was married.)
    Sound the tabret and the lute,
    The dental harp that Hebrews use;
    For the man would be a brute
    Who his music would refuse,
    Loud enough to wake the dead,
    When our cherished Reid is wed.

II
    Leave thy Presbyterian halls,
    Muse, and hie thee to St Paul's
    Knightsbridge: – not the church of Wren
    And tomb of celebrated men,
    But the fane of Pimlico
    Where Ritualistic damsels go.
    There in expectation great,
    All the Royal Household sate.
    Maids-of-Honour and Equerries,
    All were there as thick as berries;
    And that transitory horde,
    Fleeting phantoms of an hour,
    Who only share the Royal Board,
    When their Party is in power;
    Stewards, Chamberlains, and Masters
    Of the Horse, – t'would court disasters
    Did I try to tell them all.
    The Board of Green Cloth was at call;

The Bedchamber and Wardrobe gay
Poured forth Officials for the day,
And the Parliamentary Groom
Attended in a natty Brougham.

III   But there was emotion strong,
Reigning in the wanton throng.
First dubiety,
And then anxiety,
Hushed the swelling nuptial song,
And harassed the pew-opening hag.
Whence was the care?
For the Bishop was there,
With vestments in a Gladstone bag,
Ready to unite and bless.
Other cause had the distress.
Where was the Bridegroom, where?
'Was he coming, would he come?'
Rose the agitated hum,
Or was he timidly afar
Concealed in lonely Lochnagar?
'Where was the Bridegroom, where?'
Where? – Why like any other body,
With some comfortable toddy,
Seated in a Vestry chair.

IV   But now the clanging of the bell
Heralds the coming of the Bride.
As killing as a Lyddite shell,
The Bridegroom hastens to her side.
The nuptial crowd approaches
In sixty-seven coaches.
Appears the Bishop with his sleeves of lawn.
His martial namesake, drooping and forlorn,
Attends the Bridegroom without pomp or fuss,
Vir optimorum optimus –
But proud to serve, as all can see,
A Baronet and K.C.B.

V   Illegal incense taints the breeze,
And makes the congregation sneeze
While Prebendary Villiers hopes

That all the world admires his copes.
Our Reid, of deep devotion full,
Clothed in white samite, mystic, wonderful,
With trembling grasp austerely handles
A pair of spermaceti candles;
A wreath entwines his locks, for so
The early Christian's always wedded
Both Brides and Grooms
In the Catacombs, –
(Or so they think in Pimlico)
An ordeal somewhat to be dreaded
By any Presbyterian who
To the shorter Cat is true.

Thus our Baronet was wed –
May Angels flutter o'er his head.

Appendix V

Medical Report on the Queen's Death at Osborne, 23 January 1901

The Queen's health for the past 12 months had been failing, with symptoms mainly of a dyspeptic kind accompanied by impaired general nutrition, periods of insomnia and later by occasional slight and transitory attacks of aphasia, the latter indicating that the cerebral circulation had become damaged although Her Majesty's general arterial system shewed remarkably few signs of age.

The constant brain work through a long life of Royal responsibilities and the Imperial events, domestic sorrows and anxieties which have crowded into her life of later years, may no doubt be held in some measure to account for this discrepancy between the cerebral and general vessel nutrition.

The dyspepsia which tended to lower Her Majesty's naturally robust constitution was especially marked during her last visit to Balmoral. She there first manifested distinct symptoms of brain fatigue and lost notably in weight.

The signs of brain fatigue continued at Windsor and it was there in November and December that the aphasic symptoms appeared but always of an ephemeral kind and unattended by any motor paralysis.

Although it was judged best to continue the arrangements for Her Majesty's proposed visit to the Continent in the spring it was distinctly recognised by her Physicians and by those in closest personal attendance upon her, that these arrangements were purely provisional, it being particularly desired not to discourage Her Majesty in regard to her own health by suggesting doubts as to the feasibility of the change abroad to which she had been looking forward.

After manifesting unusual fatigue from the journey to Osborne on the 18th December with symptoms of nervous agitation and restlessness which lasted for two days, Her Majesty began to show improvement both in appetite and nerve tone in response to more complete quietude than she had hitherto consented to observe.

A few days before the final illness, transient but recurring symptoms of apathy and torpor with aphasic indications and increasing feebleness gave great uneasiness to her Physician. On Wednesday 16th January

The Queen showed for the first time unequivocal symptoms of mental confusion.

By an effort of will Her Majesty would for a time as it were command her brain to work and the visitor of a few minutes would fail to observe the signs of cerebral exhaustion.

On Thursday the mental confusion was more marked with considerable drowsiness; and a slight flattening was observed on the right side of the face. From this time the aphasia and facial flattening although incomplete were permanent. On Friday The Queen was a little brighter.

On Saturday evening 19th, however there was a relapse of the graver symptoms which with remissions continued until the close.

It is important to note that notwithstanding the great bodily weakness and cerebral exhaustion the heart's action was steadily and well sustained to the last; the pulse at times evincing an increased tension but being always regular and of normal frequency.

The temperature was normal throughout.

The end came with symptoms of failing power of the organic reflexes and the final scene with paresis of the pulmonary nerves, the heart beating steadily to the last.

Beyond the slight right facial flattening there was never any motor paralysis and except for occasional lapses mentioned, the mind cannot be said to have been clouded. Within a few minutes of death The Queen recognised the several Members of her family.

Signed James Reid

Notes on Sources

Abbreviations: JR-Sir James Reid; QV-Queen Victoria; *Letters-The Letters of Queen Victoria*, ed. G.E. Buckle, John Murray, 1928

Chapter 1 *The Making of a Doctor*, pp.23–31
p.31 QV's first impression of JR: *Letters, 1879–1885*, second series, vol. III, (p.221)

Chapter 2 *Arrival at Court*, pp.32–50
p.32 JR takes up position at Windsor: *Letters, 1879–1885*, second series, vol. III (p.221). The Queen notes: 'Sir William brought in Dr Reid, whom I like.'
p.33 Randall Davidson on QV: see G.K.A. Bell, *Randall Davidson*, Oxford University Press, 1938 (pp.77–8)
p.34 Sir James Clark and fresh air: Elizabeth Longford, 'Queen Victoria's Doctors', essay from *A Century of Conflict, 1850–1950*, ed. Martin Gilbert, Hamish Hamilton, 1966.
p.35 'She treated them with meticulous respect': *ibid.*
p.36 & 37 QV's Medical Household: see A.M. Cooke, 'Queen Victoria's Medical Household', *Medical History*, No. 26, 1982 (pp.307–20)
p.38 Cause of Prince Consort's death: see Daphne Bennett, *King Without a Crown*, Heinemann, 1977 (Appendix II, p.381)
p.40 Randall Davidson on Cowell: see G.K.A. Bell, *op.cit.* (p.79)
p.41 Disraeli's tribute to Ponsonby: see W. F. Monypenny and G.E. Buckle, *The Life of Benjamin Disraeli*, vol. V, John Murray, 1910 (p.210)
p.41 Bigge on Ponsonby: see *Henry Ponsonby: His Life from his Letters*, ed. Arthur Ponsonby, Macmillan, 1942 (p.402)
p.44 JR 'excited about small things': quoted by Stanley Weintraub, *Victoria, biography of a Queen*, Unwin Hyman, 1987 (p.516)
p.45 JR's 'I have no objection': I am indebted for this anecdote to another Reid grandson, Richard Ingrams, who observes, 'It is a remark that I often use myself in various circumstances.'
p.46 Campbell Bannerman on Balmoral: see Ivor Brown, *Balmoral*, Collins, 1955 (p.221)
p.47 QV on Windsor shooting incident: *Letters, 1879–1885*, second series, vol. III, (p.266)
p.50 QV on Prince Leopold's wedding: *ibid.* (p.270)

Chapter 3 *Three Deaths*, pp.51–61
p.52 Dr Hal Yarrow: quoted by Tom Cullen, *The Empress Brown*, Bodley Head, 1969 (p.179)
p.55 QV to Mrs Jessie McHardy Brown: see Tom Cullen, *The Empress Brown*, Bodley Head, 1969 (p.211), from holograph in the possession of Mrs Hilda Harris, great niece of John Brown.
p.55 QV to Ponsonby: *Henry Ponsonby*, ed. Arthur Ponsonby (p.129)
p.55 QV to Prince George: see Elizabeth Longford, *Victoria R.I.*, Weidenfeld & Nicolson, 1964 (p.457). Royal Library, Windsor, Ref. RA AB 10 and 13
p.57 QV loses use of her legs in 1861: see *Dearest Mama: Private Correspondence of Queen Victoria and the Crown Princess of Prussia, 1861–1864*, ed. Roger Fulford, Evans Bros., 1977
p.57 QV to Ponsonby: Ponsonby, *op.cit.* (p.129)
p.57 'How can I see people at dinner': Ponsonby papers
p.58 QV's first impression of Randall Davidson: see G.K.A. Bell, *Randall Davidson* (p.58)
p.58–9 Randall Davidson on QV: *ibid.* (p.95)
p.59 QV on death of Prince Leopold: *Letters, 1879–1885*, second series, vol. III (pp.489–90)
p.59 QV on Prince Leopold's funeral wishes: *ibid.* (p.492)

Chapter 4 *Two Marriages*, pp.62–73
p.65 Duke of Cambridge diary: 23 July 1885
p.67 QV on Princess Beatrice's wedding: *Letters, 1879–1885*, second series, vol. III (p.689)
p.70 'Another Battenberg on the way': *Society*, May 1889
p.70 QV on birth of Prince Leopold of Battenberg: *Letters, 1886–1901*, third series, vol. I (p.499)

Chapter 5 *The Queen's Health*, pp.74–87
p.78 Family squabbles and misunderstandings: see Elizabeth Longford, *Victoria R.I.* (p.479–80)
pp.79; 80 Political crisis over Ireland: *ibid.* (p.484), 'Lord Carnarvon, the Viceroy of Ireland, had already fatally weakened the Government by resigning over Coercion. He was the first person ever to tell Queen Victoria the unflattering truth about Ireland. There was "no loyalty to the Queen personally", he reported but a "determination to arrange their own affairs", and something would have to be done.'
p.80 QV to Ponsonby: *Henry Ponsonby*, ed. Arthur Ponsonby (p.206)

Chapter 6 *Royal Health*, pp.88–109
p.90 Crown Prince Frederick attends the Jubilee: *Letters of the Empress Frederick*, ed. Sir Frederick Ponsonby, Macmillan, 1928 (p.242)
p.92 Crown Prince Frederick to QV, 27 August 1887: Translation in Reid Papers

p.92   Mackenzie diagnoses possible cancer: M. Mackenzie to JR, 10 November 1887

p.94   QV's Journal entry for 14 November 1887: *Letters, 1886–1901*, third series, vol. I (p.306)

p.96   Mackenzie's report: *British Medical Journal*, 18 February 1888

p.100 Empress Frederick to QV, 13 June 1888: *op.cit.* (pp.314–15)

pp.101–102   Marie Mallet on Princess Louise: See *Life with Queen Victoria: Marie Mallet's Letters from Court, 1887–1901*, ed. Victor Mallet, John Murray, 1968 (p.50)

p.104 Prince Leopold's haemophilia: JR to Jenner, 28 January 1894

p.104 Princess Ena's riding accident: *ibid.*, 12 February 1894

p.107 Lady Lytton on JR: *Lady Lytton's Court Diary*, ed. Mary Lutyens, Hart-Davies, 1961 (p.81)

p.108 QV on death of Duke of Coburg: *Letters, 1886–1901*, third series, vol. III (pp.579–80)

Chapter 7 *Perquisites and Promotion*, pp.110–27

p.119 QV on JR's rheumatic attack: Royal Library, Windsor, Ref. RA ADDL. MSS. A/15

p.120 Beresford's practical joke: Sir Frederick Ponsonby, *Recollections of Three Reigns*, Eyre & Spottiswoode, 1951 (p.79)

p.122 Kaiser Wilhelm and Britain: Wilhelm's confusion about whether he was more like his father or more like his mother, more of a German or more of an Englishman, exacerbated the friction between Germany and England, and created tension within both countries. The English did not understand what right the Kaiser had to meddle in their affairs, and the Germans did not understand why their Kaiser was so fond of England. See *Kaiser Wilhelm II. New Interpretations*, ed. John C.G. Röhl and Nicholas Sombart, Cambridge University Press, 1982 (p.85)

p.125 Britain and the Sudan: see Elizabeth Longford, *Victoria R.I.* (pp.466–8, 472–5)

p.125 QV on Slatin: *Letters, 1886–1901*, third series, vol. I (p.554)

p.126 Lord Esher on Rosebery: *Journals and Letters of Reginald, Viscount Esher*, vol. I, ed. Maurice V. Brett, Nicolson & Watson, 1934 (p.187)

p.127 QV's urgency regarding Rosebery's premiership: *Letters, 1886–1901*, third series, vol. II (p.369)

Chapter 8 *Indian Affairs – Munshimania*, pp.128–57

p.128 QV studies Hindustani: *Letters, 1886–1901*, third series, vol. I (p.344)

p.146 Fleetwood Edwards to QV: 28 June, 1897, in Reid papers

p.156 Prince of Wales to Edward VII, December 1905: see Harold Nicolson, *King George the Fifth, His Life and Reign*, Constable, 1952 (p.86)

Chapter 9 *A Position of Pre-eminence*, pp.158–73

p.166 QV on Ponsonby's funeral: *Letters, 1886–1901*, third series, vol. II (p.577) p.170 QV says 'Ask Sir James': Notes from QV to Sir Fleetwood Edwards, 16 May 1898 in Reid Papers

p.171 No baronetcy for Playfair: Lord Salisbury to Bigge, 13 December 1895 in Reid papers

p.172 JR on Sir Oscar Clayton: JR to Jenner, 24 April 1889

p.172 QV on 'The Gentlemen and Sir James Reid': Sir Frederick Ponsonby, *Recollections of Three Reigns* (p.25)

Chapter 10 *Happy Marriage*, pp.174–90

p.177 Susan Baring to Margaret Spencer, August 1898: from scrapbooks belonging to JR's grandson David Reid. The definitions of Baringisms were compiled by JR's daughter Victoria Ingrams, aided by Lady Delia Peel (née Spencer), Lady Margaret Douglas-Home (née Spencer) and Mrs Arthur Pollen (née Baring).

p.183 Duchess of York to Duke of York, 21 August 1899: Royal Library, Windsor, Ref. R.A. Geo. V., cc 6/112

p.184 QV to Empress Frederick, 27 August 1899: from the Kronberg Archives

p.190 'And who shall bring me my tea?': Quoted to the author by Lady Delia Peel (née Spencer).

Chapter 11 *The End of an Era*, pp.191–221

p.193 QV arrives in Ireland: *Letters, 1886–1901*, third series, vol. III (p.521)

p.199 Princess Beatrice to Empress Frederick, 27 December 1900: from Kronberg Archives

p.199 'Managed to eat a little cold beef': *Letters, op.cit.* (p.635)

p.199 'Another year begun': *ibid.* (p.637)

p.200 'Laking's visit at Osborne': Susan Reid to Mary Reid, 12 January 1901

p.214 Susan Reid to Mary Reid, 25 January 1901: In the possession of Mrs Roma Barber, Mary Reid's granddaughter.

Chapter 12 *Starting Again*, pp.222–35

p.224 Lord Esher on Windsor: *Journals and Letters of Reginald, Viscount Esher*, vol. I, ed. Maurice V. Brett (pp.279–80)

p.228 Trial of Whitaker Wright: For a full account of the case see Harold Nicolson, *Helen's Towers*, Constable, 1937 (pp.267–75)

pp.233–4 Kaiser Wilhelm's state visit: see Philip Magnus, *King Edward the Seventh*, John Murray, 1984 (pp.398–400)

Chapter 13 *Death of the King*, pp.236–43

p.238 Sir Francis Bertie: *The Diary of Lord Bertie, 1914–1918*, vol. II, Hodder & Stoughton, 1924 (p.322)

p.241 Bulletin of Edward VII's death, 6 May 1910: 'His Majesty the King breathed his last at 11.45 tonight in the presence of Her Majesty

Queen Alexandra, the Prince and Princess of Wales, the Princess Royal, Duchess of Fyfe, the Princess Victoria, and Princess Louise, Duchess of Argyll.'

Chapter 14 *Last Years*, pp.244–56
p.245 JR to Fritz Ponsonby: 9 May 1911. Royal Library, Windsor, Ref. R.A., Geo.V. J.169/1
p.246 Lord Esher on Balmoral: *Journals and Letters of Reginald, Viscount Esher*, vol. III, ed. Maurice V. Brett (pp.279–80)
p.255 Fritz Ponsonby to Susan Reid: in David Reid's scrapbooks

Appendices *Appendix II*, pp.261–6
p.261 Lady Ponsonby: *Letters of the Empress Frederick*, ed. Sir Frederick Ponsonby.
p.263 Emperor Frederick on von Bergmann: see facsimile of Crown Prince's writing in the *B.M.J.*, 13 October 1888, vol. II (p.835). 'The same Hovell just tried before Bergmann ill treated me.'
p.264 Mackenzie's reply to the German pamphlet: see *Morell Mackenzie*, R. Scott Stevenson, Heinemann, 1946

Medical Glossary

Amyl nitrate A drug that relaxes smooth muscle, especially that of blood vessels. Given by inhalation amyl nitrate is used mainly in the treatment of angina pectoris.

Analgesic A drug that relieves pain.

Angina pectoris Pain in the centre of the chest which is induced by exercise and relieved by rest. It occurs when the demand for blood by the heart exceeds the supply of the coronary arteries.

Aperient A mild laxative.

Aphasia A disorder of language affecting the generation of speech and its understanding and not simply a disorder of articulation. It is caused by disease in the left half of the brain (the dominant hemisphere) in a right-handed person.

Arteries Are vessels which convey blood away from the heart to the tissues of the body, limbs, and internal organs.

Atropine Used for the treatment of biliary or renal colic.

Aurology Study of diseases of the ear.

Belladonna Deadly nightshade from which the drugs atropine and hyoscyamine are obtained.

Biopsy The removal of a small piece of living tissue from an organ or part of the body for microscopic examination.

Blue pill Or Mercury pill, is a purgative. It contains mercury and liquorice. It is also said to stimulate the activity of the liver.

Bromide Salts of Bromide. Introduced to clinical medicine just over 100 years ago, the bromides were for some time the standard treatment for epilepsy. Used also as a sedative in mild cases of insomnia.

Calomel Or subchloride of Mercury, is a powerful purgative.

Cannula Hollow tube designed for insertion into a body cavity, e.g. in the windpipe after tracheotomy.

Carbonate of ammonia Is the chief ingredient in sal volatile (qv).

Carbuncle Collection of boils with multiple drainage channels. The infection is usually caused by *staphylococcus aureus* and normally results in an extensive slough (skin that separates from healthy tissues after inflammation or infection) of skin.

Catheter A tube for insertion into a narrow opening so that fluids may be introduced or removed.

Cauterise To destroy tissues by the direct application of a heated instrument: cauterisation is used for the removal of small warts or other growths.

Cerebral thrombosis A blood clot affecting the brain.

Chloral hydrate Sedative and hypnotic drug.

Chlorodyne A patent medicine containing chloroform which relieves pain and is hypnotic.

Chloroform A volatile liquid formerly widely used as a general anaesthetic. Because its use as such causes liver damage and affects heart rhythm, chloroform is now used only in low concentrations as a flavouring agent and preservative, in the treatment of flatulence, and in liniments.

Cocaine An alkaloid (a nitrogen-containing substance produced by a plant) derived from the leaves of the cocoa plant (*Erythroxylon coca*) or prepared synthetically, sometimes used as a local anaesthetic in eye, ear, nose, and throat surgery. Causes feelings of exhilaration which may lead to dependence.

Colchicum Extracted from the bulb of *Colchicum autumnale*, or meadow saffron, it has long been used as a remedy for gout.

Colic Severe abdominal pain, usually of fluctuating severity, with waves of pain seconds or a few minutes apart.

Crepitation A soft fine crackling sound heard in the lungs through the stethoscope.

Croton oil Powerful purgative derived from seeds of *Croton tiglium*.

Crus (pl. crura). The crus cerebri is one of two symmetrical nerve tracts situated between the *medulla oblongata* and the cerebral hemispheres.

Cyanosis A bluish discoloration of the skin and mucous membranes.

Cyst An abnormal swelling filled with liquid or semisolid matter.

Delirium tremens A psychosis caused by alcoholism, usually seen as a withdrawal syndrome in chronic alcoholics. Typically it is precipitated by a head injury or an acute infection causing abstinence from alcohol. Vivid and terrifying visual and sensory hallucinations are symptomatic.

Dermatology Medical specialty concerned with the diagnosis and treatment of skin disorders.

Diathesis Is another name for *constitution* meaning the general condition of the body, especially with reference to its liability to certain diseases.

Dilatation Enlargement or expansion of e.g. the pupil.

Diphtheria An acute infectious disease generally affecting the throat but occasionally other mucous membranes and the skin. The disease is spread by direct contact with a patient or carrier, or by contaminated milk. Death from heart failure or general collapse can follow and the disease was often fatal in the nineteenth century before an effective immunisation programme made diphtheria rare in most Western countries.

Dover's powder Is made of 10 per cent each of powdered opium and ipecacuanha, with 80 per cent of lactose. Still one of the most popular remedies in medicine it was introduced by Capt. Thomas Dover (1660–1742).

Duodenal ulcer   An ulcer in the duodenum (the first of the three parts of the small intestine) caused by the action of acid and pepsin on the duodenal lining of a susceptible individual. It is usually associated with an increased output of stomach acid and affects people with blood group O more commonly than others. Symptoms include pain in the upper abdomen and vomiting may occur. Symptoms are relieved by antacid medicines and diet but surgery is sometimes required for a permanent cure.

Dyspepsia   Disordered digestion: usually applied to pain or discomfort in the lower chest or abdomen after eating, and sometimes accompanied by nausea or vomiting.

Dyspnoea   Laboured or difficult breathing due to obstruction to the flow of air into and out of the lungs.

Enteric fever   Typhoid or Paratyphoid fever.

Epiglottis   A thin leaf-shaped flap of cartilage, covered with mucous membrane, situated immediately behind the root of the tongue. It covers the entrance to the larynx during swallowing.

Epitaxis   Nosebleed.

Erysipelas   A streptococcal infection of the skin and underlying tissues. The affected areas, usually the face and scalp, become inflamed and swollen. The patient is ill with a high temperature. It was from time to time fatal but can now be cured with antibiotics.

Ether   A volatile liquid formerly used as an anaesthetic administered by inhalation, though now largely replaced by safer and more efficient drugs.

Expectoration   The act of spitting out material brought into the mouth by coughing.

Femur   The thigh bone.

Gangrene   Death and decay of part of the body due to deficiency or cessation of blood supply. *Dry gangrene* is death and withering of tissues caused simply by cessation of local blood circulation. *Moist gangrene* is death and putrefactive decay of tissue caused by bacterial infection.

Ginger draught   Used in cases of flatulence to stop griping.

Gleet   The discharge of purulent mucus or pus from the penis or vagina resulting from chronic gonorrhoea.

Gonorrhoea   A venereal disease that affects the genital mucous membranes of either sex. In untreated cases the infection may spread throughout the reproductive system causing sterility. Later complications can include arthritis, inflammation of the heart valves and infection of the eyes.

Granulation   The growth of small rounded outgrowths, made up of small blood vessels and connective tissue, on the healing surface of a wound (when the edges do not fit together) or an ulcer. Granulation is a normal stage in the healing process.

Haematemis The act of vomiting blood. The blood may have been swallowed (e.g. following nosebleed) but more often arises from bleeding in the oesophagus, stomach or duodenum. Common causes are gastric and duodenal ulcers, gastritis brought on by irritating food or drink, and varicose veins in the oesophagus.

Haemophilia An hereditary disorder in which the blood clots very slowly due to a deficiency of one of the coagulation factors (*antihaemophilic factor or Factor VIII*). The patient may experience prolonged bleeding following any injury or wound, and in severe cases there is spontaneous bleeding into muscles and joints. Haemophilia is controlled by a sex-linked gene, which means that it is almost exclusively restricted to males: women can carry the disease and pass it on to their sons without being affected themselves.

As far as existing evidence is conclusive Queen Victoria was the first carrier of the morbid gene in her family. Ten of Victoria's male descendants have suffered from haemophilia and seven of her female descendants have proved to be carriers. Prince Leopold, Duke of Albany, was haemophilic, and Princess Alice and Princess Beatrice carried the gene to the next generation. Through them 'the royal disease' was transmitted to the Russian and Spanish ruling families. By contributing to the hold of Rasputin on the Czarina, and by endangering the succession in Spain, haemophilia has had a considerable influence on recent European history. See: Iltis, Hugo, 'Haemophilia: The Royal Disease and the British Royal Family'. *The Journal of Heredity*, vol.39, no.4, pp.113-16, April 1948.

Haemorrhage The escape of blood from a ruptured blood vessel, externally or internally.

Hemiplegia Paralysis of one side of the body. It is caused by disease of the opposite (contralateral) hemisphere of the brain.

Henbane Or Hyocymus is a plant which grows commonly in the United States and in Europe. The preparations are made from the leaves, and have an effect in relieving pain and spasm. Also used for inducing sleep, and for the prevention of travel sickness.

Hernia The protrusion of an organ or tissue out of the body cavity in which it normally lies.

Homatropine Is an alkaloid (nitrogen-containing substance) which is used to produce dilatation of the pupil for the purpose of examining the interior of the eye.

Hyoscyamine Used for the treatment of muscular spasm.

Interstice (adj. Interstitial) a small space in a tissue or between parts of the body.

Iodide of potassium At one time used to absorb diseased tissue; iodides are salts of iodine.

Ipecacuanha A plant extract used in small doses, usually in the form of tinctures and syrups, as an expectorant to relieve coughing and to induce vomiting.

Laryngoscope   A mirror for examining the larynx and trachea.

Larynx   Is the organ of voice, and also forms one of the higher parts of the air passage. It is placed high up in front of the neck, and there forms a considerable prominence on the surface.

Laudanum   Is the popular name for tincture (alcoholic extract) of opium.

Linctus   A syrupy liquid medicine, particularly one used in the treatment of irritating coughs.

Linseed   Externally, linseed meal is used in poultices (qv); for internal use, linseed tea is an old domestic remedy for the treatment of a cough.

Lumbago   Low backache of any cause or description.

Malaria   Also known as Ague, Paludism, Jungle fever, Marsh fever, and Periodic fever, Malaria is a disease caused by the presence of certain parasites in the blood. It is transmitted by the *Anopheles mosquito* and is confined mainly to tropical and subtropical areas. Bouts of fever occur periodically varying from mild to very severe, amounting to fatal. A dreaded complication is blackwater fever associated with malignant tertian Malaria, and occurs in Central Africa, India and the Far East.

Maltese fever   Also known as Mediterranean fever; Rock fever; Neapolitan fever; Levant fever; Undulant fever; and Brucellosis, is a fever of long duration which principally occurs on the shores and islands of the Mediterranean, but is found also in many other countries.

Medula oblongata   (Myelencephalon) The extension within the skull of the upper end of the spinal cord, forming the lowest part of the brainstem.

Morphine   A potent analgesic and narcotic drug used mainly to relieve severe and persistent pain. It is administered by mouth or injection; common side effects are loss of appetite, nausea, constipation, and confusion.

Motor   Is a term applied to those nerves and tracts of fibres in the brain and spinal cord by which impulses are sent to the muscles, thus causing movements. Motor Paralysis is the inability to move.

Mucous membrane   The moist membrane lining many tubular structures and cavities, including the nasal sinuses, respiratory tract, gastrointestinal tract, biliary, and pancreatic systems.

Mucus   A viscous or sticky fluid secreted by mucous membranes in many parts of the body, including the mouth, bronchial passages, and gut. Mucus acts as a protective barrier over the surfaces of the membranes, as a lubricant, and as a carrier of enzymes.

Mustard poultice   Used externally it is made into a paste with water, and spread on brown paper, or made up with linseed into a poultice, and applied to the chest and abdomen when the organs in these cavities are inflamed.

Narcotic A drug that induces stupor and insensibility and relieves pain. The term is used particularly for morphine and other derivatives of opium, but is also applied to other drugs that depress brain function (e.g. general anaesthetics and hypnotics).

Neoplasm A new and abnormal growth: any benign or malignant tumour.

Neuralgia A severe burning or stabbing pain often following the course of a nerve.

Neuritis Inflammation of a peripheral nerve.

Nitrate of silver Caustic application.

Nitric acid A strong corrosive mineral acid the concentrated form of which is capable of producing severe burns of the skin. Swallowing the acid leads to intense burning pain and ulceration of the mouth and throat. Treatment is by immediate administration of alkaline solutions, followed by milk or olive oil.

Nodule A small swelling or aggregation of cells.

Nucleus (Nuclear Cataract) Means the central body in a cell, around which something may grow. A cataract is any opacity in the lens of the eye, resulting in blurred vision.

Nutrient enemata Given when the stomach is seriously deranged and cannot retain or digest food, but are not widely used today. A nutrient enema consists of dextrose, 5 per cent solution in normal saline solution, warmed to 100°F (38°C), and is administered very slowly through a small funnel and catheter tube.

Ophthalmoscope An instrument for examining the interior of the eye.

Opiate One of a group of drugs derived from opium, including apomorphine, codein, morphine and papaverine.

Opium An extract from the white Indian poppy *Papaver somniferum*, which relieves pain and induces euphoria followed by stupor and insensibility. Prolonged use may lead to dependence and, in severe cases, death may occur.

Paregoric A medicine that soothes pain.

Paresis of the pulmonary nerves Muscular weakness caused by disease of the nervous system of the lungs.

Pathology The study of disease processes with the aim of understanding their nature and causes. This is achieved by observing samples of blood, urine, faeces, and diseased tissue obtained from the living patient or at autopsy.

Perichondritis Inflammation of cartilage and surrounding soft tissues, usually due to chronic infection.

Peritonitis Inflammation of the peritoneum (serous membrane of the abdominal cavity). Secondary peritonitis is due to perforation or rupture of an abdominal organ, e.g. the appendix.

Phlebitis Inflammation of the wall of a vein which is most commonly seen in the legs as a complication of varicose veins. Thrombosis (blood clot) commonly develops.

Phthisis A former name for: 1. Any disease resulting in wasting of tissues; 2. Pulmonary tuberculosis.

Placebo A medicine that is ineffective but may help to relieve a condition because the patient has faith in its powers.

Podophyllin A resin derived from the root of *Podophyllum peltatum,* a plant growing in the United States and Canada, or from *Podophyllum emodi,* a plant which grows in the Himalayas. It has a purgative action but is seldom used for this purpose now.

Polypoid (adj.) Having the appearance of a polyp which is a growth, usually benign, intruding from a mucous membrane.

Potassium iodide At one time its chief use was to cause absorption of the unhealthy tissues in syphilis upon which it acted with great rapidity when taken into the system.

Poultice A preparation of hot moist material applied to any part of the body to increase local circulation, alleviate pain, or soften the skin to allow matter to be expressed from a boil.

Prolapse The downward displacement of an organ or a part of an organ from its normal position. This may happen if the supporting tissues are weak. The womb and rectum are most commonly affected by this condition.

Ptosis Drooping of the upper eyelid, for which there are several causes. In the instance described in Princess Ena's illness, as a result of her fall, *ptosis* was caused by a disorder of the third cranial nerve (*oculomotor nerve*) and accompanied by paralysis of eye movement causing double vision and enlarged pupil.

Pulmonary congestion Congestion of the lungs.

Pulmonary consumption i.e. Pulmonary Tuberculosis. An infectious disease affecting the lungs caused by the bacillus *Mycobacterium tuberculosis,* and resulting in the wasting of tissues. In the nineteenth century it proved to be fatal in many cases, but is now curable by antibiotics.

Purulent (adj.) Forming, consisting of, or containing pus.

Radium A radioactive metallic element that emits alpha and gamma rays during its decay into other elements. The gamma radiation is employed in radiotherapy for the treatment of cancer. Because radon, a radioactive gas, is released from radium the metal must be enclosed in gas-tight containers during use. By present day standards it would seem that Reid was misusing radium and failing to take adequate precautions.

Rhinoscopy Examination of the interior of the nose.

Rhonchus An abnormal musical noise produced by air passing through narrowed bronchi. It is heard through a stethoscope usually when the patient breathes out.

Rigor An abrupt attack of shivering and a sensation of coldness accompanied by a rapid rise in body temperature. This often marks the onset of a fever and may be followed by a feeling of heat, with copious sweating.

Sal volatile   Another name for aromatic solution of ammonia, a liquid of burning taste and great stimulating powers. It is used as an expectorant in cough mixtures, and is valuable as a stimulant in faints.

Scabies   Skin infection caused by the itch mite, *Sarcoptes scabiei*. Scabies is typified by severe itching (particularly at night), red papules, and often secondary infection. Commonly affected areas are the groin, penis, nipples, and the skin between the fingers.

Septic pneumonia   Pneumonia (inflammation of the substance of the lungs) arising as a part of other diseases of which it forms a serious complication; as opposed to broncho-pneumonia, or lobar pneumonia.

Septicaemia   Is an infection of the blood due to the multiplication of bacteria in the blood stream.

Shingles   *Herpes zoster:* Usually starts with pain along the distribution of a nerve (often in the face, chest, or abdomen), followed by the development of small blisters. The disease subsides in about three weeks, though sometimes severe pain may persist for many months in the area of the affected nerve. The virus that causes shingles can also cause chickenpox in children.

Soda draught   Sodium bicarbonate, a salt of sodium that neutralises acid and is used to treat stomach and digestive disorders.

Stertor   Snoring type of noisy breathing heard in deeply unconscious patients.

Strychnine   A poisonous alkaloid produced in the seeds of the East Indian tree *Strychnos nux-vomica*. In small doses it was formerly widely used in 'tonics', and as a stimulant.

Subacute   Describes a disease that progresses more rapidly than a chronic (i.e. disease of long duration involving very slow changes) condition but does not become acute (i.e. disease of rapid onset, severe symptoms, and brief duration).

Subcutaneous   Means anything pertaining to the loose cellular tissue beneath the skin.

Syncope   Fainting.

Syphilis   Chronic venereal (sexually transmitted) disease caused by the bacterium *Treponema pallidum*, resulting in the formation of lesions throughout the body.

Tannin   Or tannic acid is an uncrystallisable white or yellowish-white powder which is soluble in water or glycerin. Glycerin of tannin was painted on to the throat and acted as an astringent, diminishing the secretion of mucus. As with all astringents, when applied to a raw spot there would be initial discomfort. Linseed meal was the normal substance used for poultices.

Thorax The chest, adj. thoracic.

Thyrotomy Surgical incision of either the thyroid cartilage (the largest cartilage in the larynx which forms the priminence of the Adam's apple in front of the neck) or of the thyroid gland itself.

Tincture An alcoholic extract of a drug derived from a plant.

Tincture iodi Antiseptic.

Trachea Windpipe.

Tracheal rale When breathing there is a fine crackling sound in the windpipe, caused by congested lungs. Occurs frequently just before dying.

Tracheitis Inflammation of the windpipe. Tracheitis causes soreness in the chest and painful coughing and is often associated with bronchitis.

Tracheotomy A surgical operation in which a hole is made into the trachea through the neck to relieve obstruction to breathing. A curved metal, plastic, or rubber tube is usually inserted through the hole and held in position by tapes tied round the neck.

Trional A drug used as a narcotic.

Typhoid fever An infection of the digestive system by the bacterium *Salmonella typhi*, causing general weakness, high fever, a rash of red spots on the chest and abdomen, chills, sweating, and in serious cases inflammation of the spleen and bones, delirium and haemorrhage. It is transmitted through food or drinking water contaminated by the faeces or urine of patients or carriers. In the nineteenth century there was no vaccination to provide immunity.

Tyramine An amine (derivative of ammonia) naturally occurring in cheese. It acts as a stimulant.

Umbilical hernia Is most common in young children, and appears as a bulge at the naval. A hernia becomes *strangulated* (gangrenous) and painful when cut off from the blood supply.

Ventral hernia A hernia which protrudes at some accidental opening on the abdomen as, for example, through the scar of an operation wound.

Vessel Is a tube conveying a body fluid, especially a blood vessel or a lymphatic vessel.

Bibliography

Anon., *Uncensored Recollections*, J.B. Lippincott, 1924

Antrim, Louisa, Countess of, *Recollections*, London, 1937

Ashdown, Dulcie M., *Ladies-in-Waiting*, Arthur Barber, 1976

Auchincloss, Louis, *Persons of Consequence: Queen Victoria and Her Circle*, Weidenfeld & Nicolson, 1979

Baring, Maurice, *The Puppet Show of Memory*, Heinemann, 1922

Barlow, Helen & Andrew, *Sir Thomas Barlow, Three Selected Lectures & a Biographical Sketch*, Dawsons of Pall Mall, 1965

Battiscombe, Georgina, *Queen Alexandra*, Constable, 1969

——, *The Spencers of Althorp*, Constable, 1984

Bell, G.K.A., *Randall Davidson, Archbishop of Canterbury*, Oxford University Press, 1938

Bennett, Daphne, *King Without a Crown*, Heinemann, 1977

——, *Vicky: Princess Royal of England and German Empress*, Collins Harvill, 1971

Benson, E.F., *Queen Victoria*, Longmans, 1935

Bertie, Sir Francis Leveson, *The Diary of Lord Bertie of Thame, 1914–1918*, ed. Lady Algernon Gordon Lennox, Hodder & Stoughton, 1924

Blake, Robert, *Disraeli*, Eyre & Spottiswoode, 1966

Bolitho, Henry Hector, *Victoria, the Widow, and her Son*, Cobden-Sanderson, 1934

Broadbent, M.E. (ed.), *Life of Sir William Henry Broadbent*, John Murray, 1909

Brown, Ivor, *Balmoral. The History of a Home*, Collins, 1955

Buchanan, Meriel, *Queen Victoria's Relations*, Cassell, 1954

Buckle, G.E. and W.F. Monypenny, *The Life of Benjamin Disraeli, Earl of Beaconsfield*, 6 vols, John Murray, 1910

Cecil, Lady Gwendolen, *Life of Robert, Marquis of Salisbury*, 4 vols, Hodder & Stoughton, 1921–32

Cheyne, W., *Lister and his Achievement*, Longmans, 1925

Clark, Ronald W., *Balmoral: Queen Victoria's Highland Home*, Thames and Hudson, 1981

Cowles, Virginia, *Edward VII and his Circle*, Hamish Hamilton, 1956

——, *The Kaiser*, Collins, 1963

Cullen, Tom, *The Empress Brown*, The Bodley Head, 1969

Cust, Sir Lionel, *King Edward VII and his Court: Some Reminiscences*, John Murray, 1930

Duff, David, *Hessian Tapestry*, Frederick Muller, 1967

——, *The Shy Princess*, Evans Brothers, 1958

——, *Victoria Travels, Journeys of Queen Victoria between 1830 and 1900, with extracts from her journal*, Frederick Muller, 1970

Emden, Paul H., *Behind the Throne*, Hodder & Stoughton, 1934

Esher, Viscount, *Journals and Letters of Reginald, Viscount Esher*, 4 vols, ed. Maurice V. Brett, Nicolson & Watson, 1934–38

Fulford, Roger (ed.), *Dearest Mama: Private Correspondence of Queen Victoria and the Crown Princess of Prussia, 1861–1864*, Evans Brothers, 1977

——, *Beloved Mama: Private Correspondence of Queen Victoria and the German Crown Princess, 1878–1885*, Evans Brothers, 1981

Godlee, R.J., *Lord Lister*, Oxford, 1924

Hennessy, James Pope, *Queen Mary, 1867–1953*, George Allen & Unwin, 1959

—— (ed.), *Queen Victoria at Windsor and Balmoral. Letters from Princess Victoria of Prussia*, George Allen & Unwin, 1959

Hibbert, Christopher, *The Court at Windsor*, Longmans, 1964

——, *The Court of St James's*, Weidenfeld & Nicolson, 1979

——, *Edward VII: A Portrait*, Allen Lane, 1976

Hough, Richard, *Advice to a Grand-daughter: Letters from Queen Victoria to Princess Victoria of Hesse*, Heinemann, 1975

——, *Louis and Victoria. The First Mountbattens*, Hutchinson, 1974

Housman, Laurence, *Victoria Regina*, Jonathan Cape, 1934

Iltis, Hugo, 'Haemophilia: The Royal Disease and the British Royal Family', *The Journal of Heredity*, vol. 39, no. 4, pp.113–16, April 1948

James, Robert Rhodes, *Rosebery: A Biography of Archibald Philip, Fifth Earl of Rosebery*, Weidenfeld & Nicolson, 1963

Lee, Sidney, *Queen Victoria: A Biography*, Smith, Elder, 1902

Lees-Milne, James, *The Enigmatic Edwardian, The Life of Reginald 2nd Viscount Esher*, Sidgwick & Jackson, 1986

Longford, Elizabeth (ed.), *Louisa, Lady in Waiting: The Personal Diaries and Albums of Louisa, Lady in Waiting to Queen Victoria and Queen Alexandra*, Jonathan Cape, 1979

——, 'Queen Victoria's Doctors', essay from *A Century of Conflict, 1850–1950*, ed. Martin Gilbert, Hamish Hamilton, 1966

——, *Victoria R.I.*, Weidenfeld & Nicolson, 1964

Ludwig, Emil, *Kaiser Wilhelm II*, Putnam's, 1926

Lytton, Edith, Countess of, *Lady Lytton's Court Diary, 1895–1899*, ed. Mary Lutyens, Hart-Davis, 1961

Mackenzie, Morell, *The Fatal Illness of Frederick the Noble*, Sampson Low, 1888

Magnus, Philip, *Gladstone. A Biography*, John Murray, 1954

——, *King Edward the Seventh*, John Murray, 1964

Mallet, Marie, *Life with Queen Victoria: Marie Mallet's Letters from Court, 1887–1901*, ed. Victor Mallet, John Murray, 1968

Bibliography

Marie Louise, Princess, *My Memories of Six Reigns*, Evans Brothers, 1956

Massie, Robert K., *Nicholas and Alexandra*, Victor Gollancz, 1968

Matson, John, *Dear Osborne: Queen Victoria's Family Life in the Isle of Wight*, Hamish Hamilton, 1978

Millar, Delia, *Queen Victoria's Life in the Scottish Highlands, depicted by her watercolour artists*, Philip Wilson, 1985

Morley, John, *The Life of William Ewart Gladstone*, 3 vols, Macmillan, 1903

Neele, George P., *Railway Reminiscences*, McCorquodale, 1904

Nicolson, Harold, *Helen's Tower*, Constable, 1937

——, *King George the Fifth. His Life and Reign*, Constable, 1952

Paget, Stephen (ed.), *Memoirs & Letters of Sir James Paget*, Longmans, 1901

Ponsonby, Arthur, *Henry Ponsonby: His Life from his Letters*, Macmillan, 1942

Ponsonby, Sir Frederick (ed.), *Letters of the Empress Frederick*, Macmillan, 1928

——, *Recollections of Three Reigns*, Eyre & Spottiswoode, 1951

——, *Sidelights on Queen Victoria*, Macmillan, 1930

Ponsonby, Magdalen, *Mary Ponsonby: A Memoir, Some Letters, and a Journal*, John Murray, 1927

Prothero, Rowland E., *A Memoir of H.R.H. Prince Henry of Battenberg*, John Murray, 1897

Reid, Dr James, 'Case of Aortic Embolism', *British Medical Journal*, 1873

——, 'Erysipelas during Puerperal Condition', *ibid.*, 1874

Rodd, Sir Rennel, *Frederick, Crown Prince and Emperor*, David Stott, 1888

Röhl, John C.G. and Nicolaus Sombart (eds), *Kaiser Wilhelm II: New Interpretations*, Cambridge University Press, 1982

Rose, Kenneth, *King George V*, Weidenfeld & Nicolson, 1983

——, *The Later Cecils*, Weidenfeld & Nicolson, 1975

St Aubyn, Giles, *Edward VII: Prince and King*, Collins, 1979

Semon, Sir Felix, *The Autobiography*, eds. H.C. Semon and T.A. McIntyre, Jarrolds, 1926

Stevenson, R. Scott, *Morell Mackenzie*, Heinemann, 1946

Strachey, Lytton, *Queen Victoria*, Chatto & Windus, 1921

Tisdall, E.E.P., *Queen Victoria's John Brown*, Stanley Paul, 1938

——, *Queen Victoria's Private Life, 1837–1901*, Jarrolds, 1961

Victoria, Queen, *Leaves from the Journal of our Life in the Highlands from 1848 to 1861*, ed. Arthur Helps, Smith, Elder, 1868

——, *More Leaves from the Journal of a Life in the Highlands from 1862 to 1882*, Smith, Elder, 1884

——, *The Letters of Queen Victoria, 1862–1885*, second series, 3 vols, ed. G.E. Buckle, John Murray, 1926–28

——, *The Letters of Queen Victoria, 1886–1901*, third series, 3 vols, ed. G.E. Buckle, John Murray, 1930–32

——, *The Private Life of the Queen. By One of Her Majesty's Servants*, C. Arthur Pearson, 1897

Warner, Marina, *Queen Victoria's Sketchbook*, Macmillan, 1979

Watson, Francis, *Dawson of Penn*, Chatto & Windus, 1950
Weintraub, Stanley, *Victoria, Biography of a Queen*, Unwin Hyman, 1987
Youngson, A.J., *The Scientific Revolution in Victorian Medicine*, Billing & Sons Ltd, Croom Helm, London, 1979
Dictionary of National Biography, Oxford University Press, 1975
Black's Medical Dictionary – William A.R. Thomson, M.D., Thirty Third Edition, Adam & Charles Black, 1981.

Index

ELAND

61 Exmouth Market, London EC1R 4QL
Email: info@travelbooks.co.uk

Eland was started thirty years ago to revive great travel books that had
fallen out of print. Although the list soon diversified into biography and
fiction, all the books are chosen for their interest in spirit of place. One of
our readers explained that for him reading an Eland is like listening to an
experienced anthropologist at the bar – she's let her hair down and is telling
all the stories that were just too good to go into the textbook.

Eland books are for travellers, and for readers who are content to travel
in their own minds. They open out our understanding of other cultures,
interpret the unknown and reveal different environments, as well as
celebrating the humour and occasional horrors of travel. We take
immense trouble to select only the most readable books and therefore
many readers collect the entire, hundred-volume series.

You will find a very brief description of our books on the
following pages. Extracts from each and every one of them can be
read on our website, at www.travelbooks.co.uk. If you would
like a free copy of our catalogue, email us
or send a postcard.

ELAND

'One of the very best travel lists' WILLIAM DALRYMPLE

Libyan Sands
RALPH BAGNOLD
An heroic account of an infatuation with the
Model T Ford and the Sahara

An Innocent Anthropologist
NIGEL BARLEY
An honest, funny, affectionate and
compulsively irreverent account of fieldwork
in West Africa

Memoirs of a Bengal Civilian
JOHN BEAMES
Sketches of 19th-century India
painted with the richness of Dickens

Jigsaw
SYBILLE BEDFORD
An intensely remembered autobiographical
novel about an inter-war childhood

A Visit to Don Otavio
SYBILLE BEDFORD
The hell of travel and the Eden of arrival
in post-war Mexico

Journey into the Mind's Eye
LESLEY BLANCH
An obsessive love affair with Russia and
one particular Russian

Japanese Chronicles
NICOLAS BOUVIER
Three decades of intimate experiences
throughout Japan

The Way of the World
NICOLAS BOUVIER
A 1950s road trip to Afghanistan,
by a legendary young sage

The Devil Drives
FAWN BRODIE
Biography of Sir Richard Burton,
explorer, linguist and pornographer

Travels into Bokhara
ALEXANDER BURNES
Nineteenth-century espionage in Central Asia

Turkish Letters
OGIER DE BUSBECQ
Eyewitness history at its best: Istanbul
during the reign of Suleyman the
Magnificent

An Ottoman Traveller
EVLIYA ÇELEBI
Travels in the Ottoman Empire,
by the Pepys of 17th-century Turkey

Two Middle-Aged Ladies in Andalusia
PENELOPE CHETWODE
An infectious, personal account
of a fascination with horses,
God and Spain

My Early Life
WINSTON CHURCHILL
From North West Frontier to Boer War
by the age of twenty-five

A Square of Sky
JANINA DAVID
A Jewish childhood in the Warsaw
ghetto and hiding from the Nazis

Chantemesle
ROBIN FEDDEN
A lyrical evocation of childhood
in Normandy

Viva Mexico!
CHARLES FLANDRAU
Five years in turn-of-the-century
Mexico, described by an enchanted Yankee

Travels with Myself and Another
MARTHA GELLHORN
Five journeys from hell by a great
war correspondent

The Trouble I've Seen
MARTHA GELLHORN
Four stories of the Great Depression,
offering profound insight into the
suffering of poverty

The Weather in Africa
MARTHA GELLHORN
Three novellas set amongst the
white settlers of East Africa

The Last Leopard
DAVID GILMOUR
The biography of Giuseppe di Lampedusa,
author of The Leopard

Walled Gardens
ANNABEL GOFF
A portrait of the Anglo-Irish: sad,
absurd and funny

Africa Dances
GEOFFREY GORER
The magic of indigenous culture
and the banality of colonisation

Cinema Eden
JUAN GOYTISOLO
Essays from the Muslim
Mediterranean

Goodbye Buenos Aires
ANDREW GRAHAM-YOOLL
A portrait of an errant father,
and of the British in Argentina

A State of Fear
ANDREW GRAHAM-YOOLL
A journalist witnesses Argentina's
nightmare in the 1970s

A Pattern of Islands
ARTHUR GRIMBLE
Rip-roaring adventures and a passionate
appreciation of life in the Southern Seas

Warriors
GERALD HANLEY
Life and death among the Somalis

Morocco That Was
WALTER HARRIS
All the cruelty, fascination and
humour of a pre-modern kingdom:
Morocco in the 19th and early 20th century

Far Away and Long Ago
W H HUDSON
A childhood in Argentina, and a hymn to
nature

Palestine Papers 1917–22
ED. DOREEN INGRAMS
History caught in the making

Holding On
MERVYN JONES
The story of a London dockland street,
and the families who lived there

Mother Land
DMETRI KAKMI
A minutely observed Greek childhood on a
Turkish island in the 1960s

Red Moon & High Summer
HERBERT KAUFMANN
A coming-of-age novel following a
young singer in his Tuareg homeland

Three Came Home
AGNES KEITH
A mother's ordeal in a Japanese
prison camp

Peking Story
DAVID KIDD
The ruin of an ancient Mandarin
family under the new communist order

Scum of the Earth
ARTHUR KOESTLER
Koestler's escape from a collapsing France
in World War II

The Hill of Kronos
PETER LEVI
A poet's radiant portrait of Greece

A Dragon Apparent
NORMAN LEWIS
Cambodia, Laos and Vietnam
on the eve of war

Golden Earth
NORMAN LEWIS
Travels in Burma